New Perspectives on

THE INTERNET
2nd EDITION

Brief

JAMES T. PERRY
University of San Diego

GARY P. SCHNEIDER
University of San Diego

ONE MAIN STREET, CAMBRIDGE, MA 02142

Australia • Canada • Mexico • Singapore • Spain • United Kingdom • United States

New Perspectives on The Internet—Brief, 2nd Edition is published by Course Technology.

Managing Editor	**Greg Donald**
Senior Editor	**Donna Gridley**
Senior Product Manager	**Rachel Crapser**
Product Manager	**Karen Shortill**
Product Manager	**Catherine Donaldson**
Associate Product Manager	**Melissa Dezotell**
Editorial Assistant	**Jill Kirn**
Developmental Editor	**Catherine Skintik**
Production Editor	**Jennifer Goguen**
Text Designer	**Meral Dabcovich**
Cover Art Designer	**Douglas Goodman**

© 2000 by Course Technology, a division of Thomson Learning.
Thomson Learning is a trademark used herein under license.

For more information contact:
Course Technology
1 Main Street
Cambridge, MA 02142
Or find us on the World Wide Web at: http://www.course.com.

For permission to use material from this text or product, contact us by
- Web: www.thomsonrights.com
- Phone: 1-800-730-2214
- Fax: 1-800-730-2215

All rights reserved. This publication is protected by federal copyright law. No part of this publication may be reproduced, stored in a retrieval system, used to make a derivative work (such as a translation or adaptation), or transmitted in any form or by any means—graphic, electronic, or mechanical, including photocopying, recording, or Web distribution—without prior permission in writing from Course Technology.

Trademarks

Course Technology and the Open Book logo are registered trademarks and CourseKits is a trademark of Course Technology. Custom Edition is a registered trademark of Thomson Learning.

The Thomson Learning Logo is a registered trademark used herein under license.

Some of the product names and company names used in this book have been used for identification purposes only and may be trademarks or registered trademarks of their respective manufacturers and sellers.

Disclaimer

Course Technology reserves the right to revise this publication and make changes from time to time in its content without notice.

ISBN 0-619-01995-6

Printed in the United States of America

1 2 3 4 5 6 7 8 9 10 BM 04 03 02 01 00

PREFACE
The New Perspectives Series

About New Perspectives

Course Technology's **New Perspectives Series** is an integrated system of instruction that combines text and technology products to teach computer concepts, the Internet, and microcomputer applications. Users consistently praise this series for innovative pedagogy, use of interactive technology, creativity, accuracy, and supportive and engaging style.

How is the New Perspectives Series different from other series?

The **New Perspectives Series** distinguishes itself by **innovative technology**, from the renowned Course Labs to the state-of-the-art multimedia that is integrated with our Concepts texts. Other distinguishing features include **sound instructional design, proven pedagogy,** and **consistent quality**. Each tutorial has students learn features in the context of solving a realistic case problem rather than simply learning a laundry list of features. With the **New Perspectives Series,** instructors report that students have a complete, integrative learning experience that stays with them. They credit this high retention and competency to the fact that this series incorporates critical thinking and problem-solving with computer skills mastery. In addition, we work hard to ensure accuracy by using a multi-step quality assurance process during all stages of development. Instructors focus on teaching and students spend more time learning

Choose the coverage that's right for you

New Perspectives applications books are available in the following categories:

Brief
2-4 tutorials

Introductory
6 or 7 tutorials, or Brief + 2 or 3 more

Comprehensive
Introductory + 4 or 5 more tutorials. Includes Brief Windows tutorials and Additional Cases

Advanced
Quick Review of basics + in-depth, high-level coverage

Office
Office suite components + integration + Internet

Custom Editions
Choose from any of the above to build your own Custom Editions or CourseKits

Brief: approximately 150 pages long, two to four "Level I" tutorials, teaches basic application skills. The book you are holding is a Brief book.

Introductory: approximately 300 pages long, four to seven tutorials, goes beyond the basic skills. These books often build out of the Brief book, adding two or three additional "Level II" tutorials.

Comprehensive: approximately 600 pages long, eight to twelve tutorials, all tutorials included in the Introductory text plus higher-level "Level III" topics. Also includes two Windows tutorials and three or four fully developed Additional Cases.

Advanced: approximately 600 pages long, cover topics similar to those in the Comprehensive books, but offer the highest-level coverage in the series. Advanced books assume students already know the basics, and therefore go into more depth at a more accelerated rate than the Comprehensive titles. Advanced books are ideal for a second, more technical course.

Office: approximately 800 pages long, covers all components of the Office suite as well as integrating the individual software packages with one another and the Internet.

Custom Books The New Perspectives Series offers you two ways to customize a New Perspectives text to fit your course exactly: *CourseKits*™—two or more texts shrinkwrapped together. We offer significant price discounts on *CourseKits*™. *Custom Editions*® offer you flexibility in designing your concepts, Internet, and applications courses. You can build your own book by ordering a combination of topics bound together to cover only the subjects you want. There is no minimum order, and books are spiral bound. Contact your Course Technology sales representative for more information.

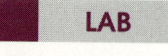

What course is this book appropriate for?

New Perspectives on The Internet— Brief, 2nd Edition can be used in any course in which you want students to learn all the most important topics of using the internet, including the history of the internet, getting connected, basic e-mail and integrated browser e-mail software, and the basics of browsing. It is particularly recommended for a short course on internet concepts. This book assumes that students have learned basic Windows 95 or Windows NT navigation and file management skills from Course Technology's *New Perspectives on Microsoft Windows 95—Brief*, *New Perspectives on Microsoft Windows NT Workstation 4.0—Introductory*, or an *equivalent* book.

Proven Pedagogy

Tutorial Case Each tutorial begins with a problem presented in a case that is meaningful to students. The case turns the task of learning how to use an application into a problem-solving process.

45-minute Sessions. Each tutorial is divided into sessions that can be completed in about 45 minutes to an hour. Sessions allow instructors to more accurately allocate time in their syllabus, and students to better manage their own study time.

Step-by-Step Methodology We make sure students can differentiate between what they are to *do* and what they are to *read*. Through numbered steps – clearly identified by a gray shaded background – students are constantly guided in solving the case problem. In addition, the numerous screen shots with callouts direct students' attention to what they should look at on the screen.

TROUBLE? Paragraphs These paragraphs anticipate the mistakes or problems that students may have and help them continue with the tutorial.

"Read This Before You Begin" Page Located opposite the first tutorial's opening page for each level of the text, the Read This Before You Begin Page helps introduce technology into the classroom. Technical considerations and assumptions about software are listed to save time and eliminate unnecessary aggravation. Notes about the Student Disks help instructors and students get the right files in the right places, so students get started on the right foot.

Quick Check Questions Each session concludes with meaningful, conceptual Quick Check questions that test students' understanding of what they learned in the session. Answers to the Quick Check questions are provided at the end of each tutorial.

Reference Windows Reference Windows are succinct summaries of the most important tasks covered in a tutorial and they preview actions students will perform in the steps to follow.

Task Reference Located as a table at the end of the book, the Task Reference contains a summary of how to perform common tasks using the most efficient method, as well as references to pages where the task is discussed in more detail.

End-of-Chapter Review Assignments, Case Problems, Internet Assignments and Lab Assignments Review Assignments provide students with additional hands-on practice of the skills they learned in the tutorial using the same case presented in the tutorial. These Assignments are followed by three to four Case Problems that have approximately the same scope as the tutorial case but use a different scenario. In addition, some of the Review Assignments or Case Problems may include Exploration Exercises that challenge students, encourage them to explore the capabilities of the program they are using, and/or further extend their knowledge. Each tutorial also includes instructions on getting to the text's Student Online Companion page, which contain the Internet Assignments and other related links for the text. Internet Assignments are additional exercises that integrate the skills the students learned in the tutorial with the World Wide Web. Finally, if a Course Lab accompanies a tutorial, Lab Assignments are included after the Case Problems.

New Perspectives on The Internet—Brief, 2nd Edition Instructor's Resource Kit for this title contains:

- Instructor's Manual in Word 97 format
- Sample Syllabus
- Data Files
- Solution Files
- Course Labs
- Course Test Manager Testbank
- Course Test Manager Engine
- Figure files
- WebCT

These supplements come on CD-ROM. If you don't have access to a CD-ROM drive, contact your Course Technology customer service representative for more information.

The New Perspectives Supplements Package

Electronic Instructor's Manual Our Instructor's Manuals include tutorial overviews and outlines, technical notes, lecture notes, solutions, and Extra Case Problems. Many instructors use the Extra Case Problems for performance-based exams or extra credit projects. The Instructor's Manual is available as an electronic file, which you can get from the Instructor Resource Kit (IRK) CD-ROM or download it from **www.course.com**.

Data Files Data Files contain all of the data that students will use to complete the tutorials, Review Assignments, and Case Problems. A Readme file includes instructions for using the files. See the "Read This Before You Begin" page for more information on Data Files.

Solution Files Solution Files contain every file students are asked to create or modify in the tutorials, Tutorial Assignments, Case Problems, and Extra Case Problems. A Help file on the Instructor's Resource Kit includes information for using the Solution files.

Course Labs: Concepts Come to Life These highly interactive computer-based learning activities bring concepts to life with illustrations, animations, digital images, and simulations. The Labs guide students step-by-step, present them with Quick Check questions, let them explore on their own, test their comprehension, and provide printed feedback. Lab icons at the beginning of the tutorial and in the tutorial margins indicate when a topic has a corresponding Lab. Lab Assignments are included at the end of each relevant tutorial. The Labs available with this book and the tutorials in which they appear are:

Tutorial 2   Tutorial 3

Figure Files Many figures in the text are provided on the IRK CD-ROM to help illustrate key topics or concepts. Instructors can create traditional overhead transparencies by printing the figure files. Or they can create electronic slide shows by using the figures in a presentation program such as PowerPoint.

Course Test Manager: Testing and Practice at the Computer or on Paper Course Test Manager is cutting-edge, Windows-based testing software that helps instructors design and administer practice tests and actual examinations. Course Test Manager can automatically grade the tests students take at the computer and can generate statistical information on individual as well as group performance.

Online Companions: Dedicated to Keeping You and Your Students Up-To-Date Visit our faculty sites and student sites on the World Wide Web at www.course.com. Here instructor's can browse this text's password-protected Faculty Online Companion to obtain an online Instructor's Manual, Solution Files, Student Files, and more. Students can also access this text's Student Online Companion, which contains Data files other useful links.

Acknowledgments

Creating a quality textbook is a collaborative effort between author and publisher. We work as a team to provide the highest quality book possible. The authors want to acknowledge the work of the seasoned professionals at Course Technology. We thank Mac Mendelsohn, Vice President of Product Development, for his initial interest in and continual support of our work on this book. It was Mac's vision for a book focused on the Internet, rather than on a specific software application, that motivated us to take on this project. We offer a special thank you to Martha Wagner, our former Course Technology sales representative, for introducing us to Mac. For the many years we have known Martha, she has always been an enthusiastic and committed professional—devoted to her business and her customers. In addition we thank Rachel Crapser, Senior Product Manager; Karen Shortill, Product Manager; Jennifer Goguen, Production Editor; and John Bosco's team of Quality Assurance testers for being terrific, positive, and supportive members of a great publishing team. We also thank our Developmental Editor, Cat Skintik. Her sharp eyes caught all the small (and sometimes not-so-small) mistakes and made the manuscript better. We offer our heartfelt thanks to the Course Technology organization as a whole. The people at Course Technology have been, by far, the best publishing team with which we have ever worked.

We want to thank the following reviewers for their insightful comments and suggestions at various stages of the book's development: Cathy Fothergill, Kilgore College; Don Lopez, The Clovis Center; Suzanne Nordhaus, Lee College; Sorel Reisman, California State University, Fullerton; T. Michael Smith, Austin Community College; and Bill Wagner, Villanova University. Margaret Beeler and Pamela Drotman provided helpful comments on early drafts of the outline for this book.

Finally, we want to express our deep appreciation for the continuous support and encouragement of our spouses, Nancy Perry and Cathy Cosby. They demonstrated remarkable patience as we worked both ends of the clock to complete this book on a very tight schedule. Without their support and cooperation, we would not have attempted to write this book. We also thank our children for tolerating our absences while we were busy writing.

James T. Perry
Gary P. Schneider

Dedication

To my oldest daughter, Jessica Perry
  Finally, you have learned to soar. Keep giving life your best. — J.T.P.

To the memory of my brother, Bruce Schneider. — G.P.S.

BRIEF CONTENTS

Preface   iii

The Internet—Level 1 Tutorials   WEB 1.01

Read This Before You Begin   WEB 1.02

Tutorial 1   WEB 1.03

Introduction to the Internet and the World Wide Web

	SESSION 1.1	WEB 1.04
	SESSION 1.2	WEB 1.17

Tutorial 2   WEB 2.01

Basic E-Mail: Integrated Browser E-Mail Software

	SESSION 2.1	WEB 2.02
	SESSION 2.2	WEB 2.13
	SESSION 2.3	WEB 2.33

Tutorial 3   WEB 3.01

Browser Basics

	SESSION 3.1	WEB 3.02
	SESSION 3.2	WEB 3.17
	SESSION 3.3	WEB 3.41

Appendix E   WEB E.03

Eudora   WEB E.03

Appendix F   WEB F.01

Pine   WEB F.01

Index   1

Task Reference   11

Reference Window List

Sending a message using Messenger	WEB 2.18
Using Messenger to receive and read an e-mail message	WEB 2.21
Saving an attached file	WEB 2.22
Replying to a sender's message	WEB 2.24
Forwarding an e-mail message	WEB 2.25
Deleting an e-mail message	WEB 2.27
Adding an address to the address book	WEB 2.29
Creating a mailing list	WEB 2.31
Sending a message using Outlook Express	WEB 2.37
Using Outlook Express to receive and read an e-mail message	WEB 2.39
Saving an attached file	WEB 2.41
Replying to a message	WEB 2.42
Forwarding an e-mail message	WEB 2.43
Deleting an e-mail message	WEB 2.46
Entering a new e-mail address in the address book	WEB 2.47
Creating a group address entry	WEB 2.49
Hiding or showing a toolbar	WEB 3.19
Entering a URL in the Location field	WEB 3.21
Creating a Bookmarks folder	WEB 3.24
Creating a bookmark in a bookmarks folder	WEB 3.25
Saving a bookmark to a floppy disk	WEB 3.26
Using hyperlinks and the mouse to navigate between Web pages	WEB 3.27
Changing the default home page	WEB 3.30
Printing the current Web page	WEB 3.32
Opening the NetHelp - Netscape window	WEB 3.35
Saving a Web page to a floppy disk	WEB 3.37
Copying text from a Web page to a WordPad document	WEB 3.38
Saving an image from a Web page on a floppy disk	WEB 3.40
Hiding and restoring the toolbars	WEB 3.44
Entering a URL in the Address Bar	WEB 3.45
Creating a new Favorites folder	WEB 3.48
Moving an existing favorite into a new folder	WEB 3.50
Using hyperlinks and the mouse to navigate between Web pages	WEB 3.51
Changing the Home toolbar button settings	WEB 3.55
Printing the current Web page	WEB 3.56
Getting Help in Internet Explorer	WEB 3.58
Saving a Web page to a floppy disk	WEB 3.60
Copying text from a Web page to a WordPad document	WEB 3.61
Saving an image from a Web page on a floppy disk	WEB 3.63

Tutorial Tips

These tutorials will help you learn about Internet concepts. The tutorials are designed to be worked through at a computer. Each tutorial is divided into sessions. Watch for the session headings, such as Session 1.1 and Session 1.2. Each session is designed to be completed in about 45 minutes, but take as much time as you need. It's also a good idea to take a break between sessions.

Before you begin, read the following questions and answers. They will help you use the tutorials.

Where do I start?
Each tutorial begins with a case, which sets the scene for the tutorial and gives you background information to help you understand what you will be doing. Read the case before you go to the lab. In the lab, begin with the first session of a tutorial.

How do I know what to do on the computer?
Each session contains steps that you will perform on the computer to learn how to use the Internet. Read the text that introduces each series of steps. The steps you need to do at a computer are numbered and are set against a shaded background. Read each step carefully and completely before you try it.

How do I know if I did the step correctly?
As you work, compare your computer screen with the corresponding figure in the tutorial. Don't worry if your screen display is somewhat different from the figure. The important parts of the screen display are labeled in each figure. Check to make sure these parts are on your screen.

What if I make a mistake?
Don't worry about making mistakes—they are part of the learning process. Paragraphs labeled "TROUBLE?" identify common problems and explain how to get back on track. Follow the steps in a TROUBLE? paragraph only if you are having the problem described. If you run into other problems:

- Carefully consider the current state of your system, the position of the pointer, and any messages on the screen.
- Complete the sentence, "Now I want to…" Be specific, because identifying your goal will help you rethink the steps you need to take to reach that goal.
- If you are working on a particular piece of software, consult the Help system.
- If the suggestions above don't solve your problem, consult your technical support person for assistance.

How do I use the Reference Windows?
Reference Windows summarize the procedures you will learn in the tutorial steps. Do not complete the actions in the Reference Windows when you are working through the tutorial. Instead, refer to the Reference Windows while you are working on the assignments at the end of the tutorial.

How can I test my understanding of the material I learned in the tutorial?
At the end of each session, you can answer the Quick Check questions. The answers for the Quick Checks are at the end of that tutorial.

After you have completed the entire tutorial, you should complete the Review Assignments and Case Problems. They are carefully structured so that you will review what you have learned and then apply your knowledge to new situations.

What if I can't remember how to do something?
You should refer to the Task Reference at the end of the book; it summarizes how to accomplish tasks using the most efficient method.

Before you begin the tutorials, you should know the basics about your computer's operating system. You should also know how to use the menus, dialog boxes, Help system, and My Computer. Now that you've read Tutorial Tips, you are ready to begin.

LEVEL I

New Perspectives on

THE
INTERNET

2nd Edition

TUTORIAL 1   WEB 1.03
Introduction to the Internet and the World Wide Web
History, Potential, and Getting Connected

TUTORIAL 2   WEB 2.01
Basic E-Mail: Integrated Browser E-Mail Software
Evaluating E-Mail Alternatives

TUTORIAL 3   WEB 3.01
Browser Basics
Introduction to Netscape Navigator and Microsoft Internet Explorer

Read This Before You Begin

To the Student

Data Disks
To complete the Level I tutorials, Review Assignments, and Case Problems in this book, you need two Data Disks. Your instructor will either provide you with Data Disks or ask you to make your own.

If you are making your own Data Disks, you will need two blank, formatted, high-density disks. You will need to copy onto your disks a set of folders from a file server, a standalone computer, or the Web. Your instructor will tell you which computer, drive letter, and folders contain the files you need. You could also download the files by going to www.course.com, clicking Data Disk Files, and following the instructions on the screen.

The following table shows you which folders go on your disks, so that you will have enough disk space to complete all the tutorials, Review Assignments, and Case Problems:

Data Disk 1
Write this on the disk label:
Data Disk 1: Tutorial 2
Put this folder on the disk:
Tutorial.02

Data Disk 2
Write this on the disk label:
Data Disk 2: Tutorial 3
Put this folder on the disk:
Tutorial.03

When you begin each tutorial, be sure you are using the correct Data Disk. See the inside back cover of this book for more information on Data Disk files, or ask your instructor or technical support person for assistance.

Course Labs
The tutorials in this book feature two interactive Course Labs to help you understand e-mail and multimedia concepts. There are Lab Assignments at the end of Tutorials 2 and 3 that relate to these Labs.

To start a Lab, click the **Start** button on the Windows taskbar, point to **Programs**, point to **Course Labs**, point to **New Perspectives Applications**, and click the name of the Lab you want to use.

Using Your Own Computer
If you are going to work through this book using your own computer, you need:

- **Computer System** Netscape Navigator 4.0 or higher OR Microsoft Internet Explorer 4.0 or higher and Windows 95 or higher must be installed on your computer. This book assumes a complete installation of the Web browser software and its components, and that you have an existing e-mail account and an Internet connection. Because your Web browser may be different from the ones used in the figures or the book, your screens may differ slightly at times.

- **Data Disks** You will not be able to complete the tutorials or exercises in this book using your own computer until you have Data Disks.

- **Course Labs** See your instructor or technical support person to obtain the Course Lab software for use on your own computer.

Visit Our World Wide Web Site
Additional materials designed especially for you are available on the World Wide Web.
Go to http://www.course.com.

To the Instructor

The Data files and Course Labs are available on the Instructor's Resource Kit for this title. Follow the instructions in the Help file on the CD-ROM to install the programs to your network or standalone computer. For information on creating Data Disks, see the "To the Student" section above. To complete the tutorials in this book, students must have a Web browser, an e-mail account, and an Internet connection.

You are granted a license to copy the Data Files to any computer or computer network used by students who have purchased this book.

TUTORIAL 1

OBJECTIVES

In this tutorial you will:

- Obtain an overview of the tools and information that are available on the Internet

- Learn what computer networks are and how they work

- Find out how the Internet and World Wide Web began and grew

- Compare and evaluate different methods for connecting to the Internet

INTRODUCTION TO THE INTERNET AND THE WORLD WIDE WEB

History, Potential, and Getting Connected

CASE

Tropical Exotics Produce Company

Lorraine Tomassini, the owner of the Tropical Exotics Produce Company (TEPCo), is concerned about the firm's future. She started TEPCo 10 years ago to import organically grown exotic fruits and vegetables from South America, Africa, and Asia to the U.S. market. The TEPCo product line includes items such as babaco, cherimoya, feijoa, African horned melon, malanga, and tamarillo. The business has grown rapidly and thrived financially, but Lorraine is worried that TEPCo is failing to use technology effectively. She already knows that this weakness has caused TEPCo to lose customers and suppliers to competitors.

You started work as an intern at TEPCo six months ago to learn more about international business while you attend college. Justin Jansen and Arti Rao have been with the firm for about five years and are Lorraine's key assistants. During this week's meeting with you, Justin, and Arti, Lorraine expressed concern that TEPCo has become internally focused and might be missing major trends that affect its worldwide suppliers. She worries that reading newspapers for market information and staying in touch with suppliers by telephone are time-consuming, ineffective strategies. She recalled the events of the last year, when bad weather in Costa Rica destroyed most of their suppliers' sapote crop and TEPCo received the reports too late to change its customer price schedule.

Justin mentioned that he knew some people who followed weather reports from all over the world using the Internet, which he explained was a worldwide collection of computers, connected together to allow communication. He also suggested that TEPCo might be able to attract new customers by creating a World Wide Web site on a computer connected to the Internet. Arti looked worried as she noted that TEPCo's five computers were not even connected to each other, much less to a worldwide network of computers. Lorraine knew that colleges and universities had been involved in the Internet for years and asked you to do some research on ways that TEPCo might use the Internet. You agreed to undertake the project so you could learn more about international business in general.

SESSION 1.1

The Internet offers anyone connected to it a vast array of communication tools and information resources. This session explains what the Internet and World Wide Web are, describes how they have grown from their beginnings in the military and research communities, and outlines some of the resources available on them.

Internet and World Wide Web: Amazing Developments

The **Internet**—a large collection of computers all over the world that are connected to one another in various ways—is one of the most amazing technological developments of the twentieth century. Using the Internet, you can communicate with other people throughout the world through **electronic mail** (or **e-mail**); read online versions of newspapers, magazines, academic journals, and books; join discussion groups on almost any conceivable topic; participate in games and simulations; and obtain free computer software. In recent years, the Internet has allowed commercial enterprises to connect. Today, all kinds of businesses provide information about their products and services on the Internet. Many of these businesses use the Internet to market and sell their products and services. The part of the Internet known as the **World Wide Web** (or the **Web**), is a subset of the computers on the Internet that are connected to each other in a specific way that makes those computers and their contents easily accessible to all computers in that subset. The Web has helped to make Internet resources available to people who are not computer experts. Figure 1-1 shows some of the tools and resources available on the Internet today.

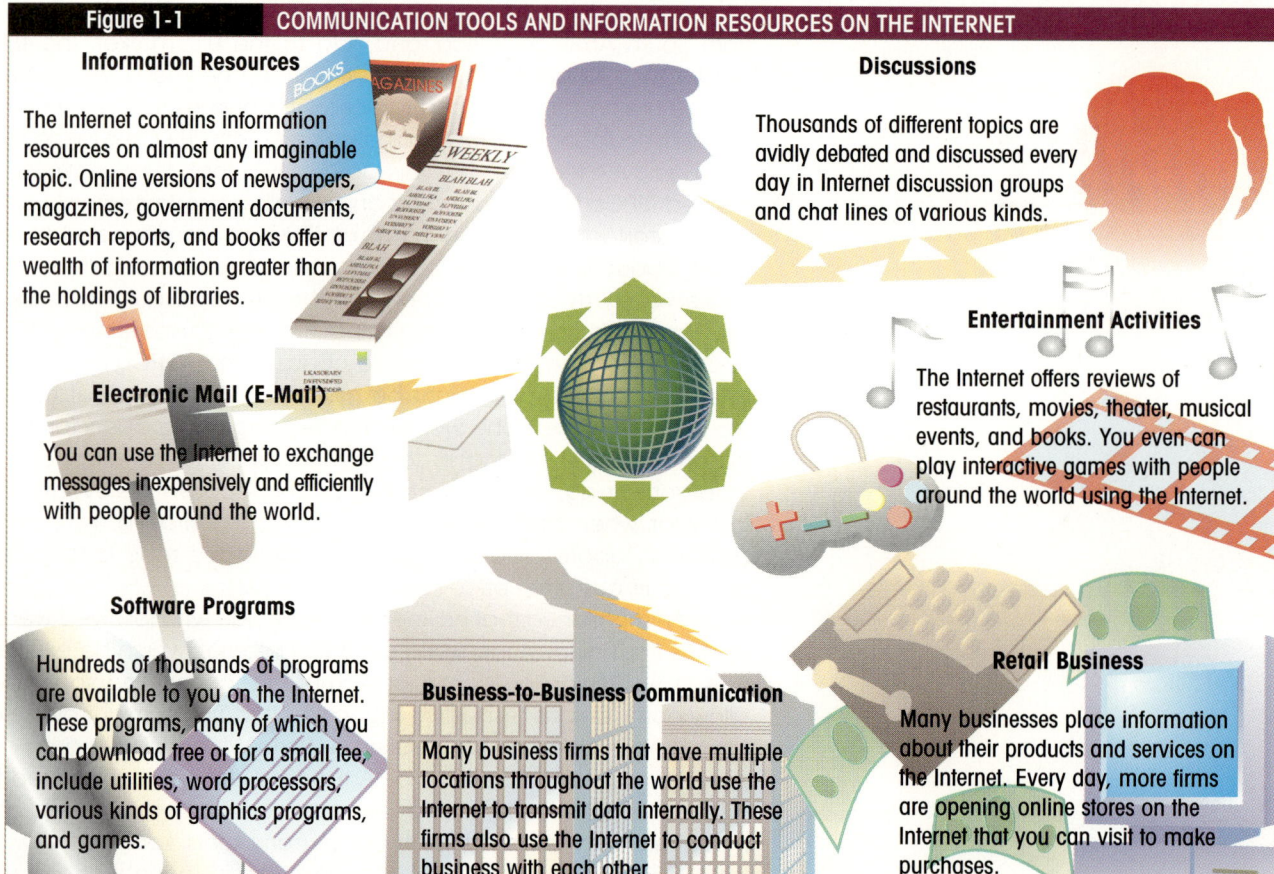

Figure 1-1   COMMUNICATION TOOLS AND INFORMATION RESOURCES ON THE INTERNET

Information Resources
The Internet contains information resources on almost any imaginable topic. Online versions of newspapers, magazines, government documents, research reports, and books offer a wealth of information greater than the holdings of libraries.

Discussions
Thousands of different topics are avidly debated and discussed every day in Internet discussion groups and chat lines of various kinds.

Electronic Mail (E-Mail)
You can use the Internet to exchange messages inexpensively and efficiently with people around the world.

Entertainment Activities
The Internet offers reviews of restaurants, movies, theater, musical events, and books. You even can play interactive games with people around the world using the Internet.

Software Programs
Hundreds of thousands of programs are available to you on the Internet. These programs, many of which you can download free or for a small fee, include utilities, word processors, various kinds of graphics programs, and games.

Business-to-Business Communication
Many business firms that have multiple locations throughout the world use the Internet to transmit data internally. These firms also use the Internet to conduct business with each other.

Retail Business
Many businesses place information about their products and services on the Internet. Every day, more firms are opening online stores on the Internet that you can visit to make purchases.

As you begin Lorraine's research project, you remember Arti's comment that TEPCo does not have its computers connected to each other. You decide to learn more about what computer networks are and how to connect computers to each other to form those networks.

Computer Networks

After talking with Adolfo Segura, the director of your school's computer lab, you realize that you will have some good news for Arti. Adolfo explained to you that he linked the lab computers to each other by inserting a network interface card into each computer and connecting cables from each card to the lab's main computer, called a server. Adolfo told you that a **network interface card** (**NIC**) is a card or other device used to connect a computer to a network of other computers. A **server** is a general term for any computer that accepts requests from other computers that are connected to it and shares some or all of its resources, such as printers, files, or programs, with those computers.

Client/Server Local Area Networks

The server runs software that coordinates the information flow among the other computers, which are called **clients**. The software that runs on the server computer is called a **network operating system**. Connecting computers this way, in which one server computer shares its resources with multiple client computers, is called a **client/server network**. Client/server networks commonly are used to connect computers that are located close together (for example, in the same room or building). Because the direct connection from one computer to another through NICs only works over relatively short distances (no more than a few thousand feet), this kind of network is called a **local area network** (**LAN**). Figure 1-2 shows a typical client/server LAN.

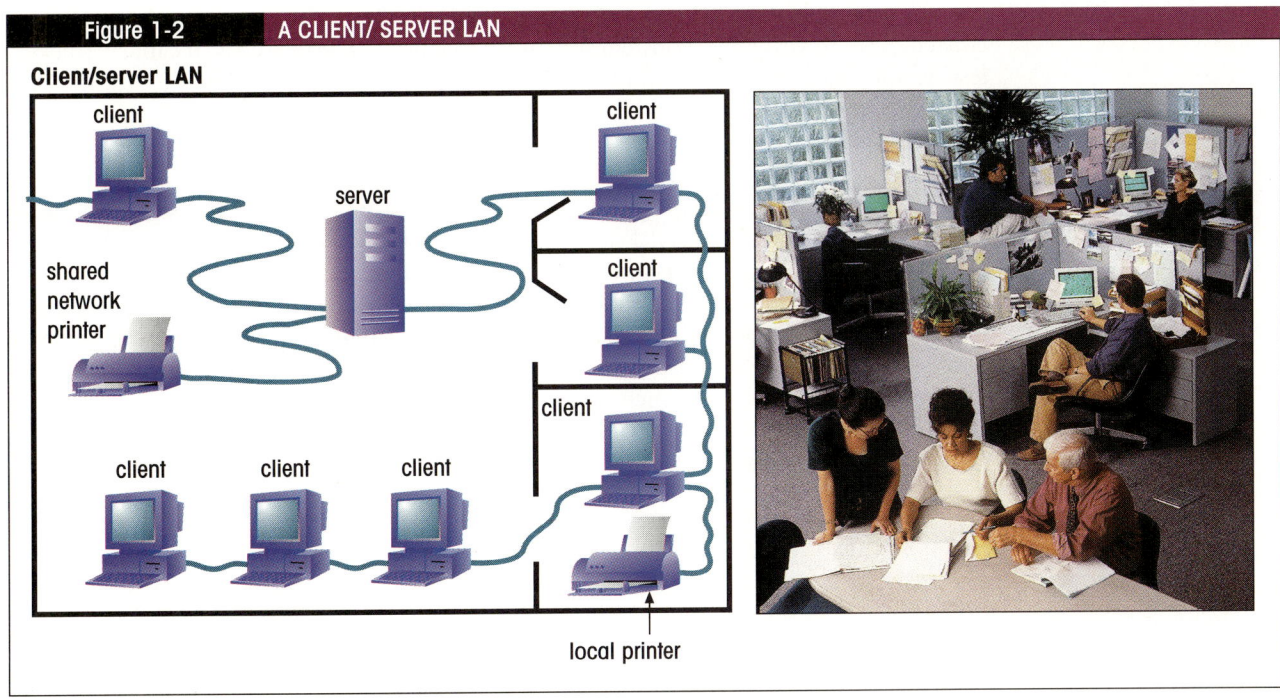

Figure 1-2 A CLIENT/SERVER LAN

The good news for Arti is that both the NICs and the cable that connects them are fairly inexpensive. Arti's first step is to select one of TEPCo's more powerful computers to be the server. A server can be a powerful personal computer (PC) or a larger computer such as a minicomputer or a mainframe computer. **Minicomputers** and **mainframe computers** are larger, more expensive computers that businesses and other organizations use to process large volumes of work at high speeds. For many years, even the largest PCs were not powerful enough to be servers, but this has changed in the past few years.

Next, Arti will need to buy the network operating system software and have a network technician install it on the server. This software is more expensive than the operating system software for a standalone computer; however, you find that having the computers connected in a client/server network offers TEPCo some potential cost savings. For example, by connecting each computer to the server, each computer now has its own printer and its own tape drive for backups because a client/server network lets computers on the network share printers and tape drives.

Connecting Computers to a Network

As you talk with Adolfo, you learn more about computer networks. You find that not all LANs use the same kind of cables to connect their computers. The oldest cable type is called **twisted-pair**, which is the type of cable that telephone companies have used for years to wire residences and businesses. Twisted-pair cable has two or more insulated copper wires that are twisted around each other and enclosed in another layer of plastic insulation. The wires are twisted to reduce interference from other nearby current-carrying wires. The type of twisted-pair cable that telephone companies have used for years to transmit voice signals is called **Category 1** cable. Category 1 cable transmits information more slowly than the other cable types, but it is also much less expensive. **Coaxial cable** is an insulated copper wire that is encased in a metal shield that is enclosed with plastic insulation. The signal-carrying wire is completely shielded, so it resists electrical interference much better than twisted-pair cable. Coaxial cable also carries signals about 20 times faster than Category 1 twisted-pair; however, it is considerably more expensive. Because coaxial cable is thicker and less flexible than twisted-pair, it is harder for installation workers to handle and thus is more expensive to install. You might recognize coaxial cable because most cable television connections still use coaxial cable. In the past 20 years, cable manufacturers have developed better versions of twisted-pair cable. The current standard for twisted-pair cable used in computer networks is **Category 5**. Category 5 twisted-pair cable carries signals between 10 and 100 times faster than coaxial cable and is as easy to install as Category 1 cable. The most expensive cable type is **fiber-optic cable**, which does not use an electrical signal at all. Fiber-optic cable transmits information by pulsing beams of light through very thin strands of glass. Fiber-optic cable transmits signals much faster than either coaxial cable or Category 5 twisted-pair cable. Because it does not use electricity, fiber-optic cable is completely immune to electrical interference. Fiber-optic cable is lighter and more durable than coaxial cable, but it is harder to work with and much more expensive than either coaxial cable or Category 5 twisted-pair cable. Figure 1-3 shows these three types of cable.

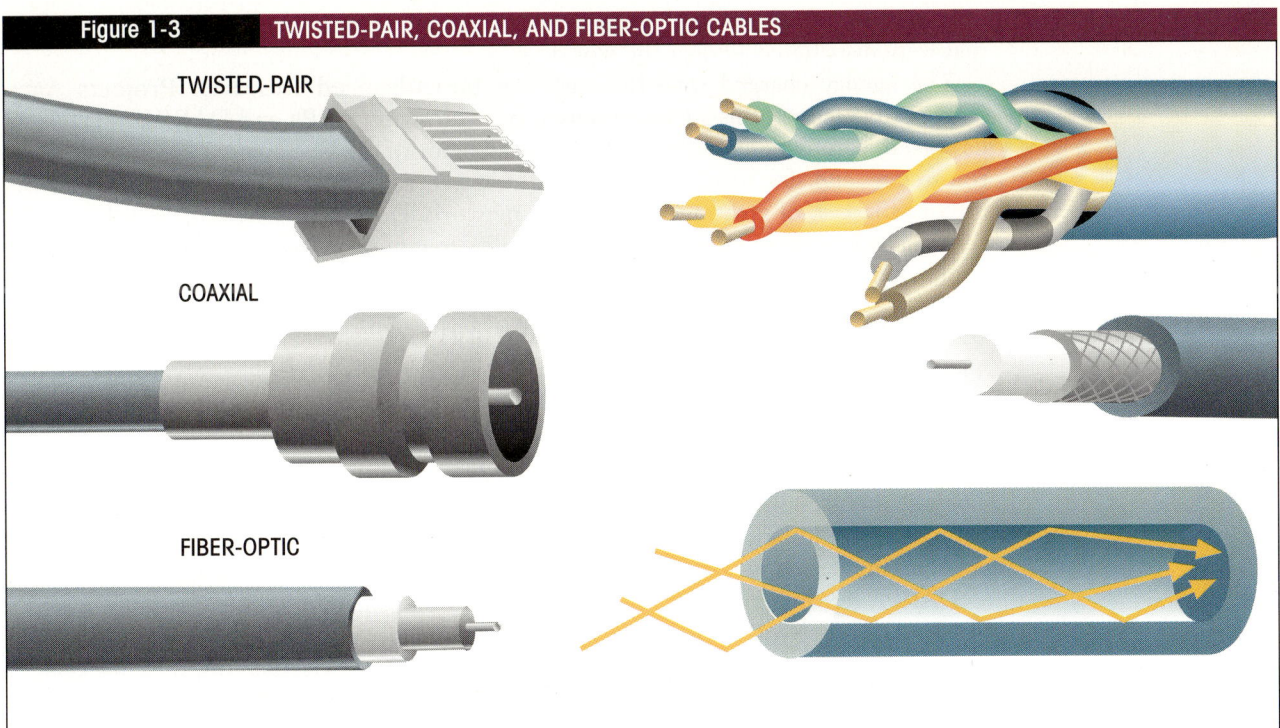

Figure 1-3 TWISTED-PAIR, COAXIAL, AND FIBER-OPTIC CABLES

Perhaps the most intriguing way to connect computers in a LAN is to avoid cable all together. **Wireless networks** are becoming more common as the cost of the wireless transmitters and receivers that plug into NICs continues to drop. Wireless LANs are especially welcome in organizations that occupy old buildings. Many cities have structures that were built before electricity and telephones were widely available. These buildings have no provision for running wires through walls or between floors, so a wireless network can be the best option for connecting resources.

Wide Area Networks

You know that your school has several computer labs in different buildings, so you ask Adolfo whether the individual labs are connected to each other as a larger LAN. Adolfo explains that each computer lab is its own client/server LAN, but that these individual networks are connected to each other as part of the school's **wide area network (WAN)**. Adolfo remembers that you came to him with questions about the Internet and tells you that **internet** (lowercase "i") is short for **interconnected network**. The computer lab LANs are networks, and the school's WAN is a network of networks, or an internet. You look a little puzzled, so Adolfo continues to explain that *any* network of networks is called an internet. However, the school's WAN is connected to an internet called the Internet (capital "I"). The **Internet** is a specific worldwide collection of interconnected networks whose owners have voluntarily agreed to share resources and network connections with each other. You decide that your project is starting to become interesting and head toward the campus library to find out more about this huge interconnected network called the Internet.

How the Internet Began

In the early 1960s, the U.S. Department of Defense (DOD) became very concerned about the possible effects of nuclear attack on its computing facilities. The DOD realized that the weapons of the future would require powerful computers for coordination and control. The powerful computers of that time were all large mainframe computers, so the DOD began examining ways to connect these computers to each other and also to weapons installations that were distributed all over the world.

The agency charged with this task was the **Advanced Research Projects Agency**. (During its lifetime, this agency has used two acronyms, ARPA and DARPA; this book uses its current acronym, **DARPA**.) DARPA hired many of the best communications technology researchers and, for many years, funded research at leading universities and institutes to explore the task of creating a worldwide network. DARPA researchers soon became concerned about computer networks' vulnerability to attack and worked hard to devise ways to eliminate the need for network communications to rely on a central control function.

Circuit Switching vs. Packet Switching

The early models for networked computers were the telephone companies; most early WANs used leased telephone company lines for their connections. In telephone company systems of that time, a telephone call established a single connection between sender and receiver. Once the connection was established, all data then traveled along that single path. The telephone company's central switching system selected specific telephone lines, or **circuits**, that would be connected to create the single path. This centrally controlled, single-connection method is called **circuit switching**.

DARPA researchers turned to a different method of sending information, packet switching. In a **packet switching** network, files and messages are broken down into packets that are labeled electronically with codes for their origin and destination. The packets travel from computer to computer along the network until they reach their destination. The destination computer collects the packets and reassembles the original data from the pieces in each packet. Each computer that an individual packet encounters on its trip through the network determines the best way to move the packet forward to its destination. Computers that perform this function on networks are often called **routers**, and the programs they use to determine the best path for packets are called **routing algorithms**.

By 1967, DARPA researchers had published their plan for a packet switching network and in 1969, they connected the first computer switches at the University of California at Los Angeles, SRI International, the University of California at Santa Barbara, and the University of Utah. This experimental WAN, called the **ARPANET**, grew over the next three years to include over 20 computers and used the **Network Control Protocol (NCP)**. A **protocol** is a collection of rules for formatting, ordering, and error-checking data sent across a network.

Open Architecture Philosophy

As more researchers connected to the ARPANET, interest in the network grew in the academic community. The next several years saw many technological developments that increased the speed and efficiency with which the network operated. One reason for the project's success was its adherence to an **open architecture** philosophy; that is, each network could continue using its own protocols and data-transmission methods internally. Conversion to NCP occurred only when the data moved out of the local network and onto the ARPANET. The original purpose of the ARPANET was to connect computers in the field that were controlling a wide range of diverse weapons systems, so the ARPANET could not force its protocol or structure onto those individual component networks. This open approach was quite different from the closed architecture designs that companies such as IBM and Digital Equipment Corporation were using to build networks for their customers during this period. The open architecture philosophy included four key points:

- Independent networks should not require any internal changes to be connected to the Internet.
- Packets that do not arrive at their destinations must be retransmitted from their source network.
- The router computers do not retain information about the packets they handle.
- No global control will exist over the network.

One of the new developments of this time period that was rapidly adopted throughout the ARPANET was a set of new protocols developed by Vincent Cerf and Robert Kahn. These new protocols were the **Transmission Control Protocol** and the **Internet Protocol**, which usually are referred to by their combined acronym, **TCP/IP**. TCP includes rules that computers on a network use to establish and break connections; IP includes rules for routing of individual data packets. These two protocols were technically superior to the NCP that ARPANET had used since its inception and gradually replaced that protocol. TCP/IP continues to be used today in LANs and on the Internet. The term *Internet* was first used in a 1974 article about the TCP protocol written by Cerf and Kahn. The importance of the TCP/IP protocol in the history of the Internet is so great that many people consider Vincent Cerf to be the Father of the Internet.

ARPANET's successes were not lost on other network researchers. Many university and research institution computers used the UNIX operating system. When TCP/IP was included in a version of UNIX, these institutions found it easier to create networks and interconnect them. A number of TCP/IP-based networks—independent of the ARPANET—were created in the late 1970s and early 1980s. The National Science Foundation (NSF) funded the **Computer Science Network (CSNET)** for educational and research institutions that did not have access to the ARPANET. The City University of New York started a network of IBM mainframes at universities, called the **Because It's Time** (originally, "There") **Network (BITNET)**.

Birth of E-Mail: A New Use for Networks

Although the goals of ARPANET were still to control weapons systems and transfer research files, other uses for this vast network began to appear in the early 1970s. In 1972, an ARPANET researcher named Ray Tomlinson wrote a program that could send and receive messages over the network. E-mail had been born and became widely used very quickly; in 1976, the Queen of England sent an e-mail message over the ARPANET. By 1981, the ARPANET had expanded to include over 200 networks and was continuing to develop faster and more effective network technologies; for example, ARPANET began sending packets via satellite in 1976.

More New Uses for Networks Emerge

The number of network users in the military and education research communities continued to grow. Many of these new participants used the networking technology to transfer files and access computers remotely. The TCP/IP suite included two tools for performing these tasks. **File Transfer Protocol (FTP)** enabled users to transfer files between computers, and **Telnet** let users log in to their computer accounts from remote sites. Both FTP and Telnet still are widely used on the Internet today for file transfers and remote logins, even though more advanced techniques facilitate multimedia transmissions such as realtime audio and video clips. The first e-mail mailing lists also appeared on these networks. A **mailing list** is an e-mail address that takes any message it receives and forwards it to any user who has subscribed to the list.

Although file transfer and remote login were attractive features of these new TCP/IP networks, their improved e-mail and other communications facilities attracted many users in the education and research communities. For example, BITNET would run mailing list software (called **LISTSERV**) on its IBM mainframe computers that provided automatic control and maintenance for the mailing lists. In 1979, a group of students and programmers at Duke University and the University of North Carolina started **Usenet**, an acronym for **User's News Network**. Usenet allows anyone that connects with the network to read and post articles on a variety of subjects.

Usenet survives on the Internet today, with over a thousand different topic areas, called **newsgroups**. Going even farther from the initial purpose of TCP/IP networks, researchers at the University of Essex wrote a program that allowed users to assume character roles and play an adventure game. This adventure game let multiple users play at the same time and interact with each other. These games continue on the Internet today and are called **MUDs**, which originally stood for **multiuser dungeon**, although many users now consider the term an acronym for **multiuser domain**, or **multiuser dimension**.

Although the people using these networks were developing many creative applications, the number of persons who had access to the networks was limited to members of the research and academic communities. The decade from 1979 to 1989 would be the time in which these new and interesting network applications were improved and tested with an increasing number of users. The TCP/IP set of protocols would become more widely used as academic and research institutions realized the benefits of having a common communications network. The explosion of PC use during that time also would help more people become comfortable with computing.

Interconnecting the Networks

The early 1980s saw continued growth in the ARPANET and other networks. The **Joint Academic Network (Janet)** was established in the United Kingdom to link universities there. Traffic increased on all of these networks and, in 1984, the Department of Defense (DOD) split the ARPANET into two specialized networks: ARPANET would continue its advanced research activities, and **MILNET** (for **Military Network**) would be reserved for military uses that required greater security. That year also saw a new addition to CSNET, named the **National Science Foundation Network (NSFnet)**. By 1987, congestion on the ARPANET caused by a rapidly increasing number of users on the limited-capacity leased telephone lines was becoming severe. To reduce the government's traffic load on the ARPANET, the NSFnet merged with BITNET and CSNET to form one network. The resulting NSFnet awarded a contract to Merit Network, Inc., IBM, Sprint, and the State of Michigan to upgrade and operate the main NSFnet backbone. A **network backbone** includes the long-distance lines and supporting technology that transports large amounts of data between major network nodes. The NSFnet backbone connected 13 regional WANs and six supercomputer centers. By the late 1980s, many other TCP/IP networks had merged or established interconnections. Figure 1-4 summarizes how the individual networks described in this section combined to become the Internet as we know it today.

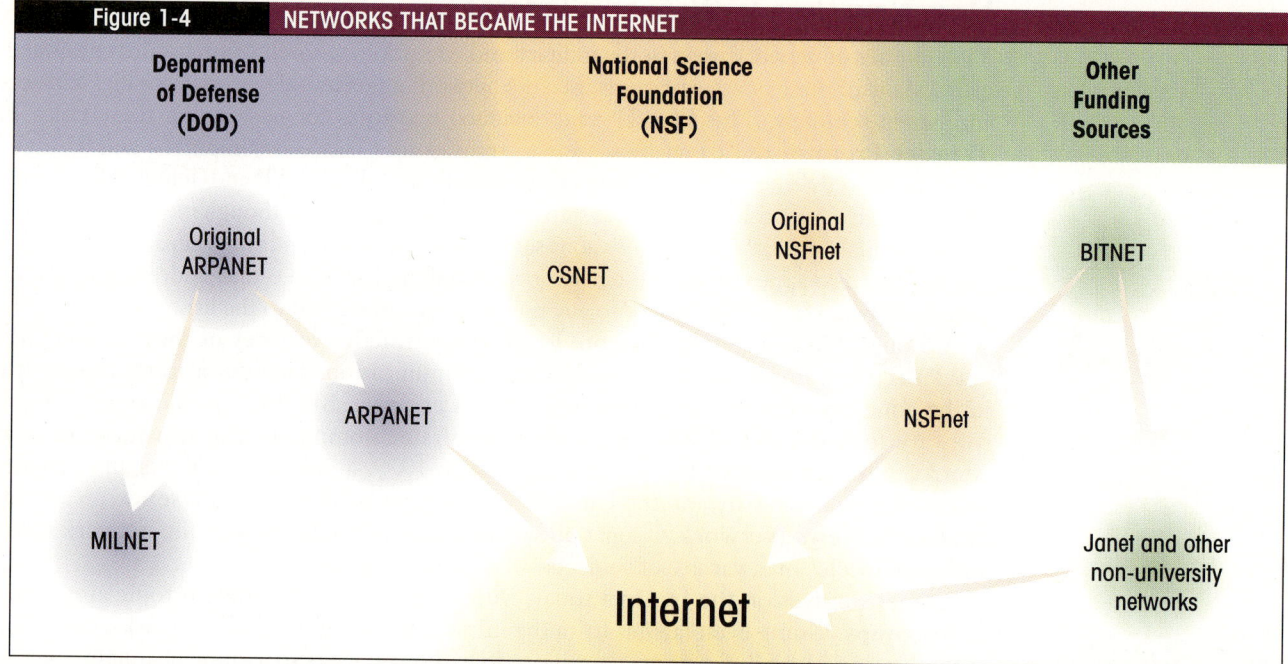

Figure 1-4 NETWORKS THAT BECAME THE INTERNET

Commercial Interest Increases

As PCs became more powerful, affordable, and available during the 1980s, firms increasingly used them to construct LANs. Although these LANs included e-mail software that employees could use to send messages to each other, businesses wanted their employees to be able to communicate with people outside their corporate LANs. The National Science Foundation (NSF) prohibited commercial network traffic on the networks it funded, so businesses turned to commercial e-mail services. Larger firms built their own TCP/IP-based WANs that used leased telephone lines to connect field offices to corporate headquarters. Today, we use the term **intranet** to describe LANs or WANs that use the TCP/IP protocol but do not connect to sites outside the firm. In 1989, the NSF permitted two commercial e-mail services, MCI Mail and CompuServe, to establish limited connections to the Internet that allowed their commercial subscribers to exchange e-mail messages with the members of the academic and research communities who were connected to the Internet. These connections allowed commercial enterprises to send e-mail directly to Internet addresses and allowed members of the research and education communities on the Internet to send e-mail directly to MCI Mail and CompuServe addresses. The NSF justified this limited commercial use of the Internet as a service that would primarily benefit the Internet's noncommercial users.

People from all walks of life—not just scientists or academic researchers—started thinking of these networks as a global resource that we now know as the Internet. Information systems professionals began to form volunteer groups such as the **Internet Engineering Task Force (IETF)**, which first met in 1986. The IETF is a self-organized group that makes technical contributions to the engineering of the Internet and its technologies. IETF is the main body that develops new Internet standards.

Just as the world was coming to realize the value of these interconnected networks, however, it also became aware of the threats to privacy and security posed by these networks. In 1988, Robert Morris launched a program called the **Internet Worm** that used weaknesses in e-mail programs and operating systems to distribute itself to over 6,000 of the 60,000 computers that were then connected to the Internet. The Worm program created multiple copies of itself on the computers it infected. The large number of program copies consumed the processing power of the infected computer and prevented it from running other programs. This event brought international attention and concern to the Internet.

Although the network of networks that is now known as the Internet had grown from four computers on the ARPANET in 1969 to over 300,000 computers on many interconnected networks by 1990, the greatest growth in the Internet was yet to come.

Growth of the Internet

A formal definition of Internet, which was adopted in 1995 by the Federal Networking Council, appears in Figure 1-5.

Figure 1-5 — THE FEDERAL NETWORKING COUNCIL'S OCTOBER 1995 RESOLUTION TO DEFINE THE TERM INTERNET

RESOLUTION: The Federal Networking Council (FNC) agrees that the following language reflects our definition of the term "Internet." "Internet" refers to the global information system that—

(i) is logically linked together by a globally unique address space based on the Internet Protocol (IP) or its subsequent extensions/follow-ons;

(ii) is able to support communications using the Transmission Control Protocol/Internet Protocol (TCP/IP) suite or its subsequent extensions/follow-ons, and/or other IP-compatible protocols; and

(iii) provides, uses or makes accessible, either publicly or privately, high level services layered on the communications and related infrastructure described herein.

Source: http://www.fnc.gov/Internet_res.html

Many people find it interesting to note that a formal definition of the term did not appear until 1995. The Internet was a phenomenon that surprised an unsuspecting world. The researchers who had been so involved in the creation and growth of the Internet accepted it as part of their working environment. People outside the research community were largely unaware of the potential offered by a large interconnected set of computer networks.

From Research Project to Information Infrastructure

By 1990, the Internet had become a well-functioning grid of useful technology. Much of the funding for these networks had come from the U.S. government, through its DOD and the NSF. The NSFnet alone consumed over $200 million from 1986 to 1995 on research and development. Realizing that the Internet was no longer a research project, the DOD finally closed the research portion of its network, the ARPANET. The NSF also wanted to turn over the Internet to others so it could return its attention and funds to other research projects.

In 1991, the NSF further eased its restrictions on Internet commercial activity and began implementing plans to privatize much of the Internet eventually. The first parts of the NSFnet on which it encouraged commercial activity were the local and regional nodes, which allowed time for private firms to develop long-haul network capacity similar to that of the NSFnet national network backbone. Businesses and individuals connected to the Internet in ever-increasing numbers. Figure 1-6 shows the number of Internet host computers from 1991 through 1999. As you can see, the growth has been dramatic.

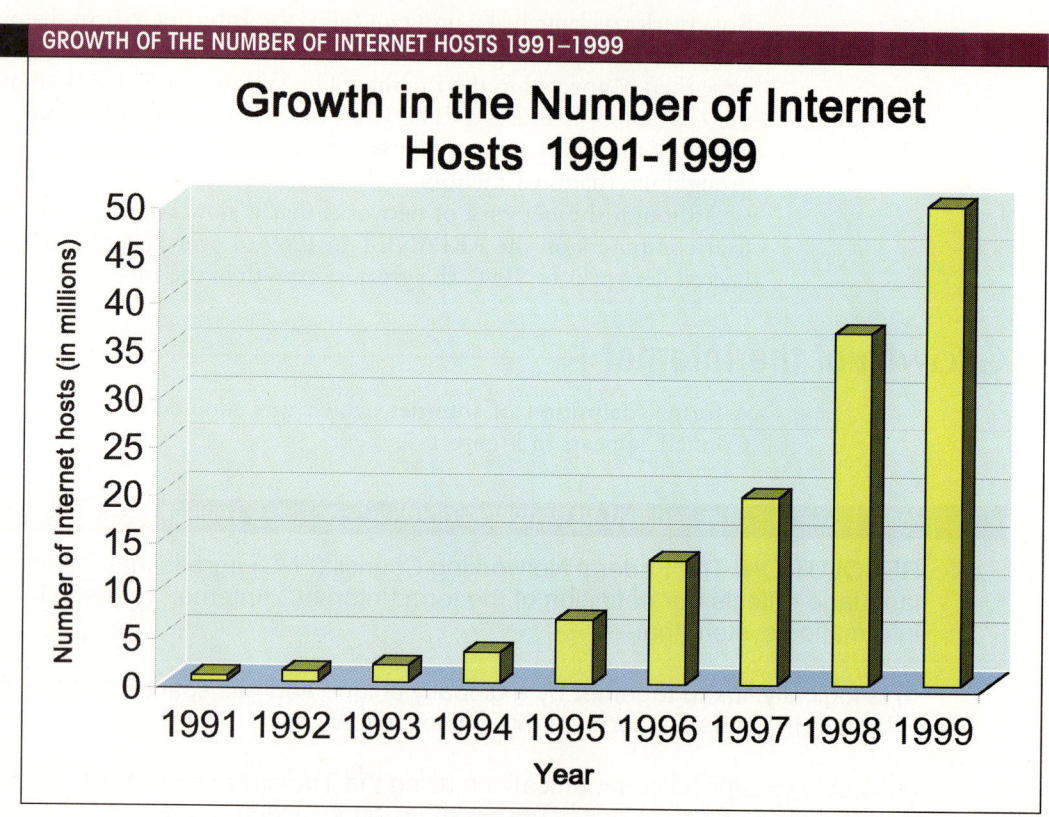

Figure 1-6 GROWTH OF THE NUMBER OF INTERNET HOSTS 1991–1999

The numbers in Figure 1-6 probably understate the true growth of the Internet in recent years for two reasons. First, the number of hosts connected to the Internet includes only directly connected computers. In other words, if a LAN with 100 PCs is connected to the

Internet through only one host computer, those 100 computers appear as one host in the count. Because the number and size of LANs has increased steadily in recent years, the host count probably is understated. Second, the number of computers is only one measure of growth. Internet traffic now carries more files that contain graphics, sound, and video, so Internet files have become larger. A given number of users sending video clips will use much more of the Internet's capacity than the same number of users will use by sending e-mail messages or text files. Many people are surprised to learn that no one knows how many users are on the Internet. The Internet has no central management or coordination, and the routing computers do not maintain records of the packets they handle. Therefore, no one has the capability to know how many individual e-mail messages or files travel on the Internet.

New Structure for the Internet

As NSFnet converted the main traffic-carrying backbone portion of its network to private firms, it organized the network around the four network access points (NAPs) shown in Figure 1-7. A different company now operates each of these NAPs, as shown in Figure 1-7.

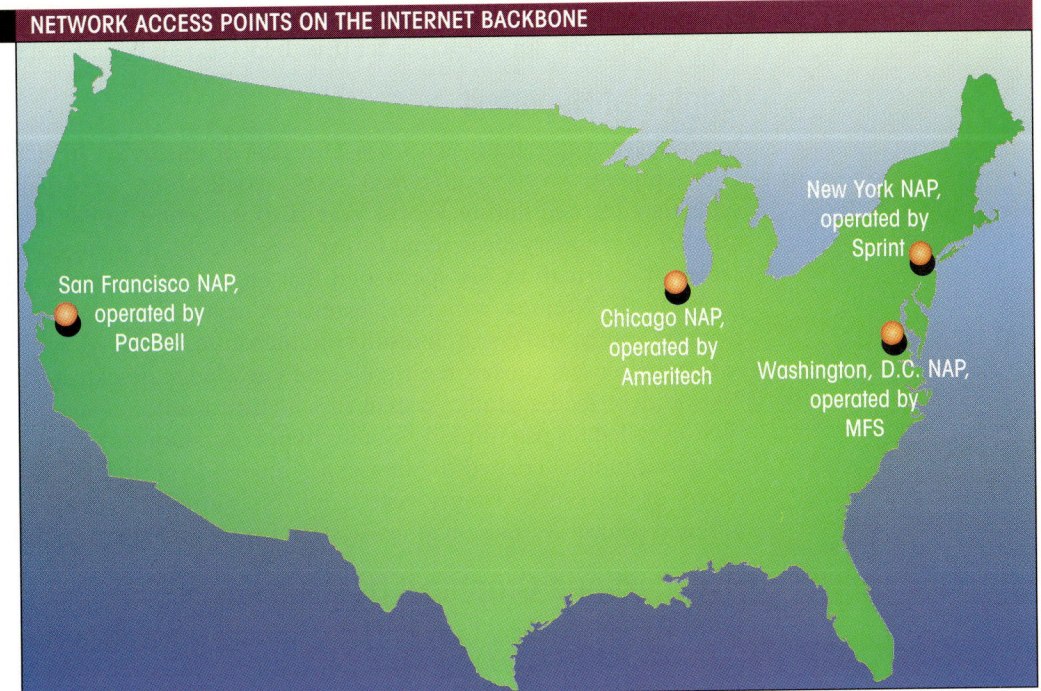

Figure 1-7 NETWORK ACCESS POINTS ON THE INTERNET BACKBONE

These four companies sell access to the Internet through their NAPs to organizations and businesses. The NSFnet still exists for government and research use, but it uses these same NAPs for long-range data transmission.

With over 20 million connected computers and an estimate of between 50 and 150 million worldwide Internet users, the Internet faces some challenges. The firms that sell network access have enough incentive to keep investing in the network architecture because they can recoup their investments by attracting new Internet users. However, the existing TCP/IP numbering system that identifies users will run out of addresses in a few years if the Internet continues its current rate of growth. Groups like the IETF are working on a new addressing scheme that will allow existing users to continue accessing the Internet while the new system is implemented.

In less than 30 years, the Internet has become one of the most amazing technological and social accomplishments of the century. Millions of people use a complex, interconnected network of computers that run thousands of different software packages. The computers are located in almost every country of the world. Over one billion dollars changes hands over the Internet in exchange for all kinds of products and services. All of this activity occurs with no central coordination point or control. Even more interesting is that the Internet began as a way for the military to maintain control while under attack.

The opening of the Internet to business enterprise helped increase its growth dramatically in recent years. However, another development worked hand-in-hand with the commercialization of the Internet to spur its growth. That development was the technological advance known as the World Wide Web.

World Wide Web

The World Wide Web (the Web) is more a way of thinking about information storage and retrieval than it is a technology. Because of this, its history goes back many years. Two important innovations played key roles in making the Internet easier to use and more accessible to people who were not research scientists: hypertext and graphical user interfaces (GUIs).

Origins of Hypertext

In 1945, Vannevar Bush, who was Director of the U.S. Office of Scientific Research and Development, wrote an *Atlantic Monthly* article about ways that scientists could apply the skills they learned during World War II to peacetime applications. The article included a number of visionary ideas about future uses of technology to organize and facilitate efficient access to information. He speculated that engineers eventually would build a machine that he called the **Memex**, a memory extension device that would store all of a person's books, records, letters, and research results on microfilm. Bush's Memex would include mechanical aids to help users consult their collected knowledge quickly and flexibly. In the 1960s, Ted Nelson described a similar system in which text on one page links to text on other pages. Nelson called his page-linking system **hypertext**. Douglas Englebart, who also invented the computer mouse, created the first experimental hypertext system on one of the large computers of the 1960s. Twenty years later, Nelson published *Literary Machines*, in which he outlined project **Xanadu**, a global system for online hypertext publishing and commerce.

Hypertext and Graphical User Interfaces Come to the Internet

In 1989, Tim Berners-Lee and Robert Calliau were working at CERN-The European Laboratory for Particle Physics and were trying to improve the laboratory's research document-handling procedures. CERN had been connected to the Internet for two years, but its scientists wanted to find better ways to circulate their scientific papers and data among the high-energy physics research community throughout the world. Independently, they each proposed a hypertext development project.

Over the next two years, Berners-Lee developed the code for a hypertext server program and made it available on the Internet. A **hypertext server** is a computer that stores files written in the hypertext markup language and lets other computers connect to it and read those files. **Hypertext markup language** (**HTML**) is a language that includes a set of codes (or **tags**) attached to text. These codes describe the relationships among text elements. For example, HTML includes tags that indicate which text is part of a header element, which text is part of a paragraph element, and which text is part of a numbered list element. One important type of tag is the hypertext link tag. A **hypertext link**, or **hyperlink**, points to another location in the same or another HTML document. You can use several different types of software to read HTML documents, but most people use a Web browser such as Netscape Navigator or Microsoft Internet Explorer. A **Web browser** is software that lets users read (or browse) HTML documents and move from one HTML document to another through the text formatted with hypertext link tags in each file. If the HTML documents are on computers connected to the Internet, you can use a Web browser to move from an HTML document on one computer to an HTML document on any other computer on the Internet. HTML is based on **Standard Generalized Markup Language** (**SGML**), which organizations have used for many years to manage large document-filing systems.

An HTML document differs from a word-processing document because it does not specify *how* a particular text element will appear. For example, you might use word-processing software to create a document heading by setting the heading text font to Arial, its font size to 14 points, and its position to centered. The document would display and print these exact settings whenever you opened the document in that word processor. In contrast, an HTML document would simply include a heading tag with the text. Many different programs can read an HTML document. Each program recognizes the heading tag and displays the text in whatever manner each program normally displays headers. Different programs might display the text differently.

A Web browser presents an HTML document in an easy-to-read format in its graphical user interface. A **graphical user interface (GUI)** is a way of presenting program output to users that uses pictures, icons, and other graphical elements instead of just displaying text. Almost all PCs today use a GUI such as Microsoft Windows or the Macintosh user interface.

Berners-Lee and Calliau called their system of hyperlinked HTML documents the World Wide Web. The Web caught on quickly in the scientific research community, but few people outside that community had software that could read the HTML documents. In 1993, a group of students led by Marc Andreessen at the University of Illinois wrote **Mosaic**, the first GUI program that could read HTML and use HTML documents' hyperlinks to navigate from page to page on computers anywhere on the Internet. Mosaic was the first Web browser that became widely available for PCs.

The Web and Commercialization of the Internet

Programmers quickly realized that a functional system of pages connected by hypertext links would provide many new Internet users with an easy way to locate information on the Internet. Businesses quickly recognized the profit-making potential offered by a worldwide network of easy-to-use computers. In 1994, Andreessen and other members of the University of Illinois Mosaic team joined with James Clark of Silicon Graphics to found Netscape Communications. Their first product, the Netscape Web browser program based on Mosaic, was an instant success. Netscape became one of the fastest growing software companies ever. Microsoft created its Internet Explorer Web browser and entered the market soon after Netscape's success became apparent. A number of other Web browsers exist, but these two products dominate the market today.

The number of **Web sites**, which are computers connected to the Internet that store HTML documents, has grown even more rapidly than the Internet itself to nearly 8 million sites. Each Web site might have hundreds, or even thousands, of individual Web pages, so the amount of information on the Web is astounding. Figure 1-8 shows the phenomenal growth in the Web during its short lifetime.

As more people obtain access to the Web, commercial uses of the Web and a variety of nonbusiness uses will greatly increase. Although the Web has grown rapidly, many experts believe that it will grow at an increasing rate for the foreseeable future.

| Figure 1-8 | GROWTH OF THE WORLD WIDE WEB |

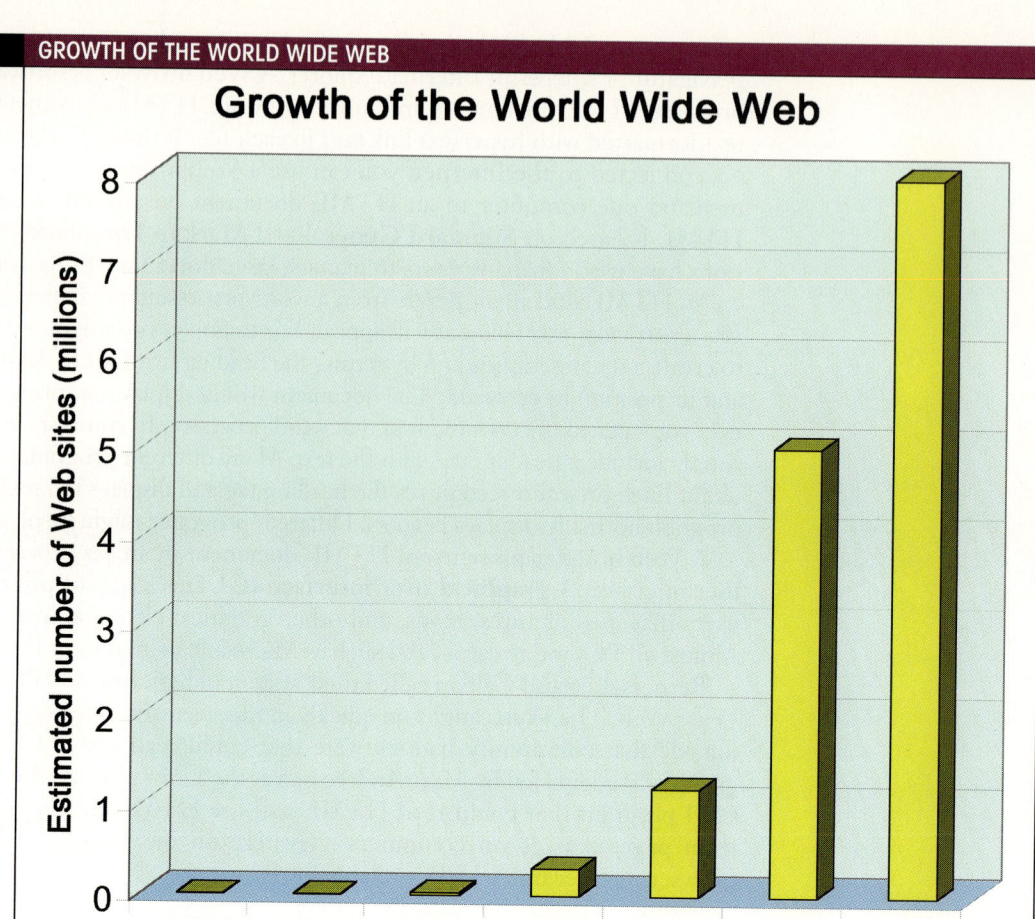

Session 1.1 QUICK CHECK

1. Name three resources that computers connected to a client/server LAN can share.
2. The fastest and most expensive way to connect computers in a network is _____ cable.
3. Telephone companies use centrally controlled circuit switching to connect telephone callers and transmit data. Name and briefly describe the switching method used by the Internet.
4. What is the technical term for the collection of rules that computers follow when formatting, ordering, and error-checking data sent across a network?
5. The networks that became the Internet were originally designed to transmit files; however, early in its history, people found other uses for the Internet. Name three of those uses.
6. What is an intranet?

7. Name and briefly describe two key factors that contributed to the Internet's rapid growth in the 1990s.
8. What type of software can network users run on their computers to access HTML documents that are stored on other computers?

You have obtained a good background for your report on how TEPCo might use the Internet and the Web by learning about their histories. You are convinced that the Internet can help Lorraine and her assistants manage the company better, identify new customers, and stay in contact with suppliers. You decide that the next logical step in your research is to identify ways that TEPCo can connect to the Internet. In the next session, you will learn how to evaluate Internet connection options.

SESSION 1.2

You can connect your computer to the Internet in several different ways. This session presents an overview of connection options and explains how you can choose the one that is right for you.

Connection Options

Remember that the Internet is a set of interconnected networks. Therefore, you cannot become a part of the Internet unless you are part of a communications network, whether it is a LAN, an intranet, or through a telephone connection. Each network that joins the Internet must accept some responsibility for operating the network by routing message packets that other networks pass along. As you consider your project for TEPCo, you become concerned that Justin and Arti are not going to want to become involved in something this complex. After all, they are exotic-produce experts—not computer wizards!

Business of Providing Internet Access

As you continue your research, you learn more about the NAPs (network access points) that maintain the core operations and long-haul backbone of the Internet. You find that they do not offer direct connections to individuals or small businesses. Instead, they offer connections to large organizations and businesses that, in turn, provide Internet access to other businesses and individuals. These firms are called **Internet access providers** (**IAPs**) or **Internet service providers** (**ISPs**). Most of these firms call themselves ISPs because they offer more than just access to the Internet. ISPs usually provide their customers with the software they need to connect to the ISP, browse the Web, send and receive e-mail messages, and perform other Internet-related functions such as file transfer and remote login to other computers. ISPs often provide network consulting services to their customers and help them design Web pages. Some ISPs have developed a full range of services that include network management, training, and marketing advice. Some larger ISPs not only sell Internet access to end users, but also market Internet access to other ISPs, which then sell access and service to their own business and individual customers. This hierarchy of Internet access appears in Figure 1-9.

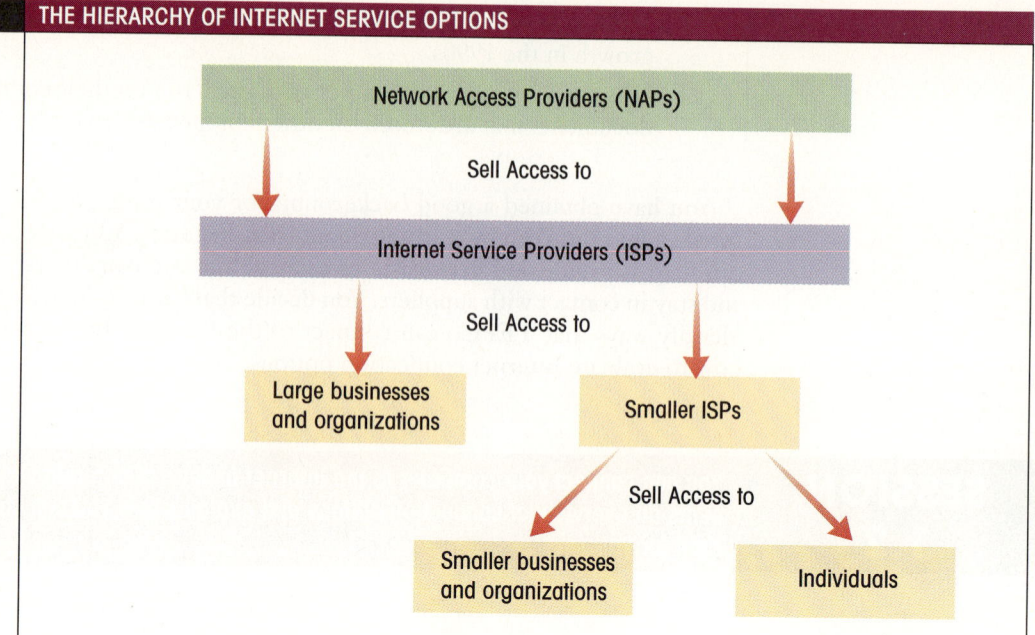

Figure 1-9   THE HIERARCHY OF INTERNET SERVICE OPTIONS

Connection Bandwidth

Of the differences that exist among service providers at different levels of the access hierarchy, one of the most important is the connection bandwidth that an ISP can offer. **Bandwidth** is the amount of data that can travel through a communications circuit in one second. The bandwidth that an ISP can offer you depends on the type of connection it has to the Internet and the kind of connection you have to the ISP.

The bandwidth for a network connection between two points always is limited to the narrowest bandwidth that exists in any part of the network. For example, if you connect to an ISP through a regular telephone line, your bandwidth is limited to the bandwidth of that telephone line, regardless of the bandwidth connection that the ISP has to the Internet. Bandwidth is measured in multiples of **bits per second (bps)**. Discussions of Internet bandwidth often use the terms **kilobits per second (Kbps)**, which is 1,024 bps; **megabits per second (Mbps)**, which is 1,048,576 bps; and **gigabits per second (Gbps)**, which is 1,073,741,824 bps. Most LANs run either an Ethernet network, which has a bandwidth of 10 Mbps, or Fast Ethernet, which operates at 100 Mbps. When you extend your network beyond a local area, the speed of the connection depends on what type of connection you use.

One way to connect computers or networks over longer distances is to use regular telephone service (sometimes referred to as **POTS**, or **plain old telephone service**). Regular telephone service to most U.S. residential and business customers provides a maximum bandwidth of between 28.8 Kbps and 56 Kbps. These numbers vary because the United States has a number of different telephone companies that do not all use the same technology. Some telephone companies offer a higher grade of service that uses one of a series of protocols called **Digital Subscriber Line** or **Digital Subscriber Loop (DSL)**. The first technology that was developed using a DSL protocol is called **Integrated Services Digital Network (ISDN)**. ISDN service has been available in various parts of the United States since 1984. Although considerably more expensive than regular telephone service, ISDN offers bandwidths of up to 128 Kbps. ISDN is much more widely available in Australia, France, Germany, Japan, and Singapore than in the United States because the regulatory structure of the telecommunications industries in these countries encouraged rapid deployment of this new technology. All technologies based on the DSL protocol require the implementing telephone company to install modems at its switching stations, which can be very expensive. New technologies that use the DSL protocol are currently being implemented around the world. One of those, **Asymmetric Digital Subscriber Line**

(**ADSL**, also abbreviated **DSL**), offers transmission speeds ranging from 16 to 640 Kbps from the user to the telephone company and from 1.5 to 9 Mbps from the telephone company to the user.

Larger firms can connect to an ISP using higher-bandwidth telephone company connections called **T1** (1.544 Mbps) and **T3** (44.736 Mbps) connections. These connections are much more expensive than POTS or ISDN connections; however, organizations that must link hundreds or thousands of individual users to the Internet require the greater bandwidth of T1 and T3 connections. The NAPs currently operate the Internet backbone using a variety of connections. In addition to T1 and T3 lines, the NAPs use newer **Asynchronous Transfer Mode (ATM)** connections that have bandwidths of up to 622 Mbps. Improved ATM methods are being developed that will provide bandwidths exceeding 1 Gbps. NAPs also use satellite and radio communications links to transfer data over long distances. The NAPs are working with a group of universities and the National Science Foundation (NSF) to develop a network called **Internet 2** that will have backbone bandwidths that exceed 1 Gbps.

A new connection option that is available in parts of the United States is to connect to the Internet through a cable television company. The cable company transmits data in the same cables it uses to provide television service. Only a few cable operators around the country currently have the necessary cable installed to offer this service; however, many cable operators are planning to upgrade their facilities during the next few years. Cable can deliver up to 10 Mbps to an individual user and can accept up to 768 Kbps from an individual user. These speeds far exceed those of existing POTS and ISDN connections and are comparable to speeds provided by the ADSL technologies currently being implemented by telephone companies.

An option that is particularly appealing to users in remote areas is connecting via satellite. Using a satellite-dish receiver, you can download at a bandwidth of approximately 400 Kbps. Unfortunately, you cannot send information to the Internet using a satellite dish, so you must also have an ISP account to send files or e-mail. Figure 1-10 summarizes the bandwidths for various types of connections currently in use on the Internet.

Figure 1-10 BANDWIDTHS FOR VARIOUS TYPES OF INTERNET CONNECTIONS

TYPE OF SERVICE	SPEED	TYPICAL USES
Regular telephone service	28.8 Kbps to 56 Kbps	Individual and small business users connecting to ISPs
Integrated Services Digital Network (ISDN)	128 Kbps	Individual and small business users connecting to ISPs
Asymmetric Digital Subscriber Line (ADSL or DSL)	16 Kbps to 640 Kbps (upload) 1.5 Mbps to 9 Mbps (download)	Individual and small business users connecting to ISPs
Cable modem	Up to 768 Kbps (upload) Up to 10 Mbps (download)	Individual and small business users connecting to ISPs
T1 leased line	1.544 Mbps	Large businesses and other organizations connecting to ISPs and ISPs connecting to other ISPs
T3 leased line	44.736 Mbps	Large businesses and other organizations connecting to ISPs, ISPs connecting to other ISPs, ISPs connecting to NAPs, and portions of the Internet backbone
Asynchronous Transfer Mode (ATM) Line	622 Mbps	Internet backbone

As you evaluate the information you have gathered about ways Lorraine might connect TEPCo to the Internet, you realize that there are four ways that individuals or small businesses can link to the Internet. The first way, which is only for individuals, is a connection through your school or employer. The second option is to connect through an ISP. The third option is to connect through a cable television company. The fourth option is to use a combination of satellite download and an upload method. Next, you will learn about some of the advantages and disadvantages of each connection method that you have identified for your analysis and report to Lorraine.

Connecting Through Your School or Employer

One of the easiest ways to connect to the Internet is through your school or employer, if it already has an Internet connection. The connection is either free or very reasonably priced. However, by using your school or employer to connect to the Internet, you must comply with its rules. In some cases, this can outweigh the cost advantage.

Connecting Through Your School

Most universities and community colleges are connected to the Internet, and many offer Internet access to their students, faculty members, and other employees. In most schools, you can use computers in computing labs or in the library to access the Internet. Many schools provide a way to connect your own computer through the school's network to the Internet. The form of connection will depend on what your school offers. An increasing number of schools have dormitory rooms wired with LAN connections so students can connect using their own computers. Some schools even provide the computers as part of their tuition or housing charge.

Dialing in

Most schools or businesses, whether or not they have LANs in their buildings, provide telephone numbers that you can call and connect your computer through a modem. **Modem** is short for **modulator-demodulator**. When you connect your computer, which communicates using digital signals, to another computer through a telephone line, which uses analog signals, you must perform a signal conversion. Converting a digital signal to an analog signal is **modulation**; converting that analog signal back into digital form is called **demodulation**. A modem performs both functions; that is, it acts as a modulator-demodulator. If you use a modem to connect to the Internet, you will need to install software that implements a protocol that makes your modem connection appear to be a TCP/IP connection. Two of the most frequently used software packages are the **serial line Internet protocol (SLIP)** and the **point-to-point protocol (PPP)**. Usually, this software automatically chooses the correct protocol (either SLIP or PPP) when you install it, based on your description of the connection you are making.

Connecting Through Your Employer

Your employer might offer you a connection to the Internet through the computer you use in your job. This computer might be connected through a LAN to the Internet, or you might have to use a modem to connect it. Before you attempt to connect to the Internet this way, make sure that your employer permits personal use of company computing facilities. Remember, your employer owns the computers you use as an employee. In most of the world, this gives your employer the right to examine any e-mail or files that you transmit or store using those computers. A number of schools retain similar rights under the law or through policies they publish in their student handbooks.

Acceptable Use Policies

Most schools and employers have an **acceptable use policy (AUP)** that specifies the conditions under which you can use their Internet connections. Some organizations require you to sign a copy of the AUP before they permit you to use their computing facilities; others simply include it as part of your student or employee contract. AUPs often include provisions that require you to respect copyright laws, trade secrets, the privacy of other users, and standards of common decency. Many AUPs expressly prohibit you from engaging in commercial activities, criminal activities, or specific threat-making or equipment-endangering practices.

Many provisions in AUPs are open to honest misunderstanding or disagreement in interpretation. It is extremely important for you to read and understand any AUP with which you must comply when you use computing facilities at your school or employer. AUPs often include punitive provisions that include revocation of user accounts and all rights to use the network. Some AUPs state that a user can be expelled or fired for serious violations.

Advantages and Disadvantages

Although accessing the Internet through your school or employer might be the least expensive option, you might decide that the restrictions on your freedom of expression and actions are too great. For example, if you wanted to start a small business on the Web, you would not want to use your school account if its AUP has a commercial-activity exclusion. An important concern when using your employer's computing facilities to connect to the Internet is that the employer generally retains the right to examine any files or e-mail messages that you transmit through those facilities. Carefully consider whether the limitations placed on your use of the Internet are greater than the benefits of the low cost of this access option.

Connecting Through an Internet Service Provider

Depending on where you live, you might find that an ISP is the best way for you to connect to the Internet. In major metropolitan areas, many ISPs compete for customers and, therefore connection fees often are reasonable. Smaller towns and rural areas have fewer ISPs and, thus might be less competitive. When you are shopping for an ISP, you will want to find information such as:

- The monthly base fee and number of hours it provides
- The hourly rate for time used over the monthly base amount
- Whether the telephone access number is local or long distance
- Which specific Internet services are included
- What software is included
- What user-support services are available

Advantages and Disadvantages

ISPs are the best option for many Internet users, in part because they usually provide reliable connectivity at a reasonable price. The terms of their AUPs often are less restrictive than those imposed by schools on their students or employers on their employees. You should examine carefully the terms of the service agreement, and you always should obtain references from customers who use an ISP before signing any long-term contract.

Some ISPs limit the number of customers they serve, whereas others guarantee that you will not receive a busy signal when you dial in. These are significant factors in the quality of service you will experience. Remember, each ISP has a limited amount of bandwidth in its connection to the Internet. If your ISP allows more new customers to subscribe to its service than leave each month, each remaining user will have proportionally less bandwidth available. Be especially wary of ISPs that offer a large discount if you sign a long-term agreement. The quality of service might deteriorate significantly over time if the ISP adds many new customers without expanding its bandwidth.

You also should find out whether the ISP has an AUP and, if so, you should examine its terms carefully. Some ISPs have restrictive policies. For example, an ISP might have an entirely different fee structure for customers who use their Internet access for commercial purposes. Carefully outline how you plan to use your Internet connection and decide what services you want before signing any long-term contract with an ISP.

Connecting Through Your Cable Television Company

One of the more recent developments in the Internet access business is the cable modem. A **cable modem** performs a function similar to that of a regular modem; that is, it converts digital computer signals to analog signals. However, instead of converting the digital signals into telephone-line analog signals, a cable modem converts them into radio-frequency analog signals that are similar to television transmission signals. The converted signals travel to and from the cable company on the same lines that carry your cable television service. The cable company maintains a connection to the Internet and otherwise operates much like the ISPs discussed previously, which deliver an Internet connection through telephone lines.

To install a cable modem, the cable company first installs a **line-splitter**, a device that divides the combined cable signals into their television and data components, and then connects the television (or televisions) and the cable modem to the line-splitter. Most cable companies that offer this service rent the required line-splitter and cable modem to each customer.

Advantages and Disadvantages

The main advantage of a cable television connection to the Internet is its high bandwidth. A cable connection can provide very fast downloads to your computer from the Internet, as much as 170 times faster than a telephone line connection. Although upload speeds are not as fast, they are still about 14 times faster than a telephone line connection. The cost usually is higher than—and often more than double—what competing ISPs charge. However, if you consider that the cable connection might save you the cost of a second telephone line, the net benefit can be significant. The greatest disadvantage for most people right now is that the cable connection is simply not available in their area yet. Because cable companies must invest in expensive upgrades to offer this service, it might not become available in many parts of the U.S. for many years. You should remember that, other than the nature of the connection, a cable company is the same as any other ISP. Therefore, all of the issues outlined in the previous section about contracting with ISPs apply equally to dealing with your cable company.

Connecting Via Satellite

Many rural areas in the United States do not have cable television service and never will because their low population density makes it too expensive: A cable company cannot afford to run miles of cable to reach one or two isolated customers. People in these areas often buy satellite receivers to obtain television signals. Recently, Internet connections via satellite became available. The satellite connection is downlink only, so you also must have another connection through an ISP that uses telephone lines to handle the uplink half of the connection.

Advantages and Disadvantages

The major advantage of a satellite connection is speed. Although the speeds are not as great as those offered by cable modems, they are about five to ten times greater than telephone connections. The speed increase is in one direction only, so you still send information to the Internet through a modem and telephone lines to an ISP. An ISP still is involved in this connection option, so all of the advantages and disadvantages outlined earlier also apply to a satellite connection. The cost of the satellite dish antenna and receiver still is fairly high, but prices are slowly dropping as more people become aware of this connection option. For users in remote areas, this technology often offers the best connection solution.

Session 1.2 QUICK CHECK

1. To connect to the Internet, your computer must be part of a(n) _____.
2. What services do ISPs usually offer their customers?
3. How much greater bandwidth does ISDN offer over telephone service?
4. The Internet backbone today uses a combination of technologies to transmit data over long distances. Name and briefly describe three of these technologies.
5. Explain briefly how a modem enables a computer to transmit information over regular telephone lines.

6. Many schools and businesses have adopted acceptable use policies (AUPs). Describe the purpose of an AUP.
7. What conditions would lead you to consider connecting to the Internet via satellite?

You now have collected a great deal of information about the origins and history of the Internet and the Web. As you conducted your research project for TEPCo, you learned about some of the information and tools that exist on the Internet. You also gathered information about ways to connect to the Internet. Now you are ready to prepare your report for Lorraine and recommend a plan of action for connecting TEPCo to the Internet.

PROJECTS

1. **Diagramming School Networks** Your school probably has a number of computer networks. At most schools, you can find information about computing facilities from the department of academic computing or the school library. Identify what LANs and WANs you have on your campus, and determine whether any or all of them are interconnected. Draw a diagram that shows the networks, their connections to each other, and their connection to the Internet.

2. **DARPA Alternatives** The DARPA researchers that laid the foundation for the Internet were conducting research on ways to coordinate weapons control. They chose to develop a computer network that could operate without a central control mechanism. Think about alternative directions that the DARPA researchers might have taken to achieve their objective. Select one of these alternative directions, and discuss whether you think that approach would have given birth to something like the Internet. Describe how you think it would differ from the Internet and Web that exist today.

3. **School Cabling Choices** Select two or three buildings on your campus that have computers in offices, dormitory rooms, or computing labs. Find out from the appropriate office administrator, dormitory official, or lab supervisor what kind of computer cable the school uses to connect the computers. Evaluate the school's cabling choices. Would you make the same decisions? Why or why not?

4. **Using the Web and E-Mail** Describe three ways in which you might use the Web or e-mail to identify part-time job and internship opportunities that relate to your major.

5. **Acceptable Use Policy Evaluation** Obtain a copy of your school's or employer's acceptable use policy (AUP). Outline the main restrictions it places on student (or employee) activities. Compare those restrictions with the limits it places on faculty (or employer) activities. Analyze and evaluate any differences in treatment. If there are no differences, discuss whether the policy should be rewritten to include differences. If your school or employer has no policy, outline the key elements that you believe should be included in such a policy for your school or employer.

6. **Commercialization of the Internet** Many people who have been involved with the Internet for many years believe that the National Science Foundation (NSF) made a serious mistake when it opened the Internet to commercial traffic. Discuss the advantages and disadvantages of this policy decision. Do you think that the Internet would be as successful as it is today if no commercial activity were allowed?

7. **The Web and the Memex Machine** Vannevar Bush died before the Web came into existence. Speculate on what he would have thought about the Web. Would he have seen it as the embodiment of his Memex machine? Why or why not?

8. **Evaluating ISPs** Contact three ISPs in your area and obtain information about their Internet access and related services. You can find ISPs in your local telephone directory (try headings such as "Internet Services," "Computer Networks," or "Computer On-Line Services"), or look for advertisements in your local or student newspaper. Summarize the services and the charges for each service by ISP. Which ISP would you recommend for an individual? Why? Which ISP would you recommend for a small business? Why?

Quick Check Answers

Session 1.1

1. Printers, scanners, digital cameras, data files, programs, and so forth.
2. fiber-optic
3. The Internet uses packet switching, a method in which files and messages are broken down into packets that are labeled electronically with codes for their origin and destination. The packets travel along the network until they reach the destination computer, which collects the packets and reassembles the original data from the pieces in each packet.
4. protocol
5. e-mail, mailing lists, Usenet newsgroups, and adventure gaming
6. A LAN or WAN that uses the TCP/IP protocol but does not connect to sites outside a particular business firm or other organization.
7. Commercialization and the development of the WWW. Commercialization opened the Internet's potential to persons outside the academic and research communities, and the WWW graphical user interface (GUI) helped these new participants effectively use and add value to the Internet.
8. Web browser software

Session 1.2

1. network
2. Software to connect to the ISP, browse the Web, send and receive e-mail messages, transfer files, and log in to remote computers. Also, some ISPs provide network-consulting services and network management, training, and marketing advice.
3. two to four times
4. Leased telephone lines, satellite links, and radio communications links. Leased telephone lines include T1 lines, T3 lines, and Asynchronous Transfer Mode (ATM) connections. Satellite and radio links are used for the parts of the Internet that cross oceans and connect to remote locations.
5. A modem converts a computer's digital signals into analog signals that will travel over regular telephone lines (modulation). When the analog signal arrives at its destination, another modem converts the analog signals back into digital signals (demodulation).
6. An AUP specifies the conditions under which you can use your school's or your employer's Internet connection. AUPs often prohibit users from engaging in commercial activities, criminal activities, or specific threat-making or equipment-endangering practices.
7. Persons who live in remote areas that are not served by cable television providers would consider connecting to the Internet via satellite if they desired a faster connection than that available through regular telephone lines.

TUTORIAL 2

OBJECTIVES

In this tutorial you will:

- Learn about e-mail and how it works
- Set up and use two popular e-mail programs
- Send and receive e-mail messages
- Print an e-mail message
- Forward and reply to e-mail messages
- Create folders to save your e-mail messages
- File and delete e-mail messages and folders
- Create and maintain an electronic address book

LABS

E-mail

BASIC E-MAIL: INTEGRATED BROWSER E-MAIL SOFTWARE

Evaluating E-Mail Alternatives

CASE

Sidamo's Carpets

Sidamo's Carpets is a large retail store that has been selling fine Oriental rugs since 1930. Ifram Sidamo opened his store on one floor of a large department store in Syracuse, New York. In the early days, Sidamo's sold all of its rugs to walk-in customers. Most new customers learned about Sidamo's through other customers who raved about Sidamo's high quality and variety of handmade rugs from Iran, India, Pakistan, and China.

Sidamo's Carpets has grown considerably over the years, both in size and sales volume. Today, Sidamo's boasts of customers from all over the United States as well as from many other countries. No longer a regional company, Sidamo's is now housed in a single, large store on the outskirts of Syracuse. With over 7,000 Oriental rugs in stock, Sidamo's offers a complete line of Oriental rugs that range in size from small mat and scatter rugs to large carpets. Over the past three years, Sidamo's has used extensive advertising campaigns to broaden its visibility. Barbara Goldberg, Sidamo's vice president of marketing, estimates that more than half of Sidamo's sales are from customers who have never visited Sidamo's showroom. Interestingly, 42 percent of all sales are to repeat customers.

Typically, a customer would see a Sidamo's advertisement in a magazine and then call the toll-free number to inquire about available rugs. This system has worked well so far, but Barbara believes that Sidamo's could serve a growing number of customers better—especially repeat customers—if it provided e-mail as an alternative way of contacting the Sidamo's sales staff. Barbara has hired you to put the new e-mail system in place. Your job includes evaluating available e-mail systems and overseeing the software's installation. Eventually, you will train the sales staff so they can use the new e-mail system efficiently and effectively.

SESSION 2.1

In this session, you will learn what e-mail is, how it travels to its destination, and the parts of a typical e-mail message. You will find out about signature files and how to use them. You will set up an e-mail client program to send, receive, print, delete, file, forward, reply to, and respond to e-mail messages. Finally, you will use an address book to manage your e-mail addresses.

What Is E-Mail and How Does It Work?

Electronic mail, or **e-mail**, is one of the most prevalent forms of business communication and the most popular use of the Internet. In fact, many people view the Internet as an electronic highway that transports e-mail messages, without realizing that the Internet provides a wide variety of services. E-mail travels across the Internet to its destination and is deposited in the recipient's electronic mailbox. While similar to other forms of correspondence, including letters and memos, e-mail has the added advantage of being fast and inexpensive. Instead of traveling through a complicated, expensive, and frequently slow mail delivery service such as a postal system, e-mail travels quickly, efficiently, and inexpensively to its destination across the city or around the world. You can send a message any time you want, without worrying about when the mail is picked up or delivered or adding any postage. In business and recreation today, people rely on e-mail as an indispensable way of sending messages and data to each other. Businesses today depend on e-mail to deliver mission-critical and time-sensitive information to other businesses, customers, and employees internal to the organization.

E-mail travels across the Internet like other forms of information—that is, in small packets, which are reassembled at the destination and delivered to the addressee, whose address you specify in the message. When you send an e-mail message to its addressee, the message is sent to a **mail server**, which is a hardware and software system that determines from the recipient's address one of several electronic routes to send your message. When you send an e-mail message to another person, the message is routed from one computer to another and is passed through several mail servers. Each mail server determines the next leg of the journey for your message until it finally arrives at the recipient's electronic mailbox.

Sending e-mail employs one of the many technologies used on the Internet. Special **protocols**, or rules that determine how the Internet handles message packets flowing on it, are used to interpret and transmit e-mail. **SMTP (Simple Mail Transfer Protocol)** decides which paths your e-mail message takes on the Internet. SMTP handles outbound mail; another protocol called **POP (Post Office Protocol)** takes care of incoming messages. POP is a standard, extensively used protocol that is part of the Internet suite of recognized protocols. Other protocols used to deliver mail include **IMAP (Internet Message Access Protocol)** and **MIME (Multipurpose Internet Mail Extensions)**. IMAP is a protocol for retrieving mail messages from a server, and MIME protocol specifies how to encode nontext data, such as graphics and sound, so they can travel over the Internet.

When an e-mail message arrives at its destination mail server, the mail server's software handles the details of distributing the e-mail locally, much like a mail-room worker unbundles a bag of mail and places letters and packages into individual departmental or personal mail slots. When the server receives a new message, it is not saved directly on the recipient's individual computer, but rather, it is held on the mail server. When you check for new e-mail messages, you use a program stored on your personal computer (PC) to request the mail server to deliver any stored mail to your PC. The software that requests mail delivery from the mail server to your PC is known as **mail client software**. You will learn about two popular e-mail client programs—Netscape Messenger and Microsoft Outlook Express—in Sessions 2.2 and 2.3, respectively.

Anatomy of an E-Mail Message

An e-mail message consists of two major parts: the message header and the message body. The **message header** contains all the information about the message, and the **message body** contains the actual message. A message header contains the recipient's e-mail address (To), the sender's e-mail address (From), and a subject line (Subject), which indicates the topic of the message. In addition, the message header can contain a carbon copy (or courtesy copy) address (Cc), a blind carbon copy (or blind courtesy copy) address (Bcc), and, sometimes, an attachment filename. Normally, your name automatically appears in the From line when you send a message. When you receive an e-mail message, the date and time it was sent and other information is added to the message automatically.

Figure 2-1 shows a message that Barbara Goldberg wrote to Ifram Sidamo, the company president. The memo contains an attached file named 800LineSale.xls. This file is a spreadsheet composed using a spreadsheet program and then attached to the message. Notice that Ifram's e-mail address appears in the To line. When Ifram receives Barbara's message, Barbara's name and e-mail address will appear in the From line. Following good e-mail etiquette, Barbara included a short Subject line so Ifram can quickly determine the content of the message. The Cc line indicates that the marketing department will receive a copy of the message. Sylvia Sidamo, Ifram's vice president of sales, will also receive a copy of the message, but Sylvia's e-mail address is on the Bcc line, so neither Ifram nor the marketing department will know that she also received a copy of the message. Each of the message parts is described next.

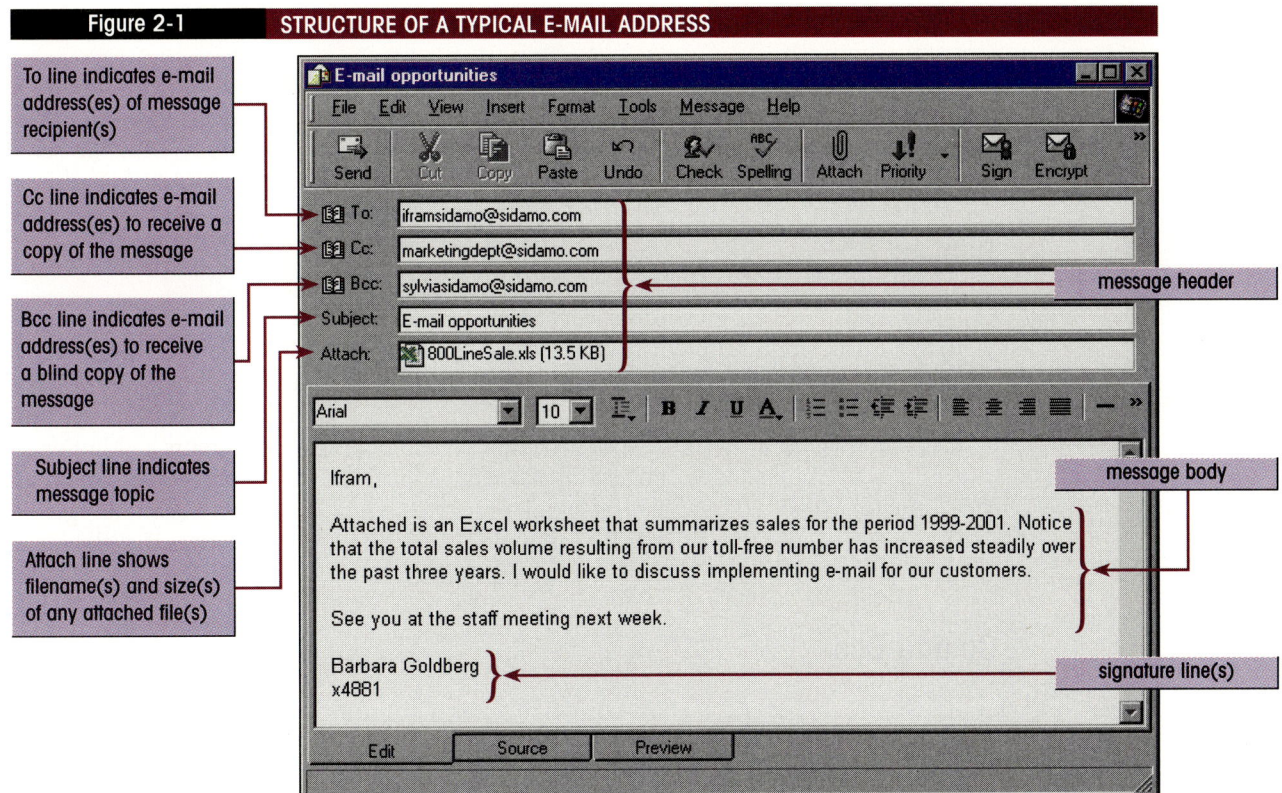

Figure 2-1 STRUCTURE OF A TYPICAL E-MAIL ADDRESS

To

You type the recipient's full e-mail address in the **To line** of an e-mail header. Usually, the To line is at the top of the header. Be careful to type the address correctly; otherwise, the e-mail cannot be delivered. You can send mail to multiple people by typing a comma between the individual e-mail addresses. There is no real limit on the number of addresses you can type in the To line or in the other parts of the e-mail header that require an address. Figure 2-2 shows the message header for a message that Barbara is sending to three people.

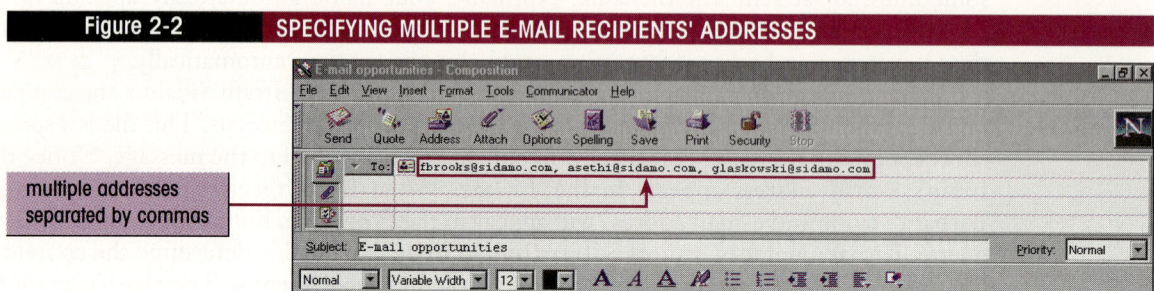

Figure 2-2 SPECIFYING MULTIPLE E-MAIL RECIPIENTS' ADDRESSES

multiple addresses separated by commas

Sometimes, the To address contains one physical mailing address that is not one person's address, but rather, a message to a special service called a **mailing list**. In a mailing list, the single e-mail address contains dozens or even thousands of individual e-mail addresses.

From

The **From line** of an e-mail message includes the sender's e-mail address. Most e-mail programs automatically insert the sender's e-mail address into all messages. Even if you don't insert your e-mail address in an outgoing message, the recipient *always* sees the sender's e-mail address in the message—in other words, you cannot send anonymous e-mail.

Subject

The content of the **Subject line** is very important. Often, the person receiving your message will scan an abbreviated display of incoming messages, looking for the most interesting or important messages based on the contents of the Subject line. If the Subject line is blank, then the recipient might not read the associated message immediately. It is always best to include a message subject so the reader has a hint of the message's contents and importance. For example, a subject line such as "Just checking" is far less informative and certainly less interesting than "Urgent: new staff meeting time." The e-mail message shown in Figure 2-1, for example, contains the subject "E-mail opportunities" and thus indicates that the message concerns e-mail.

Cc and Bcc

You can use the optional **carbon copy (Cc)** and the **blind carbon copy (Bcc)** header lines to send mail to people who should be aware of the e-mail message but who are not the message's main addressees. When an e-mail message is delivered, every recipient can see the addresses of other recipients, except for those who receive a blind carbon copy. Neither the primary recipient (in the To line) nor those recipients on the carbon copy list are aware of those recipients on the blind carbon copy list because Bcc addresses are hidden from messages sent to people on the To and Cc lists. Recipients on the Bcc list are unaware of others who receive blind copies. For example, if you send a thank you message to a salesperson for performing a task especially well, you might consider sending a blind carbon copy to that person's supervisor. That way, the supervisor knows a customer is happy and that the praise was unsolicited.

Attachments

Because of the way the messaging system is set up, you can send only plain-text messages using SMTP—the protocol that handles outgoing e-mail. When you need to send a more complex document, such as a Word document or an Excel worksheet, you send it along as an attachment. An **attachment** is encoded so that it can be carried safely over the Internet, to "tag along" with the message. Frequently, the attached file is the most important part of the e-mail message, and the message body contains a brief statement such as "The worksheet you requested is attached." Barbara's e-mail message contains an attachment whose location and filename (on Barbara's computer) appear in the Attach line in the header. The attachment is stored on Barbara's computer on drive C with the filename 800LineSale.xls. You can attach more than one file to an e-mail message, and files can be delivered to more than one recipient at the same time. E-mail attachments provide a convenient way of transmitting electronic documents of various types to a colleague down the hall or on the other side of the world.

When you receive an e-mail message with an attached file, you can preview it within the message or save it and review it later. E-mail programs differ in how they handle and display attachments. Several e-mail programs identify an attached file with an icon that represents the program associated with that file type. In addition to an icon, several programs also display an attached file's size in kilobytes (a **kilobyte** is approximately 1,000 characters) and indicate the attached file's name. Other e-mail programs display an attached file in a preview window when they recognize the attached file's format and can start a program to display the file. In any case, you can always save the file and later execute a program associated with the file type.

With most e-mail client programs, you can easily detach an attached file, examine the file, and save it. An icon representing an attached file accompanies the file. To open the attached file, you click the icon. If a worksheet is attached to an e-mail message, for example, a spreadsheet program on your computer starts and opens the worksheet. Similarly, a Word file opens inside the Word program when you click the icon representing the Word file inside your e-mail message. Saving an open attachment is simple. Usually, you click File on the menu bar, and then click Save or Save As in the program displaying the attached file. Then, you indicate the disk and folder into which you want to save the attached file.

Message Body and Signature Files

Most often, people use e-mail to write short, quick messages. However, e-mail messages can be dozens or hundreds of pages long, although the term *pages* has little meaning in the e-mail world. Few people using e-mail think of a message in terms of page-sized chunks; e-mail is more like an unbroken scroll with no physical page boundaries.

Frequently, an e-mail message includes an optional **signature** that identifies more detailed information about the sender. You can sign a message by typing your name and other information at the end of the message for each message you send, or you can create a signature file. A **signature file** contains the information you routinely type at the end of your e-mail messages. You can instruct your e-mail program to insert the signature file into every message automatically to save a lot of time. The signature usually contains the sender's name, title, and company name. Signature files often contain a complete nonelectronic address, facsimile telephone number, and a voice phone number. Periodically, signature files include graphics, such as a company logo, or the sender's favorite quotation or saying. Enclosing a signature file in an e-mail message ensures that e-mail recipients can contact you in a variety of ways besides using your e-mail address. For example, in Figure 2-1, Barbara's signature file contains her full name and her internal company phone extension.

Signatures can be either formal or informal, or a hybrid. A **formal signature** typically contains the sender's name, title, company name, company address, telephone and fax numbers, and e-mail address. **Informal signatures** can contain graphics or quotations that express a more casual style found in correspondence between friends and acquaintances. Most e-mail software programs automatically include a signature at the end of each e-mail message you send. You can easily modify your signature or choose not to include it in selected messages. Most e-mail programs allow you to create multiple signature files so you can choose which one to include when sending a message.

When you create a signature, don't overdo it. A signature that is extremely long is in bad taste—especially if it is much longer than the message. It is best to keep a signature to a few lines that identify alternative ways to contact you. Figure 2-3 shows two examples of signatures. The top signature is informal and typical of one you might send to a friend. The bottom signature is Barbara's formal signature that she uses for all external business correspondence to identify herself, her title, and her mailing and telephone information.

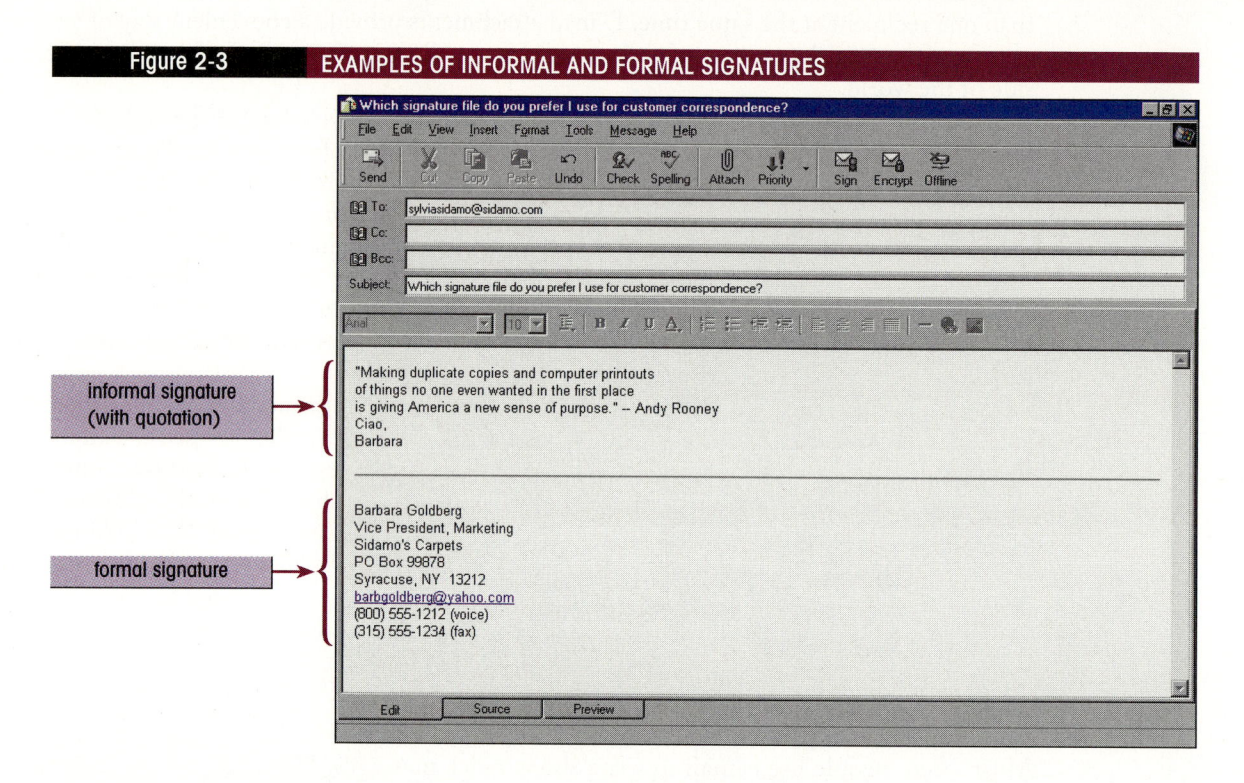

Figure 2-3   EXAMPLES OF INFORMAL AND FORMAT SIGNATURES

E-Mail Addresses

E-mail addresses, also called Internet addresses, uniquely identify an individual or organization that is connected to the Internet. They are like telephone numbers—when you want to call anyone in the world, you dial a series of numbers that route your call through a series of switchboards until your call reaches its destination. For example, calling a friend in San Diego from another country requires you to dial the country code for the United States first (the country code varies according to the country from which you are calling). Then, you must know the area code for the part of San Diego in which your friend lives, and dial that three-digit number. Finally, you dial the last seven digits of your friend's local number. Like telephone numbers, e-mail addresses consist of a series of numbers. Usually, addresses consist of three or four groups of numbers that are separated by periods. For instance, the number 192.55.87.1 is an **Internet Protocol address**, or more commonly an **IP address**, which corresponds to a single computer connected to the Internet. The IP address uniquely identifies the computer at the organization you want to contact. To route an e-mail message to an *individual* whose mail is stored on a particular computer, you must identify that person by his or her account name, or **user name**, and also by the computer on which mail is stored. The two parts of an e-mail address—the user name and the computer name—are separated by an "at" sign (@). Barbara Goldberg, for example, uses the user name *barbgoldberg* to access her e-mail. If her account were stored on a Sidamo computer whose address is 194.206.126.204, then one form of her e-mail address would be barbgoldberg@194.206.126.204.

Fortunately, you rarely have to use numeric IP addresses. Instead, you use **host names**, which are unique names that are equivalent to IP addresses. Barbara Goldberg's address using a host name is simply *barbgoldberg@sidamo.com*, which is much easier to remember and certainly less error prone. A full e-mail address consists of your user name, followed by an @ sign, followed by the host name (or address). A user name usually specifies a person within an organization, although it can sometimes refer to an entire group. Sometimes, you can select your own user name, but frequently the organization through which you obtain an e-mail account has rules about acceptable user names. Some organizations insist that the user name consist of a person's first initial followed by up to seven characters of the person's last name. Other institutions prefer that your user name contain your full first and last names separated by an underscore character (for example, Barbara_Goldberg). Occasionally, you can pick a nickname such as "ziggy" or "bigbear" as your user name. When typing e-mail addresses, the usage of upper- and lower-case letters does matter, and the *spelling* is important. When mail cannot be delivered, the electronic postmaster sends the mail back to you and indicates the addressee is unknown—just like conventional mail.

The host name (or host address) is the second part of an e-mail address. The host name specifies the computer to which the mail is to be delivered on the Internet. Host names contain periods, which are usually pronounced "dot," to divide the host name. The most specific part of the host name appears first in the host address followed by more general destination names. Barbara's host name, sidamo.com (and pronounced "sidamo dot com"), contains only two names separated by a period. The suffix *com* in the address indicates that this company falls into the large, general class of commercial locations.

Host names can consist of more than two parts. For example, Figure 2-4 shows that the host name *condor.cs.missouri.edu* contains four parts. Clusters of related computers are sometimes given related names such as earth, wind, and fire. In this address, *condor* is one of several related computers. Where is this computer located? The second name, *cs*, is a common abbreviation for computer science. In all likelihood, the computer belongs to a computer science department. Judging by the third part of the host name, *missouri*, it's a good bet that the institution is located in Missouri or at the University of Missouri. The *edu* host name suffix indicates the organization is an educational institution of some sort. Taken together, the host name parts strongly point to the University of Missouri's computer science department. With a little imagination and experience, you can decipher most host names and determine the location of the computers to which the names refer.

> **Figure 2-4 HOST NAME ELEMENTS**
>
> condor.cs.missouri.edu
>
> computer name | abbreviation for computer science department | state name | host name suffix

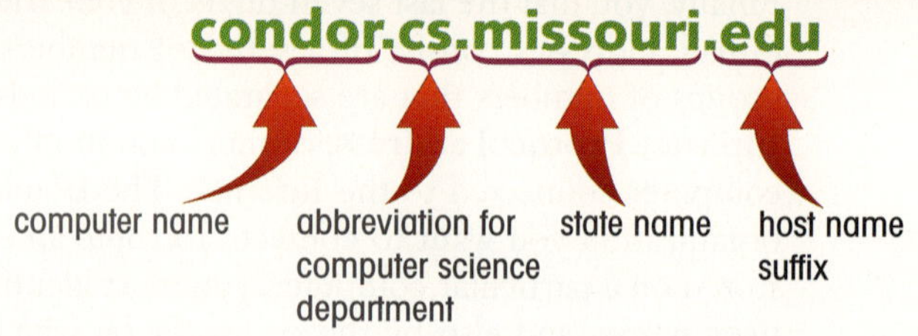

E-Mail Programs

Several programs for managing e-mail are available today because no single program works on all computers. The good news is that you can use any e-mail program to send mail to people with different e-mail clients. The recipient will be able to read your mail and you will be able to read mail from other people, regardless of which e-mail programs are used. If you have an Internet service provider (ISP) with a PPP or SLIP connection, then you can choose from a large selection of e-mail client programs that run on your PC and periodically check the mail server for incoming mail. On the other hand, you might have to use the e-mail program provided by your college or university if you have a dial-up connection that does not provide access to the Internet. Some e-mail programs—called **shareware**—are free or very inexpensive, and others are not. Some e-mail programs are software clients that run on your computer and receive mail from the mail server. Other e-mail programs run strictly on a server machine that you access from your personal computer, which acts as a dumb terminal. A **dumb terminal** is an otherwise "smart" computer that passes all your keystrokes to another computer to which you are connected and does not attempt to do anything else during the e-mail session. Examples of popular e-mail clients operating in the Windows environment are Netscape Messenger, Microsoft Outlook Express, and Eudora. A widely used e-mail program running on larger, multiuser computers is Pine. Especially popular on university campuses, Pine is a simple system that accepts and displays only plain-text messages. In your future personal and professional life, chances are good that you will encounter a different system from the one you are currently using, so it's a good idea to learn about different e-mail clients.

Free E-Mail Clients

Several free e-mail programs are available on the Internet. Some free programs require you to access e-mail through the Web, and others have a proprietary program that you install on your computer. Examples of free e-mail programs that you access from any Web browser include Yahoo!Mail, ExciteMail, and HotMail. Another program is Juno, which is an example of a free proprietary e-mail program that was one of the earliest free e-mail services. One advantage that these e-mail services share is that you can have e-mail service without being affiliated with an organization. Before these free e-mail services came to the Internet, many people who were not students or employees of a company could not use e-mail. Now, anyone with an Internet connection can use these services to send and receive e-mail messages.

To use e-mail provided by HotMail, ExciteMail, or Yahoo!Mail, you apply for an e-mail account. In order to apply for an e-mail account, you visit the Web site of the company offering free e-mail with your Web browser. (You will learn about Web browsers in Tutorial 3.) When you apply for free e-mail, you will probably be asked to supply a small amount of information about yourself. Then, you choose a user name and secret password. Next, the e-mail service checks to see that no one else has applied for the same user name you requested. If the user name is available, then you are immediately enrolled in the e-mail service. On the other hand, if someone already has the user name you selected, the service will ask you to try a different user name or change the one you chose slightly by adding digits to the end of it.

Once you have one of the Web-based e-mail accounts, such as Yahoo!Mail, you can send and receive e-mail. A big advantage of Web-based e-mail accounts is that you can get your e-mail from any computer with a Web browser and Internet access. In other words, you can access your e-mail account in Mexico City, Hong Kong, or any other place where there is public access to a Web browser. This is an advantage for people who travel a lot and do not want to incur long-distance telephone charges when accessing their own e-mail server from another city or country.

Juno and other similar services offer a different type of free e-mail service. First, you must install its free software on your computer, and then you activate a Juno e-mail account. The program automatically dials the Juno computer and establishes an e-mail account with a user name and password of your choosing—subject to the user name not being assigned already. Subsequently, you can access your e-mail from the same computer on which you installed it. The big disadvantage of Juno and systems like it is that you must install the Juno program on any computer on which you want to access your e-mail, which is sometimes impractical for people who travel a lot and use different computers to access their e-mail.

You might wonder how these companies can provide free e-mail—after all, nothing is free! The answer is advertising. With each e-mail message you receive, you also receive some sort of advertisement—either large or small—in the message itself or stored on your computer. Advertising revenues pay for free e-mail, so you must decide whether you are willing to put up with a little advertising for the free e-mail service. Most users of these free services agree that seeing some ads is a small price to pay for the great convenience e-mail provides.

Setting Up and Using Your E-Mail Client

Many ISPs support POP (Post Office Protocol) or SMTP (Simple Mail Transfer Protocol), whereby the mail server receives mail and stores it until you use your mail client software to request the mail server to deliver mail to your computer. Similarly, when you send e-mail from your computer, that mail is forwarded across the Internet until it reaches its destination. Once e-mail reaches the mail server at the addressee's location, it is stored. Subsequently, e-mail is downloaded from the server to a user on request. In either case—sending or receiving and reading e-mail—a client program must notify the mail server to deliver the mail or accept outgoing mail.

Your message might not be sent to the mail server immediately, depending on how the e-mail client is configured on your computer. A message can be **queued**, or temporarily held with other messages, and sent when you either exit the program or check to see if you received any new e-mail.

Remember, e-mail correspondence can be formal or informal, but you should still follow the rules of good writing and grammar. After typing the content of your message—even a short message—it is always a good idea to check your typing and spelling. Most mail systems do not allow you to retract mail after you send it, so you should examine your messages carefully *before* sending them. Always exercise politeness and courtesy in your messages. Don't write anything in an e-mail message that you wouldn't want someone else to post on a public bulletin board.

Receiving Mail

The mail server is always ready to process mail; in theory, it never sleeps. That means that when you receive e-mail, it is held on the mail server until you start the e-mail client on your PC and ask the server to retrieve your mail. Most clients allow you to save delivered mail in any of several standard or custom mailboxes or folders on your PC. However, the mail server is a completely different story. Once the mail is delivered to your PC, one of two things can happen to it on the server: either the server's copy of your mail is deleted, or it is preserved and marked as delivered or read. Marking mail as **delivered** or **read** is the server's way of identifying new mail from mail that you have read. For example, when Barbara receives mail on the Sidamo mail server, she might decide to save her accumulated mail—even after she reads it—so she has an archive of all of her received e-mail messages. On the other hand, Barbara might want to delete old mail to save space on the mail server. Both methods have advantages. Saving old mail on the server lets you access your mail from any PC that can connect to your mail server. On the other hand, if you automatically delete mail after reading it, you don't have to worry about storing and organizing messages that you don't need, which requires less effort.

Printing a Message

Reading mail on the computer is fine, but there are times when you will need to print a copy of some or all of your messages. Other times, you need to file your mail in an appropriate mailbox and deal with it later or simply file it for safekeeping. You also might find that you don't need to keep or file certain messages, so you can read and immediately delete them. Most client programs provide these facilities to help you manage your electronic correspondence.

The majority of programs let you print a message during or after you compose it or after mail has been received or sent. The Print command usually appears on the File menu in a GUI program, or there is a Print button on the toolbar. In a character-based program, the Print command is usually a key combination, such as Ctrl + P.

Filing a Message

Most clients let you create separate mailboxes or folders in which to store related messages. You can create new mailboxes or folders when needed, rename existing mailboxes and folders, or delete folders and their contents when you no longer need them. You can move mail from the incoming mailbox or folder to any other mailbox or folder to file it. Some programs let you use a **filter** to move incoming mail into one or several mailboxes or folders automatically based on the content of the message. If your client does not allow the use of filters, you can filter the messages manually by reading them and filing them in the appropriate folder.

Forwarding a Message

You can forward any message that you receive to one or more recipients. When you **forward** a message to another recipient, a copy of the original message is sent to the new recipient you specify, without the original sender's knowledge. You can forward a misdirected message to another recipient, or you can forward a message to someone who was not included in the original message routing list.

For example, suppose you receive a message intended for someone else, or the message requests information that you do not have but you know a colleague who does know the information. In either case, you can forward the message you received to the person who can deal with the request best. When you forward a message, your e-mail address and name appear automatically on the From line, and most e-mail clients amend the Subject line with the text "Fwd," "Forward," or something similar to indicate that the message is being forwarded. You simply fill in the To line and then send the message. Optionally, the message you received is quoted. A **quoted** message is a copy of the sender's original message that is returned to the sender with your comments added. Each line of the quoted message is preceded by a special mark (usually the greater than symbol, >). When you respond to a message someone sent to you, it is a good idea to include parts of the sender's message, or the quoted message. That way, the receiver can recall his or her original statement or question and therefore better understand your "yes, I agree with you" response.

Replying to a Message

When you **reply** to a message, the e-mail client automatically formats a new, blank message and addresses it to the sender. Replying to a message is a quick way of sending a response to someone who sent a message to you. When you reply to a message, the client automatically addresses a new message to the sender of the original message. Most clients will copy the entire message from the original message and place it in the response window. Usually, a special mark, such as >, appears at the beginning of each line of the response to indicate the text of the original message. When you are responding to more than one question, it is a good idea to type your responses below the original questions. That way, the recipient can better understand the context of your responses. When you respond to a message that has been sent to a number of people—perhaps some people received the message as a carbon copy—be careful about responding. You can choose to respond to all the original recipients or just to the sender.

Deleting a Message

On most e-mail clients, deleting a message is a two-step process in order to avoid accidental deletions of important messages. First, you temporarily delete a message by placing it in a "trash" folder or by marking it for deletion. Then, you permanently delete the trash or marked messages by emptying the trash or by indicating to the client to delete the messages. It is a good idea to delete unneeded mail.

Maintaining an Address Book

E-mail addresses are sometimes difficult to remember and type, especially when you send many e-mail messages to the same recipients. You can use an **address book** to save e-mail addresses and convenient nicknames to remember them by. The features of an e-mail address book vary by e-mail client. Usually, you can organize information about individuals or companies. Each entry in the address book can contain an individual's full e-mail address (or a group e-mail address that represents several individual addresses), a person's real name, and the person's complete contact information. In addition, some e-mail clients allow you to include notes for each address book entry. You can assign a unique nickname to each entry so it is easier to refer to e-mail addresses when you need them.

After saving entries in your address book, you can refer to them at any point while you are composing, replying to, or forwarding a message. You can review your address book and sort the entries in alphabetical order by nickname, or you can view them in last name order. Of course, you can switch between several sort orders any time you want—even as you are creating a message.

Creating a Multi-Address Entry

What happens if you need to send the same e-mail message to different recipients? You could send the message to all recipients by typing their nicknames in the To line and separating them with a comma. But what if you need to send a message to an entire department or the entire sales staff? You can create a handy address entry called a distribution list. A **distribution list**, or a **group mailing list**, is a single nickname that represents more than one individual e-mail address. For example, you might use the nickname "Web Site" to save the e-mail addresses of your partners on a Web site project. When you need to send a message to your partners, you just type "Web Site" in the To line, and then the client will send the same message to each individual's e-mail address.

Session 2.1 QUICK CHECK

1. True or False: E-mail travels across the Internet in small clusters.
2. The special rules governing how information is handled on the Internet are collectively called _____.
3. An e-mail message consists of two parts: the message _____ and the message _____.
4. Explain why it is a good practice to include a Subject line in your e-mail messages.
5. True or False: You use the Bcc line in an e-mail message to send copies of a message to others without the principal addressee knowing who received a copy.
6. Can you send a spreadsheet file over the Internet? If so, how?
7. The four-part number comprising an Internet address is known as a(n) _____ address.
8. Why is it important to include part of the sender's message in your reply?
9. What advantage(s) does a distribution list or mailing list provide when sending a message to many recipients?

Now that you understand some basic information about e-mail and e-mail client software, you are ready to start using your e-mail client. If you are using Netscape Messenger, your instructor will assign Session 2.2; if you are using Microsoft Outlook Express, your instructor will assign Session 2.3. The authors recommend, however, that you read both sessions in order to be familiar with both e-mail clients. In the future, you might encounter a different e-mail client on a public or employer's computer, so it is important to be familiar with both clients. Fortunately, most e-mail clients work the same, so it is easy to use other programs once you master the basics.

TUTORIAL 2 BASIC E-MAIL: INTEGRATED BROWSER E-MAIL SOFTWARE WEB 2.13 INTERNET

SESSION 2.2

In this session you will learn how to use Netscape Messenger to send and receive e-mail. You will learn how to print, file, save, delete, respond to, and forward e-mail messages. Finally, you will organize your e-mail addresses in an address book.

Netscape Messenger Client

You continue to express your enthusiasm for your newly assigned task of evaluating e-mail software. **Netscape Messenger**, or simply **Messenger**, is the e-mail client that is an integral part of the Netscape Communicator suite. You installed Netscape Communicator and are anxious to start using Messenger. Barbara stopped by to ask you a few questions about the program and wants you to use Messenger to e-mail items, such as the weekly marketing meeting agenda, to members of the marketing department staff. You start Messenger by using the Start menu or by double-clicking a desktop icon, if one is installed. Figure 2-5 shows the Message List window. When you open Messenger, a window opens containing mailbox folders in the left pane, message summary lines in the upper-right panel, and the selected message's contents in the lower-right panel. (Your Message List window might look different from the one shown in Figure 2-5.)

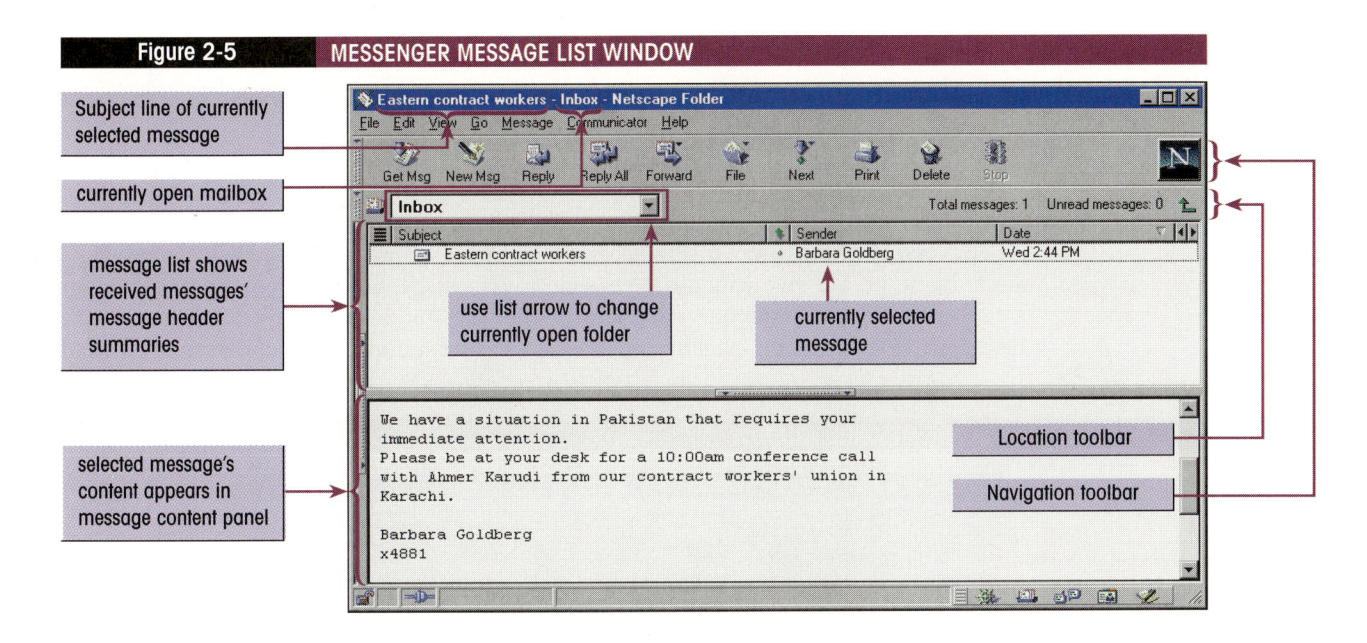

Figure 2-5 MESSENGER MESSAGE LIST WINDOW

- Subject line of currently selected message
- currently open mailbox
- message list shows received messages' message header summaries
- use list arrow to change currently open folder
- currently selected message
- selected message's content appears in message content panel
- Location toolbar
- Navigation toolbar

Messenger uses four different windows to furnish the tools you need to manage your e-mail: the Message List, Netscape Message Center, Netscape Message, and Composition windows. When you start Messenger, the Message List window shown in Figure 2-5 opens. The Message List window opens the **Inbox**, which is one of several mailboxes, and displays its contents in two panels. The top panel shows a summary of messages, called **message header summaries**. The lower panel, or the **message content panel**, shows the contents of a selected message header summary.

The **Netscape Message Center** window contains a list of your mailboxes, mail folders, and discussion groups. You open the Netscape Message Center window by clicking Communicator on the menu bar and then clicking Messenger. When you open the Netscape Message Center window, you can see the mailboxes on your computer (see Figure 2-6). Mailboxes in the list shown in Figure 2-6 include Inbox, Unsent Messages, Drafts, Sent, Trash, and Samples. News, another item on the Local Mail list, contains mail from **newsgroups**, which are Internet discussion groups on a specified topic. The Inbox contains your incoming mail messages.

Figure 2-6   NETSCAPE MESSAGE CENTER WINDOW

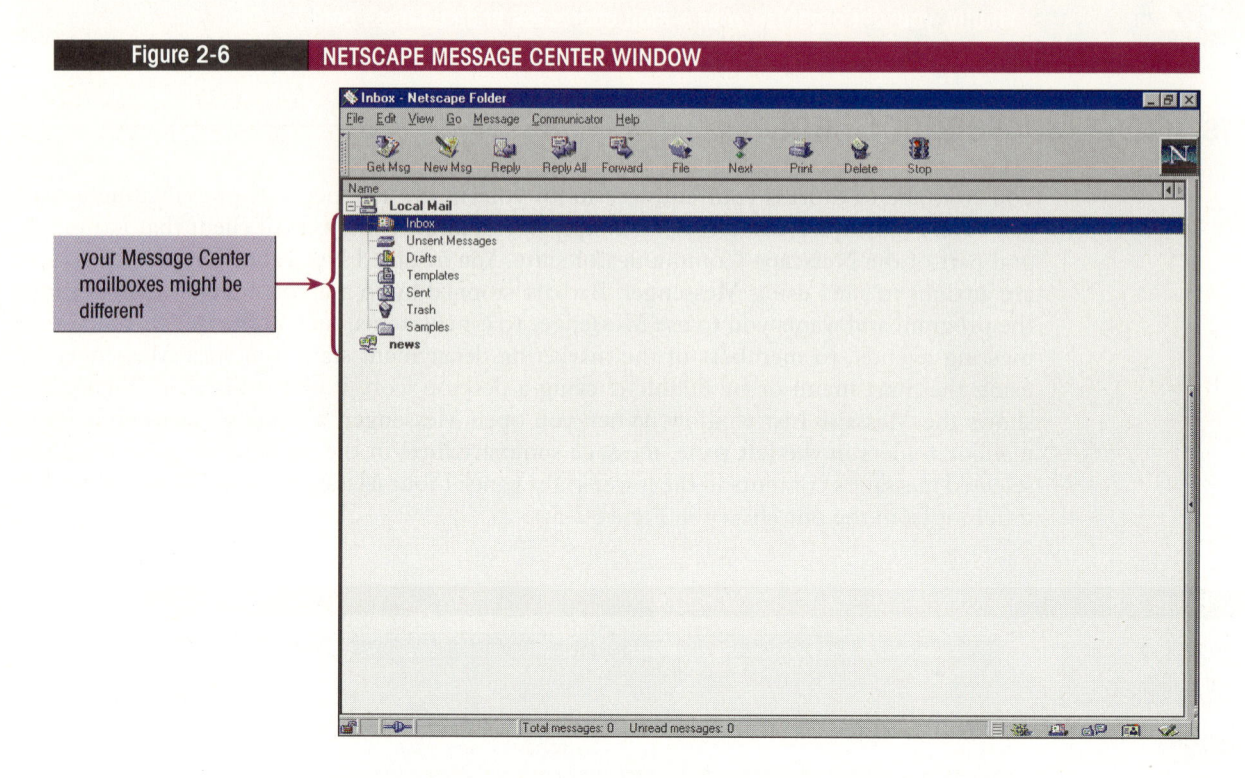

your Message Center mailboxes might be different

The **Netscape Message window**, shown in Figure 2-7, shows your individual messages. You use the Netscape Message window to respond to a message, file it in one of several mailboxes, forward a message to someone else, print a message, or delete it. You open the Netscape Message window by double-clicking any message header summary in the Message List window.

Figure 2-7   NETSCAPE MESSAGE WINDOW

Navigation toolbar

Location toolbar

message's subject appears in the title bar

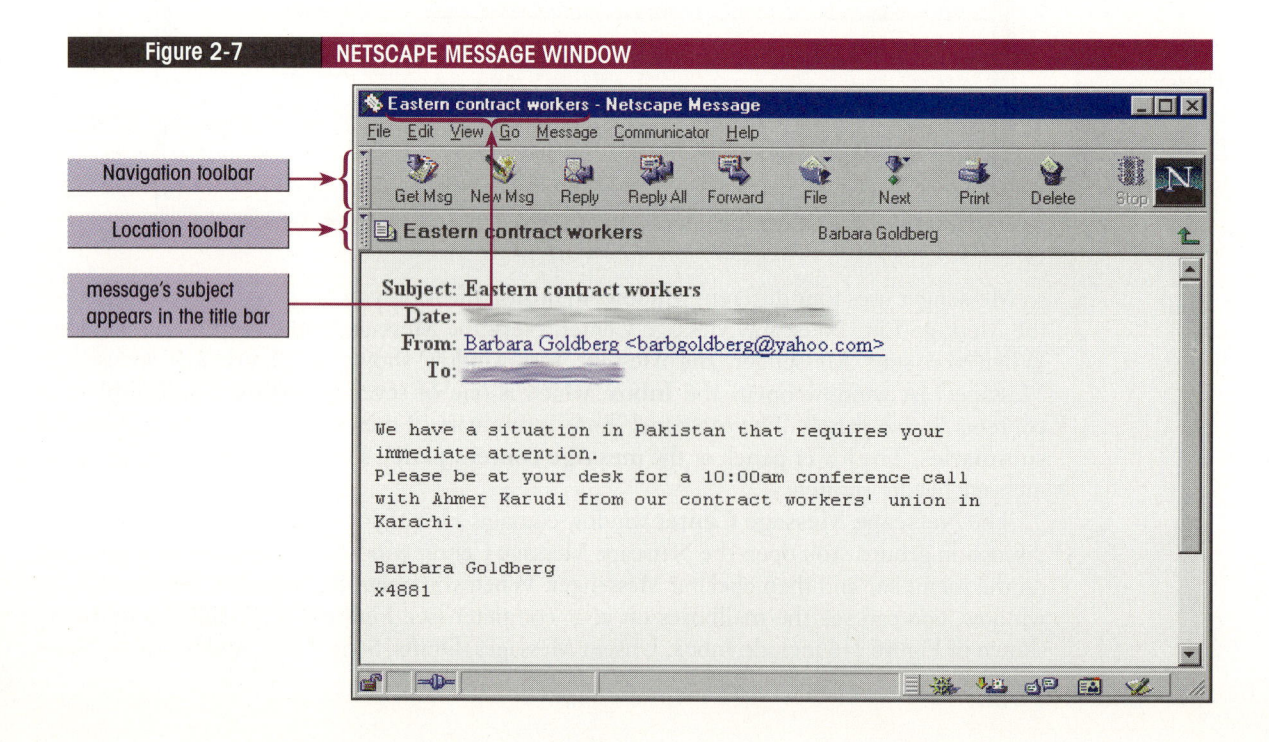

TUTORIAL 2 BASIC E-MAIL: INTEGRATED BROWSER E-MAIL SOFTWARE   WEB 2.15   INTERNET

You use the **Composition window**, shown in Figure 2-8, to create messages. You open the Composition window by clicking the New Message button on the Navigation toolbar in the Message List or Netscape Message windows. The Composition window toolbar contains buttons to send e-mail, quote (paste) information from another person's e-mail message, use the address book to find someone's e-mail address, attach files, check spelling, save an e-mail message as a draft, or stop a current message after sending it. When you start a new message, you will see the To, From, Cc, and Bcc lines in the Composition window.

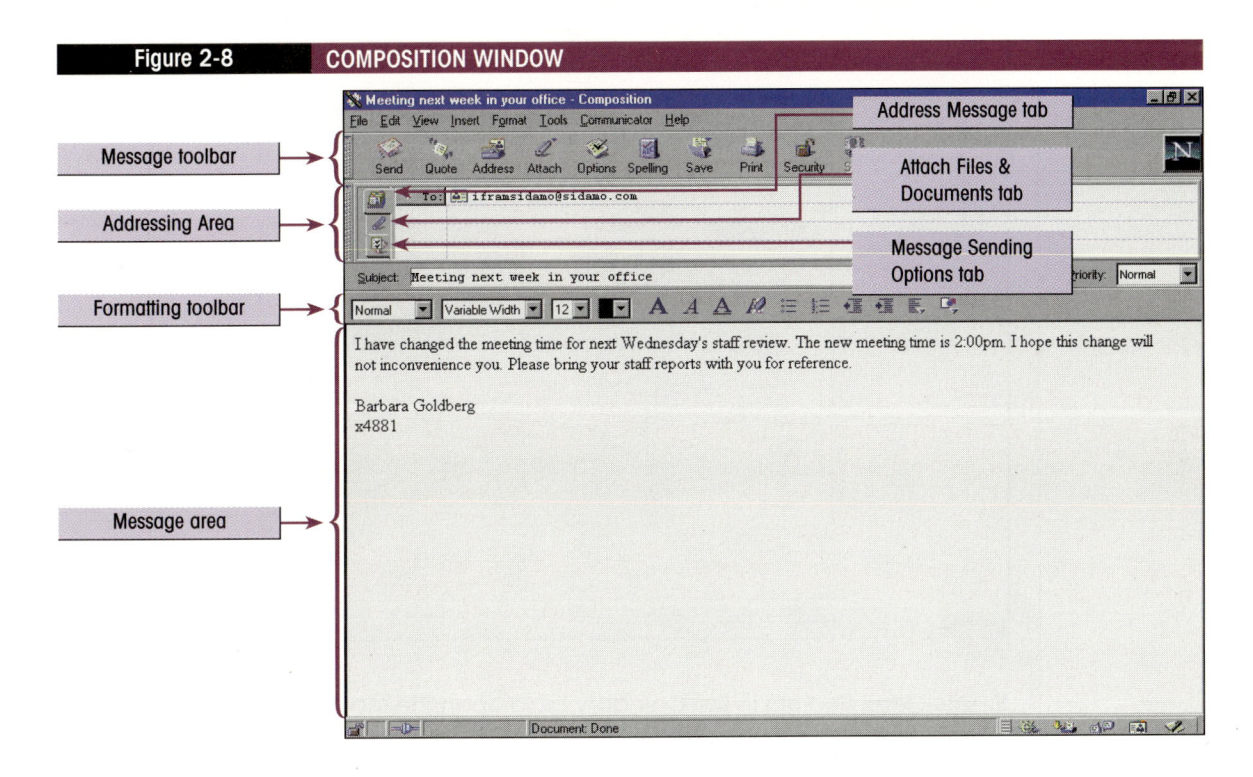

Figure 2-8   COMPOSITION WINDOW

Labels: Message toolbar, Addressing Area, Formatting toolbar, Message area, Address Message tab, Attach Files & Documents tab, Message Sending Options tab

Setting Up E-Mail

You are eager to start using Messenger to see if Sidamo's customers can use it to contact sales representatives. Cost is not a consideration because the Netscape Communicator suite—including Netscape Messenger—is free. Your first step is to start and configure Messenger so it fetches and sends *your* e-mail.

To start and initialize Messenger for use on a public computer:

1. Click the **Start** button on the Windows taskbar, point to **Programs**, point to **Netscape Communicator**, and then click **Netscape Messenger** to start the program. The Message List window opens (see Figure 2-5).

2. Click the **New Msg** button on the Navigation toolbar to open the Composition window (see Figure 2-8). If necessary, click the **Maximize** button on the Composition window title bar so the window fills the desktop.

3. Click **Edit** on the menu bar, and then click **Preferences**. The Preferences window opens and shows the preferences for the Mail & Newsgroups category.

4. If necessary, click the **plus sign** to the left of the Mail & Newsgroups category to show the different settings that you can change. (After you click the plus sign, it changes to a minus sign.) To set up your e-mail information, you will change the settings in the Mail Servers category. See Figure 2-9.

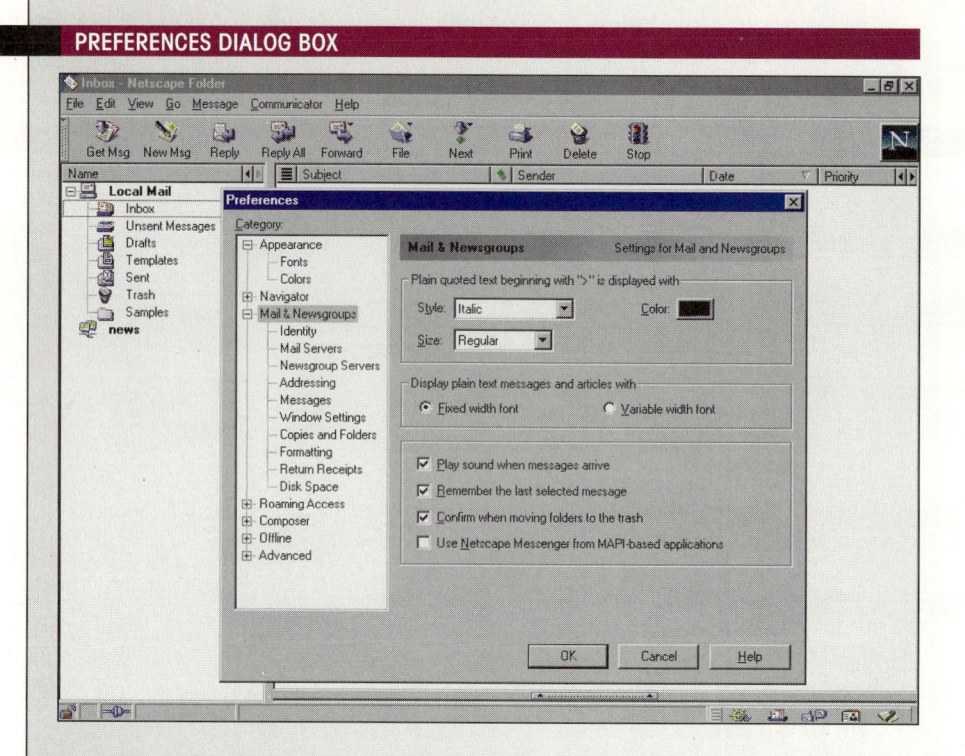

Figure 2-9 **PREFERENCES DIALOG BOX**

5. Click **Mail Servers** in the Category list to open the Mail Servers settings on the right side of the window.

   TROUBLE? If you (or someone else) already set up your account, then go to Step 4 in the next set of steps ("To change your e-mail name").

6. If the Incoming Mail Servers text box is empty, then click the **Add** button. Otherwise, click the **Edit** button. In either case, type the name of the server that processes your incoming mail. (Your instructor or lab manager will provide you with this name.) Usually, your incoming mail server name is POP, POP3, or IMAP followed by a domain name.

7. Click the **Server Type** list arrow and select the server type (ask your instructor).

8. Type your e-mail user name in the User Name text box (see Figure 2-10) and click the **OK** button.

TUTORIAL 2 BASIC E-MAIL: INTEGRATED BROWSER E-MAIL SOFTWARE   WEB 2.17   INTERNET

| Figure 2-10 | **CONFIGURING MESSENGER FOR BARBARA GOLDBERG** |

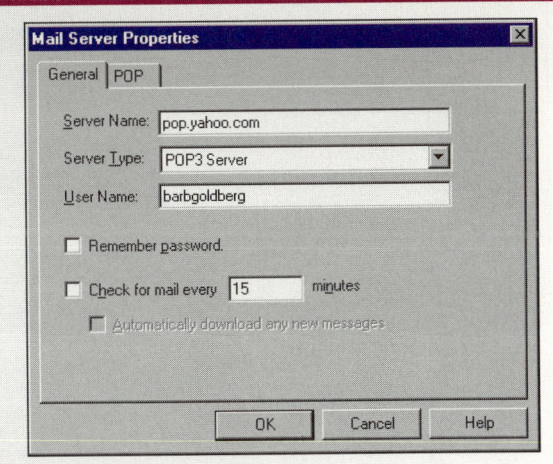

[Mail Server Properties dialog box showing General/POP tabs with Server Name: pop.yahoo.com, Server Type: POP3 Server, User Name: barbgoldberg, Remember password checkbox, Check for mail every 15 minutes checkbox, Automatically download any new messages checkbox, and OK, Cancel, Help buttons]

9. In the Outgoing mail (SMTP) server text box, type the name of the server that processes your outgoing mail. Your instructor or technical support person will provide you with this name. Usually, your outgoing mail server name is either SMTP or MAIL followed by a domain name. Press the **Tab** key to move to the Outgoing mail server user name text box.

10. Type your e-mail address (or login name) in the Mail server user name text box.

11. Click the **Choose** button. The Directory dialog box opens. Select drive A and click the **OK** button.

If you want your mail to remain on the mail server so you can read it from any computer, then check the Leave messages on server after retrieval check box. (In the Preferences dialog box, click the Mail & Newsgroups plus sign, click Mail Servers, and then click the Edit button. In the Mail Server Properties dialog box, click the POP tab and check the Leave messages on the server check box.) Otherwise, the server will delete your e-mail messages from the mail server after you retrieve your e-mail. You aren't finished configuring Messenger yet—you still need to set up the way that your e-mail is identified to its recipients.

To change your e-mail name:

1. Click **Identity** in the Category list to open the Identity settings in the right side of the window.

2. If necessary, click in the Your name text box, and then type your first and last names. Type your name the way you want it to appear in the message summary header when recipients receive your messages.

3. Press the **Tab** key to move the insertion point to the Email address text box, and then type your full e-mail address. Figure 2-11 shows the Identity tab for Barbara Goldberg. The values you enter in the Identity panel have no affect on your ability to send or receive e-mail; these text boxes only identify a name and associated address in the From text box of your outgoing e-mail messages.

Figure 2-11   ADDING YOUR IDENTITY INFORMATION

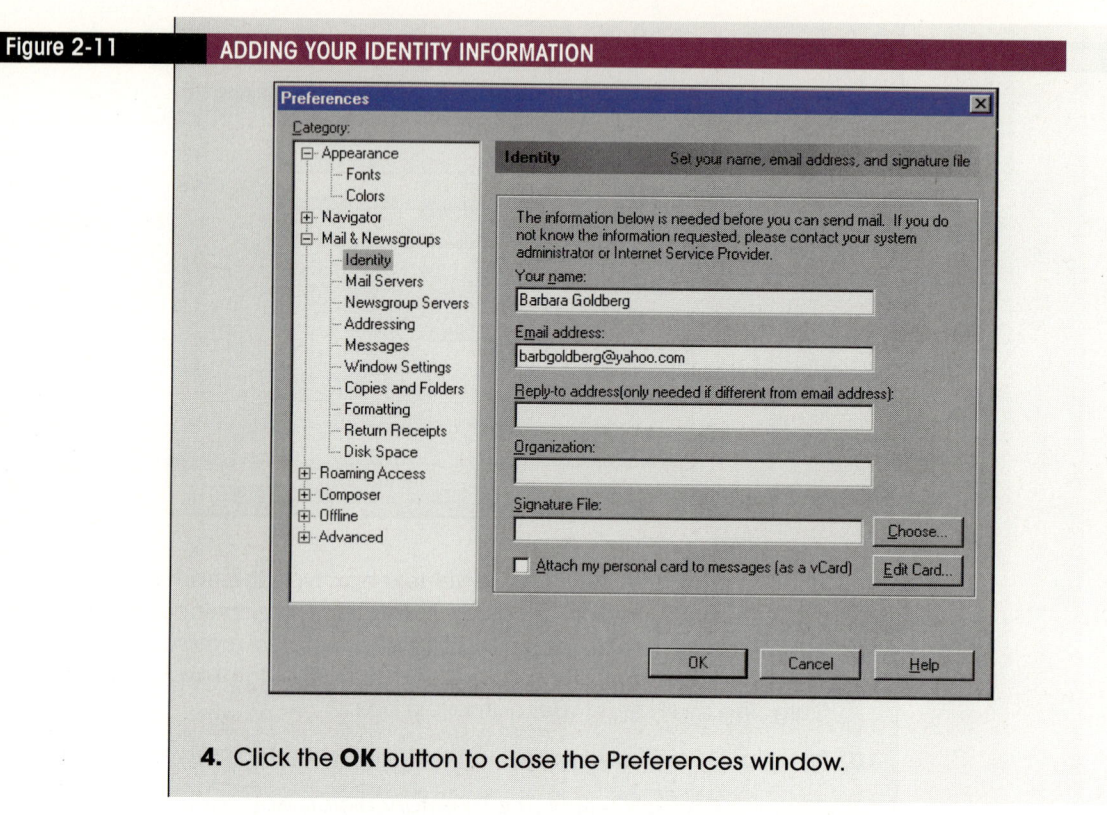

4. Click the **OK** button to close the Preferences window.

Now your copy of Messenger is set up to send and receive messages, so you are ready to send a message to Barbara.

Note: In this tutorial, you will send messages to a real mailbox with the address barbgoldberg@yahoo.com. Follow the instructions carefully so you use the correct address. Messages sent to this mailbox are deleted without being opened or read, so do not send important messages to this address.

Sending a Message Using Messenger

You decide to use Messenger to send a message with an attached file to Barbara. You will send a carbon copy of the message to your own e-mail address to make sure that the message and attached file are sent correctly. The Composition window is open, so you are ready to start typing Barbara's e-mail address.

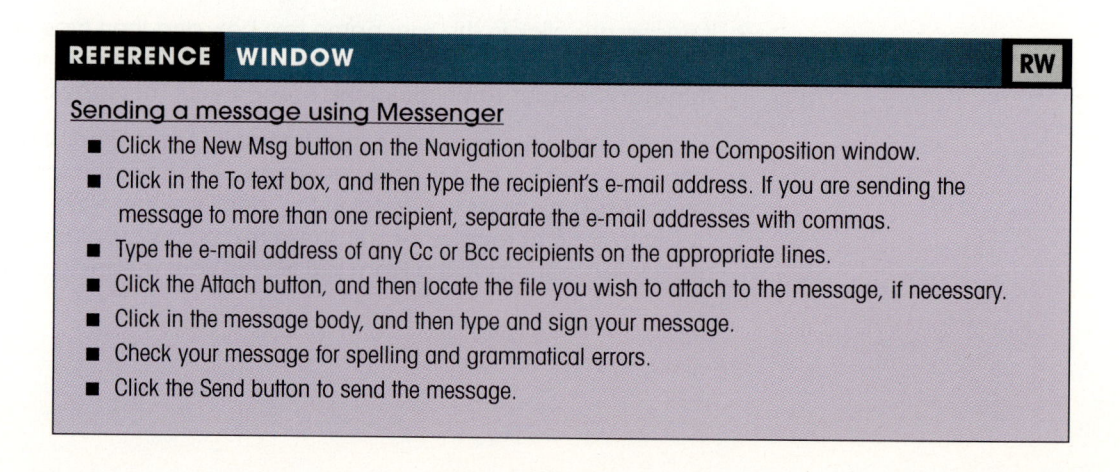

REFERENCE WINDOW

Sending a message using Messenger
- Click the New Msg button on the Navigation toolbar to open the Composition window.
- Click in the To text box, and then type the recipient's e-mail address. If you are sending the message to more than one recipient, separate the e-mail addresses with commas.
- Type the e-mail address of any Cc or Bcc recipients on the appropriate lines.
- Click the Attach button, and then locate the file you wish to attach to the message, if necessary.
- Click in the message body, and then type and sign your message.
- Check your message for spelling and grammatical errors.
- Click the Send button to send the message.

To send a message with an attachment:

1. Click in the To text box, and then type **barbgoldberg@yahoo.com**.

   TROUBLE? Make sure that you use the address barbgoldberg@yahoo.com, instead of barbgoldberg@sidamo.com. If you type Barbara's e-mail address incorrectly, your message will be returned with an error message attached.

2. Click the empty box below the To button in the message header. When the second To button appears (below the first one), click it to show a list of alternate text boxes, and then click **Cc:** in the list. A Cc button replaces the To button on the second line of the message header.

3. Type your full e-mail address in the Cc text box so you will receive a copy of your own message. It is a good idea to save a copy of all electronic correspondence as a reference. Most e-mail programs allow you to choose whether to save a copy of the messages you send.

   TROUBLE? If you make a typing mistake on a previous line, use the arrow keys or click the insertion point to return to a previous line so you can correct your mistake. If the arrow keys do not move the insertion point backward or forward in the header block, then press Shift + Tab or the Tab key to move backward or forward, respectively.

4. Click in the **Subject** text box, and then type **Test message**.

5. Click the **Attach** button on the Message toolbar, and then click **File** in the drop-down list. The Enter file to attach dialog box opens.

6. Make sure your Data Disk is in drive A. Click the **Look in** list arrow, and select **3½ Floppy (A:)** to display the list of folders on your Data Disk.

7. Double-click the **Tutorial.02** folder to open it, and then double-click the file named **Market.wri** to close the dialog box. The Attach Files & Documents tab changes color, and the filename appears on the first line of the Addressing Area. The color change indicates one or more files are attached to the message.

8. Click the **Address Message** tab to see the message recipients' addresses again.

9. Click in the message body, and then type **Please let me know that this message arrived safely and that you are able to read it and the attached file with no difficulty. I'm testing Netscape Messenger and want to make sure that it is working properly.**

10. Press the **Enter** key twice, and then type your first and last name to sign your message. See Figure 2-12.

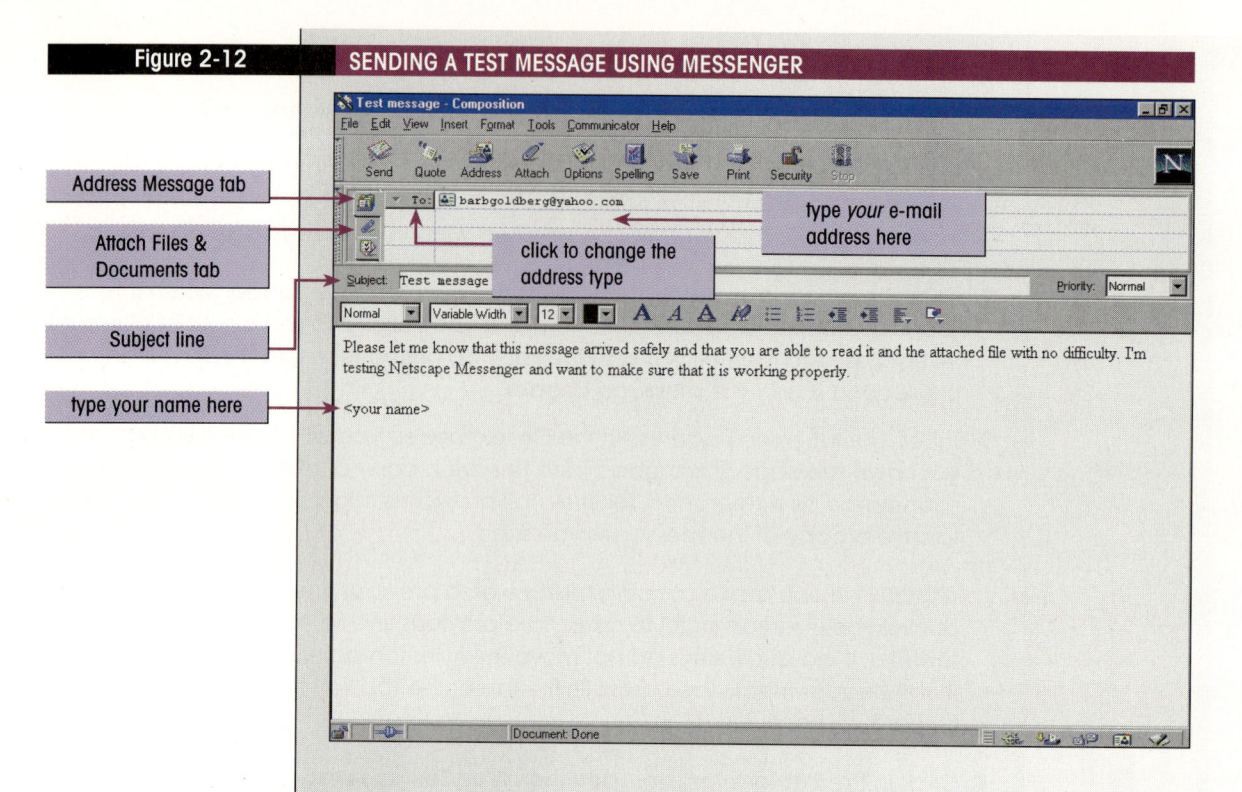

Figure 2-12 SENDING A TEST MESSAGE USING MESSENGER

Callouts on figure:
- Address Message tab
- Attach Files & Documents tab
- Subject line
- type your name here
- click to change the address type
- type *your* e-mail address here

Message body shown:
Please let me know that this message arrived safely and that you are able to read it and the attached file with no difficulty. I'm testing Netscape Messenger and want to make sure that it is working properly.

<your name>

---

11. Click the **Spelling** button on the Message toolbar to check your spelling before sending the message. If necessary, correct any typing errors. When you are finished, click the Done button to close the Check Spelling dialog box.

12. Click the **Send** button on the Message toolbar to send the message. The Composition window closes, and the message is sent to the mail server for delivery to Barbara. The Message List window reappears.

> **TROUBLE?** If you see a message that says "No SMTP server has been specified in the Mail & Newsgroups Preferences," then you did not provide enough information about your mail server and your login name. Return to the Composition window, click Edit on the menu bar, click Preferences, click the Mail & Newsgroups category, click the Mail Servers category, and then ask your instructor or technical support person for the correct mail server user name, outgoing mail (SMTP) server name, and incoming mail server. After entering this information, click the OK button and repeat Step 12 to continue.

Depending on your system configuration, Messenger might not send your message immediately. Instead, it might queue (hold) the message until you connect to your Internet service provider (ISP). When you are ready to send your messages, you can send all the queued messages at once when you connect to your ISP.

Receiving and Reading a Message

When you receive new mail, messages that you have not opened have a closed envelope with a downward-pointing green arrow to their left in the message list summaries, and messages that you have opened have a closed envelope next to them. Messages that have an attached file have a paperclip icon attached to the envelope in their message summaries. Next, you will check your e-mail to see if you received the Cc copy of the message you sent to Barbara.

> **REFERENCE WINDOW**
>
> **Using Messenger to receive and read an e-mail message**
> - Click the Get Msg button on the Navigation toolbar.
> - Type your password in the text box, and then click the OK button.
> - Double-click the summary line of any received message to read it.

To check for incoming mail:

1. Click the **Get Msg** button on the Navigation toolbar in the Message List window. The Password Entry dialog box opens.

2. Type your password in the text box, and then click the **OK** button. Depending on your system configuration, you might have to connect to your ISP to get your new mail. Within a few moments, your mail server transfers all new mail to your Inbox. You should see the Cc message that you sent to yourself when you mailed the test message to Barbara.

   TROUBLE? If you do not see any incoming messages in your Inbox, then you either did not receive any new mail or you might be looking in the wrong mailbox. If necessary, click the list arrow next to the mailbox name on the Location toolbar, which is just above the message summary list, and then click Inbox. If you still don't have any mail messages, wait a few moments and then repeat Steps 1 and 2 until you receive a message. Sometimes mail delivery slows down at peak times during the day.

3. Click the summary line for the copy of the test message that you just received in the message list. The Netscape Message window opens and shows the full message, including the header lines. The paperclip icon to the right of the sender's name indicates that the message contains an attached file. See Figure 2-13.

Figure 2-13   REVIEWING NEW E-MAIL

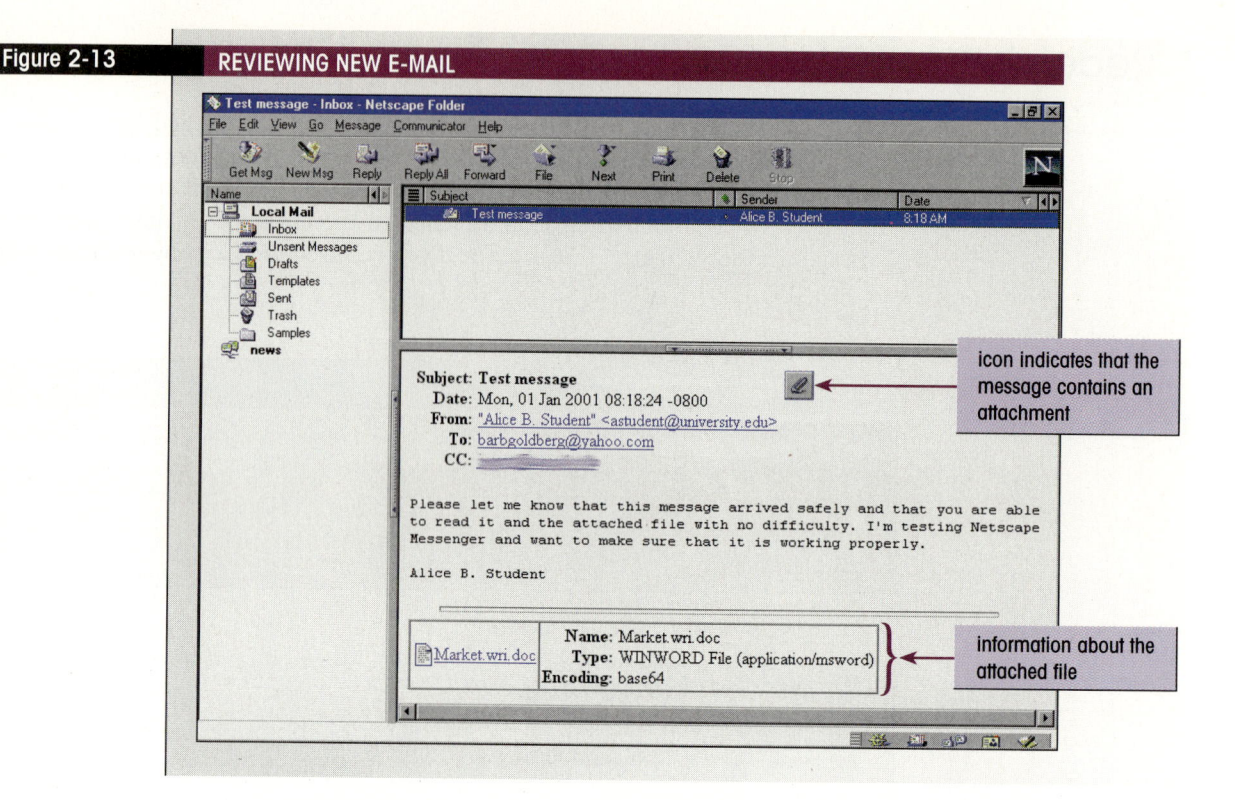

icon indicates that the message contains an attachment

information about the attached file

You received your Cc copy of the test message that you sent to Barbara, and the paperclip icon indicates that you received an attached file with the message. Now you can open the attachment in a preview window, or save it for viewing later. Open the attachment next.

Saving an Attached File

You want to make sure that your attached file was sent properly, so you decide to open it in the preview window. After you are finished looking at an attached file, you can decide whether to save or delete it from your system.

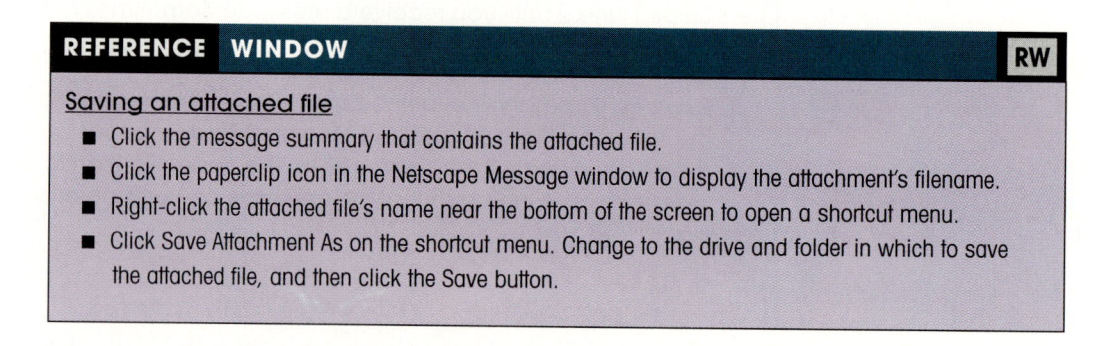

REFERENCE WINDOW   RW

Saving an attached file
- Click the message summary that contains the attached file.
- Click the paperclip icon in the Netscape Message window to display the attachment's filename.
- Right-click the attached file's name near the bottom of the screen to open a shortcut menu.
- Click Save Attachment As on the shortcut menu. Change to the drive and folder in which to save the attached file, and then click the Save button.

To save an e-mail attachment:

1. Click the paperclip icon in the Netscape Message window to show the attachment's filename.

2. Right-click the attachment name **Market.wri** icon near the bottom of the screen. (You might need to scroll down the window to see the icon.) A shortcut menu opens.

3. Click **Save Attachment As** on the shortcut menu to open the Save As dialog box.

4. Click the **Save in** list arrow, and then select the drive that contains your Data Disk.

5. Double-click the **Tutorial.02** folder to open it. Change the suggested filename to **Memo1.wri** (see Figure 2-14).

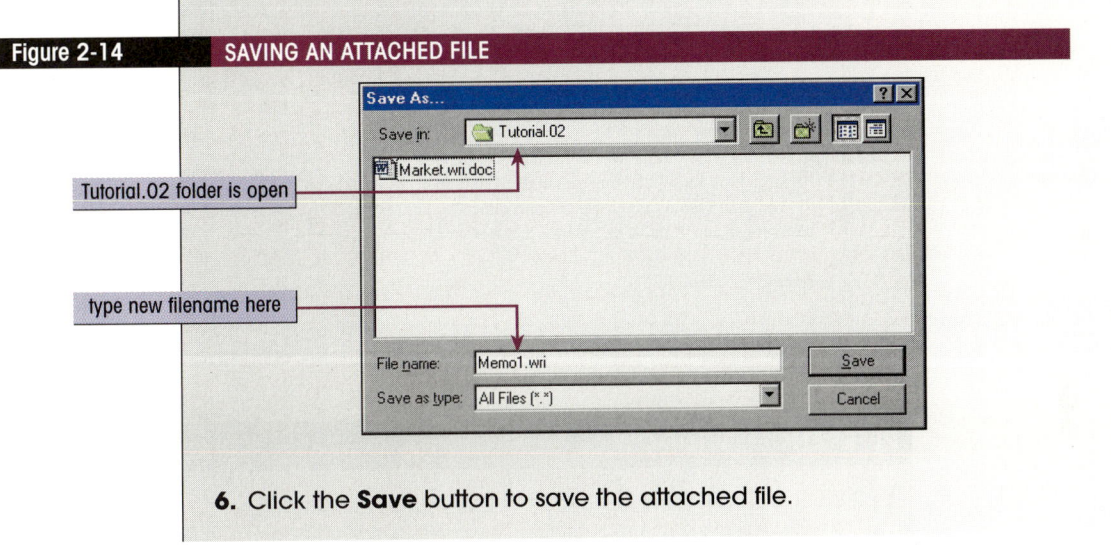

Figure 2-14 SAVING AN ATTACHED FILE

Tutorial.02 folder is open

type new filename here

6. Click the **Save** button to save the attached file.

Replying to and Forwarding Messages

You can forward any message you receive to someone else. Similarly, you can respond to the sender of a message quickly and efficiently to respond to a sender's message. You will reply to and forward messages extensively as you use e-mail.

Replying to an E-Mail Message

To reply to a message, select the message summary line in the Message List window and click the Reply to sender only button—it is labeled Reply—on the Navigation toolbar to respond to the sender. To reply to all the recipients, click the Reply All button. Messenger opens a Composition window and places the original sender's address in the message header To text box. You can leave the Subject line as is or modify it. Most systems, including Messenger, will copy the entire body from the original message and place it in the response window. Usually, a special mark in one edge of the response indicates what part is the original message. After typing your response, you click the Composition window Send button to send your response to the original message's author.

If you are responding to a question, it is a good idea to intersperse your responses below each question from the original message so the recipient can better understand the context of your responses. When you respond to a message that was sent to a number of people—perhaps some people received the message as a carbon copy—be careful how you respond. You can choose to respond to all the original recipients or just to the sender. Figure 2-15 shows the Composition window that opens when you reply to a message sent by Alice B. Student.

Figure 2-15 REPLYING TO A MESSAGE

vertical line indicates the body of the sender's original message

---

REFERENCE WINDOW

Replying to a sender's message
- Click the message summary of the message to which you want to reply in order to select it.
- Click either the Reply or the Reply All button located on the Navigation toolbar. The Composition window opens. The Composition window will include a To line with the address of the sender or the sender and all recipients, depending on your selection. You can type other recipients' e-mail addresses in the message header as needed.
- The Subject line includes the subject of the original message, plus "Re:" to indicate that this is a reply message. You can change the Subject line by editing it, if necessary.
- The message body includes one blank line at the top of the window, and the text of the original message, which is indicated with a vertical blue line in the left margin. You can type a message on the blank line (use as much space as you require). You can also delete any of the original message that you don't need. For example, you might type a message such as, "I received your message today, thank you." at the top of your reply message.
- Send the message by clicking the Send button on the Message toolbar.

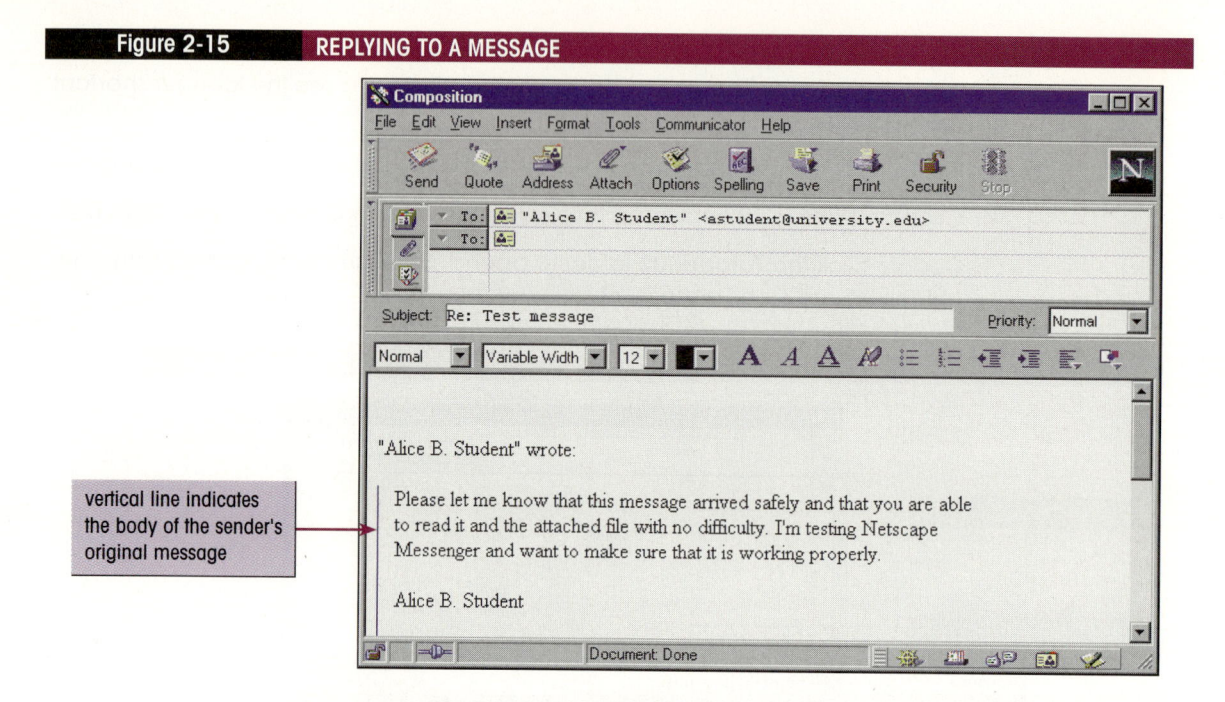

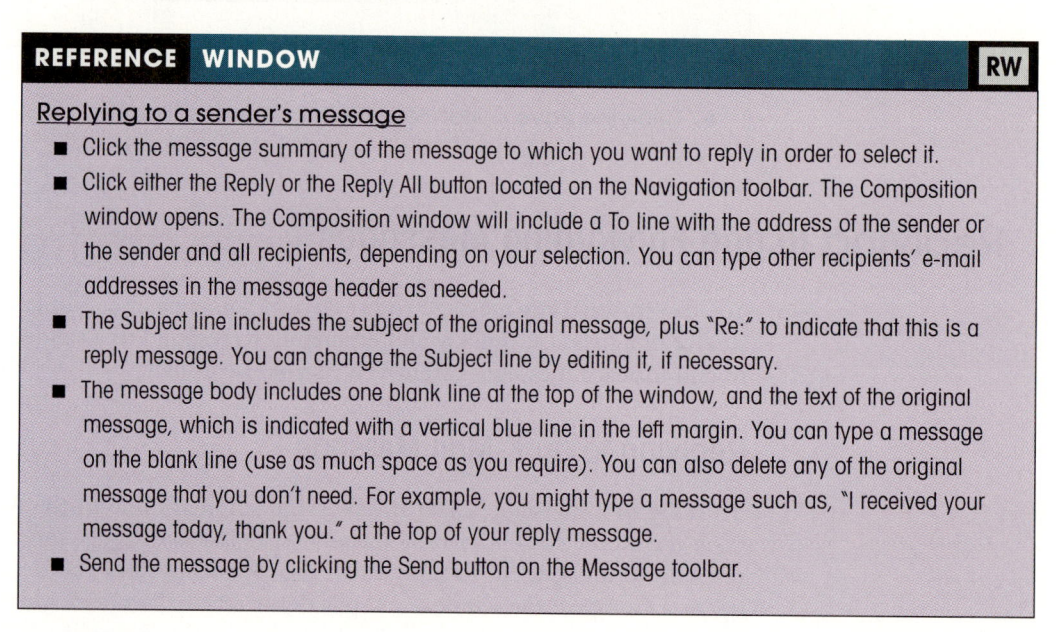

Forwarding an E-Mail Message

When you forward a message, it is copied from your Inbox folder and travels to the person to whom you are forwarding the message. To forward an existing mail message to another user, open the folder containing the message (usually, the Inbox folder) in the Message List window, double-click the message summary to open a full Message window, click Message on the menu bar, click Forward As, and then click Quoted. The Composition window opens and displays the message to forward along with a full message header. The forwarded message is marked with a line to the left side. You can include your own comments along with the message itself. Figure 2-16 shows the Composition window for forwarding a message. You can forward a message to more than one person by including each e-mail address in the To, Cc, or Bcc text boxes as necessary.

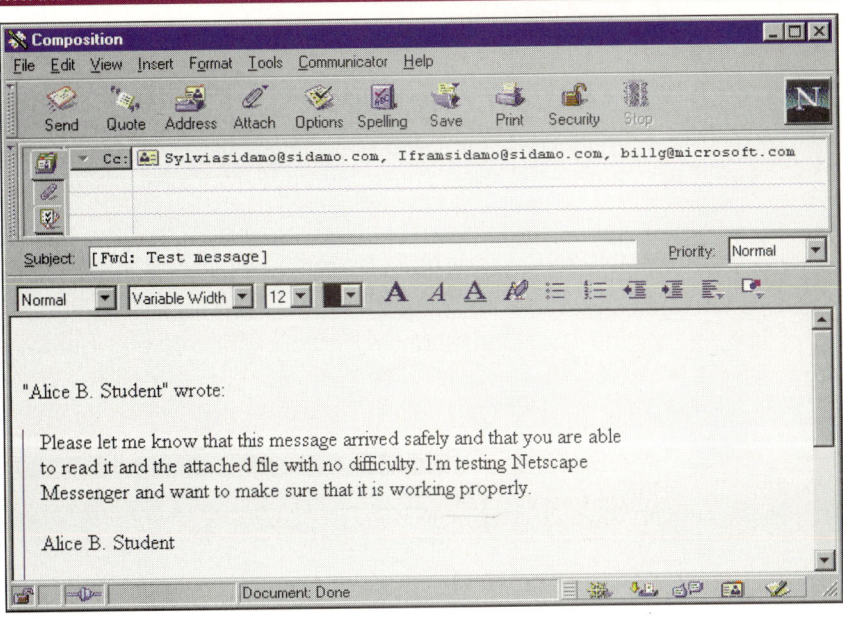

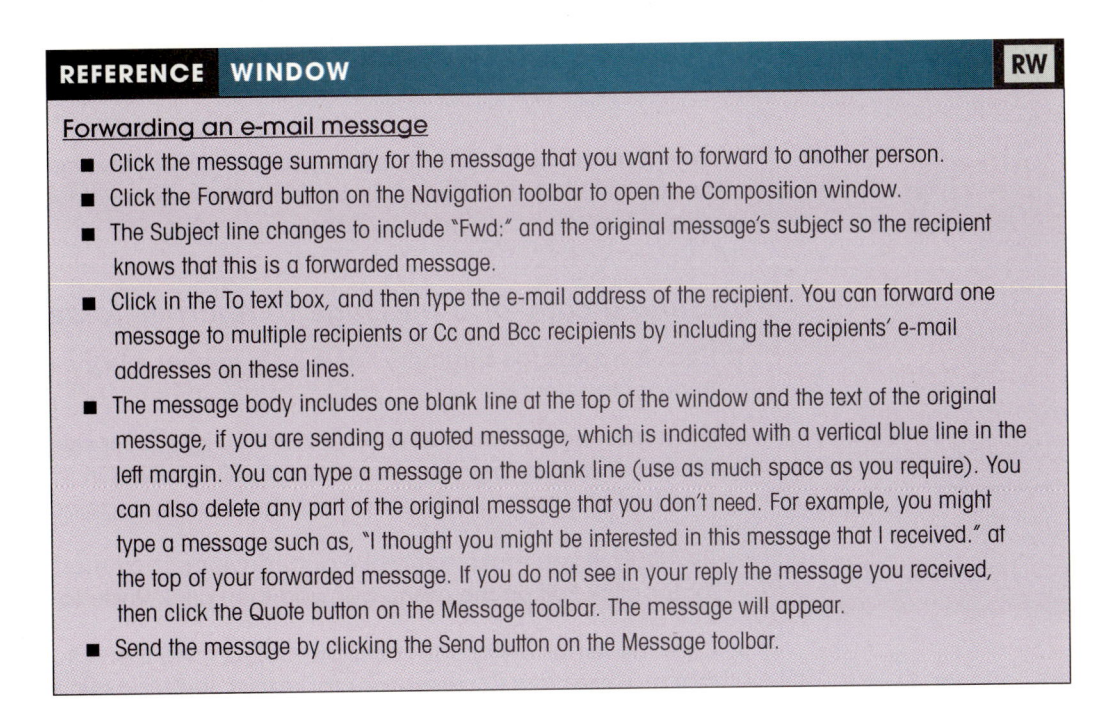

Figure 2-16 FORWARDING A MESSAGE

[Screenshot of Composition window showing a forwarded message with Cc: Sylviasidamo@sidamo.com, Iframsidamo@sidamo.com, billg@microsoft.com; Subject: [Fwd: Test message]; body shows "Alice B. Student" wrote: Please let me know that this message arrived safely and that you are able to read it and the attached file with no difficulty. I'm testing Netscape Messenger and want to make sure that it is working properly. Alice B. Student]

REFERENCE WINDOW

Forwarding an e-mail message
- Click the message summary for the message that you want to forward to another person.
- Click the Forward button on the Navigation toolbar to open the Composition window.
- The Subject line changes to include "Fwd:" and the original message's subject so the recipient knows that this is a forwarded message.
- Click in the To text box, and then type the e-mail address of the recipient. You can forward one message to multiple recipients or Cc and Bcc recipients by including the recipients' e-mail addresses on these lines.
- The message body includes one blank line at the top of the window and the text of the original message, if you are sending a quoted message, which is indicated with a vertical blue line in the left margin. You can type a message on the blank line (use as much space as you require). You can also delete any part of the original message that you don't need. For example, you might type a message such as, "I thought you might be interested in this message that I received." at the top of your forwarded message. If you do not see in your reply the message you received, then click the Quote button on the Message toolbar. The message will appear.
- Send the message by clicking the Send button on the Message toolbar.

Filing and Printing an E-Mail Message

You can use Messenger mail folders to file your e-mail messages by category. When you file a message, you move it from the Inbox to another folder. You can also make a *copy* of a message in the Inbox and save it in another folder. You will make a copy of your Cc message and save it in a folder named "Marketing" for safekeeping. You can create other folders to suit your individual working style.

To create a new folder:

1. Click **File** on the menu bar in the Message List window, and then click **New Folder**. The New Folder dialog box opens.

2. Type **Marketing** in the Name text box to name the new folder. You will create this folder as a sub-folder of the Inbox folder.

3. Make sure that the Create as a subfolder of list box shows the Inbox. If it doesn't, then click the list arrow and click **Inbox**. See Figure 2-17.

Figure 2-17 CREATING A NEW MAIL FOLDER

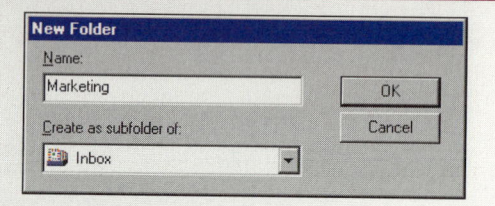

[New Folder dialog box showing Name: Marketing, Create as subfolder of: Inbox, with OK and Cancel buttons]

4. Click the **OK** button to create the new folder.

After you create the Marketing folder, you can transfer messages to it. Besides copying or transferring mail from the Inbox, you can select any other mail folder's messages for transfer to another folder.

To send a copy of a message to another folder:

1. Click the message summary for your Cc message in the Message List window in order to select it.

2. Click **Message** on the menu bar, point to **Copy Message**, point to **Inbox**, and then click **Marketing**. Your Cc message still appears in the Inbox. Now, make sure that you have copied and filed your Cc message correctly.

    TROUBLE? If you make a mistake and move or copy messages to the wrong folder, click Edit on the menu bar, and then click Undo to cancel the action.

3. Click the **list arrow** on the Location toolbar, and then click **Marketing** to open that mailbox. Your Cc message appears in the Marketing mailbox.

When you need to file a message, you follow a similar procedure.

TUTORIAL 2 BASIC E-MAIL: INTEGRATED BROWSER E-MAIL SOFTWARE   WEB 2.27   INTERNET

To file a message in another folder:

1. Select the message summary for your Cc message in the Marketing folder.

2. Click the **File** button on the Navigation toolbar, and then click **Trash**. The message is removed from the Marketing folder and is transferred to the Trash folder.

Moving or copying several messages at once is a snap. Hold down the Ctrl key and click each message summary in the Message List window that you want to move. Then click Message on the menu bar. Next, point to either Move Message or Copy Message, and then click the folder to which you want to move or copy the group of messages.

You might need to print important messages in the future, so you want to make sure that you can print and file messages in a safe place.

To print an e-mail message:

1. Click the **Inbox** to return to that folder.

2. Right-click the message summary for your Cc message in the Inbox window to open the shortcut menu that shows the actions you can take.

3. Click **Print Message** on the shortcut menu, and then click the **OK** button in the Print dialog box to send the message to the printer.

You can print a message at any time—when you receive it, before you send it, or after you file it.

Deleting an E-Mail Message

You saved and printed your Cc message, so now you can delete the message and the Marketing folder that you created. Deleting messages in the Inbox mailbox and other mailboxes is easy. When you delete a message, you are really just moving it to the Trash mailbox. To remove messages permanently, click File on the menu bar, and then click Empty Trash on Local Mail. If you are using a public PC in a university computer laboratory, it is always a good idea to delete all your messages and then empty the trash before you leave the computer. Otherwise, the next person who uses Messenger will be able to access and read your messages.

REFERENCE WINDOW   RW

Deleting an e-mail message
- Right-click the message summary to delete, and then click Delete Message on the shortcut menu.
- To delete the message permanently, click File on the menu bar, and then click Empty Trash on Local Mail.

To delete a message and empty the trash:

1. Right-click the message summary line for your Cc message. See Figure 2-18.

Figure 2-18 DELETING A MESSAGE

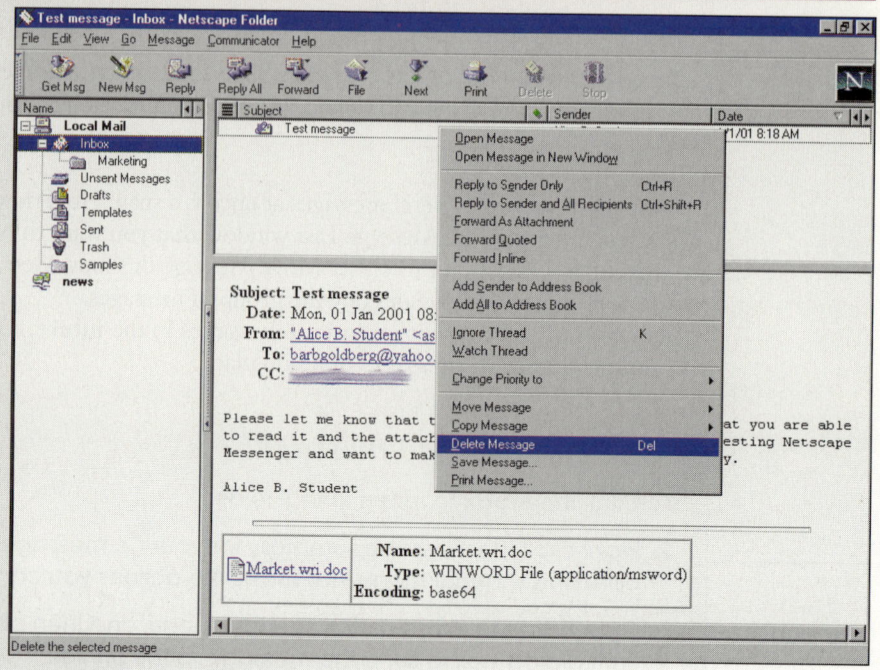

[Screenshot of Netscape Folder Inbox showing a Test message with a right-click shortcut menu displayed. The menu includes options: Open Message, Open Message in New Window, Reply to Sender Only (Ctrl+R), Reply to Sender and All Recipients (Ctrl+Shift+R), Forward As Attachment, Forward Quoted, Forward Inline, Add Sender to Address Book, Add All to Address Book, Ignore Thread (K), Watch Thread, Change Priority to, Move Message, Copy Message, Delete Message (Del) — highlighted, Save Message, Print Message. Status bar reads "Delete the selected message".]

2. Click **Delete Message** on the shortcut menu to delete the message. The message is moved from the Inbox to the special folder named Trash.

   TROUBLE? If you deleted a message you wanted to keep, you can recover it by clicking Edit on the menu bar and then clicking Undo. To remove the message completely, you must empty the contents of the Trash folder.

3. Click **File** on the menu bar, and then click **Empty Trash on Local Mail**. Any deleted messages or folders are permanently removed.

To delete a folder, you follow the same process.

To delete a user-created folder:

1. Click the **Marketing** folder and then right-click the **Marketing** folder.

2. Click **Delete Folder** on the shortcut menu.

3. The dialog box appears asking if you want to move the selected folders into the Trash. Click **OK**. The folder moves to the Trash folder.

   TROUBLE? If you deleted a folder you wanted to keep, you can recover it by clicking Edit on the menu bar and then clicking Undo.

4. To remove the folder completely, click **File** on the menu bar, and then click **Empty Trash on Local Mail**. Any deleted messages or folders are permanently removed.

Maintaining an Address Book

As you send e-mail to different people, you will probably find it burdensome and sometimes errorprone to type their e-mail addresses, especially long and difficult ones. As you use e-mail to contact business associates and friends, you will want to save their addresses in an address book.

Adding an Address to the Address Book

You can access the address book by clicking Communicator on the menu bar and then clicking Address Book. To create a new address, you open the address book and then click the New Card button so you can enter information into the text boxes in the New Card dialog box for each person, including the person's first and last names and complete e-mail address information. If you enter a short name in the Nickname text box, then you can use that name to address a new message. After you click the OK button in the New Card dialog box, Messenger adds the new contact information to your address book.

You are eager to add information to your address book. Begin by entering Barbara Goldberg's contact information into your Messenger address book.

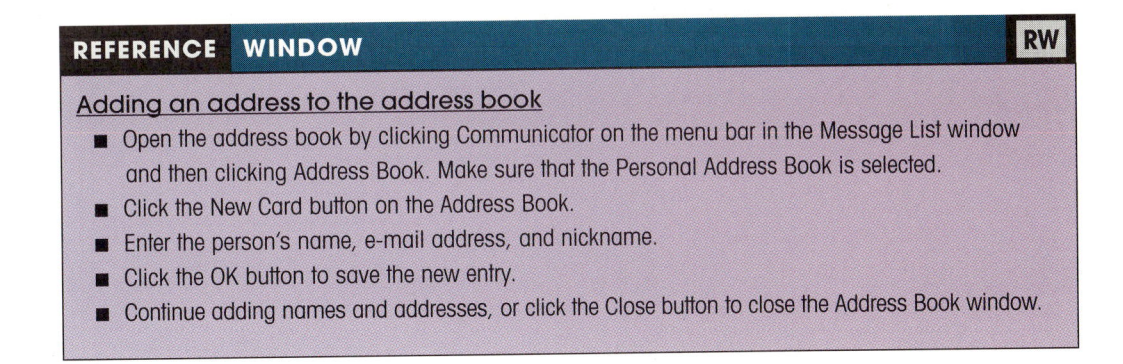

REFERENCE WINDOW RW

Adding an address to the address book
- Open the address book by clicking Communicator on the menu bar in the Message List window and then clicking Address Book. Make sure that the Personal Address Book is selected.
- Click the New Card button on the Address Book.
- Enter the person's name, e-mail address, and nickname.
- Click the OK button to save the new entry.
- Continue adding names and addresses, or click the Close button to close the Address Book window.

To add an e-mail address to the address book:

1. Click **Communicator** on the menu bar in the Message List window, and then click **Address Book** to open the Address Book window. See Figure 2-19.

Figure 2-19 ADDRESS BOOK WINDOW

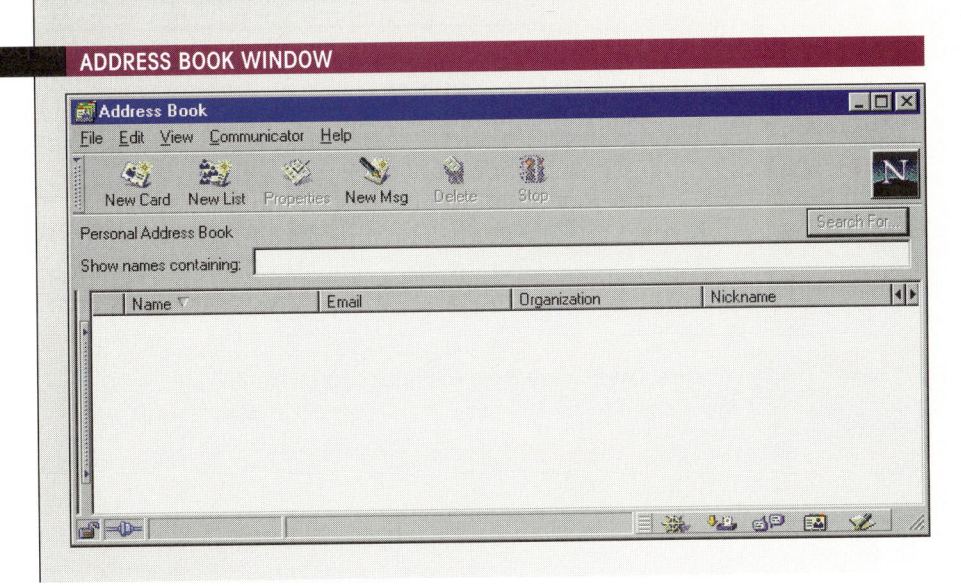

2. Click the **New Card** button on the Address Book toolbar. The New Card dialog box opens. You use this dialog box to add addresses to your address book. The Name tab stores information about a person's e-mail address. You can use the Contact tab to store postal mail address information and other personal information.

3. Make sure that the **Personal Address Book** is selected in the list box that appears at the top of the New Card dialog box. If it is not selected, click the list arrow and then click Personal Address Book.

4. Type **Barbara** in the First Name text box, and then press the **Tab** key to go to the Last Name text box.

5. Type **Goldberg**, and then press the **Tab** key two times to go to the Email text box.

6. Type **barbgoldberg@yahoo.com**, press the **Tab** key to go to the Nickname text box, and then type **Barbara**. Your New Card dialog box looks like Figure 2-20.

Figure 2-20 ENTERING A NEW ADDRESS IN THE ADDRESS BOOK

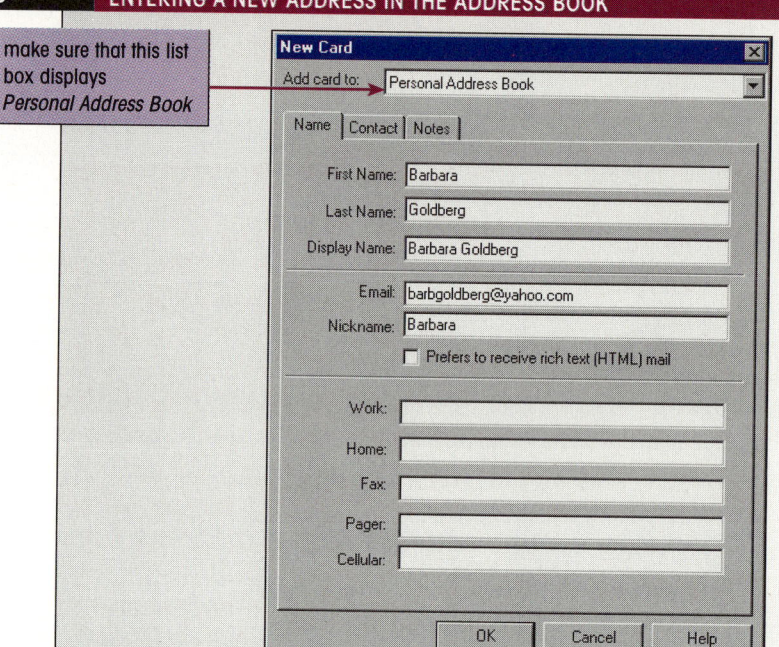

make sure that this list box displays *Personal Address Book*

7. Click the **OK** button to store your new address entry.

8. Repeat Steps 3 through 7 to create address cards for the following members of the marketing department:

First Name	Last Name	E-mail Address	Nickname
Gary	**Kildare**	gkildare@sidamo.com	**Gary**
Faye	**Borthman**	fborthman@sidamo.com	**Faye**
Fran	**Brooks**	fbrooks@sidamo.com	**Fran**

9. When you are finished adding the addresses, click the **Close** button on the Address Book window title bar to close it.

With these entries now in your address book, you can easily insert even the most complicated e-mail address in any of the message text boxes as you compose a message. To insert an e-mail address into a new message's address line, open the address book, select the address, and then click the To, Cc, or Bcc buttons as needed. You can edit an address book entry while viewing the address book by either double-clicking the name or right-clicking the name and then clicking Properties. Another handy facility lets you easily add new names to your address book. Whenever you receive mail from someone not in your address book, right-click the message summary line in the Message List window, and then click Add Sender to Address Book on the shortcut menu to add the sender's e-mail address to your address book.

Creating a Multi-Address Entry

You can use Messenger to create a distribution list, or a **mailing list**, which is an address entry consisting of more than one e-mail address in a single group. A mailing list is helpful when you want to send one message to several people simultaneously.

Barbara frequently sends messages to each member of the marketing department. She asks you to create a mailing list entry in her address book so she can type one nickname for the group of e-mail addresses, instead of typing each address separately.

REFERENCE WINDOW

Creating a mailing list
- Click Communicator on the menu bar in the Message List window, and then click Address Book to open the Address Book window.
- Click the New List button on the Address Book toolbar.
- Enter the mailing list's name in the List Name text box.
- Enter the mailing list's nickname in the List Nickname text box.
- Enter the individual nicknames or e-mail address information of the individual group members.
- Click the OK button to create the list.

To create a mailing list address entry:

1. Click **Communicator** on the menu bar in the Message List window, and then click **Address Book** to open the Address Book window. Maximize the Address Book window, if necessary.

2. Click the **New List** button on the Address Book toolbar. The Mailing List dialog box opens. You will add a group name, a nickname, and the individual e-mail addresses for the group to your mailing list entry.

3. Type **Marketing List** in the List Name text box, and then press the **Tab** key to go to the List Nickname text box.

4. Type **mkt** in the List Nickname text box. Now, when Barbara needs to send a message to every member of the marketing department, she can type "mkt" on the To line.

5. Click **OK** to create the list. The Address Book window reappears. Next, add the individual e-mail addresses to the mailing list.

6. Double-click the **Marketing List** entry in the address book to open the list.

7. Press the **Tab** key three times to move to the address list, and then type **Fran**. You already added Fran's address to the address book. After you start typing Fran's name, Messenger recognizes it. Press the **Enter** key to add Fran's address to the list.

8. Repeat Step 5 to add Faye Borthman and Gary Kildare to the mailing list. Press the **Enter** key after entering each name to add the name to the mailing list and to move to the next line in the address list. Figure 2-21 shows the marketing list after three names have been entered.

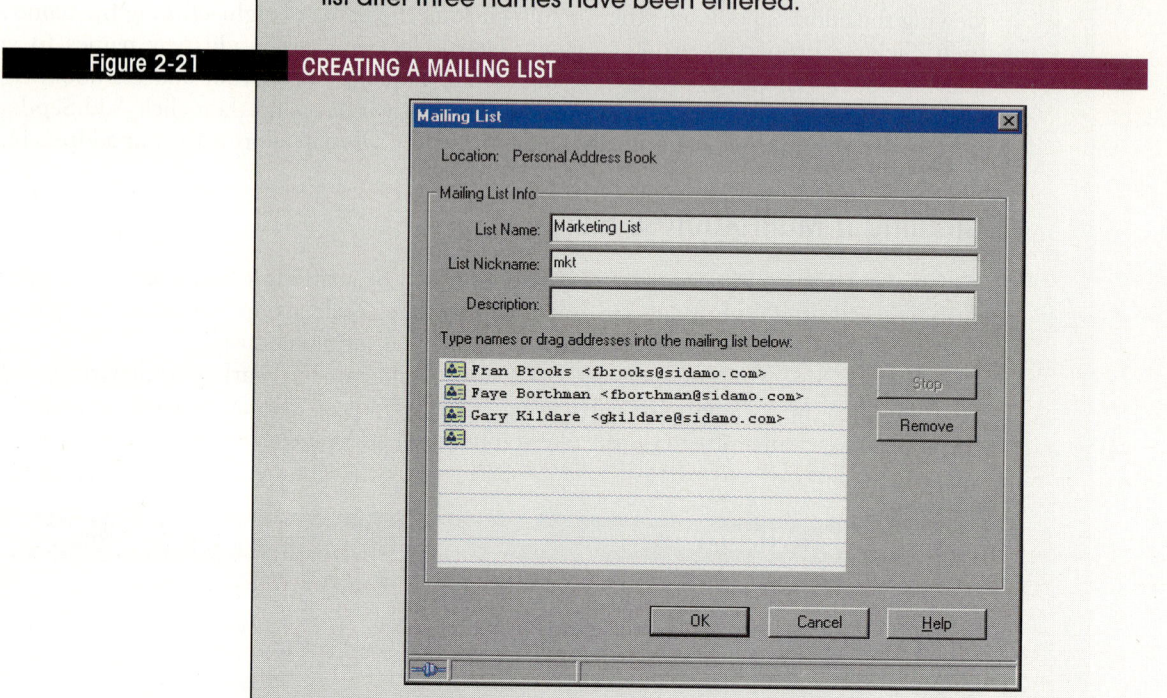

Figure 2-21   CREATING A MAILING LIST

9. Click the **OK** button to close the Mailing List dialog box. Now, the Marketing List entry appears in the Address Book window. See Figure 2-22.

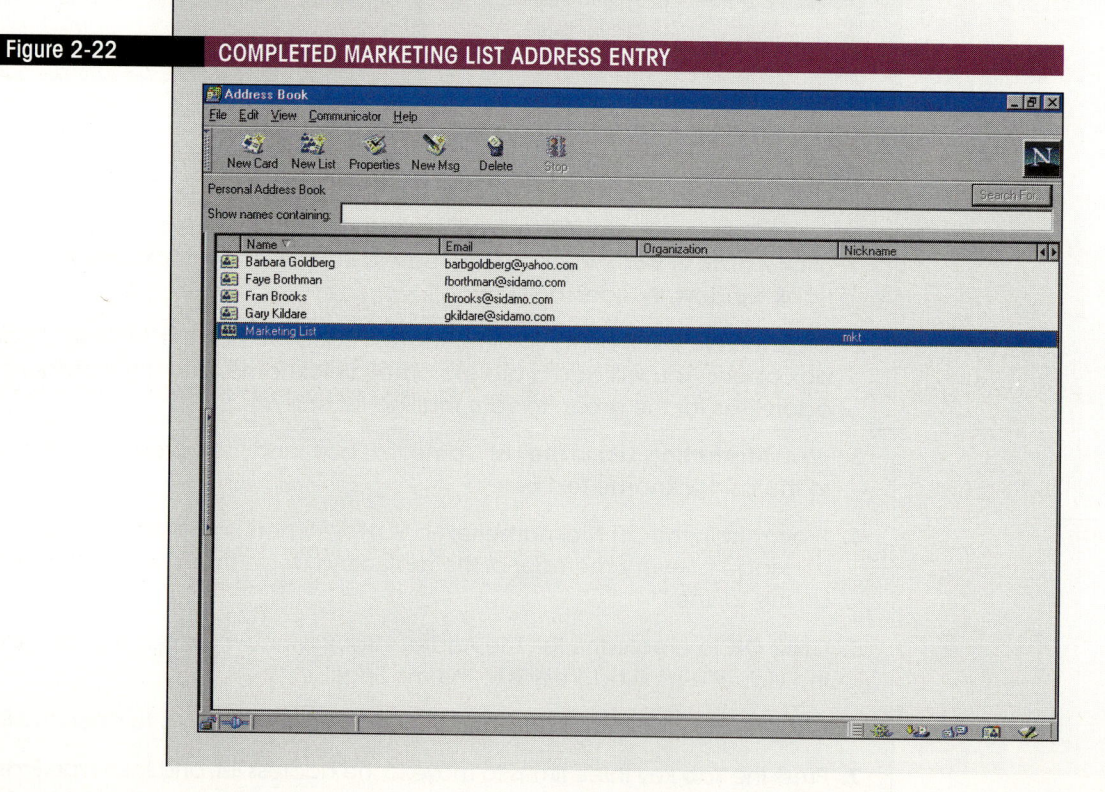

Figure 2-22   COMPLETED MARKETING LIST ADDRESS ENTRY

TUTORIAL 2 BASIC E-MAIL: INTEGRATED BROWSER E-MAIL SOFTWARE   WEB 2.33

10. Close the Address Book by clicking the **Close** button.

11. Close all open Netscape windows, and then close your dial-up connection, if necessary.

When you need to modify a mailing list, you can delete one or more members from the group by opening the address book, double-clicking the list name, and then deleting a member's name by selecting it and clicking the Remove button. You can add members to an existing list by opening the mailing list and typing the new member's name.

Session 2.2 QUICK CHECK

1. Netscape Messenger is known as an e-mail _____ because it runs on a PC and it sends requests for mail delivery to the mail server.

2. What is perhaps the most important potential disadvantage of using mail programs such as Netscape Messenger? *Hint:* What happens when you read mail in another location?

3. When you delete an e-mail message in a mail program, are the messages deleted immediately? If not, then how do you delete mail messages permanently?

4. You can organize mail by placing messages into _____.

5. Discuss whether or not it is important to include parts of the original message when replying to the sender.

6. If you store people's e-mail addresses in an address book, then you can type a(n) _____ in place of a person's e-mail address and Netscape Messenger will automatically fill in the correct e-mail address.

7. When you assemble several e-mail addresses under a single address book entry, you are creating a(n) _____ list.

If your instructor assigns Session 2.3, continue reading. Otherwise, complete the Review Assignments at the end of this tutorial.

SESSION 2.3

In this session you will learn how to use Microsoft Outlook Express to send and receive e-mail. You will learn how to print, file, save, delete, respond to, and forward e-mail messages. Finally, you will organize your e-mail addresses in an address book.

Microsoft Outlook Express Client

Microsoft Outlook Express, or simply **Outlook Express**, is an e-mail client that supports all the standard e-mail functions you learned about in Session 2.1 to send and receive mail. You can access Outlook Express from within a Web browser or from any Microsoft Office program.

You are eager to continue your evaluation of e-mail software. You start Outlook Express by double-clicking its icon on the Windows desktop or by using the Start menu. Figure 2-23 shows the Outlook Express Inbox window.

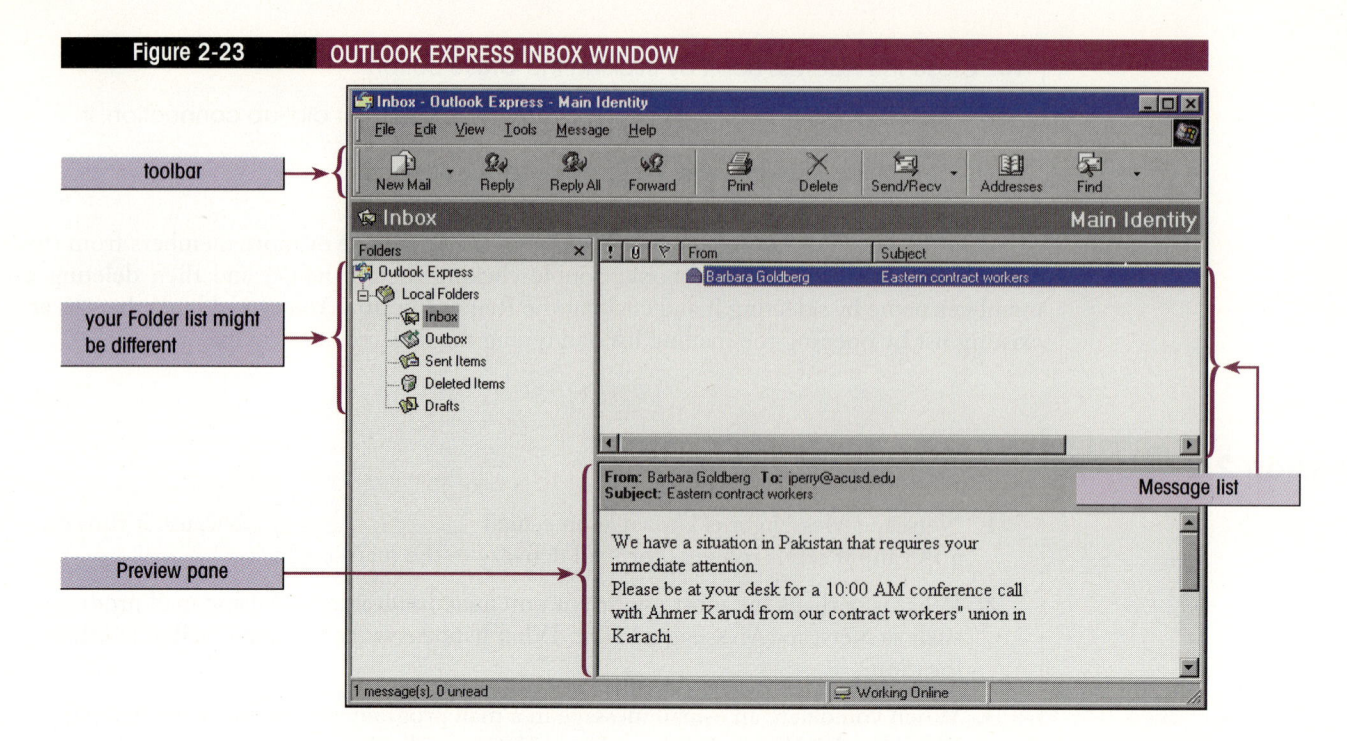

Figure 2-23 OUTLOOK EXPRESS INBOX WINDOW

[Screenshot of Outlook Express Inbox window with callouts: **toolbar**, **your Folder list might be different**, **Preview pane**, **Message list**]

Three panels appear on the screen: the Folder list on the left side, the Message list in the upper-right pane, and the Preview pane in the lower-right pane. The **Folder list** displays a list of folders for receiving, saving, and deleting mail messages. Your folders might be different from those that appear in Figure 2-23. The **Inbox** folder holds messages you have received, the **Outbox** folder holds messages waiting to be sent, the **Sent Items** folder contains copies of messages you sent, and the **Deleted Items** folder contains messages you deleted from other folders.

The Message list contains summary information for each message that you receive, including the message priority, an indication for an attached file, the sender's name, and the message's subject. The message summary that is selected in the Message list appears in the Preview pane. The Preview pane is normally located below the message list and reveals part of the message's contents. You can customize each of the panels to display different information, so Figure 2-23 might be slightly different from what you see in your copy of Outlook Express.

Setting Up E-Mail

You are eager to get started using Outlook Express. These steps assume that Outlook Express is already installed on your computer. First, you want to set up Outlook Express so it will retrieve your mail from a publicly accessible computer. Cost is not a consideration because the Microsoft Outlook Express program is free. Your first step is to start and configure Outlook Express so it fetches and sends *your* e-mail.

> ### To start and initialize Outlook Express for use on a public computer:
>
> 1. Click the **Start** button on the Windows taskbar, point to **Programs**, point to **Internet Explorer**, and then click **Outlook Express** to start the program. The Inbox folder opens (see Figure 2-23).

TUTORIAL 2 BASIC E-MAIL: INTEGRATED BROWSER E-MAIL SOFTWARE   WEB 2.35   INTERNET

TROUBLE? If a graphic Microsoft Outlook Express screen appears when you start Outlook Express, click the Read Mail icon to go directly to your Inbox.

TROUBLE? If a Browse for Folder dialog box opens when you first try to start Outlook Express, click the Outlook Express folder, and then click the OK button.

TROUBLE? If the Internet Connection Wizard starts, click the Cancel button.

TROUBLE? If you cannot find the Outlook Express program on your computer, ask your instructor or technical support person for assistance.

2. Click **Tools** on the menu bar, click **Accounts**, and then, if necessary, click the **Mail** tab so you can set up your mail account settings.

TROUBLE? If you (or someone else) already set up your account, then click the Close button in the Internet Accounts dialog box and skip the remainder of these steps.

3. Click the **Add** button in the Internet Accounts dialog box, and then click **Mail**, if necessary. The Internet Connection Wizard starts. You use the Wizard to identify yourself and the settings for your mail server and user name. See Figure 2-24.

Figure 2-24 | INTERNET CONNECTION WIZARD DIALOG BOX

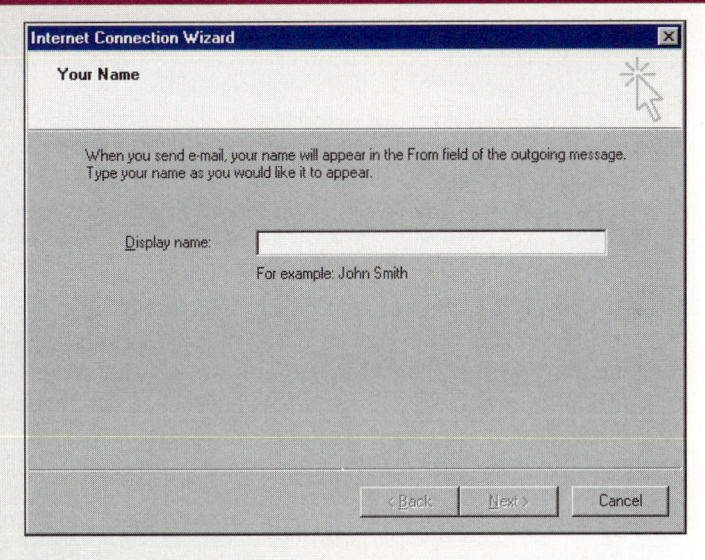

4. Type your first and last name in the Display name text box, and then click the **Next** button to go to the next dialog box, where you enter your e-mail address.

5. Type your full e-mail address (such as student@university.edu) in the E-mail address text box, and then click the **Next** button. The next dialog box asks you for your incoming and outgoing mail server names.

6. Enter the name of your incoming and outgoing mail servers in the text boxes where indicated. Your instructor or technical support person will provide you with this information. Usually, your outgoing mail server name is either SMTP or MAIL followed by a domain name. Your incoming mail server name is typically POP, POP3, or IMAP followed by a domain name. When you are finished, click the **Next** button to continue.

7. In the Account name text box type your Internet mail logon, as supplied by your instructor or technical support person. Make sure that you type only your login name and not your domain name. Enter your password in the Password text box.

8. Clear the **Remember password** check box and click the **Next** button.

9. Click the **Finish** button to save the mail account information and close the Internet Connection Wizard. The Internet Accounts dialog box reappears, and your account is listed on the Mail tab. Figure 2-25 shows Barbara Goldberg's information.

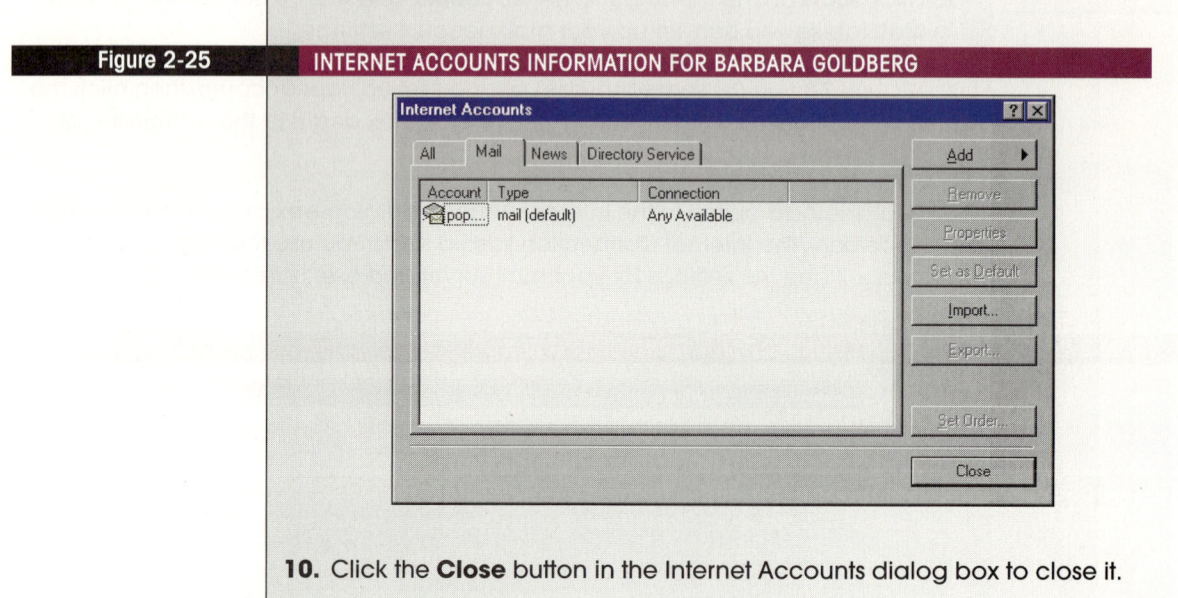

Figure 2-25   INTERNET ACCOUNTS INFORMATION FOR BARBARA GOLDBERG

10. Click the **Close** button in the Internet Accounts dialog box to close it.

Now, your copy of Outlook Express is set up to send and receive messages, so you are ready to send a message to Barbara. *Note:* In this tutorial, you will send messages to a real mailbox with the address barbgoldberg@yahoo.com. Follow the instructions carefully so you use the correct address. Messages sent to this mailbox are deleted without being opened or read, so do not send important messages to this address.

Sending a Message Using Outlook Express

You decide to use Outlook Express to send a message with an attached file to Barbara. You will send a carbon copy of the message to your own e-mail address to make sure that the message and attached file are sent correctly.

TUTORIAL 2 BASIC E-MAIL: INTEGRATED BROWSER E-MAIL SOFTWARE   WEB 2.37   INTERNET

> **REFERENCE WINDOW**
>
> **Sending a message using Outlook Express**
> - Click the New Mail button on the toolbar to open the New Message window.
> - Click in the To text box, and then type the recipient's e-mail address. If you are sending the message to more than one recipient, separate the e-mail addresses with commas. If necessary, click the View menu in the New Message window and then click the All Headers selection to display the Bcc line in your New Message window.
> - Type the e-mail address of any Cc of Bcc recipients on the appropriate lines.
> - Click the Attach button on the toolbar, and then locate the file to attach to the message, if necessary.
> - Click in the message body, and then type and sign your message.
> - Check your message for spelling and grammatical errors.
> - Click the Send button to send the message.

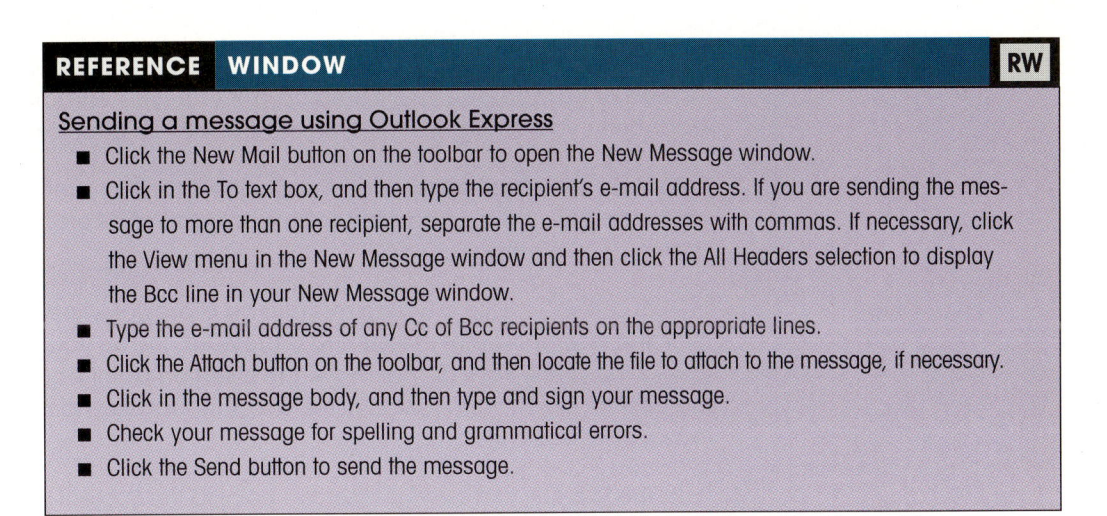

To send a message:

1. Make sure that the Inbox is selected in the Folder list, and then click the **New Mail** button on the toolbar to open the New Message window. If necessary, click the **Maximize** button on the New Message window. See Figure 2-26. The New Message window contains its own menu bar, toolbar, message display area, and text boxes in which you enter address and subject information.

Figure 2-26   NEW MESSAGE WINDOW

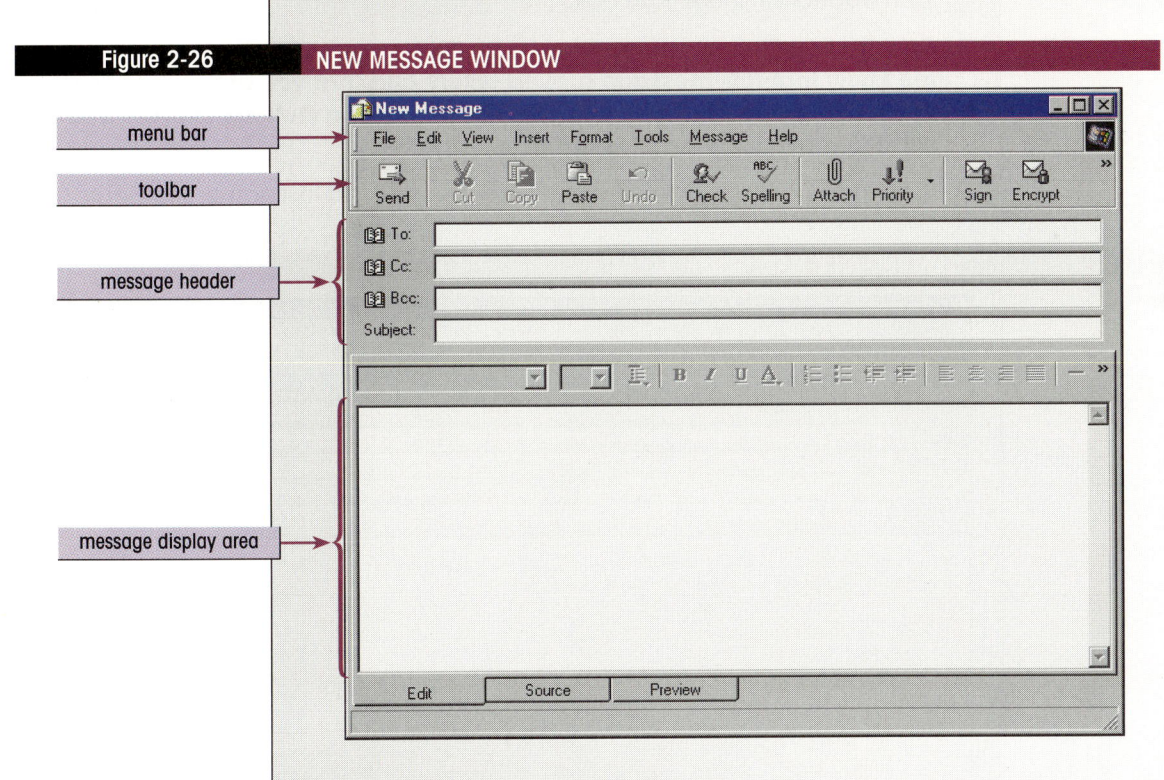

- menu bar
- toolbar
- message header
- message display area

2. Type **barbgoldberg@yahoo.com** in the To text box, and then press the **Tab** key to move to the Cc line.

TROUBLE? Make sure that you use the address barbgoldberg@yahoo.com, instead of barbgoldberg@sidamo.com. If you type Barbara's e-mail address incorrectly, your message will be returned with an error message attached.

3. Type your full e-mail address on the Cc line in order to receive a copy of your own message. It is a good idea to save a copy of all electronic correspondence as a reference.

TROUBLE? If you make a typing mistake on a previous line, use the arrow keys or click the insertion point to return to a previous line so you can correct your mistake. If the arrow keys do not move the insertion point backward or forward in the header block, then press Shift + Tab or the Tab key to move backward or forward, respectively.

4. Press the **Tab** key to move the insertion point to the Subject line, and then type **Test message**. Notice that the title bar now shows "Test message" as the window title.

5. Click the **Attach** button on the New Message window toolbar. The Insert Attachment dialog box opens.

6. Make sure your Data Disk is in drive A. Click the **Look in** list arrow, and then click **3½ Floppy (A:)** to display the contents of your Data Disk.

7. Double-click **Tutorial.02** to open that folder, and then double-click the **Market.wri** file. The Insert Attachment dialog box closes, and the attached file's icon appears in the Attach box.

8. Click the insertion point in the message display area, and then type **Please let me know that this message arrived safely and that you are able to read it and the attached file with no difficulty. I'm testing Outlook Express and want to make sure that it is working properly.**

9. Press the **Enter** key twice, and then type your first and last name. See Figure 2-27.

Figure 2-27 SENDING AN E-MAIL MESSAGE

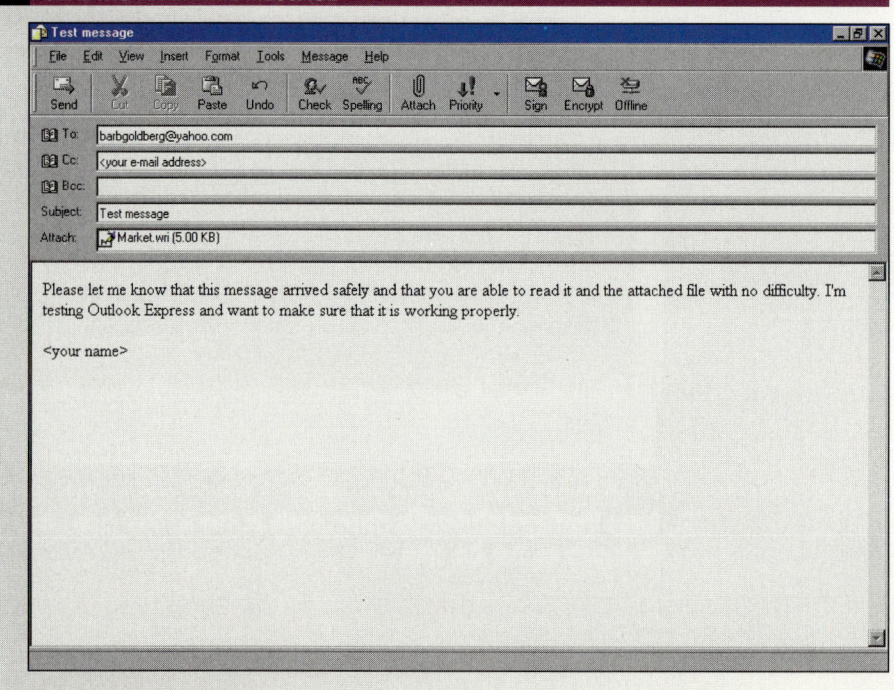

10. Click **Tools** on the menu bar, and then click **Spelling** to check your spelling before sending the message. If necessary, correct any typing errors. When you are finished, click the **OK** button to close the Check Spelling dialog box.

   TROUBLE? If the Spelling command is dimmed on the Tools menu, then your computer does not have the spelling feature installed. Press the Esc key to close the menu, and then continue with Step 11.

11. Click the **Send** button on the toolbar to mail the message. The Test message window closes and the message is placed in the Outbox. The Outlook Express window reappears.

Depending on your system configuration, Outlook Express might not send your message(s) immediately. It might queue (hold) the message(s) until you connect to your Internet service provider (ISP). If you want to examine the setting and change it, click Tools on the menu bar, and then click Options. Select the Send tab. If the Send messages immediately check box has a check mark, then mail goes out as soon as you click the Send button on the toolbar. Otherwise, the message is held and sent when you connect again.

Receiving and Reading a Message

When you receive new mail, messages that you have not opened have a closed envelope to their left in the Message list, and messages that you have opened have an open envelope next to them. You will check for new mail next.

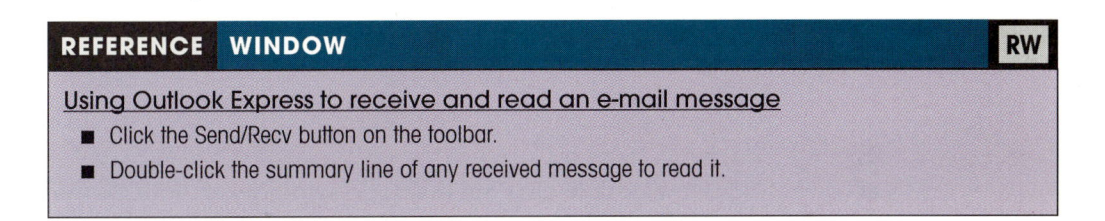

REFERENCE WINDOW — RW

Using Outlook Express to receive and read an e-mail message
- Click the Send/Recv button on the toolbar.
- Double-click the summary line of any received message to read it.

To check for incoming mail:

1. Click the **Send/Recv** button on the toolbar. Depending on your system configuration, you might have to connect to your ISP to get your new mail. Within a few moments, your mail server transfers all new mail to your Inbox. You should see the Cc message that you sent to yourself. Notice that the Inbox folder in the Folder list is bold, but other folders are not. A bold folder indicates that it contains unread mail. Unread messages have a closed envelope to their left in the Message list, whereas read messages have an open envelope next to them.

   TROUBLE? If an Outlook Express message box opens and tells you that it could not find your host, click the Hide button to close the message box, click Tools on the menu bar, click Accounts, and then click the Properties button. Verify that your incoming and outgoing server names are correct, and then repeat Step 1. If you still have problems, ask your instructor or technical support person for help.

TROUBLE? If you do not see any incoming messages in your Inbox, then you either did not receive any new mail or you might be looking in the wrong mailbox. If necessary, click the Inbox folder in the Folder list. If you still don't have any mail messages, wait a few moments, and then repeat Step 1 until you receive a message.

2. Click the message summary for your Cc message in the Message list pane to open it in the Preview pane. See Figure 2-28.

Figure 2-28   **RECEIVING A NEW MESSAGE**

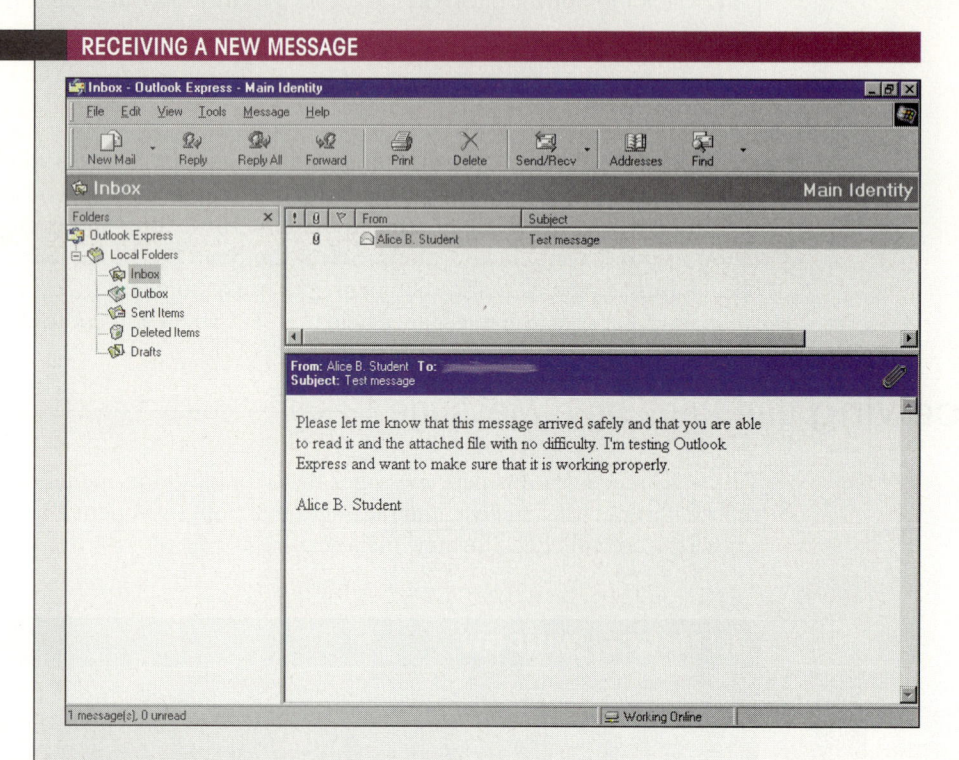

3. Now, double-click the message summary for your Cc message in the Message list to open the Test message window with the full message content.

4. Click the **Close** button on the Test message title bar to close the window. You return to the Inbox window.

You received your Cc copy of the test message that you sent to Barbara, and the paperclip icon indicates that you received an attached file with the message. Either open the attachment in a preview window or save it for viewing later. Open the attachment next.

Saving an Attached File

You want to make sure that your attached file was sent properly, so you decide to open it in the preview window. After you are finished looking at an attached file, you can decide whether to save or delete it from your system.

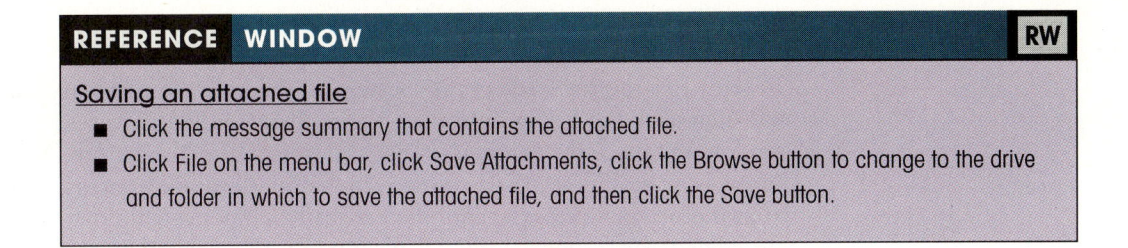

TUTORIAL 2 BASIC E-MAIL: INTEGRATED BROWSER E-MAIL SOFTWARE   WEB 2.41   INTERNET

> **REFERENCE WINDOW**
>
> **Saving an attached file**
> - Click the message summary that contains the attached file.
> - Click File on the menu bar, click Save Attachments, click the Browse button to change to the drive and folder in which to save the attached file, and then click the Save button.

To save an e-mail attachment:

1. Click the message summary for your Cc message in the Message list.
2. Click **File** on the menu bar, and then click **Save Attachments**.
3. Click the **Browse** button and move to the top of the Browse for Folder dialog box, if necessary. Double-click the drive icon that contains your Data Disk.
4. Select the **Tutorial.02** folder, if necessary, and click **OK**. See Figure 2-29.

Figure 2-29   SAVING AN ATTACHED FILE

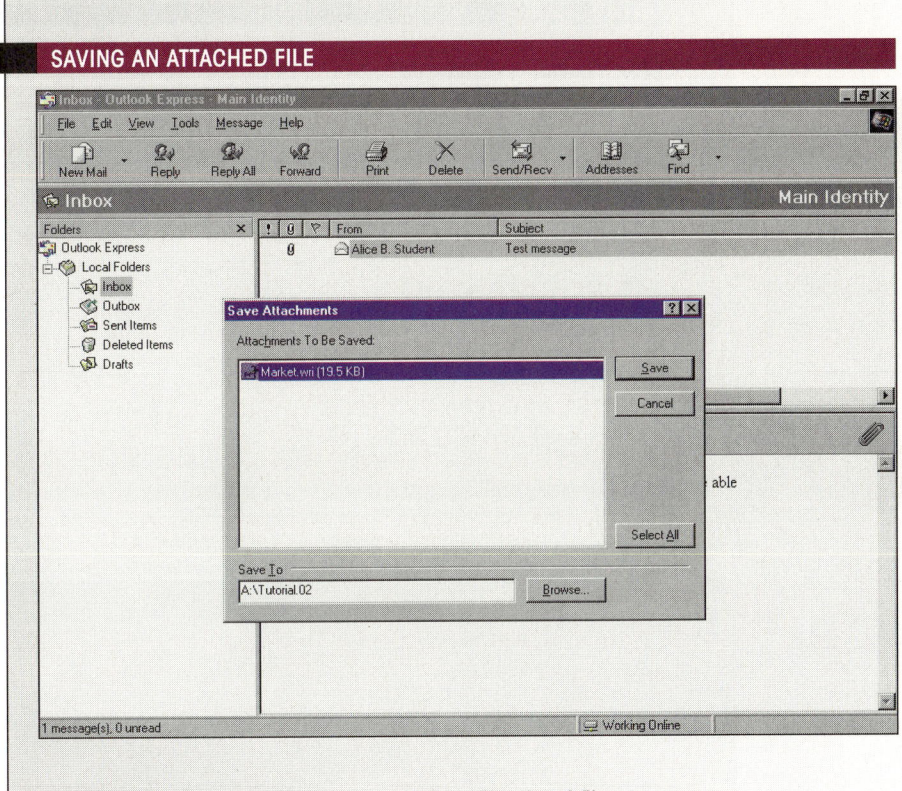

5. Click the **Save** button to save the attached file.

Replying to and Forwarding Messages

You can forward any message you receive to someone else. Similarly, you can respond to the sender of a message quickly and efficiently by replying to a message. You will use both extensively as you use e-mail.

Replying to an E-Mail Message

To reply to a message, select the message in the message summary list (or from any folder), and then click the Reply button on the toolbar. Outlook Express will open a new message window and place the original sender's address in the To text box. You can leave the Subject line as is or modify it. Most systems, including Outlook Express, will copy the entire body from the original message and place it in the response window. Usually, a special mark in one edge of the response indicates what part is the original message. You click the Send button in the Re: window to send the message to the original author.

If you are responding to a question, it is a good idea to type your responses below each question from the original message to help the recipient better understand the context of your responses. When you respond to a message that was sent to a number of people—perhaps some people received the message as a carbon copy—be careful how you respond. You can choose to respond to all the original recipients or just to the sender. Figure 2-30 shows the window that you would use to reply to a message sent by Alice B. Student.

Figure 2-30   REPLYING TO A MESSAGE

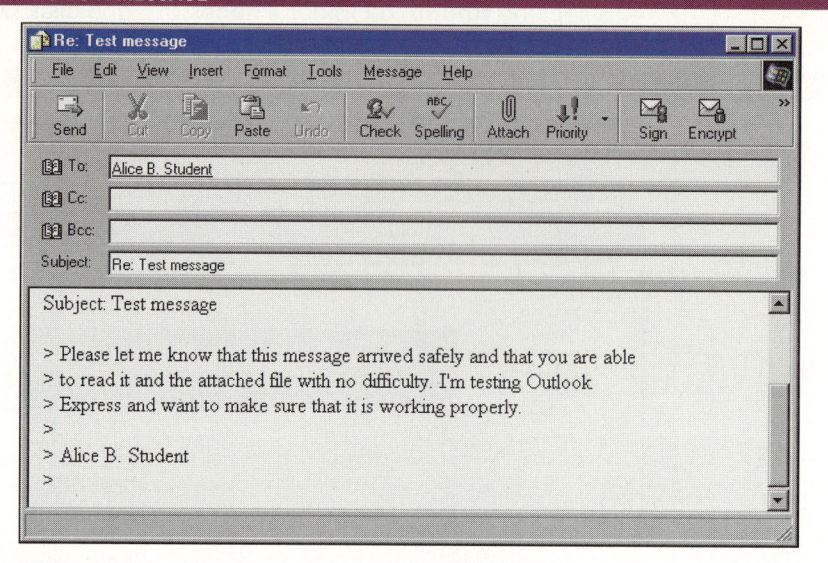

```
Re: Test message
File  Edit  View  Insert  Format  Tools  Message  Help

Send  Cut  Copy  Paste  Undo  Check  Spelling  Attach  Priority  Sign  Encrypt

To:       Alice B. Student
Cc:
Bcc:
Subject:  Re: Test message

Subject: Test message

> Please let me know that this message arrived safely and that you are able
> to read it and the attached file with no difficulty. I'm testing Outlook
> Express and want to make sure that it is working properly.
>
> Alice B. Student
>
```

REFERENCE WINDOW

Replying to a message
- Click the message summary of the message to which you want to reply.
- Click the Reply button on the toolbar. A new message window opens. The message window will include a To line with the address of the sender or the sender and all recipients, depending on your selection. You can type other recipients' e-mail addresses in the message header as needed. Maximize the window, if necessary.
- The Subject line includes the subject of the original message plus "Re:" to indicate that this is a reply message. You can change the Subject line by editing it, if necessary.
- The message body includes one blank line at the top of the window, and the text of the original message contains either a vertical black line to its left or greater than (>) symbols next to each original line. You can type a message on the blank line (and use as much space as you require). You can delete any of the original message that you don't need. For instance, you might type a message such as, "I thought you might be interested in this message that I received." at the top of your message.
- Send the message by clicking the Send button on the toolbar.

Forwarding an E-Mail Message

When you forward a message, it is copied from your Inbox folder and travels to the person to whom you are forwarding the message. To forward an existing mail message to another user, open the folder containing the message (the Inbox folder usually), select the message in the Message list, and then click the Forward button on the toolbar. The Fw: window opens. Type the address of the recipient in the To text box. If you want to forward the message to several people, type their addresses in the To text box (or Cc text box) and separate each e-mail address with a semicolon or comma. Finally, click the Send button on the toolbar to send the message. Figure 2-31 shows the window that you use to forward a message.

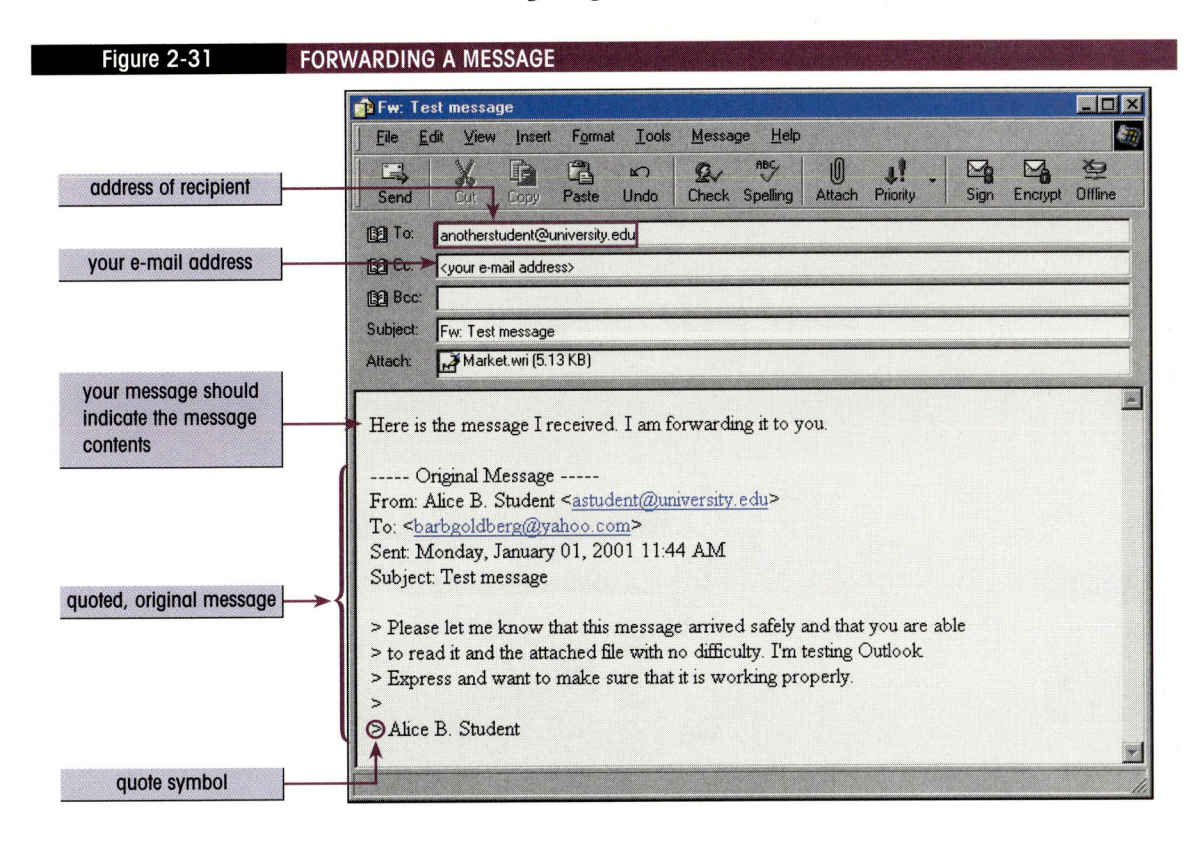

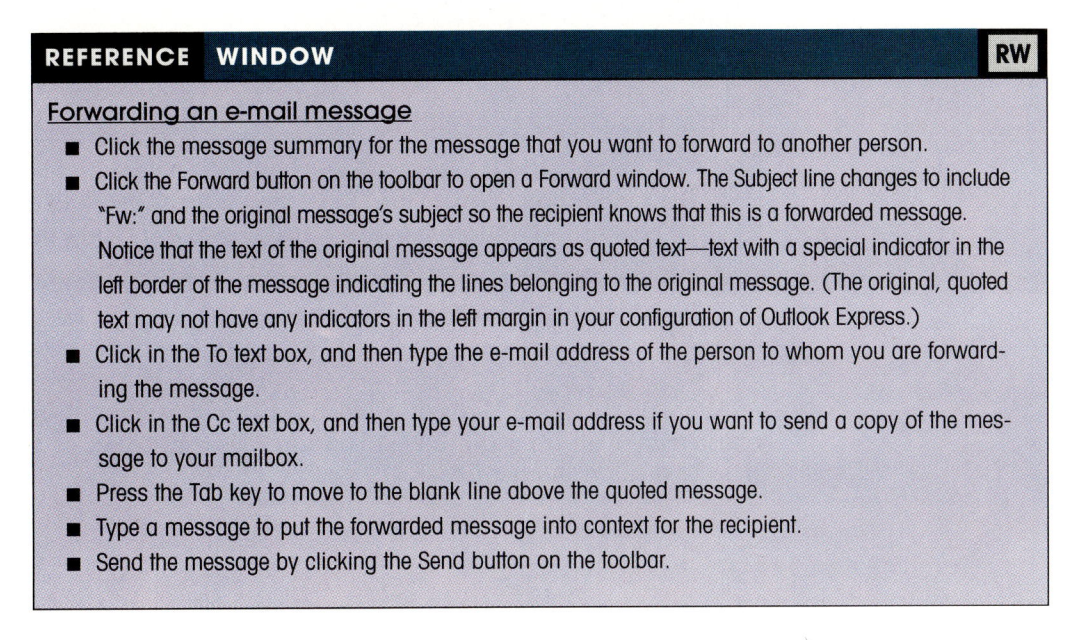

Figure 2-31   FORWARDING A MESSAGE

Callouts:
- address of recipient
- your e-mail address
- your message should indicate the message contents
- quoted, original message
- quote symbol

Window contents:
- To: anotherstudent@university.edu
- Cc: <your e-mail address>
- Bcc:
- Subject: Fw: Test message
- Attach: Market.wri (5.13 KB)

Here is the message I received. I am forwarding it to you.

----- Original Message -----
From: Alice B. Student <astudent@university.edu>
To: <barbgoldberg@yahoo.com>
Sent: Monday, January 01, 2001 11:44 AM
Subject: Test message

> Please let me know that this message arrived safely and that you are able
> to read it and the attached file with no difficulty. I'm testing Outlook
> Express and want to make sure that it is working properly.
>
> Alice B. Student

REFERENCE WINDOW

Forwarding an e-mail message
- Click the message summary for the message that you want to forward to another person.
- Click the Forward button on the toolbar to open a Forward window. The Subject line changes to include "Fw:" and the original message's subject so the recipient knows that this is a forwarded message. Notice that the text of the original message appears as quoted text—text with a special indicator in the left border of the message indicating the lines belonging to the original message. (The original, quoted text may not have any indicators in the left margin in your configuration of Outlook Express.)
- Click in the To text box, and then type the e-mail address of the person to whom you are forwarding the message.
- Click in the Cc text box, and then type your e-mail address if you want to send a copy of the message to your mailbox.
- Press the Tab key to move to the blank line above the quoted message.
- Type a message to put the forwarded message into context for the recipient.
- Send the message by clicking the Send button on the toolbar.

Occasionally, you will receive important messages, so you want to make sure that you print them and then file them in a safe place.

Filing and Printing an E-Mail Message

You can use the Outlook Express mail folders to file your e-mail messages by category. When you file a message, you move it from the Inbox to another folder. You can also make a *copy* of a message in the Inbox and save it in another folder. You will make a copy of Barbara's message and save it in a folder named "Marketing" for safekeeping. Later, you can create other folders to suit your style and working situation.

To create a new folder:

1. Click **File** on the menu bar, point to **Folder**, and then click **New**. The Create Folder dialog box opens.

2. Type **Marketing** in the Folder name text box. See Figure 2-32.

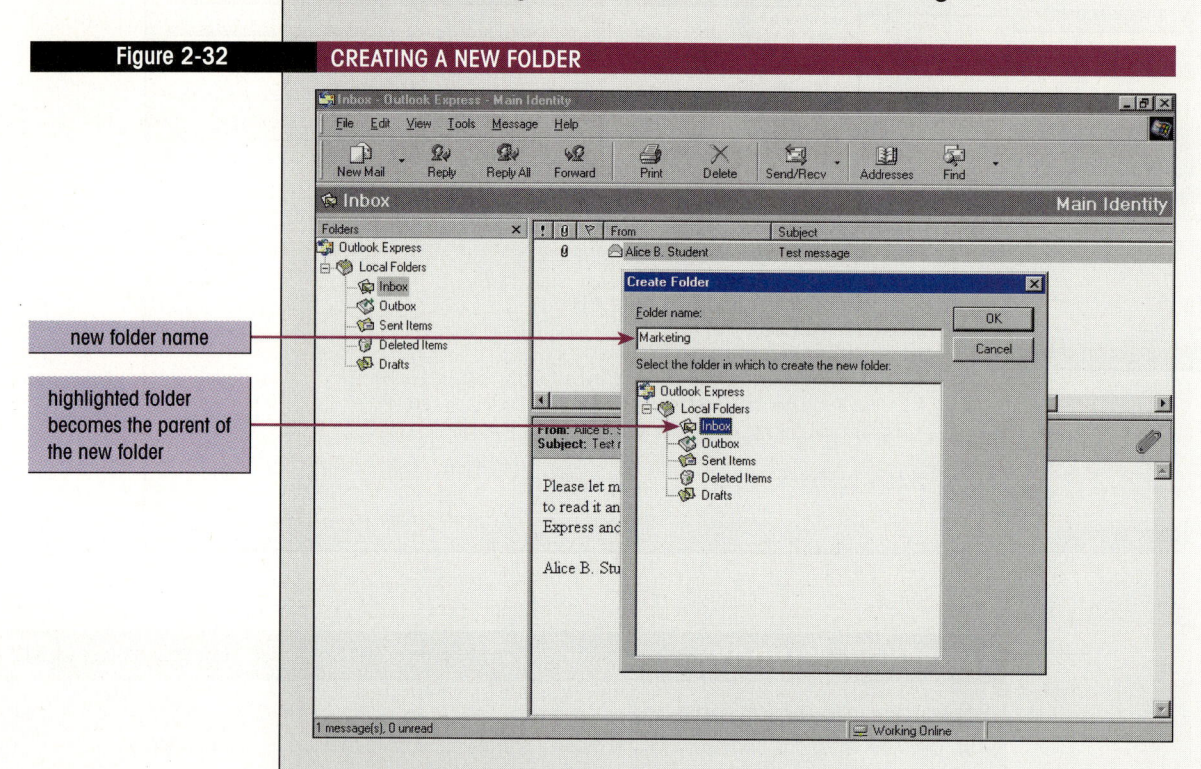

Figure 2-32   CREATING A NEW FOLDER

- new folder name
- highlighted folder becomes the parent of the new folder

3. Click the **Inbox** folder in the Select the folder in which to create the new folder list box. You will create the new Marketing folder below the Inbox folder.

4. Click the **OK** button to create the folder and close the Create Folder dialog box. The new Marketing folder appears in the Folder list.

After you create the Marketing folder, you can transfer messages to it. Besides copying or transferring mail from the Inbox, you can select messages in any other folder and then transfer them to another folder.

To send a copy of a message to another folder:

1. Click the message summary for Barbara's message in the Message list in order to select it, if necessary.

2. Click **Edit** on the menu bar, click **Copy to Folder**, click **Marketing**, and then click the **OK** button. Your Cc message still appears in the Inbox. Now, make sure that you copied and filed your Cc message correctly.

3. Click the **Marketing** folder in the Folder list to open that folder. Your Cc message appears in the Marketing folder.

When you need to move a message to another folder, you follow a similar procedure.

To move a message to another folder:

1. Click the message summary for your Cc message in the Message list.

2. Click and hold down the mouse button, and then drag the message summary for your Cc message from the Marketing folder to the **Deleted Items** folder. When the message summary is on top of the Deleted Items folder, release the mouse button. The message moves from the Inbox to the Deleted Items folder. (That is equivalent to deleting the message.)

Moving or copying several messages at once is a snap. Hold down the Ctrl key, and click each message summary in the Message list that you want to move. Then drag the selected messages to the correct folder, or use the menu commands to copy the messages and save them in a folder.

You might need to print important messages in the future, so you want to make sure that you can print and file messages in a safe place.

To print an e-mail message:

1. Open the Inbox, and then right-click your Cc message summary in the Message list to open the shortcut menu that shows the actions you can take, such as moving messages to folders, replying to a message, and other similar tasks.

2. Click **Print** on the shortcut menu. The Print dialog box opens. Click the **OK** button. The message prints within a few seconds.

You can print a message at any time—when you receive it, before you send it, or after you file it.

Deleting an E-Mail Message

When you don't need a message any longer, select the message and then click the Delete button on the toolbar. You can select multiple messages using the Ctrl key and delete them simultaneously. Also, you can delete a folder by selecting it in the Folder list and then clicking the Delete button. When you delete a message, you are simply moving it to the Deleted Items folder. To remove messages permanently, delete them from the Deleted Items folder using the same procedure. When you delete a folder, the deletion is permanent, but you receive a warning dialog box, giving you a chance to cancel your proposed folder deletion. If you are using a public PC in a university computer laboratory, it is always a good idea to delete all your messages from the Inbox and then delete them again from the Deleted Items folder before you leave the computer. Otherwise, the next person who uses Outlook Express will be able to access and read your messages.

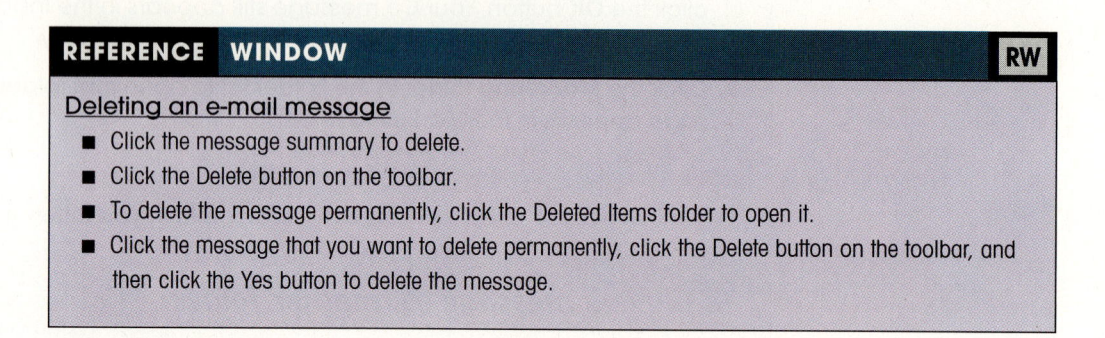

REFERENCE WINDOW

Deleting an e-mail message
- Click the message summary to delete.
- Click the Delete button on the toolbar.
- To delete the message permanently, click the Deleted Items folder to open it.
- Click the message that you want to delete permanently, click the Delete button on the toolbar, and then click the Yes button to delete the message.

To delete a message permanently:

1. Select the message summary for the message you received as a carbon copy.

2. Click the **Delete** button on the toolbar. The message is moved to the Deleted Items folder.

3. Click the **Deleted Items** folder to open it.

4. Click the message summary for the message you received that is now in the Deleted Items folder. You can press Ctrl and click more than one message summary to delete them permanently. Click the **Delete** button on the toolbar. A dialog box opens warning you that the deletion will be permanent (see Figure 2-33).

Figure 2-33 DELETING A MESSAGE

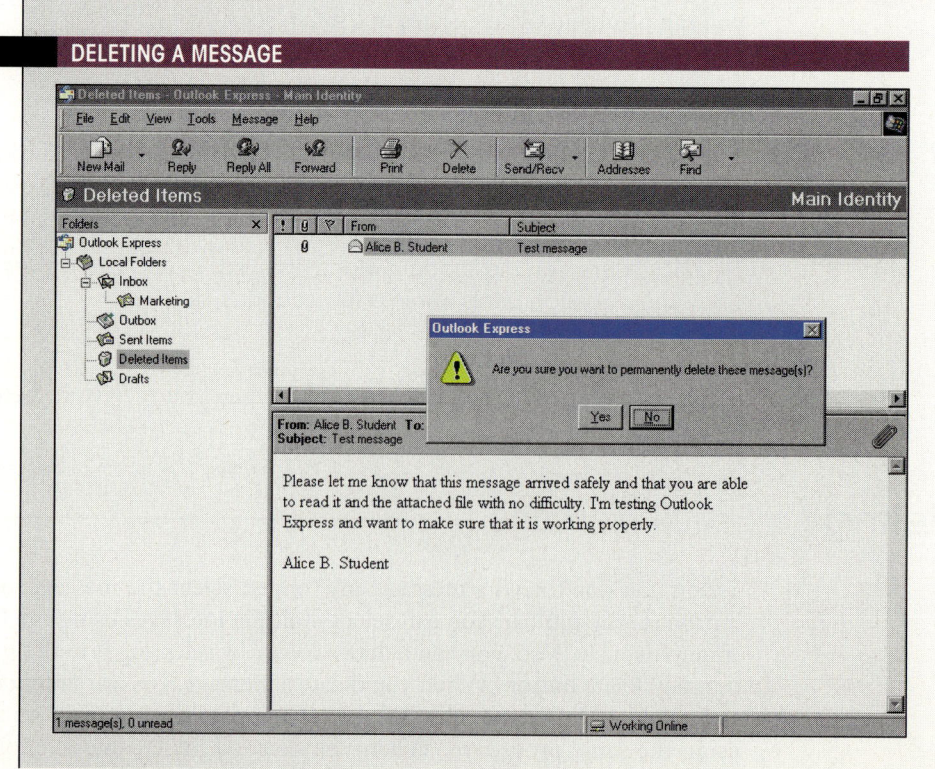

TUTORIAL 2 BASIC E-MAIL: INTEGRATED BROWSER E-MAIL SOFTWARE   WEB 2.47

> 5. Click the **Yes** button to confirm your deletion.

To delete a folder, you follow the same process.

To delete a user-created folder:

1. Right-click the **Marketing** folder in the Folder list.
2. Click **Delete** from the shortcut list of commands. A dialog box opens and asks you to confirm that it is okay to move the folder to the Deleted Items folder.
3. Click the **Yes** button.
4. Select the Marketing folder in the Deleted Items folder. (You may have to click the plus icon to open the Deleted Items folder to reveal the Marketing folder.)
5. Click the **Delete** button on the toolbar. A dialog box opens and warns you that the deletion will be permanent.
6. Click **Yes** to permanently delete the Marketing folder.
7. Click the **Inbox** folder to re-display your list of mail folders, message summary, and preview panels.

Maintaining an Address Book

As you send e-mail to different people, you will probably find it burdensome and sometimes errorprone to type their e-mail addresses, especially long and difficult ones. As you use e-mail to contact business associates and friends, you will want to save their addresses in an address book.

Adding an Address to the Address Book

You can access the address book by clicking the Addresses button on the toolbar. To create a new address, you open the address book, click the New button on the toolbar, click New Contact from the drop-down list, and then enter information into the Properties dialog box for that contact. You can enter first and last names and e-mail address information. If you enter a short name in the Nickname text box, then you can use that shortened name when you create a new message.

You are eager to add information to your address book. Begin by entering Barbara Goldberg's contact information into your Outlook Express address book.

REFERENCE WINDOW   RW

Entering a new e-mail address in the address book
- Click the Addresses button on the toolbar to open the Address Book window.
- Click the New button on the toolbar.
- Click New Contact from the drop-down list.
- Enter the person's name, e-mail address, and other information, as necessary.
- Click the OK button to add the entry to the address book.
- Repeat the steps to add more addresses, or click the Close button to close the Address Book window.

To create an address book entry:

1. Open the Address Book window by clicking the **Addresses** button on the toolbar.

2. Click the **New** button on the toolbar and click **New Contact** from the drop-down menu to open the Properties window.

3. Type **Barbara** in the First text box, and then press the **Tab** key twice to go to the Last text box.

4. Type **Goldberg** in the Last text box, and then press the **Tab** key three times to go to the Nickname text box.

5. Type **Barbara** in the Nickname text box, and then press the **Tab** key to go to the E-mail Addresses text box.

6. Type **barbgoldberg@yahoo.com** in the E-mail Addresses text box. See Figure 2-34.

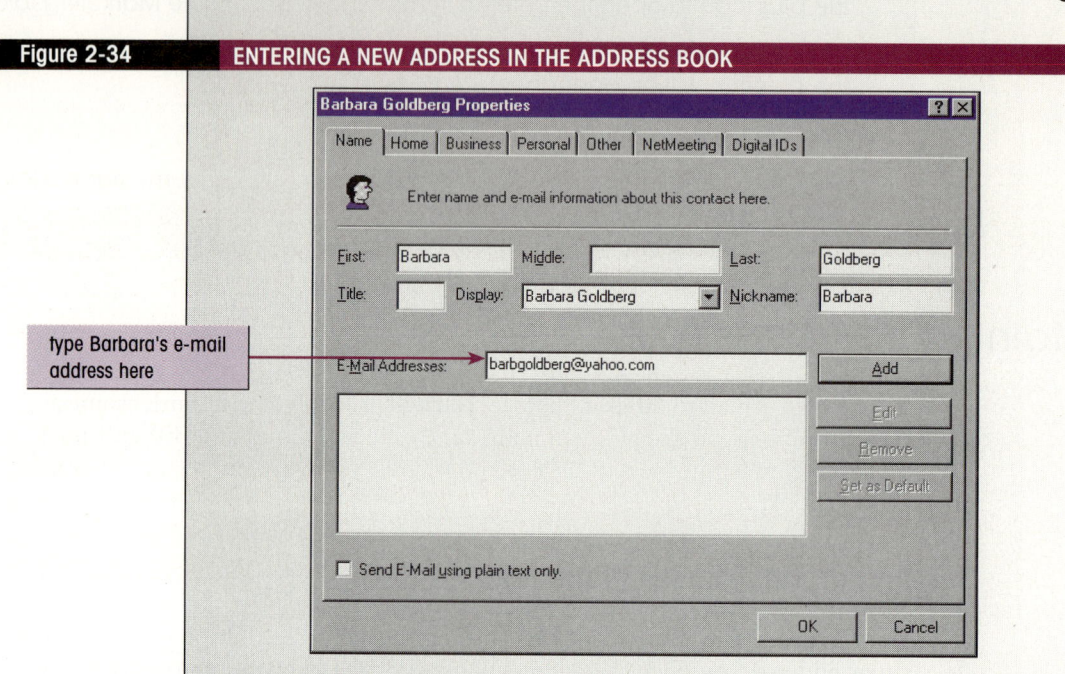

Figure 2-34   ENTERING A NEW ADDRESS IN THE ADDRESS BOOK

type Barbara's e-mail address here

7. Click the **Add** button and then click the **OK** button to close the Properties dialog box and return to the Address Book window.

8. Repeat Steps 2 through 7 to create address cards for the following members of the marketing department:

First Name	Last Name	E-mail Address	Nickname
Gary	**Kildare**	**gkildare@sidamo.com**	**Gary**
Faye	**Borthman**	**fborthman@sidamo.com**	**Faye**
Fran	**Brooks**	**fbrooks@sidamo.com**	**Fran**

9. When you are finished adding the addresses, click the **Close** button on the Address Book window title bar to close it.

With these entries in your address book, you can easily insert even the most complicated e-mail address in any of the message text boxes as you compose a message by typing the first few letters of the addressee's e-mail address. As you type one, two, or three of the first letters of the e-mail address, full addresses from the address book appear in the address text box. Edit a name by either double-clicking the name or clicking the name and clicking Properties. Another handy facility lets you easily add new names to your address book. Whenever you receive mail from someone who is not in your address book, double-click the message to display it in a window, and then right-click the "From" name. Finally, click the Add to Address Book command on the shortcut menu. The sender's e-mail address is added to your address book.

Creating a Multi-Address Entry

You can use Outlook Express to create a distribution list, or a **group**, which is an address entry consisting of more than one e-mail address in a single group. A distribution list is helpful when you want to send one message to several people simultaneously.

Barbara frequently sends messages to each member of the marketing department. She asks you to create a distribution list entry in her address book so she can type one nickname for the group of e-mail addresses, instead of having to type each address separately.

REFERENCE WINDOW

Creating a group address entry
- Click the Addresses button on the toolbar to open the Address Book window.
- Click the New button on the toolbar.
- Click New Group from the drop-down menu.
- Type the group's name in the Group Name text box.
- Click the Select Members button to add existing entries to the group.
- Add each group member's address to the group list, and then click the OK button.
- Click the OK button to finish creating the group.

To create a group address entry:

1. Click the **Addresses** button on the toolbar to open the address book.
2. Click the **New** button on the toolbar and then click New Group from the drop-down menu to open the New Group dialog box.
3. Type **mkt** in the Group Name text box to establish the group's name.
4. Click the **Select Members** button to add existing entries to the group. The Select Group Members dialog box opens so you can choose which names to add to the marketing group list.
5. Select Faye's name in the left panel, and then click the **Select** button to add it to the Members panel.
6. Repeat Step 5 to select Fran and Gary to add them to the group list. Remember to click the **Select** button after selecting each name. Figure 2-35 shows the completed group.

Figure 2-35   **CREATING AN ADDRESS GROUP**

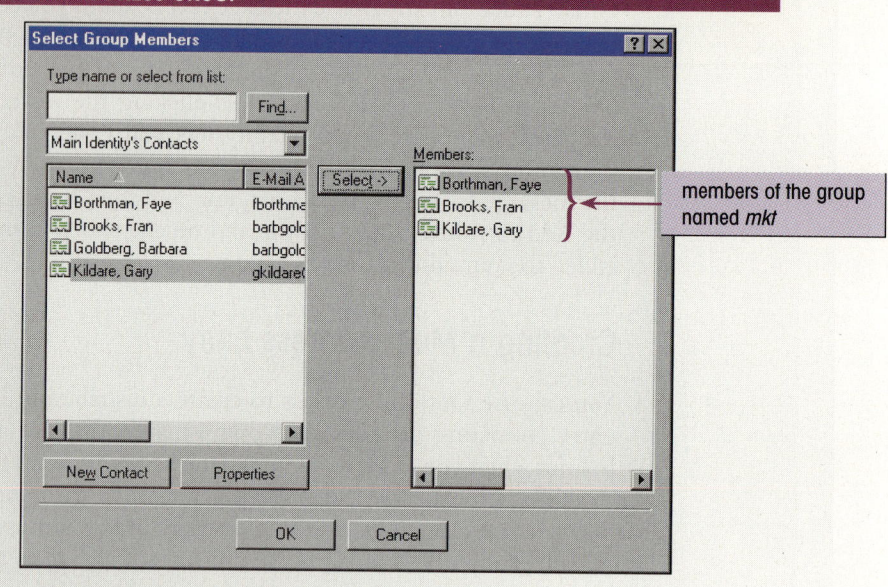

(Screenshot of Select Group Members dialog box showing Main Identity's Contacts with Borthman Faye, Brooks Fran, Goldberg Barbara, Kildare Gary on the left, and Members list on the right containing Borthman Faye, Brooks Fran, Kildare Gary — labeled "members of the group named mkt")

7. Click the **OK** button to close the Select Group Members dialog box.

8. Click the **OK** button to close the mkt Properties dialog box. Notice the new group, mkt, appears in the address book, sorted alphabetically by the Name column.

9. Close the Address Book by clicking the **Close** button.

10. Close Outlook Express, and close your dial-up connection, if necessary.

When you need to modify a group's members, you can delete one or more members from the group by opening the address book, double-clicking the group name, and then deleting a member's name by clicking the Remove button. Similarly, you can add members by clicking the Select Members button on the group's Properties dialog box. Now, whenever Barbara Goldberg wants to send mail to the marketing department members, she can select the group name *mkt* from the address book for any of a message's address text boxes (To, Cc, or Bcc for example). Clearly, group addresses are very convenient.

Session 2.3 QUICK CHECK

1. True or False: It is good etiquette to include a Subject line in your e-mail message so the recipient has a summary of a message's contents before reading it.

2. You use the _____ line to send copies of a message to other recipients without the principal addressee's knowledge.

3. When you want to send a complex document, such as a spreadsheet, it should be included in the message as a(n) _____.

4. What should you include in a message so that the receiver can contact you nonelectronically?

5. Discuss the advantages of using an electronic address book.

6. When you send the same group of people e-mail messages frequently, you can create a(n) _____ list by which you can refer to the group with a single nickname.

Now you are ready to complete the Review Assignments using the e-mail client of your choice.

REVIEW ASSIGNMENTS

You have explored two different e-mail clients, so you are ready to make a recommendation and send it to your instructor. Your status report will give an overview of either Netscape Messenger or Microsoft Outlook Express (or both programs, depending on your instructor's preferences), and then you will use your e-mail client to send the report, as a blind carbon copy, to three classmates. You will send a carbon copy of the report to yourself and then print it for your records. Finally, you will delete the message.

1. Start Messenger or Outlook Express and set up yourself as a user, if necessary.
2. Add your instructor's name and full e-mail address to the address book. Use an appropriate nickname that will be easy for you to remember.
3. Add a distribution list that consists of three classmates' e-mail addresses. Enter your classmates' full names and e-mail addresses, and assign each individual a unique nickname.
4. Create a new message.
5. Type "E-mail evaluation status report 1" on the Subject line.
6. Click the To line, and then type your instructor's nickname.
7. Click the Cc line, and then type your full e-mail address.
8. Click the Bcc line, and then type the nickname of your distribution list for your classmates so they also receive a copy of the report. (If the Bcc line is not visible, then select All Headers from the View menu.)
9. Select the message area, and then type three or more sentences describing your overall impressions about Messenger and/or Outlook Express.
10. Attach the file named Security.wri from the Tutorial.02 folder on your Data Disk to the message.
11. Leave a blank line after the end of your message, and then type your name, class name, class section, and e-mail address on four separate lines.
12. Check your spelling before you send the message and correct any mistakes.
13. Carefully proofread your message for errors, make sure that the correct recipients are indicated, and then correct any problems.
14. Send the message.
15. Wait about 15 to 30 seconds, and then manually check for new mail to see if your message arrived on the server. Retrieve your new mail, and open the new message.
16. Print the new message.
17. Permanently delete the new message from your program.
18. Exit the e-mail client.

CASE PROBLEMS

Case 1. Grand American Appraisal Company You work as an office manager for Grand American Appraisal Company, which is a national real-estate appraisal company with its corporate headquarters in Los Angeles. Grand American handles real-estate appraisal requests from all over the United States and maintains a huge inventory of approved real-estate appraisers located throughout the country. When an appraisal request is phoned into any regional office, an office staff member phones or faxes the national office to start the appraisal process. The appraisal order desk in Los Angeles receives the request and is responsible for locating a real-estate appraiser in the community in which the target property (i.e., the one to be appraised) is located. After the Los Angeles office identifies and contacts an appraiser by phone, the appraiser has two days to perform the appraisal and either phone or fax the regional office with a preliminary estimate of value for the property. The entire process of phoning the regional office and then phoning or faxing the national office is both cumbersome and expensive.

Your supervisor asks you to investigate alternatives to reduce the number of phone calls necessary to complete the appraisal cycle. You discover that Grand American requires all independent appraisers to have e-mail access and addresses. Nearly every Grand American employee has a PC connected on a LAN that ties into the larger computer on the Internet. Your job is to reduce the number of phone calls needed to set up an appraisal. You think e-mail is the solution, and you will be working with the existing e-mail system at Grand American to experiment with feasible alternatives.

Do the following:

1. Start Messenger or Outlook Express and ensure that the e-mail program has the correct settings for your mail server, your e-mail address, and your user name.

Explore

2. Use the Help system to learn how to create a signature file. (Netscape Messenger users: Create a text file in Notepad and save it. Then, click Edit, Preferences, select Identity in the Mail & Newsgroups category, and type the absolute path in the Signature File text box. Outlook Express Users: Click Tools, Options, click the Signatures tab, click the New button, and type the signature information in the Edit Signature text box.) Create a personal signature file that has three lines: your first and last name (line 1), your class and section (line 2), and your e-mail address (line 3).

3. Find a classmate and get his or her e-mail address. Your classmate will play the role of the Los Angeles order desk. Enter your classmate's nickname, full name, and e-mail address in the address book.

4. Enter your instructor's nickname, full name, and e-mail address in the address book.

5. Compose a message to your classmate. Type your classmate's nickname on the To line, type your e-mail address and your instructor's nickname on the Cc line, and then type "Request for appraisal" on the Subject line.

6. Type a short message that requests the assignment of an appraiser. Include your street address and the request date in the message.

Explore

7. Include your signature file in the message you are about to send.

8. Send the message immediately, without queuing it.

9. Wait a few seconds, and then retrieve the message that you sent to yourself.

10. Print a copy of your message, and then delete it permanently from the server and the PC.

11. Remove the signature file you created. Exit the e-mail client.

Case 2. Bridgefield Engineering Company Bridgefield Engineering Company (BECO) is a small engineering firm in Somerville, New Jersey, that manufactures and distributes heavy industrial machinery for factories worldwide. Because BECO has trouble reaching its customers around the world in different time zones, the company decided to implement an e-mail system to facilitate contact between BECO employees and their customers. BECO hired you to help employees set up and use their e-mail system to reach their customers. Your first task is to compile a list of typical industrial machines that BECO can manufacture and send it to several of BECO's marketing staff located throughout the country.

Do the following:

1. Start Messenger or Outlook Express and ensure that the e-mail program has the correct settings for your mail server, your e-mail address, and your user name.
2. Add your instructor and two classmates to the address book. Use an appropriate nickname for each person.
3. Start a new message. Use the To line to address the message to three people: yourself, your instructor, and to one of the classmates that you added to the address book in Step 2.
4. Send a blind carbon copy of the message to the second classmate that you added to the address book in Step 2.
5. In the message body, type "Bridgefield manufactures machines to your specifications. We can build borers, planers, horn presses, and a variety of other machines. E-mail us for further information."
6. Send the message to yourself.

Explore

7. Save the message in the Tutorial.02 folder on your Data Disk as BECO.txt.
8. Create a mail folder or mailbox named BECO on your client, in which you will store all mail for BECO.
9. Save the message you mailed to yourself in the BECO mail folder.
10. Create a distribution list address book entry using only the nicknames of the people that you added to the address book in Step 2. The nickname for the distribution list is classinfo.
11. Close and save the changes to your address book.
12. Delete the BECO folder and its contents from your PC.
13. Exit the e-mail client.

Case 3. Recycling Awareness Campaign You are an assistant in the mayor's office in Cleveland. The mayor has asked you to help with the recycling awareness campaign. Your job is to use e-mail to increase awareness of the recycling centers throughout the city and to encourage Cleveland's citizens and businesses to participate in the program. As it happens, you know that over 45 percent of the city's registered voters have subscribed to a particular television cable service. Of those, over 8 percent have e-mail addresses and cable modems. You decide to send an e-mail message to several key businesspeople with an invitation to help increase awareness of the program by forwarding the recycle message to their employees and colleagues. Your message includes an attached file that explains the program in detail and how to use it.

Do the following:

1. Start Messenger or Outlook Express, and ensure that the e-mail program has the correct settings for your mail server, your e-mail address, and your user name.

2. You will use the e-mail addresses of five classmates to act as the city's key businesspeople. Obtain and add the nicknames, full names, and e-mail addresses of five classmates as a distribution list named "council" in your address book. Then add the nickname, full name, and e-mail address of your instructor as a single-entry address.

3. Create a new message. Type the distribution list nickname on the To line, your e-mail address on the Cc line, and your instructor's nickname on the Bcc line. Add an appropriate subject on the Subject line.

Explore

4. Create a signature file. Your signature should include your name on line 1, your new title of "Assistant to the mayor" on line 2, and your real e-mail address on line 3.

5. Write a two- or three-line message urging the council members to encourage recycling in their districts by forwarding the attached file to their local business contacts. Thank them for reading your e-mail.

6. Attach the file named Recycle.wri that is saved in the Tutorial.02 folder on your Data Disk to the message.

7. Make sure that your signature file is added automatically to the outgoing message, proofread and spellcheck your message, and then send your message.

8. After a few moments, retrieve your e-mail message from the server and print it.

9. Forward the message to any one of the classmates in your address book. Add a message to the forwarded message that asks the recipient to forward the message to appropriate business leaders per your program objectives.

10. Save a copy of your message in a new folder named "Recycling," and then delete the original message.

11. Delete the Recycling folder and your message.

12. Remove the signature file you created. Exit the e-mail client.

Case 4. Student Birds-of-a-Feather Group In two weeks, you have a midterm exam and you want to organize a study group with your classmates. Everyone in your class has an e-mail account on the university's computer. You want to contact some classmates to find out when they might be available to get together in the next week to study for the exam. To reach these students to create a study group, you decide to use e-mail.

Do the following:

1. Start Messenger or Outlook Express and ensure that the e-mail program has the correct settings for your mail server, your e-mail address, and your user name.

2. Type the e-mail addresses of at least four group members—people in your class or friends' e-mail addresses who won't mind getting an e-mail message from you—on the To line of the new message.

3. Type your e-mail address on the Bcc line and your instructor's e-mail address on the Cc line.

4. In the message body, tell your classmates about your study group. Ask your recipients to respond to you through e-mail by a specified date so you can see who is interested.

5. Sign the message at the bottom with your full name, your course name and section number, and your e-mail address.

6. Send the message.

7. Create a new mailbox or folder named "Studygroup."

8. Check your mail for a copy of your message. When the message arrives, file a copy of the message in the Studygroup folder, and then delete the original message.

9. Print a copy of the message.

10. Delete the Studygroup folder and your message.

11. Exit the e-mail client.

Case 5. Jacopini's Student Survey During breaks from school, you work for a local company that surveys student opinions about various topics of interest to college students. The director of research, Lisa Giancone, has asked you to e-mail a short survey to three students at your university. She wants to know the name of three of their favorite music CDs, where they prefer to shop, and how much time they spend listening to music per week. Lisa asks you to create a survey using any word processing program—Word 2000, WordPad, or WordPerfect, for example—and attach the survey to the brief e-mail message. She would like to have the survey results compiled within three weeks, so you are to ask the respondents to e-mail back their answers within 15 days.

Do the following:

1. Using a word processor, create a survey that asks: 1) Name your three favorite music CDs, 2) List the names of two of your favorite stores to shop for music (online stores or not), and 3) How much time do you spend per week listening to music: 1 hour, 5 hours, or more than 5 hours. Print out the word processed document and be prepared to turn it in to your instructor.

2. Save the word processed document to your Data Disk in the Tutorial.02 folder. Call it Survey (let the word processing program assign its default extension to the file). Close your word processing program.

3. Start Messenger or Outlook Express and ensure that the e-mail program has the correct settings for your mail server, your e-mail address, and your user name.

4. Start a new e-mail message. In the To line, list the e-mail addresses of three other students in your class to whom you can mail the survey.

5. Place your e-mail address in the Cc line.

6. Also send a Cc copy of the message to barbgoldberg@yahoo.com.

7. In the Subject line enter "Music survey."

8. In the message body, write a short message indicating that the survey is part of your class assignment and that you would appreciate a quick response. Tell the student respondents that they are to detach and read the survey. Indicate that they can respond to the three questions by sending an e-mail response with the answers numbered 1 through 3 without using an attached document. They can simply indicate their answers in the e-mail response itself, in other words.

9. Type your name to sign your e-mail message.

10. Attach the word processed survey to the e-mail message.

11. Send the message.

12. When you receive the message back, print it and be prepared to turn it in to your instructor.

13. Exit the e-mail client program.

LAB ASSIGNMENTS

E-Mail E-mail that originates on a local area network with a mail gateway can travel all over the world. That's why it is so important to learn how to use it. In this Lab, you will use an e-mail simulator, so even if your school's computers don't provide you with e-mail service, you will learn the basics of reading, sending, and replying to electronic mail. See the Read This Before You Begin page for information on installing and starting this Lab.

1. Click the Steps button to learn how to work with e-mail. As you proceed through the Steps, answer all of the Quick Check questions that appear. After you complete the Steps, you will see a Quick Check summary report. Follow the instructions on the screen to print this report.

2. Click the Explore button. Write a message to re@films.org. The subject of the message is "Picks and Pans." In the body of your message, describe a movie you have recently seen. Include the name of the movie, briefly summarize the plot, and give it a thumbs up or a thumbs down. Print the message before you send it.

3. Look in your In Basket for a message from jb@music.org. Read the message, then compose a reply indicating that you will attend. Carbon copy mciccone@music.org. Print your reply, including the text of JB's original message before you send it.

4. Look in your In Basket for a message from leo@sports.org. Reply to the message by adding your rating to the text of the original message as follows:
Equipment:	Your rating:
Rollerblades	2
Skis	3
Bicycle	1
Scuba gear	4
Snowmobile	5

   Print your reply before you send it.

5. Go into the lab with a partner. You should each log into the E-mail Lab on different computers. Look at the Addresses list to find the user ID for your partner. You should each send a short e-mail message to your partner. Then, you should check your mail message from your partner. Read the message and compose a reply. Print your reply before you send it. *Note:* Unlike a full-featured mail system, the e-mail simulator does not save mail in mailboxes after you log off.

Quick Check Answers

Session 2.1

1. True
2. protocols
3. header, body
4. A recipient can quickly prioritize messages by reading the Subject line and decide when or if to read the message.
5. True
6. Yes; you can send it as an attachment to an e-mail message.
7. IP or Internet Protocol
8. so the receiver has a context for your responses
9. It is easier and faster to type a short distribution list name than several individual e-mail addresses.

Session 2.2

1. client
2. Mail messages are (optionally) deleted from the mail server and downloaded to the PC where you are located, so unless you save the messages on a disk, you won't be able to retrieve them from the server.
3. No. Most mail clients simply put the deleted messages in a special "trash" folder where they remain on the computer until the user empties the trash.
4. folders or mailboxes
5. Yes, it is important so your recipient has a context for your message.
6. nickname
7. distribution or mailing

Session 2.3

1. True
2. Bcc or blind carbon copy
3. attachment
4. a signature file with a phone number or an address
5. It makes entering e-mail addresses faster and more error-free. It also serves as a repository for address and phone information, which is another form of electronic organizer.
6. distribution or mailing

TUTORIAL 3

OBJECTIVES

In this tutorial you will:

- Learn about Web browser software and Web pages
- Learn about Web addresses and URLs
- Save and organize Web addresses
- Navigate the Web
- Use the Web to find information
- Configure and use the Netscape Navigator Web browser
- Configure and use the Microsoft Internet Explorer Web browser

LABS

The Internet: World Wide Web

BROWSER BASICS

Introduction to Netscape Navigator and Microsoft Internet Explorer

CASE

Sunset Wind Quintet

The Sunset Wind Quintet is a group of five musicians who have played together for eight years. At first, the group began by playing free concerts for local charitable organizations. As more people heard the quintet and its reputation grew, the musicians were soon in demand at art gallery openings and other functions.

Each member of the quintet is an accomplished musician. The instruments in a wind quintet include flute, oboe, clarinet, bassoon, and French horn, which are all orchestral instruments. Each quintet member has experience as a player in a symphony orchestra as well. Three quintet members—the flutist, bassoonist, and the French horn player—currently hold positions with the local orchestra. The other two quintet members—the clarinetist and the oboist—teach classes in their respective instruments at the local university.

This past summer, a booking agent asked the quintet to do a short regional tour. Although the tour was successful, the quintet members realized that none of them had any business-management skills. Marianna Rabinovich, the clarinetist, handles most of the business details for the group. The quintet members realized that business matters related to the tour were overwhelming Marianna and that they wanted to do more touring, so they hired you as their business manager.

One of your tasks will be to help market the Sunset Wind Quintet. To do this, you must learn more about how other wind quintets operate and sell their services. At one of your early meetings with the group, you found that each member of the quintet had different priorities. In addition to marketing the quintet's performances, some members felt it would be a good idea to record and sell CDs, whereas others were concerned about finding instrument-repair facilities on the road when tours extended beyond the local area.

As you discussed these issues with the quintet members, you started thinking of ways to address their concerns. Your first idea was to find trade magazines and newspapers that might describe what other small classical musical ensembles were doing. As you considered the time and cost of this alternative, you realized that the Internet and World Wide Web might offer a better way to get started.

SESSION 3.1

In this session, you will learn how Web pages and Web sites make up the World Wide Web. You will find out about things to consider when you select and use a specific software tool to find information on the Web. Finally, you will learn about some basic browser concepts.

Web Browsers

As you start to consider how you might use the Web to gather information for the Sunset Wind Quintet, you remember that one of your college friends, Maggie Beeler, earned her degree in library science. You met with Maggie at the local public library, where she is working at the reference desk. She is glad to assist you.

Maggie begins by explaining that the Web is a collection of files that reside on computers, called **Web servers**, that are located all over the world and are connected to each other through the Internet. Most computer files connected to the Internet are private; that is, only the computer's users can access them. The owners of the files that make up the Web have made their files publicly available so you can obtain access to them if you have a computer connected to the Internet.

Client/Server Structure of the World Wide Web

When you use your Internet connection to become part of the Web, your computer becomes a **Web client** in a worldwide client/server network. A **Web browser** is the software that you run on your computer to make it work as a Web client. The Internet connects many different types of computers running different operating system software. Web browser software lets your computer communicate with all of these different types of computers easily and effectively.

Computers that are connected to the Internet and contain files that their owners have made available publicly through their Internet connections are called **Web servers**. Figure 3-1 shows how this client/server structure uses the Internet to provide multiple interconnections among the various kinds of client and server computers.

Figure 3-1 CLIENT/SERVER STRUCTURE OF THE WORLD WIDE WEB

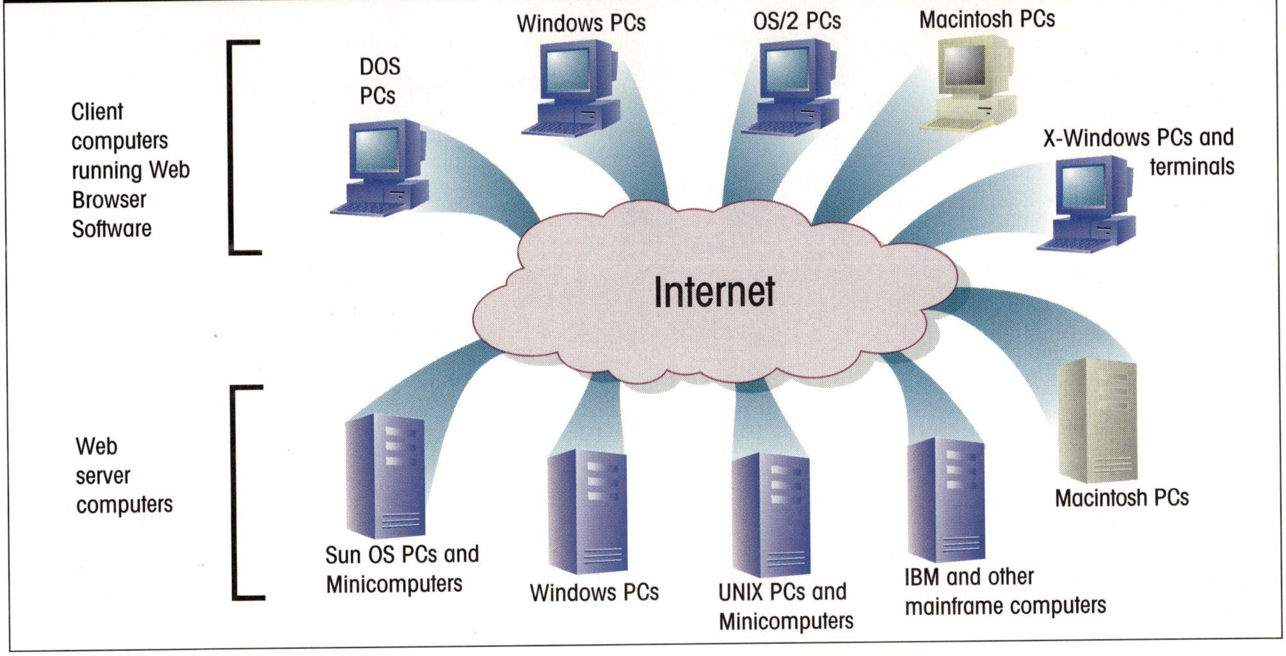

Hypertext, Links, and Hypermedia

The public files on Web servers are ordinary text files, much like the files used by word-processing software. To allow Web browser software to read them, however, the text must be formatted according to a generally accepted standard. The standard used on the Web is **Hypertext Markup Language** (**HTML**). HTML uses codes, or **tags**, to tell the Web browser software how to display the text contained in the document. For example, a Web browser reading the following line of text:

<B>A Review of the Book <I>Wind Instruments of the 18th Century</I></B>

recognizes the <B> and </B> tags as instructions to display the entire line of text in bold and the <I> and </I> tags as instructions to display the text enclosed by those tags in italics. Different Web clients that connect to this Web server might display the tagged text differently. For example, one Web browser might display text enclosed by bold tags in a blue color instead of displaying the text as bold.

HTML provides a variety of text formatting tags that you can use to indicate headings, paragraphs, bulleted lists, numbered lists, and other useful text formats in an HTML document. The real power of HTML, however, lies in its anchor tag. The **HTML anchor tag** enables you to link multiple HTML documents to each other. When you use the anchor tag to link HTML documents, you create a **hypertext link**. Hypertext links also are called **hyperlinks**, or **links**. Figure 3-2 shows how these hyperlinks can join multiple HTML documents to create a web of HTML text across computers on the Internet.

Figure 3-2   USING HYPERLINKS TO CREATE A WEB OF HTML TEXT ACROSS MULTIPLE FILE LOCATIONS

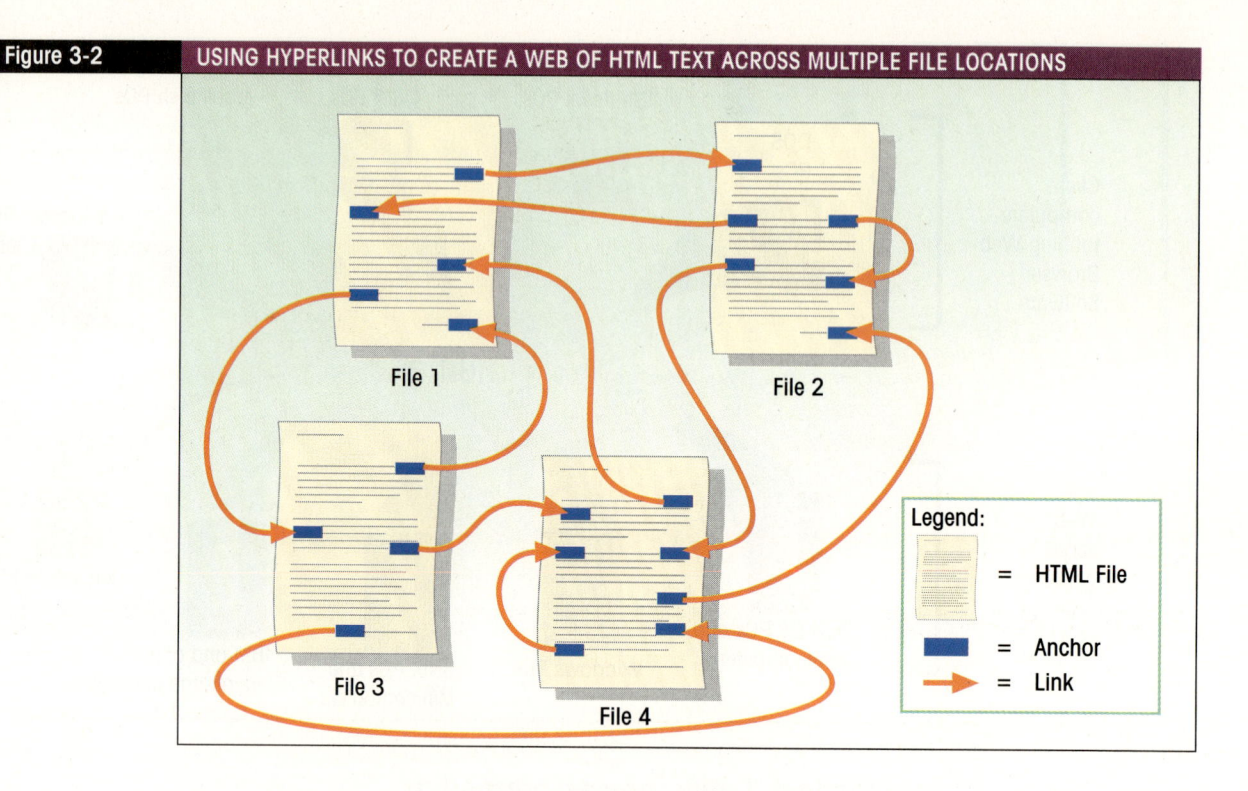

Most Web browsers display hyperlinks in a color different from other text and underline them so they are easily distinguished in the HTML document. When a Web browser displays an HTML document, people usually call the file a Web page. Maggie shows you the Web page that appears in Figure 3-3 and suggests that it might be interesting to the Sunset Wind Quintet. The hyperlinks on this Web page are easy to identify because the Web browser software that displayed this page shows the hyperlinks as red, underlined text.

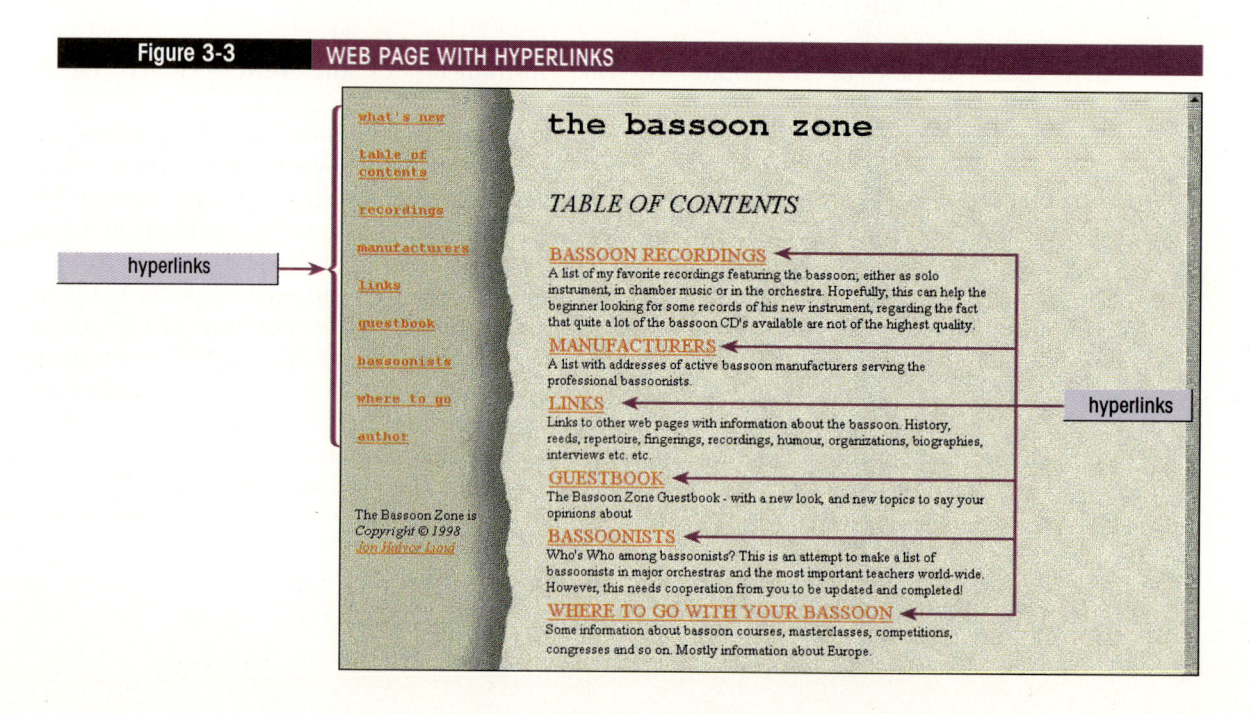

Figure 3-3   WEB PAGE WITH HYPERLINKS

Each of the hyperlinks on the Web page shown in Figure 3-3 allows the user to connect to another Web page. In turn, each of those Web pages contains hyperlinks to other pages, including one hyperlink that leads back to the Web page shown in Figure 3-3. Hyperlinks usually connect to other Web pages; however, they can lead to other media, including graphic image files, sound clips, and video files. Hyperlinks that connect to these types of files often are called **hypermedia links**. You are especially interested in learning more about these hypermedia links, but Maggie suggests you first need to understand a little more about how people organize the Web pages on their servers.

Maggie tells you that the easiest way to move from one Web page to another is to use the hyperlinks that the authors of Web pages have embedded in their HTML documents. Web page authors often use a graphic image as a hyperlink. Sometimes, it is difficult to identify which objects and text are hyperlinks just by looking at a Web page displayed on your computer. Fortunately, when you move the mouse pointer over a hyperlink in a Web browser, the pointer changes to ☝. For example, when you move the pointer over the Reservations hyperlink shown in Figure 3-4, it changes shape to indicate that if you click the Reservations text, the Web browser will open the Web page to which the hyperlink points.

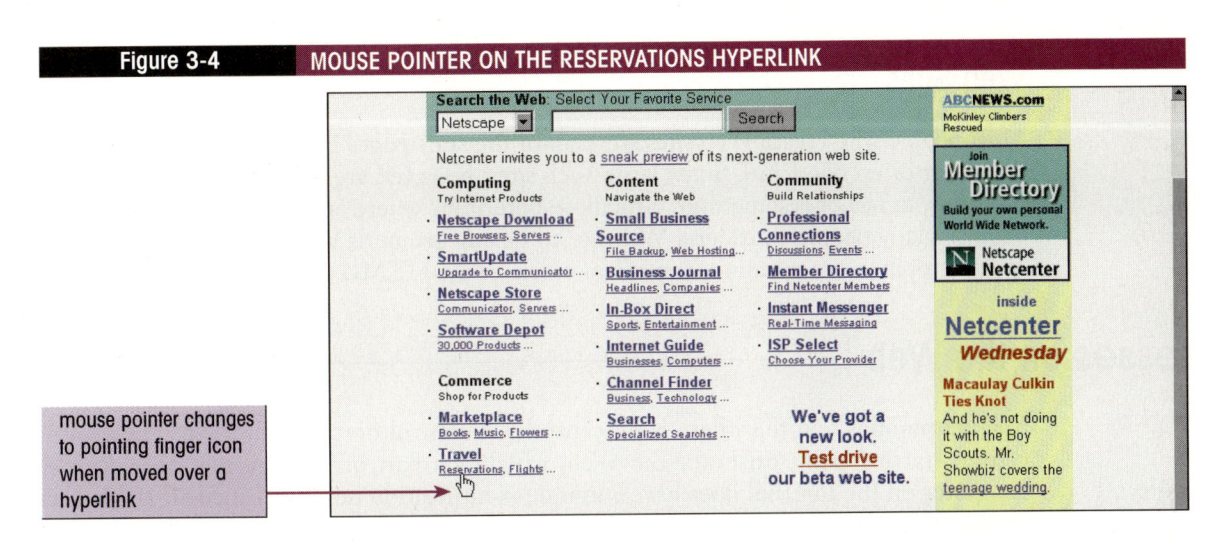

Figure 3-4   MOUSE POINTER ON THE RESERVATIONS HYPERLINK

mouse pointer changes to pointing finger icon when moved over a hyperlink

You might encounter an error message when you click on a hyperlink. Two common messages that appear in dialog boxes are the "server busy" and the "DNS entry not found" messages. Either of these messages means that your browser was unable to communicate successfully with the Web server that stores the page you requested. The cause for this inability might be temporary—in which case, you will be able to use the hyperlink later—or the cause might be permanent. The browser has no way of determining the cause of the connection failure, so it provides the same error messages in both cases. Another error message that you might receive displays as a Web page and includes the text "File not Found." This error message usually means that the Web page's location has changed permanently or that the Web page no longer exists.

Web Pages and Web Sites

Maggie explains that people who create Web pages usually have a collection of pages on one computer that they use as their Web server. A collection of linked Web pages that has a common theme or focus is called a **Web site**. The main page that all of the pages on a particular Web site are organized around and link back to is called the site's **home page**.

Home Pages

Maggie warns you that the term *home page* is used at least three different ways on the Web and that it is sometimes difficult to tell which meaning people intend when they use the term. The first definition of home page indicates the main page for a particular site: This home page is the first page that opens when you visit a particular Web site. The Bassoon Zone Table of Contents page shown in Figure 3-3 is a good example of this use. All of the hyperlinks on that page lead to pages in the Bassoon Zone site. Each page in the site links back to the Table of Contents page. The second definition of home page is the first page that opens when you start your Web browser. This type of home page might be an HTML document on your own computer. Some people create such home pages and include hyperlinks to Web sites that they frequently visit. If you are using a computer on your school's or employer's network, its Web browser might be configured to open the main page for the school or firm. The third definition of home page is the Web page that a particular Web browser loads the first time you use it. This page usually is stored at the Web site of the firm or other organization that created the Web browser software. Home pages that fall within the second or third definitions are sometimes called **start pages**.

Web Sites

Most people who create Web sites store all of the site's pages in one location, either on one computer or on one LAN. Some large Web sites, however, are distributed over a number of locations. In fact, it is sometimes difficult to determine where one Web site ends and another begins. Many people consider a Web site to be any group of Web pages that relates to one specific topic or organization, regardless of where the HTML documents are located.

Addresses on the Web

Maggie reminds you that there is no centralized control over the Internet. Therefore, no central starting point exists for the Web, which is a part of the Internet. However, each computer on the Internet does have a unique identification number, called an **IP (Internet Protocol) address**.

IP Addressing

The IP addressing system currently in use on the Internet uses a four-part number. Each part of the address is a number ranging from 0 to 255, and each part is separated from the previous part by a period, such as 106.29.242.17. You might hear a person pronounce this address as "one hundred six dot twenty-nine dot two four two dot seventeen." The combination of these four parts provides 4.2 billion possible addresses ($256 \times 256 \times 256 \times 256$). This number seemed adequate until 1998, when the accelerating growth of the Internet pushed the number of host computers from 5 to 30 million. Members of various Internet task forces are working to develop an alternative addressing system that will accommodate the projected growth; however, all of their working solutions require extensive hardware and software changes throughout the Internet.

Domain Name Addressing

Although each computer connected to the Internet has a unique IP address, most Web browsers do not use the IP address to locate Web sites and individual pages. Instead, they use domain name addressing. A **domain name** is a unique name associated with a specific IP address by a program that runs on an Internet host computer. This program, which coordinates the IP addresses and domain names for all computers attached to it, is called **DNS (domain name system) software**, and the host computer that runs this software is called a **domain name server**. Domain names can include any number of parts separated by periods; however, most domain names currently in use have only three or four parts. Domain names follow a hierarchical model that you can follow from top to bottom, if you read the name from right to left. For example, the domain name gsb.uchicago.edu is the computer connected to the Internet at the Graduate School of Business (gsb), which is an academic unit of the University of Chicago (uchicago), which is an educational institution (edu). No other computer on the Internet has the same domain name.

The last part of a domain name is called its **top-level domain**. For example, DNS software on the Internet host computer that is responsible for the "edu" domain keeps track of the IP address for all of the educational institutions in its domain, including "uchicago." Similar DNS software on the "uchicago" Internet host computer would keep track of the academic units' computers in its domain, including the "gsb" computer. Figure 3-5 shows the seven currently used top-level domain names.

Figure 3-5 TOP-LEVEL INTERNET DOMAIN NAMES

DOMAIN NAME	DESCRIPTION
com	Businesses and other commercial enterprises
edu	Postsecondary educational institutions
gov	U.S. government agency, bureau, or department
int	International organizations
mil	U.S. military unit or agency
net	Network service provider or resource
org	Other organizations, usually charitable or not-for-profit

In addition to these top-level domain names, Internet host computers outside the United States often use two-letter country domain names. For example, the domain name uq.edu.au is the domain name for the University of Queensland (uq), which is an educational institution (edu) in Australia (au). Recently, state and local government organizations in the United States have started using an additional domain name, "us." The "us" domain is also being used by U.S. primary and secondary schools as they begin to create Web presences because the "edu" domain is reserved for postsecondary educational institutions. Figure 3-6 shows 10 of the most frequently accessed country domain names.

Figure 3-6 FREQUENTLY ACCESSED INTERNET COUNTRY DOMAIN NAMES

DOMAIN NAME	COUNTRY
au	Australia
ca	Canada
de	Germany
fi	Finland
fr	France
jp	Japan
nl	Netherlands
no	Norway
se	Sweden
uk	United Kingdom

The large increase in the number of host computers on the Internet has taxed the capacity of the existing top-level domain name structure, especially that of the "com" domain. A proposal to expand the available top-level domain names is currently under consideration by the Internet Policy Oversight Committee. The seven additional top-level domain names are shown in Figure 3-7.

Figure 3-7 PROPOSED ADDITIONAL TOP-LEVEL INTERNET DOMAIN NAMES

DOMAIN NAME	DESCRIPTION
firm	Business firms
shop	Businesses that offer goods for sale
web	Entities that engage in World Wide Web-related activities
arts	Entities that engage in cultural and entertainment activities
rec	Entities that engage in recreational and entertainment activities
info	Entities that provide information services
nom	Individuals

Uniform Resource Locators

The IP address and the domain name each identify a particular computer on the Internet, but they do not indicate where a Web page's HTML document resides on that computer. To identify a Web page's exact location, Web browsers rely on Uniform Resource Locators. A **Uniform Resource Locator (URL)** is a four-part addressing scheme that tells the Web browser:

- What transfer protocol to use when transporting the file
- The domain name of the computer on which the file resides
- The pathname of the folder or directory on the computer on which the file resides
- The name of the file

The **transfer protocol** is the set of rules that the computers use to move files from one computer to another on an internet. The most common transfer protocol used on the Internet is the hypertext transfer protocol (HTTP). You can indicate the use of this protocol by typing http:// as the first part of the URL. People do use other protocols to transfer files on the Internet, but most of these protocols were used more frequently before the Web became part of the Internet. Two protocols that you still might see on the Internet are the file transfer protocol (FTP), which is indicated in a URL as ftp://, and the Telnet protocol, which is indicated in a URL as telnet://. FTP is just another way to transfer files, and Telnet is a set of rules for establishing a remote terminal connection to another computer.

The domain name is the Internet address of the computer described in the preceding section. The pathname describes the hierarchical directory or folder structure on the computer that stores the file. Most people are familiar with the structure used on Windows and DOS PCs, which uses the backslash character (\) to separate the structure levels. URLs follow the conventions established in the UNIX operating system that use the forward slash character (/) to separate the structure levels. The forward slash character works properly in a URL, even when it is pointing to a file on a Windows or DOS computer.

The filename is the name that the computer uses to identify the Web page's HTML document. On most computers, the filename extension of an HTML document is either .html or .htm. Although many PC operating systems are not case-sensitive, computers that use the UNIX operating system *are* case-sensitive. Therefore, if you are entering a URL that includes mixed-case and you do not know the type of computer on which the file resides, it is safer to retain the mixed-case format of the URL.

Not all URLs include a filename. If a URL does not include a filename, most Web browsers will load the file named index.html. The **index.html** filename is the default name for a Web site's home page. Figure 3-8 shows an example of a URL annotated to show its four parts.

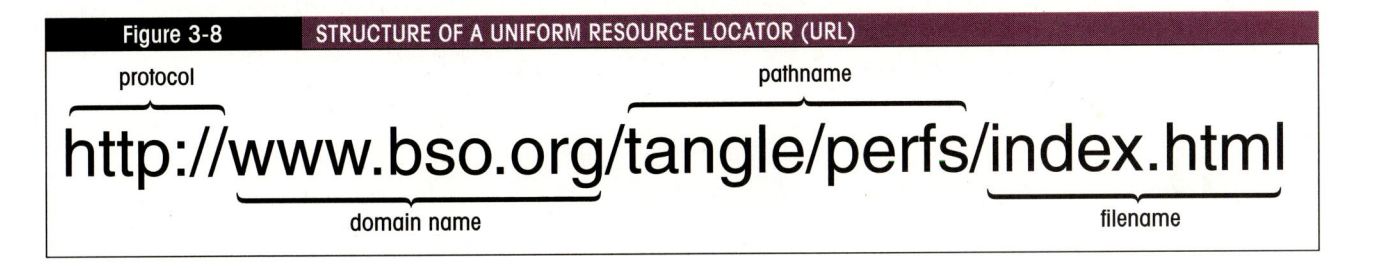

| Figure 3-8 | STRUCTURE OF A UNIFORM RESOURCE LOCATOR (URL) |

protocol — http://
domain name — www.bso.org
pathname — /tangle/perfs/
filename — index.html

The URL shown in Figure 3-8 uses the HTTP protocol and points to a computer that is connected to the Web (www) at the Boston Symphony Orchestra (bso), which is a not-for-profit organization (org). The Boston Symphony's Web page contains many different kinds of information about the orchestra. The path shown in Figure 3-8 includes two levels. The first level indicates that the information is about the orchestra's summer home at Tanglewood (tangle), and the second level indicates that the page will contain information about the orchestra's performances (perfs) at Tanglewood. The filename (index.html) indicates that this page is the home page in the Tanglewood performances folder or directory.

You tell Maggie how much you appreciate all of the help she has given you by explaining how you can use Internet addresses to find information on the Web. Now you understand that the real secret to finding good information on the Web is to know the right URLs. Maggie tells you that you can find URLs in many places; for example, newspapers and magazines often publish URLs of Web sites that might interest their readers. Friends who know about the subject area in which you are interested also are good sources. The best source, however, is the Web itself.

Main Elements of Web Browsers

Now that you know a little more about Web sites, you start to wonder how you can make your computer communicate with the Internet. Maggie tells you that there are many Web browsers that turn your computer into a Web client that communicates through an Internet service provider (ISP) or a network connection with the Web servers. Two popular browsers are **Netscape Navigator**, or simply **Navigator**, and **Microsoft Internet Explorer**, or simply **Internet Explorer**. Each browser has been released in different versions; however, the steps in this book should work for most browsers.

Maggie reminds you that most Windows programs use a standard graphical user interface (GUI) design that includes a number of common screen elements. Figures 3-9 and 3-10 show the main elements of the Navigator and Internet Explorer program windows. These two Web browsers share common Windows elements: a title bar at the top of the window, a scroll bar on the right side of the window, and a status bar at the bottom of the window.

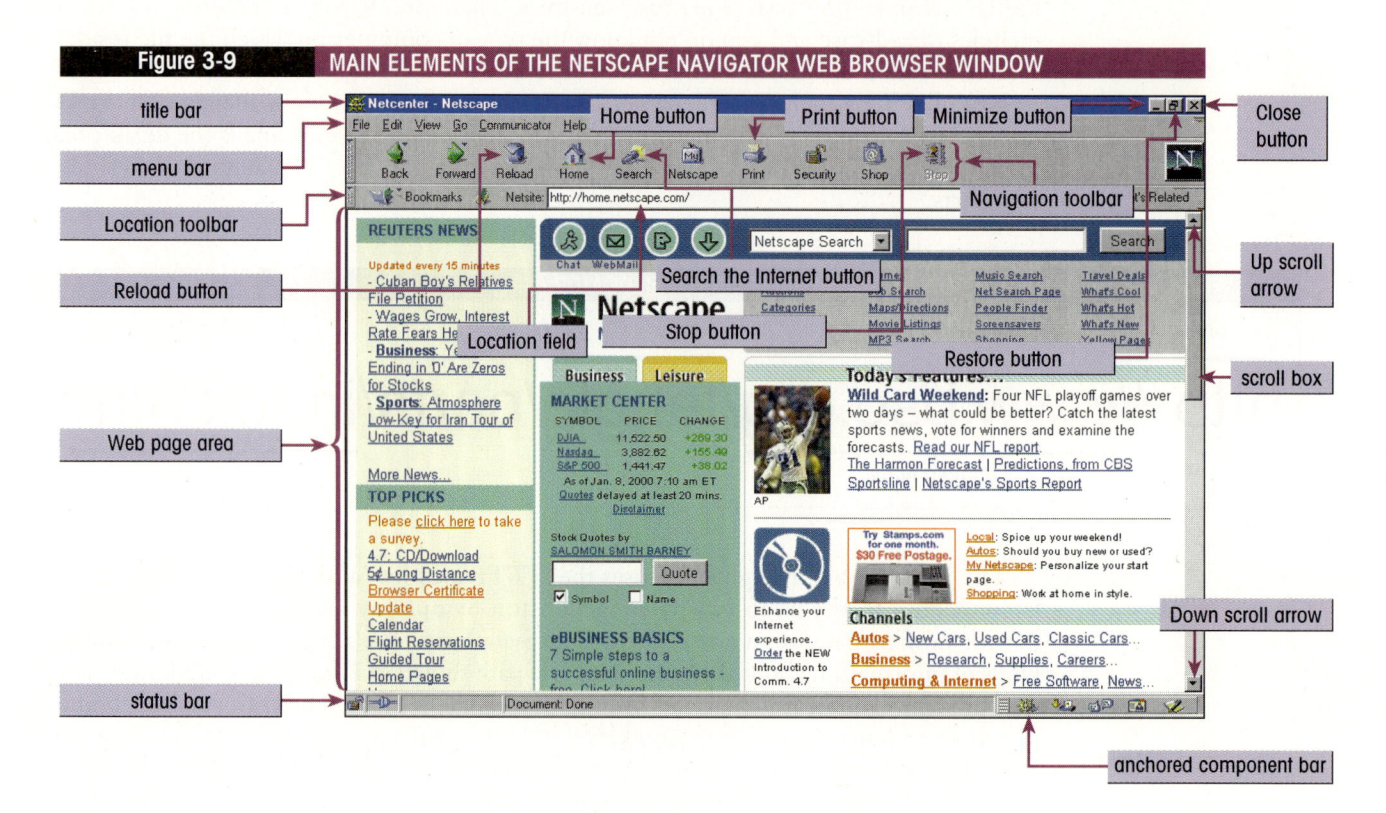

Figure 3-9 MAIN ELEMENTS OF THE NETSCAPE NAVIGATOR WEB BROWSER WINDOW

Figure 3-10 MAIN ELEMENTS OF THE MICROSOFT INTERNET EXPLORER WEB BROWSER WINDOW

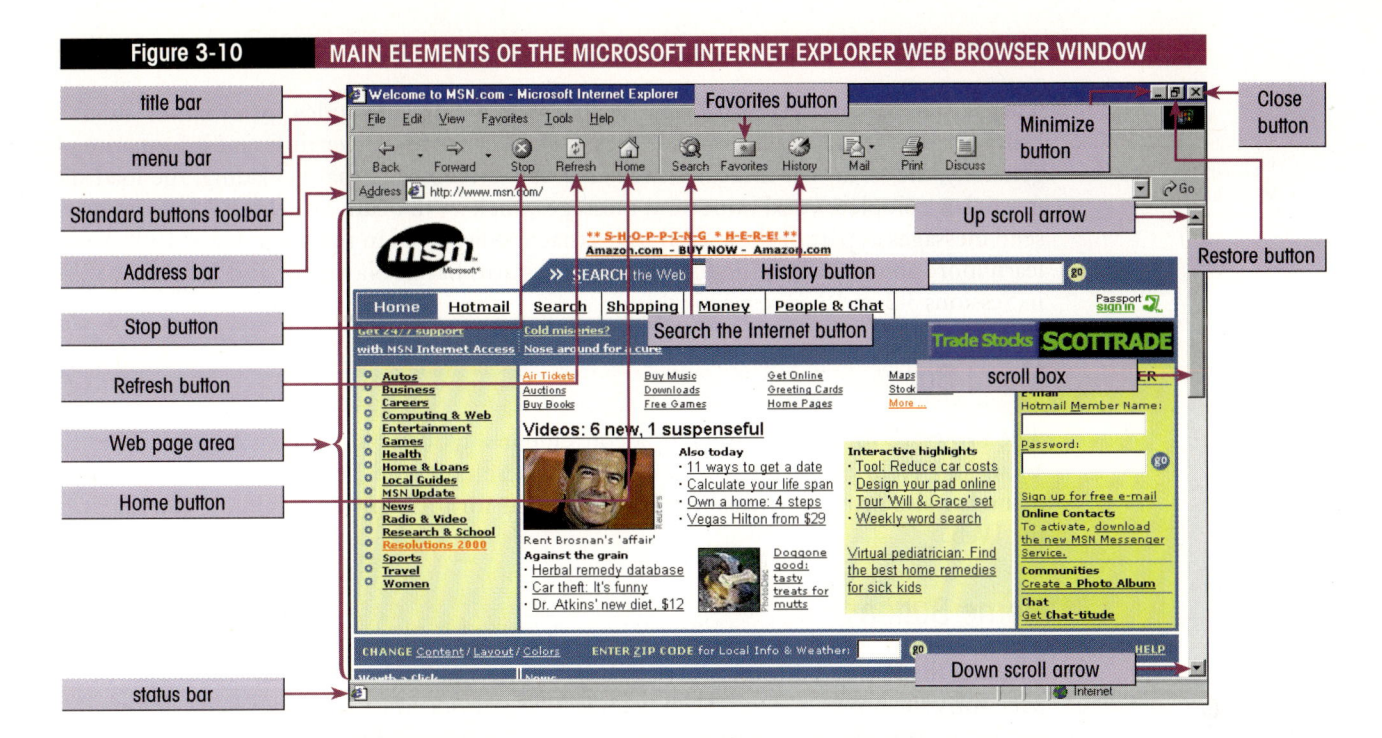

The menu bar appears below the title bar. Many of the toolbar button functions in Navigator and Internet Explorer are similar, too. Next, Maggie describes each of these elements.

Title Bar

A Web browser's **title bar** shows the name of the open Web page and the Web browser's program name. As in all Windows programs, you can double-click the title bar to resize the window quickly. The title bar contains the Minimize, Restore, and Close buttons when the window is maximized to fill the screen. To restore a resized window to its original size, click the Maximize button.

Scroll Bars

A Web page can be much longer than a regular-sized document, so you often need to use the **scroll bar** at the right side of the program window to move the page up or down through the document window. You can use the mouse to click the **Up scroll** arrow or the **Down scroll** arrow to move the Web page up or down through the window's **Web page area**. Although most Web pages are designed to resize automatically when loaded into different browser windows with different display areas, some Web pages might be wider than your browser window. When this happens, the browser places another scroll bar at the bottom of the window and above the status bar, so you can move the page horizontally through the browser. You can also click and drag the scroll box in the scroll bar to move the Web page through the window.

Status Bar

The **status bar** at the bottom of the browser window includes information about the browser's operations. Each browser uses the status bar to deliver different information, but generally, the status bar indicates the name of the Web page that is loading, the load status (partial or complete), and important messages, such as "Document: Done." Some Web sites send messages as part of their Web pages that are displayed in the status bar as well. You will learn more about the specific functions of the status bar in Navigator and Internet Explorer in Sessions 3.2 and 3.3, respectively.

Menu Bar

The browser's **menu bar** provides a convenient way for you to execute typical File, Edit, View, and Help commands. In addition to these common Windows command sets, the menu bar also provides specialized command sets for the browser that allow you to navigate the Web.

Home Button

Clicking the **Home** button in Navigator or in Internet Explorer displays the home (or start) page for your browser. Most Web browsers let you specify a page that loads automatically every time you start the program. You might not be able to do this if you are in your school's computer lab because schools often set the start page for all browsers on campus and then lock that setting. If you are using your own computer, you can choose your own start page. Some people like to use a Web page that someone else has created and made available for others to use. One example of a start page is the My Virtual Reference Desk Web page, shown in Figure 3-11.

TUTORIAL 3 BROWSER BASICS   WEB 3.13   INTERNET

Figure 3-11   MY VIRTUAL REFERENCE DESK WEB PAGE

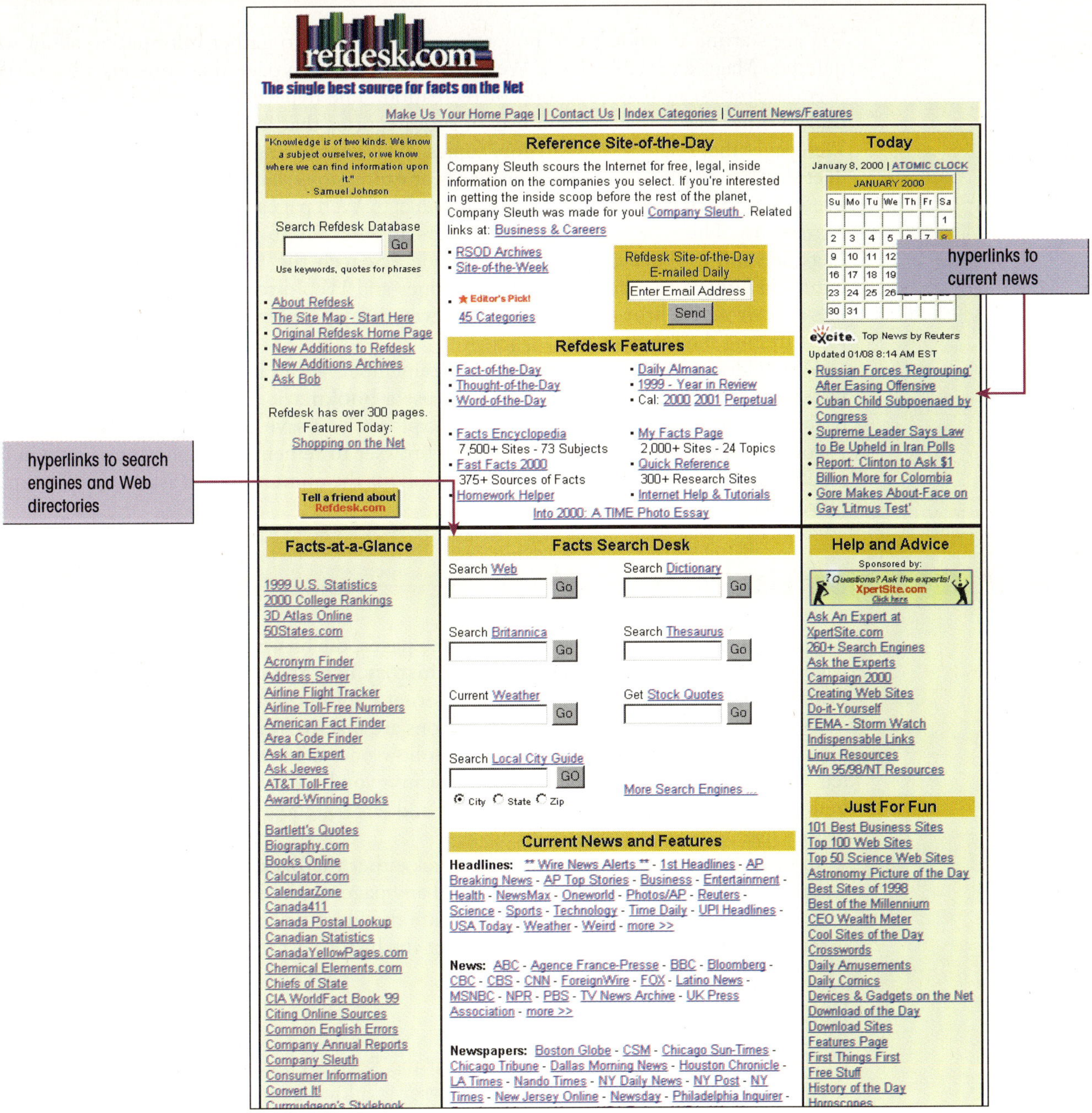

[Screenshot of refdesk.com home page with annotations: "hyperlinks to search engines and Web directories" and "hyperlinks to current news"]

Pages such as the one shown in Figure 3-11 offer links to pages that many Web users frequently visit. The people and organizations that create these pages often sell advertising space on their pages to pay the cost of maintaining their sites.

Quick Access to Web Page Directories and Guides

You are starting to understand how to use the Internet to gather information about wind quintets. Maggie explains that a **Web directory** is a Web page that contains a list of Web page categories, such as education or recreation. The hyperlinks on a Web directory page lead to other pages that contain lists of subcategories that lead to other category lists and Web pages that relate to the category topics. **Web search engines** are Web pages that conduct searches of the Web to find the words or expressions that you enter. The result of such a search is a Web page that contains hyperlinks to Web pages that contain matching text or expressions. These pages can give new users an easy way to find information on the Web. Netscape and Internet Explorer each include a **Search the Internet** button. Clicking this button in either browser opens search engines and Web directories chosen by the companies that wrote the browser software. However, many people prefer to select their own tools for searching the Internet.

Web addresses can be long and hard to remember—even if you are using domain names instead of IP addresses. In Netscape, you use a **bookmark** to save the URL of a specific page so you can return to it. In Internet Explorer, you save the URL as a **favorite** in the Favorites folder. You realize that using the browser to remember important pages will be a terrific asset as you start collecting information for the quintet, so you ask Maggie to explain more about how to return to a Web page.

Using the History List

As you click the hyperlinks to go to new Web pages, the browser stores the locations of each page you visit during a single session in a **history list**. You click the **Back** button and the **Forward** button in both Navigator and Internet Explorer to move through the history list.

When you start your browser, both buttons are inactive (dimmed) because no history list for your new session exists yet. After you follow one or more hyperlinks, the Back button lets you retrace your path through the hyperlinks you have followed. Once you use the Back button, the Forward button becomes active and lets you move forward through the session's history list.

In most Web browsers, you can right-click either the Back or Forward button to display a portion of the history list. You can reload any page on the list by clicking its name in the list. The Back and Forward buttons duplicate the functions of commands on the browser's menu commands. You will learn more about the history list in Sessions 3.2 and 3.3.

Reloading a Web Page

Clicking the **Reload** button in Navigator or the **Refresh** button in Internet Explorer loads the same Web page that appears in the browser window again. The browser stores a copy of every Web page it displays on your computer's hard drive in a **cache** folder, which increases the speed at which the browser can display pages as you navigate through the history list. The cache folder lets the browser load the pages from the client instead of from the remote Web server.

When you click the Reload button or the Refresh button, the browser contacts the Web server to see if the Web page has changed since it was stored in the cache folder. If it has changed, the browser gets the new page from the Web server; otherwise, it loads the cache folder copy. If you want to force the browser to load the page from the Web server, hold down the Shift key as you click the Reload or Refresh button.

Stopping a Web Page Transfer

Sometimes a Web page takes a long time to load. When this occurs, you can click the **Stop** button in Navigator or Internet Explorer to halt the Web page transfer from the server; you can then click the hyperlink again. A second attempt may connect and transfer the page more quickly. You also might want to use the Stop button to abort a transfer when you accidentally click a hyperlink that you do not want to follow.

Returning to a Web Page

You use a Navigator bookmark or Internet Explorer's Favorites feature to store and organize a list of Web pages that you have visited so you can return to them easily without having to remember the URL or search for the page again. Navigator bookmarks and Internet Explorer favorites each work very much like a paper bookmark that you would use in a printed book: They mark the page at which you stopped reading.

You can save as many Navigator bookmarks or Internet Explorer favorites as you want to mark all of your favorite Web pages, so you can return to pages that you frequently use or pages that are important to your research or tasks. You could even bookmark every Web page you visit!

Keeping track of many bookmarks and favorites requires an organizing system. You store bookmarks or favorites in a system folder. Netscape stores bookmarks in one file on your computer, and Internet Explorer stores *each* favorite as a separate file on your computer. Storing each favorite separately, instead of storing all bookmarks together, offers somewhat more flexibility but uses more disk space. You can organize your bookmarks or favorites in many different ways to meet your needs. For example, you might store all of the bookmarks or favorites for Web pages that include information about wind quintets in a folder named "Wind Quintet Information."

Printing and Saving Web Pages

As you use your browser to view Web pages, you will find some pages that you want to print or store for future use. Web browsers include both the print and save capabilities. Web browsers allow you to save entire Web pages or just parts of the Web page, such as selections of text or graphics.

Printing a Web Page

The easiest way to print a Web page is to click the **Print** button in Navigator or Internet Explorer. In either case, the current page (or frame) that appears in the Web page area is sent to the printer. If the page contains light colors or many graphics, you might consider changing the printing options so the page prints without the background, or with all black text. You will learn how to change the print settings for Navigator and Internet Explorer in Sessions 3.2 and 3.3, respectively.

Although printing an entire Web page is often useful, there are times when you will want to save all or part of the page to disk, as you will see next.

Saving a Web Page

When you save a Web page to disk, you save only the text portion. If the Web page contains graphics, such as photos, drawings, or icons, they will not be saved with the HTML document. To save a graphic separately, right-click the graphic in the browser window, click Save

Image As or Save Picture As on the shortcut menu, and then save the graphic to the same location to which you saved the Web's HTML document. The graphics file is specified to appear on the HTML document as a hyperlink, so you might have to change the HTML code in the Web page to identify the location of the graphic. Copying the graphics files to the same disk as the HTML document will *usually* work. You will learn more about saving a Web page and its graphics in Sessions 3.2 and 3.3.

Reproducing Web Pages and Copyright Law

Maggie explains that there might be significant restrictions on the way that you can use information or images that you copy from another entity's Web site. The United States and other countries have copyright laws that govern the use of photocopies, audio or video recordings, and other reproductions of authors' original work. A **copyright** is the legal right of the author or other owner of an original work to control the reproduction, distribution, and sale of that work. A copyright comes into existence as soon as the work is placed into a tangible form, such as a printed copy, an electronic file, or a Web page. The copyright exists even if the work does not contain a copyright notice. If you do not know whether material that you find on the Web is copyrighted, the safest course of action is to assume that it is.

You can use limited amounts of copyrighted information in term papers and other reports that you prepare in an academic setting, but you must cite the source. Commercial use of copyrighted material is much more restricted. You should obtain permission from the copyright holder before using anything you copy from a Web page. It can be difficult to determine the owner of a source's copyright if no notice appears on the Web page; however, most Web pages provide a hyperlink to the e-mail address of the person responsible for maintaining the page. That person, often called a **webmaster**, usually can provide information about the copyright status of materials on the page.

Session 3.1 QUICK CHECK

1. True or False: Web browser software runs on a Web server computer.
2. Name two things you can accomplish using HTML tags.
3. Briefly define the term *home page*.
4. Name two examples of hypermedia.
5. A local political candidate is creating a Web site to help in her campaign for office. Describe some of the things she might want to include in her Web site.
6. What is the difference between IP addressing and domain name addressing?
7. Identify and interpret the meaning of each part of the following URL: http://www.savethetrees.org/main.html
8. What is the difference between a Web directory and a Web search engine?

Now that you understand the basic function of a browser and how to find information on the Web, you are ready to start using your browser to find information for the quintet. If you are using Navigator, your instructor will assign Session 3.2; if you are using Internet Explorer, your instructor will assign Session 3.3. The authors recommend, however, that you read both sessions because you might encounter a different browser on a public or employer's computer in the future.

SESSION 3.2

In this session, you will learn how to configure the Netscape Navigator Web browser and use it to display Web pages and follow hyperlinks to other Web pages. You will learn how to copy text and images from Web pages and how to mark pages so you can return to them easily.

Starting Netscape Navigator

To be effective in searching the Web for the Sunset Wind Quintet, Maggie is sure that you will want to become familiar with Netscape Navigator, from Netscape Communications Corporation, which is part of a suite of programs called Netscape Communicator. The other programs in the Communicator suite provide e-mail, discussion groups, realtime collaboration, and Web page creation tools. This overview assumes that you have Navigator installed on your computer. You should have your computer turned on so you can see the Windows desktop.

To start Navigator:

1. Click the **Start** button on the taskbar, point to **Programs**, point to **Netscape Communicator**, and then click **Netscape Navigator**. After a moment, Navigator opens.

   TROUBLE? If you cannot find Netscape Communicator on the Programs menu, check to see if a Netscape Navigator shortcut icon appears on the desktop, and then double-click it. If you do not see the shortcut icon, ask your instructor or technical support person for help. The program might be installed in a different folder on the computer you are using.

2. If the program does not fill the screen entirely, click the **Maximize** button on the Navigator program's title bar. Your screen should look like Figure 3-12.

INTERNET   WEB 3.18   TUTORIAL 3   BROWSER BASICS

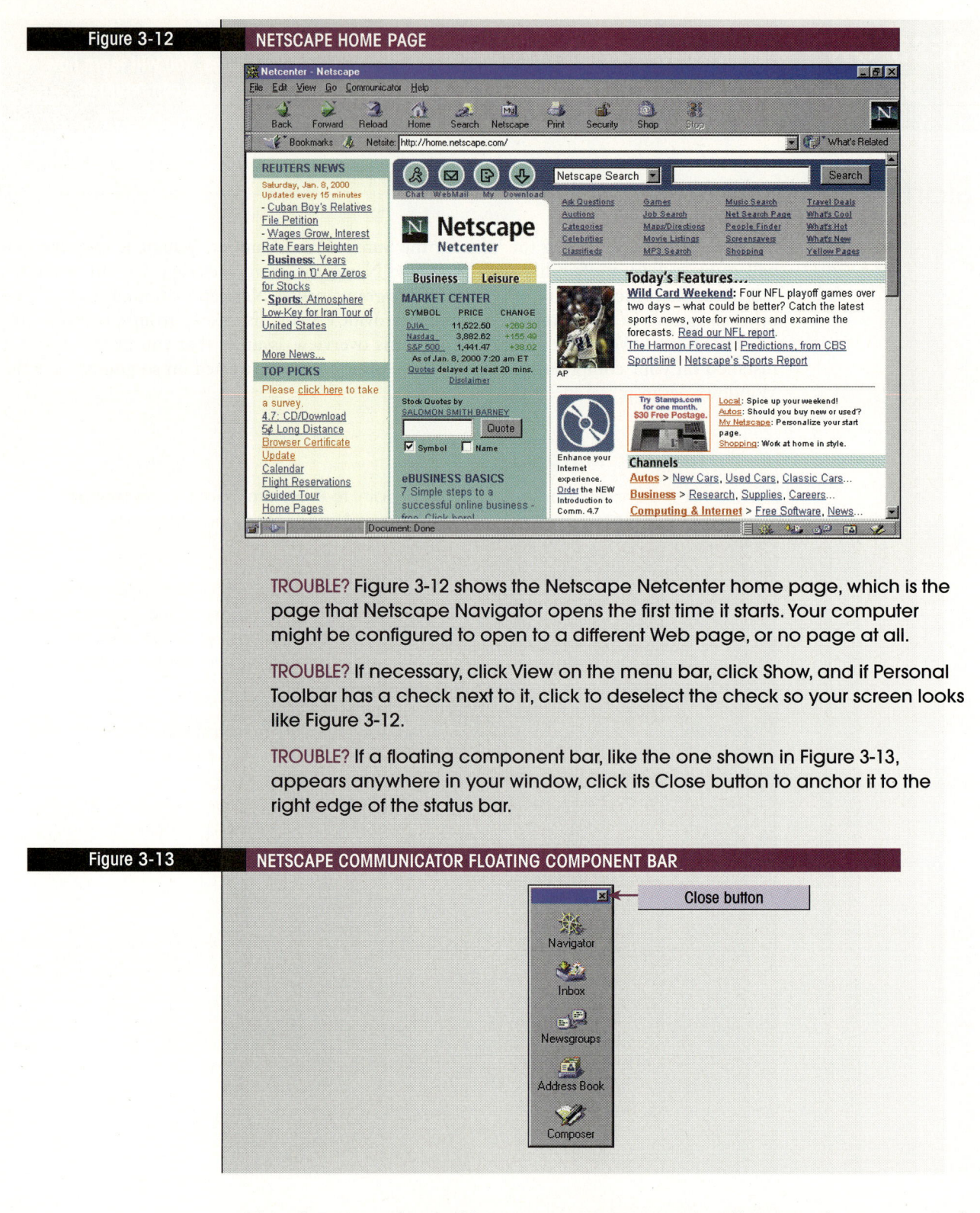

| Figure 3-12 | NETSCAPE HOME PAGE |

[Screenshot of Netscape Netcenter home page in Netscape Navigator browser, showing the URL http://home.netscape.com/, Reuters News sidebar with headlines dated Saturday, Jan. 8, 2000, Top Picks list, Market Center with stock quotes, Today's Features about Wild Card Weekend NFL playoffs, and Channels section.]

TROUBLE? Figure 3-12 shows the Netscape Netcenter home page, which is the page that Netscape Navigator opens the first time it starts. Your computer might be configured to open to a different Web page, or no page at all.

TROUBLE? If necessary, click View on the menu bar, click Show, and if Personal Toolbar has a check next to it, click to deselect the check so your screen looks like Figure 3-12.

TROUBLE? If a floating component bar, like the one shown in Figure 3-13, appears anywhere in your window, click its Close button to anchor it to the right edge of the status bar.

| Figure 3-13 | NETSCAPE COMMUNICATOR FLOATING COMPONENT BAR |

[Image of the floating component bar with Close button labeled at top, and icons for Navigator, Inbox, Newsgroups, Address Book, and Composer.]

Now that you understand how to start Navigator, you tell Maggie that you are ready to start using it to find information on the Internet. To find information, you need to know how the Navigator toolbars and menu commands work.

Using the Navigation Toolbar and Menu Commands

The Navigation toolbar includes 11 buttons that execute frequently used commands for browsing the Web. Figure 3-14 shows the Navigation toolbar buttons and describes their functions. (Depending on which version of Navigator you are using, you might see different toolbar buttons. Use online Help to get more information about buttons not pictured in Figure 3-14.)

Figure 3-14	NAVIGATION TOOLBAR BUTTONS	
BUTTON	**BUTTON NAME**	**DESCRIPTION**
Back	Back	Moves to the last previously visited Web page
Forward	Forward	Moves to the next previously visited Web page
Reload	Reload	Reloads the current page
Home	Home	Loads the program's defined start page
Search	Search	Opens a Web page that has hyperlinks to Web search engines and directories
My Netscape	My Netscape	Opens a version of the Netscape's Netcenter page that you can customize
Print	Print	Prints the current Web page
Security	Security	Shows security information about the Web page that is currently displayed
Shop	Shop	Opens the Netscape Shopping directory page
Stop	Stop	Stops the transfer of a new Web page
N	Netscape Home Page (Netcenter)	Opens the Netscape Netcenter page

In addition to the toolbar buttons, the Navigation toolbar contains a toolbar tab that you can click to hide the toolbar so there is more room to display a Web page in the Web page area. You can hide both the Navigation and Location toolbars so that the toolbar tabs fold up and remain visible, or you can hide the toolbars completely by using the options on the View menu, as you will see next.

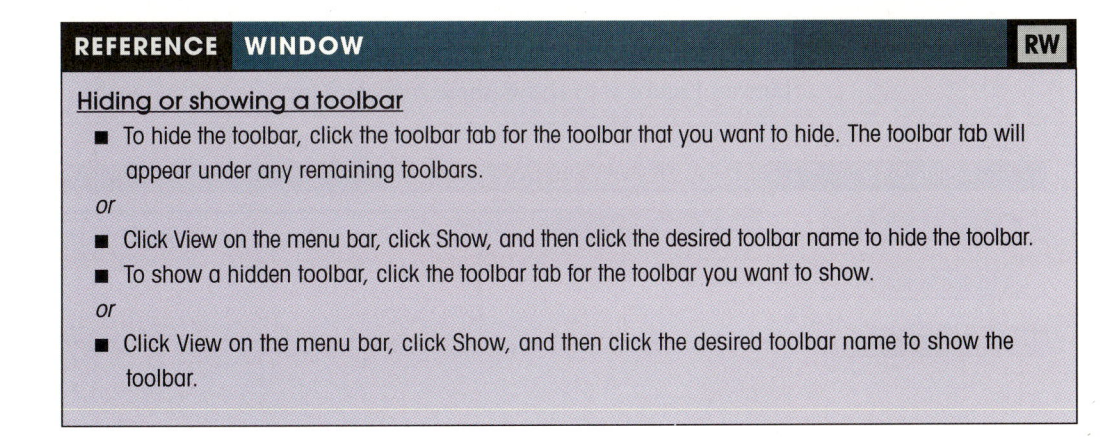

REFERENCE WINDOW RW

Hiding or showing a toolbar
- To hide the toolbar, click the toolbar tab for the toolbar that you want to hide. The toolbar tab will appear under any remaining toolbars.

or
- Click View on the menu bar, click Show, and then click the desired toolbar name to hide the toolbar.
- To show a hidden toolbar, click the toolbar tab for the toolbar you want to show.

or
- Click View on the menu bar, click Show, and then click the desired toolbar name to show the toolbar.

To hide the Navigation toolbar and then show it again:

1. Click the **Navigation toolbar** tab, which appears on the left edge of the Navigation toolbar. The toolbar will disappear and its toolbar tab appears under the Location toolbar.

2. Move the pointer to the Navigation toolbar tab below the Location toolbar and notice that the message indicates that you are pointing to the Navigation toolbar.

3. Click the **Navigation toolbar** tab. The Navigation toolbar appears above the Location toolbar.

You can use the toolbar tabs to hide or show the toolbars quickly. However, if you want to hide the toolbars and their tabs, you must use the View menu. The View menu commands are toggles. A **toggle** is like a pushbutton switch on a television set; you press the button once to turn on the television and press it a second time to turn it off.

To hide the Navigation toolbar using the View menu:

1. Click **View** on the menu bar.

2. Click **Show** and then click **Navigation Toolbar** to hide the Navigation toolbar and its toolbar tab. To see the Navigation toolbar again, you repeat the same steps.

   TROUBLE? If the Navigation Toolbar does not have a check mark next to it, then the Navigation toolbar already is hidden. Go to Step 3.

3. Click **View** on the menu bar, click **Show**, and then click **Navigation Toolbar** to show the toolbar again.

Now you are ready to use the Navigation toolbar buttons and the menu commands to browse the Web.

Using the Location Toolbar Elements

Maggie explains that there are five elements in the Location toolbar: the **Location toolbar** tab, the **Location** field, the **Page proxy** icon, the **Bookmarks** button, and the **What's Related** button. Figure 3-15 shows these five elements.

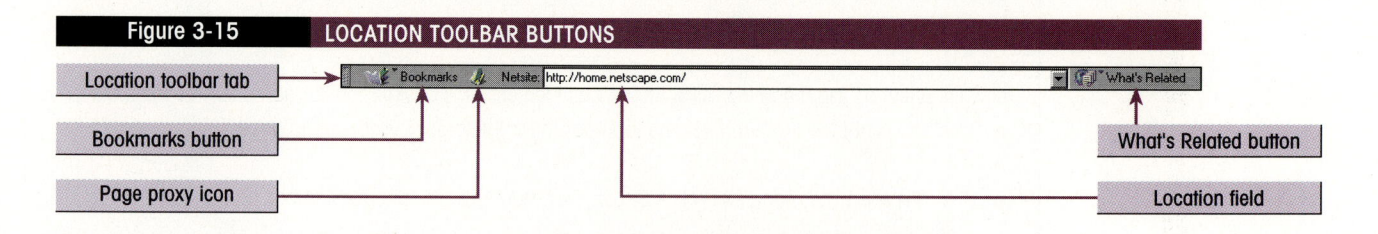

| Figure 3-15 | LOCATION TOOLBAR BUTTONS |

- Location toolbar tab
- Bookmarks button
- Page proxy icon
- What's Related button
- Location field

Hiding and Showing the Location Toolbar

You can click the Location toolbar tab or use the View menu commands to hide and show the Location toolbar, just as when you used the Navigation toolbar tab and the View menu commands to hide and show the Navigation toolbar. Clicking the Location toolbar tab hides the toolbar but keeps the tab visible so it folds up under any visible toolbars.

Entering a URL into the Location Field

Maggie tells you to use the **Location field** to enter URLs directly into Netscape Navigator. Marianna gave you the URL for the Pennsylvania Quintet, so you can see its Web page.

REFERENCE WINDOW

Entering a URL in the Location field
- Click at the end of the current text in the Location field, and then backspace over the text that you want to delete.
- Type the URL to which you want to go.
- Press the Enter key to load the URL's Web page in the browser window.

To load the Pennsylvania Quintet's Web page:

1. Click in the Location field; if there is text in the Location field, click at the end of the text, and then press the **Backspace** key to delete it.

   TROUBLE? Make sure that you delete all of the text in the Location field so the text you type in Step 2 will be correct.

2. Type **http://www.course.com/newperspectives/internet2/** in the Location field to go to the Student Online Companion page on the Course Technology Web site. In this book, you will go to the Course Technology site and then click hyperlinks to go to individual Web pages.

3. Press the **Enter** key. The Location field's label changes from "Location" to "Go to" and the Student Online Companion Web page loads, as shown in Figure 3-16. When the entire page has loaded, the Location field's label will change back to "Location."

INTERNET   WEB 3.22   TUTORIAL 3   BROWSER BASICS

Figure 3-16   STUDENT ONLINE COMPANION WEB PAGE

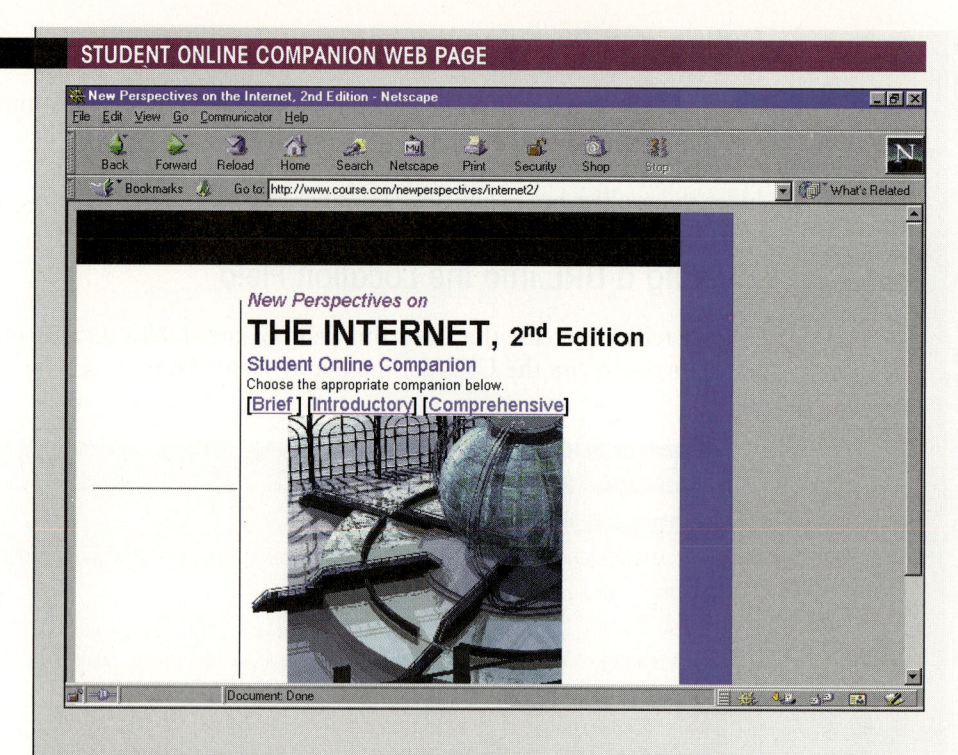

TROUBLE? If a Dial-Up Networking dialog box opens after you press the Enter key, click the Connect button. You must have an Internet connection to complete the steps in this tutorial.

4. Click the link for the book you are using to open the main page, click the **Tutorial 3** link to open the page that contains the links for this tutorial, and then click the **Session 3.2** link in the left frame to see the links in the right frame.

5. Click the **Pennsylvania Quintet** link. The Web page opens, as shown in Figure 3-17.

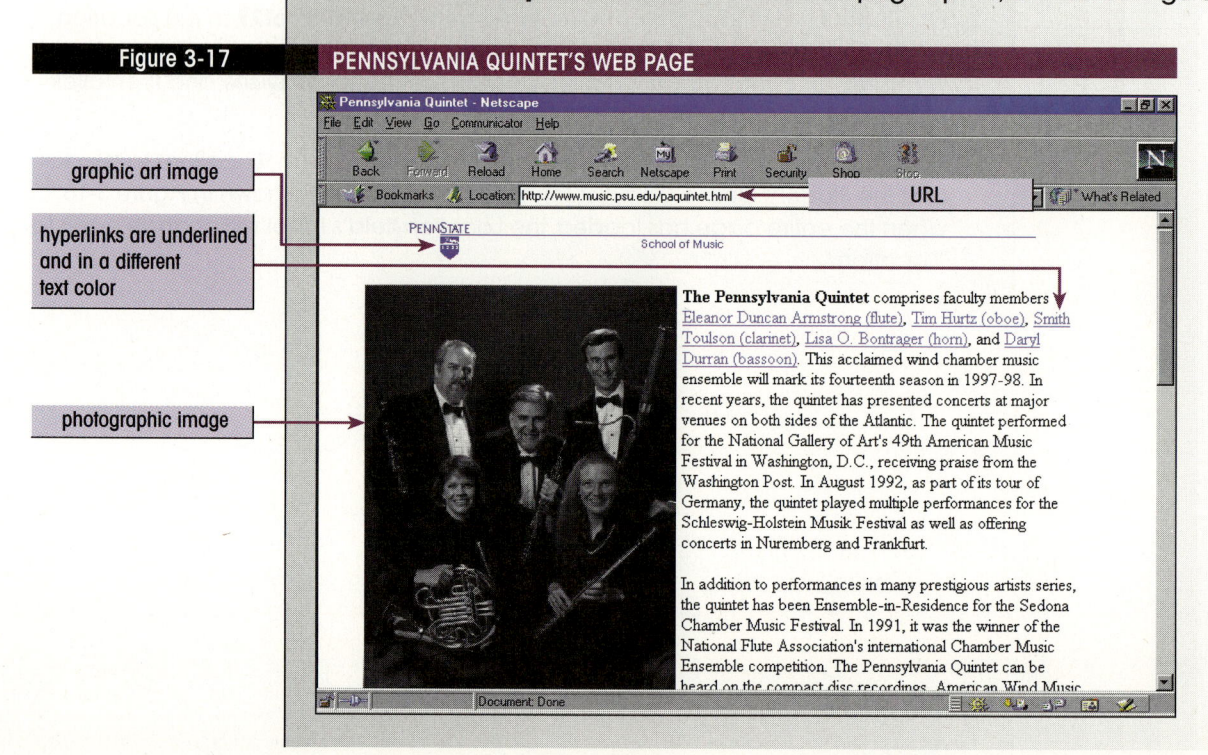

Figure 3-17   PENNSYLVANIA QUINTET'S WEB PAGE

- graphic art image
- hyperlinks are underlined and in a different text color
- photographic image
- URL

> **TROUBLE?** The Pennsylvania Quintet might change its Web page, so your Web page might look different from the one shown in Figure 3-17. If this Web page is deleted from the server, then you might see an entirely different Web page. However, the steps should work the same.
>
> 6. Read the Web page, and then click the **Back** button to return to the Student Online Companion page.

You like the format of the Pennsylvania Quintet's home page, so you want to make sure that you can go back to that page later if you need to review its contents. Maggie explains that you can write down the URL so you can refer to it later, but an easier way is to store the URL in a **bookmark file** to save in the Navigator program for future use.

Creating a Bookmark for a Web Site

You use a **bookmark** to store and organize a list of Web pages that you have visited so you can return to them easily. You use the **Bookmarks** button or the **Page proxy** icon on the Location toolbar in Netscape's bookmarking system. You can use the Bookmarks button to add new bookmarks, to open the Bookmarks menu, or to open the Bookmarks window. Figure 3-18 shows a Bookmarks menu that contains bookmarks that are sorted into categories according to the user's needs.

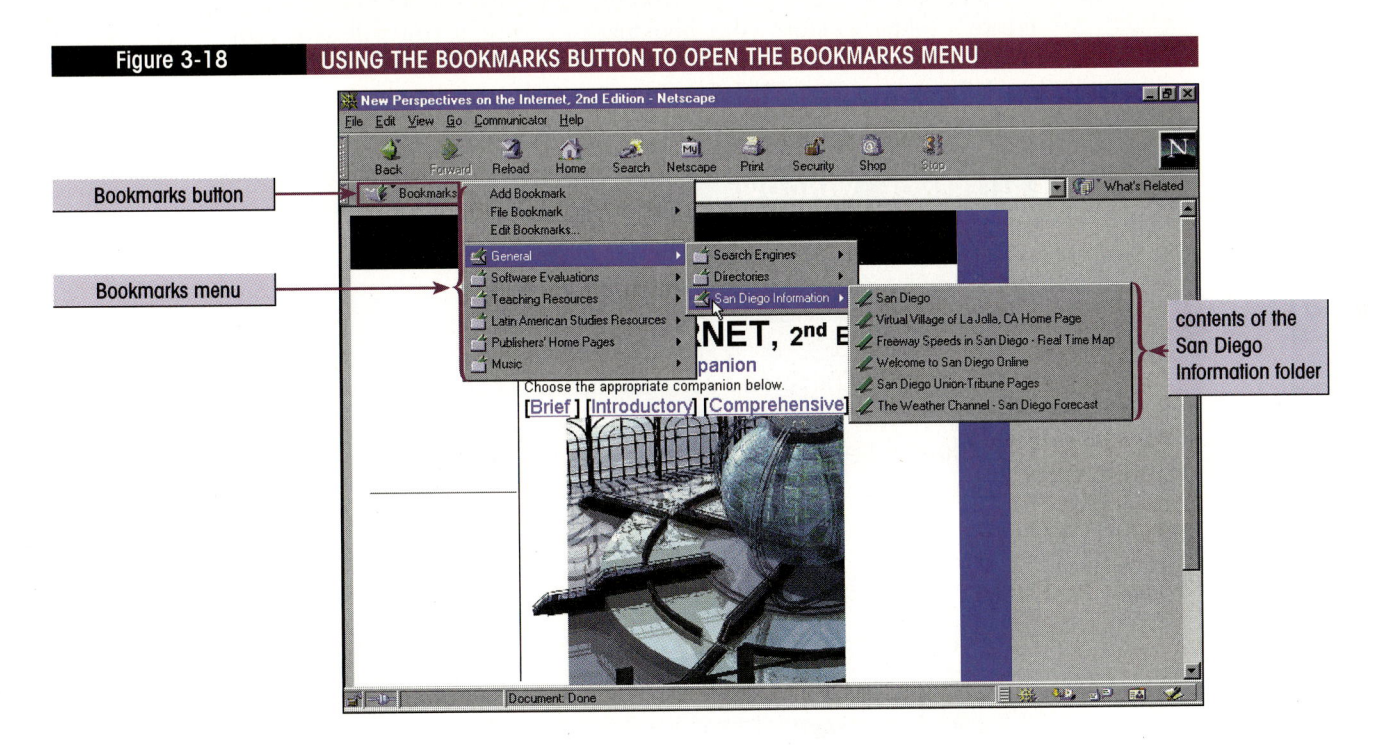

| Figure 3-18 | USING THE BOOKMARKS BUTTON TO OPEN THE BOOKMARKS MENU |

The hierarchical structure of the bookmark file is easy to see in Figure 3-18. The six Web pages shown in the San Diego Information folder provide information about San Diego.

A **Bookmarks window** provides the same information as the cascading Bookmarks menus, but it also includes tools for editing and rearranging the bookmarks. For example, you can use the Bookmarks window menu commands to create new folders, or you can use the drag and drop method to move Web pages to another folder or to move folders to new locations. Figure 3-19 shows the same set of bookmarks in the Bookmarks window, where you can see more details about the user's bookmarks and their organization.

Figure 3-19   EXAMINING BOOKMARKS IN THE BOOKMARKS WINDOW

- header
- closed folders
- bookmarks
- open folders
- URL of selected bookmark

You decide to create a bookmark for the Pennsylvania Quintet Web page. First, you will create a folder to store your bookmarks, and then you will save your bookmark in that folder. You might not work on the same computer again, so you will save a copy of the bookmark file to your Data Disk for future use.

REFERENCE WINDOW

Creating a Bookmarks folder
- Click the Bookmarks button on the Location toolbar.
- Click Edit Bookmarks to open the Bookmarks window.
- Right-click the first folder in the list, and then click New Folder on the shortcut menu to create a new folder and to open the Bookmark Properties dialog box.
- Type the name of the new folder in the Name text box, and then click the OK button to close the Bookmark Properties dialog box and create the new folder.

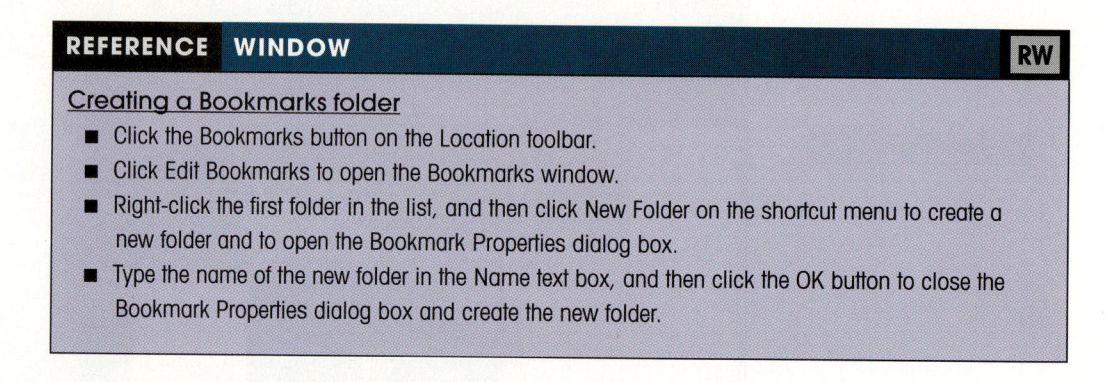

To create a new Bookmarks folder:

1. Click the **Bookmarks** button on the Location toolbar to open the Bookmarks menu, and then click **Edit Bookmarks** to open the Bookmarks window.

2. Right-click the first item in the Bookmarks window; usually, this item is "Main Bookmarks" or "Bookmarks for <name>," but it might have another title on your computer. After you right-click the first item, a shortcut menu opens.

3. Click **New Folder** on the shortcut menu to open the Bookmark Properties dialog box. The text "New Folder" appears selected in the Name text box. To change the new folder's name, you just type the new name.

TUTORIAL 3 BROWSER BASICS   WEB 3.25   INTERNET

4. Type **Wind Quintet Information** in the Name text box, and then click the **OK** button to close the Bookmark Properties dialog box and create the new Wind Quintet Information folder in the bookmark file. The new folder should appear under the first item in the Bookmarks window, as shown in Figure 3-20.

Figure 3-20   CREATING A BOOKMARK FOLDER

[Screenshot of Bookmarks - bookmark.htm window showing:
- Main Bookmarks
  - Wind Quintet Information
  - General
    - Search Engines
    - Directories
    - San Diego Information
  - Software Evaluations
  - Teaching Resources
  - Latin American Studies Resources
  - Publishers' Home Pages]

Callouts:
- new folder added
- your list of bookmarks will be different
- your first folder's name might be different

TROUBLE? If your Wind Quintet Information folder appears in a different location, don't worry. Just make sure that the folder appears in the Bookmarks window.

5. Click the **Close** button on the Bookmarks window title bar to close the Bookmarks window.

Now that you have created a folder, you can save your bookmark for the Pennsylvania Quintet's Web page in the new folder. However, first you must return to the Web page that you want to bookmark.

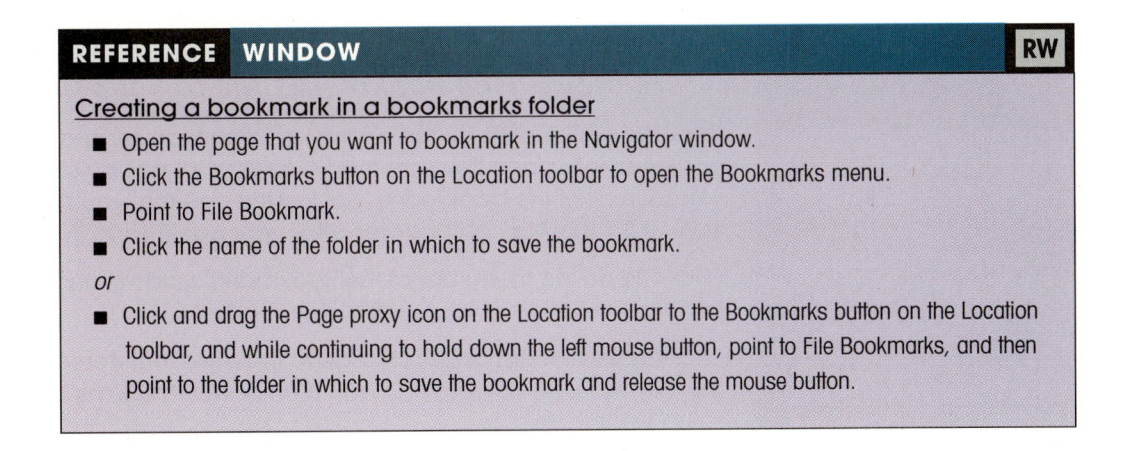

REFERENCE WINDOW   RW

Creating a bookmark in a bookmarks folder
- Open the page that you want to bookmark in the Navigator window.
- Click the Bookmarks button on the Location toolbar to open the Bookmarks menu.
- Point to File Bookmark.
- Click the name of the folder in which to save the bookmark.

or

- Click and drag the Page proxy icon on the Location toolbar to the Bookmarks button on the Location toolbar, and while continuing to hold down the left mouse button, point to File Bookmarks, and then point to the folder in which to save the bookmark and release the mouse button.

To save a bookmark for a Web page in a folder:

1. Click the **Forward** button on the Navigation toolbar to return to the Pennsylvania Quintet Web page.

2. Click the **Bookmarks** button on the Location toolbar to open the Bookmarks menu.

3. Point to **File Bookmark**, and then click the **Wind Quintet Information** folder. Now, the bookmark is saved in the correct folder. You can test your bookmark by using the bookmark to visit the site.

4. Click the **Back** button on the Navigation toolbar to go to the previous Web page.

5. Click the **Bookmarks** button on the Location toolbar, point to **Wind Quintet Information**, and then click **Pennsylvania Quintet**. The Pennsylvania Quintet page opens in the browser, which means that you created the bookmark successfully.

   TROUBLE? If the Pennsylvania Quintet page does not open, click Edit Bookmarks on the Bookmarks menu, make sure that you have the correct URL for the page, and then repeat the steps. If you still have trouble, ask your instructor or technical support person for help.

Because you might need to visit the Pennsylvania Quintet page from another client, you can save your bookmark file on your Data Disk.

REFERENCE WINDOW

Saving a bookmark to a floppy disk
- Click the Bookmarks button on the Location toolbar, and then click Edit Bookmarks to open the Bookmarks window.
- Click File on the menu bar, and then click Save As to open the Save bookmarks file dialog box.
- Click the Save in list arrow, and then change to the drive that contains your disk.
- Click the Save button to save the bookmark file and close the dialog box.

To store the revised bookmarks file to your floppy disk:

1. Click the **Bookmarks** button on the Location toolbar, and then click **Edit Bookmarks** to open the Bookmarks window. When you save your bookmarks, you save all of the bookmarks, not just the one that you need: Remember from Session 3.1 that Navigator stores *all* of your bookmarks in a single file.

2. Click **File** on the menu bar of the Bookmarks window, and then click **Save As** to open the Save bookmarks file dialog box.

3. Click the **Save in** list arrow, change to the drive that contains your Data Disk (usually, this is 3½ Floppy (A:)), and then double-click the **Tutorial.03** folder.

4. Make sure that **bookmark** appears in the File name text box, and then click the **Save** button.

   TROUBLE? Your computer might be configured to display file extensions, so you might see bookmark.htm in the File name text box, which is also correct.

   TROUBLE? If bookmark or bookmark.htm does not appear in the File name text box, click in the File name text box, type bookmark.htm, and then click the Save button.

5. Close the Bookmarks window.

When you use another computer, you can open the bookmark file from your Data Disk by starting Navigator, clicking the Bookmarks button on the Location toolbar, clicking Edit Bookmarks, clicking File on the menu bar, and then clicking Open Bookmarks File. Change to the drive that contains your Data Disk, and then open the bookmark.htm file from the disk. Your bookmark file will open in the Bookmarks window, and then you can use it as you practiced.

Hyperlink Navigation with the Mouse

Now you know how to use Navigator to find information that will help you with the Sunset Wind Quintet. Maggie tells you that the easiest way to move from one Web page to another is to use the mouse to click hyperlinks that the authors of Web pages embed in their HTML documents. You can also right-click the mouse on the background of a Web page to open a shortcut menu that includes navigation options.

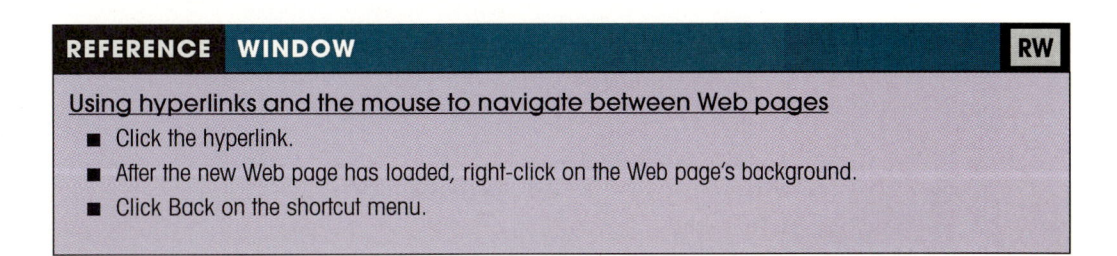

REFERENCE WINDOW   RW

Using hyperlinks and the mouse to navigate between Web pages
- Click the hyperlink.
- After the new Web page has loaded, right-click on the Web page's background.
- Click Back on the shortcut menu.

To follow a hyperlink to a Web page and return using the mouse:

1. Click the **Back** button on the Navigation toolbar to go back to the Student Online Companion page, click the **Lewis Music** link to open that page, and then point to the **Instrument Accessories** hyperlink shown in Figure 3-21 so your pointer changes to 👆.

Figure 3-21   LEWIS MUSIC HOME PAGE

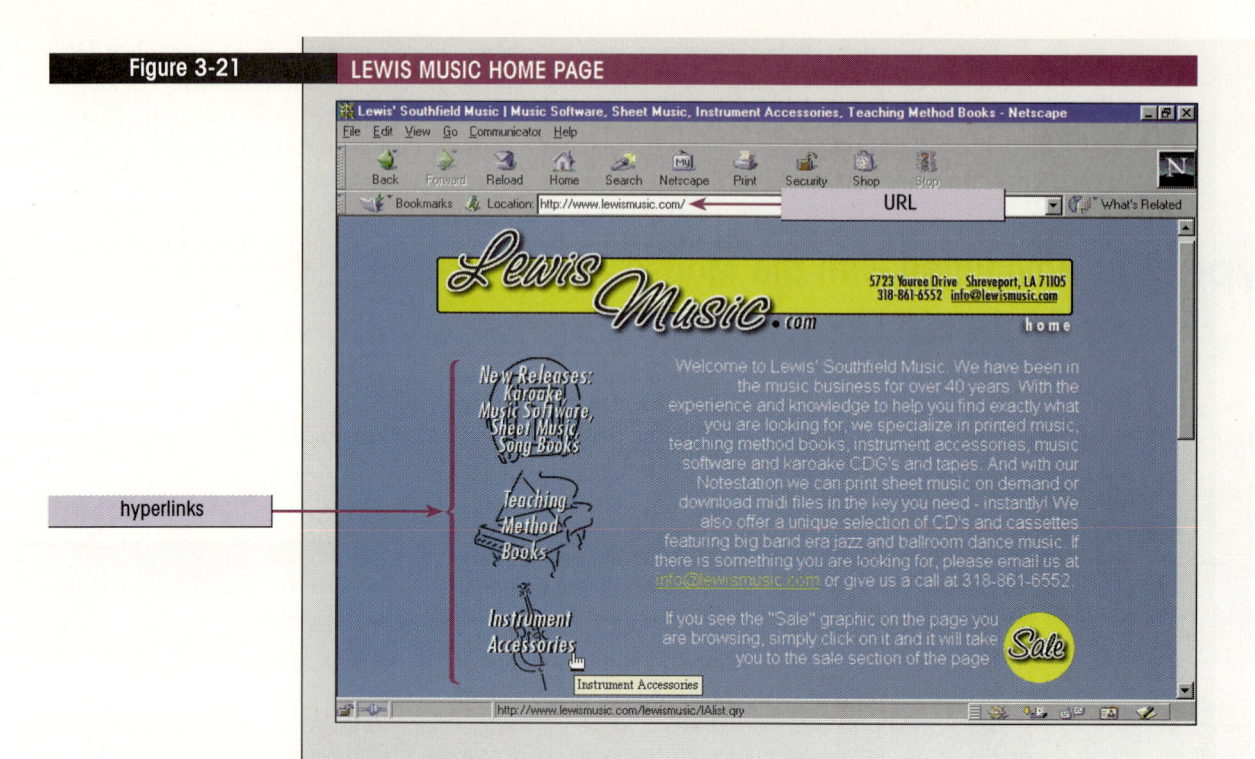

(screenshot of Lewis Music home page in Netscape, with callouts for "URL" and "hyperlinks")

2. Click the **Instrument Accessories** hyperlink to load the page. Watch the second panel in the status bar. When the shadow disappears, you know that Navigator has loaded the full page.

3. Right-click anywhere in the Web page area to open the shortcut menu, as shown in Figure 3-22.

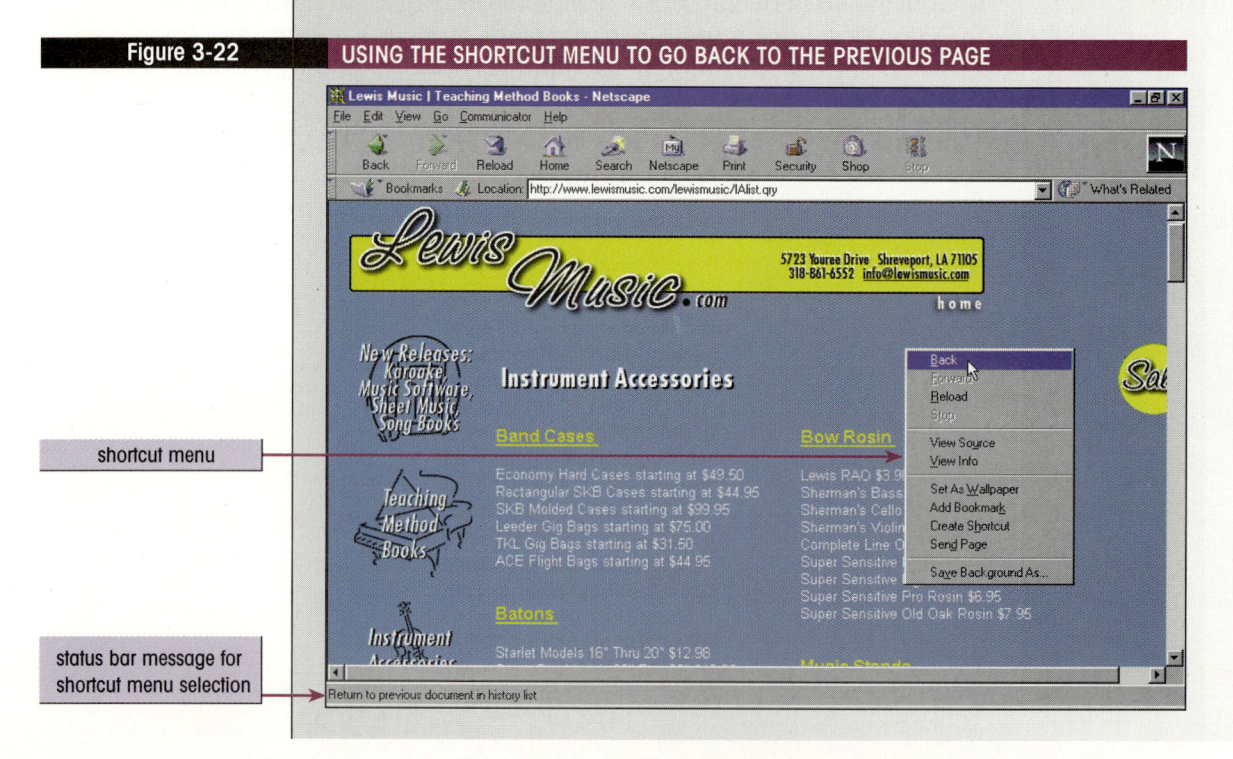

Figure 3-22   USING THE SHORTCUT MENU TO GO BACK TO THE PREVIOUS PAGE

(screenshot of Instrument Accessories page with a right-click shortcut menu visible, callouts for "shortcut menu" and "status bar message for shortcut menu selection")

TUTORIAL 3 BROWSER BASICS   WEB   3.29   INTERNET

TROUBLE? If you right-click a hyperlink, your shortcut menu will display a longer list than the one shown in Figure 3-22, and the Back item will be third in the list instead of first. If you don't see the shortcut menu shown in Figure 3-22, click anywhere outside of the shortcut menu to close it, and then repeat Step 3.

TROUBLE? Web pages change frequently, so the Instrument Accessories page you see might look different from the one shown in Figure 3-22, but right-clicking anywhere on the Web page area will still work.

4. Click **Back** on the shortcut menu to go back to the Lewis Music home page.

5. Repeat Step 4 to return to the Student Online Companion page.

You are beginning to get a good sense of how to move from one Web page to another and back again, but Maggie tells you that you have mastered only one technique of many. She explains that the Navigation toolbar and the menu bar offer many tools for accessing and using Web sites.

Using the History List

In Session 3.1 you learned that the Back and Forward buttons let you move to and from previously visited pages. These buttons duplicate the functions of the menu bar's Go command. Clicking Go opens a menu that lets you move back and forward through a portion of the history list and allows you to choose a specific Web page from that list. You also can open a full copy of the history list.

To view the history list for this session:

1. Click **Communicator** on the menu bar, click **Tools**, and then click **History** to open the History window, as shown in Figure 3-23.

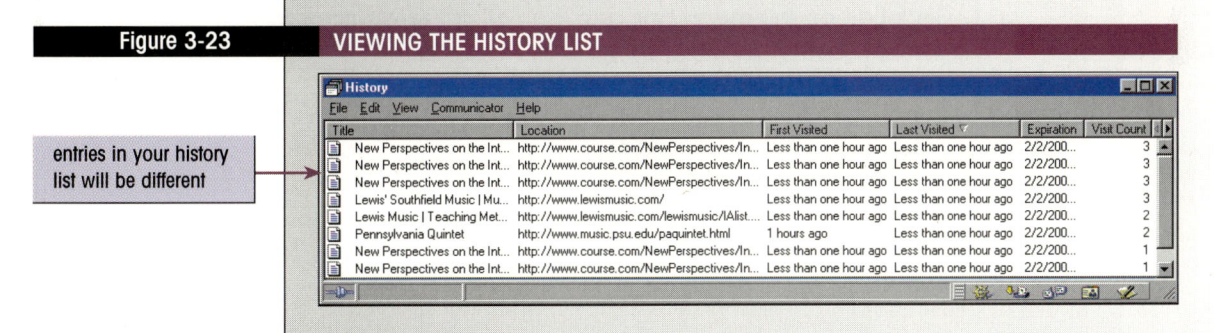

Figure 3-23   VIEWING THE HISTORY LIST

entries in your history list will be different

TROUBLE? The History window that appears on your computer might be a different size and contain different entries from the one that appears in Figure 3-23. You can resize the window by clicking and dragging its edges. You can resize the columns in the window by clicking and dragging on the edges of the column headers.

To return to a page, double-click the page in the list. You can change the way that pages are listed by using the commands on the View menu; for example, you can list the pages by title or in the order in which you visited them.

2. Click the **Close** button on the History window title bar to close it.

Reloading a Web Page

You learned in Session 3.1 that clicking the **Reload** button on the Navigator toolbar loads again the Web page that currently appears in the browser window. You can force Navigator to get the page from the Web server by pressing the Shift key when you click the Reload button.

Going Home

The **Home** button displays the home (or start) page for your copy of Navigator. You can go to the Netscape Netcenter page, which is the software's default installation home page, by clicking the **Netscape Home Page** button on the Navigator toolbar. You cannot change the page that loads by clicking the Navigator Home Page button, but you can change the default URL that opens when you click the Home button by using the Preferences dialog box.

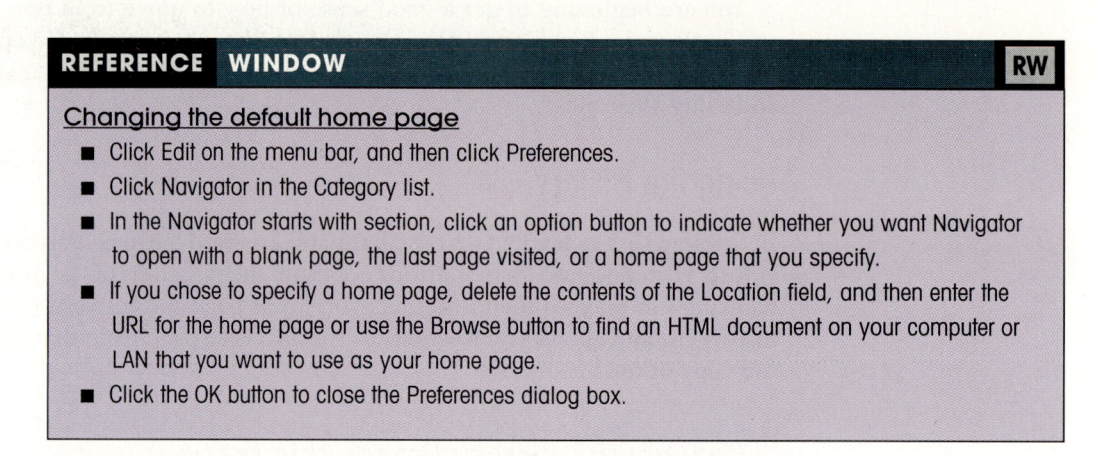

REFERENCE WINDOW

Changing the default home page
- Click Edit on the menu bar, and then click Preferences.
- Click Navigator in the Category list.
- In the Navigator starts with section, click an option button to indicate whether you want Navigator to open with a blank page, the last page visited, or a home page that you specify.
- If you chose to specify a home page, delete the contents of the Location field, and then enter the URL for the home page or use the Browse button to find an HTML document on your computer or LAN that you want to use as your home page.
- Click the OK button to close the Preferences dialog box.

To modify the Home navigation button settings:

1. Click **Edit** on the menu bar, and then click **Preferences** to open that dialog box.

2. Click **Navigator** in the Category list. See Figure 3-24.

TUTORIAL 3 BROWSER BASICS   WEB 3.31   INTERNET

Figure 3-24 **CHANGING THE HOME PAGE**

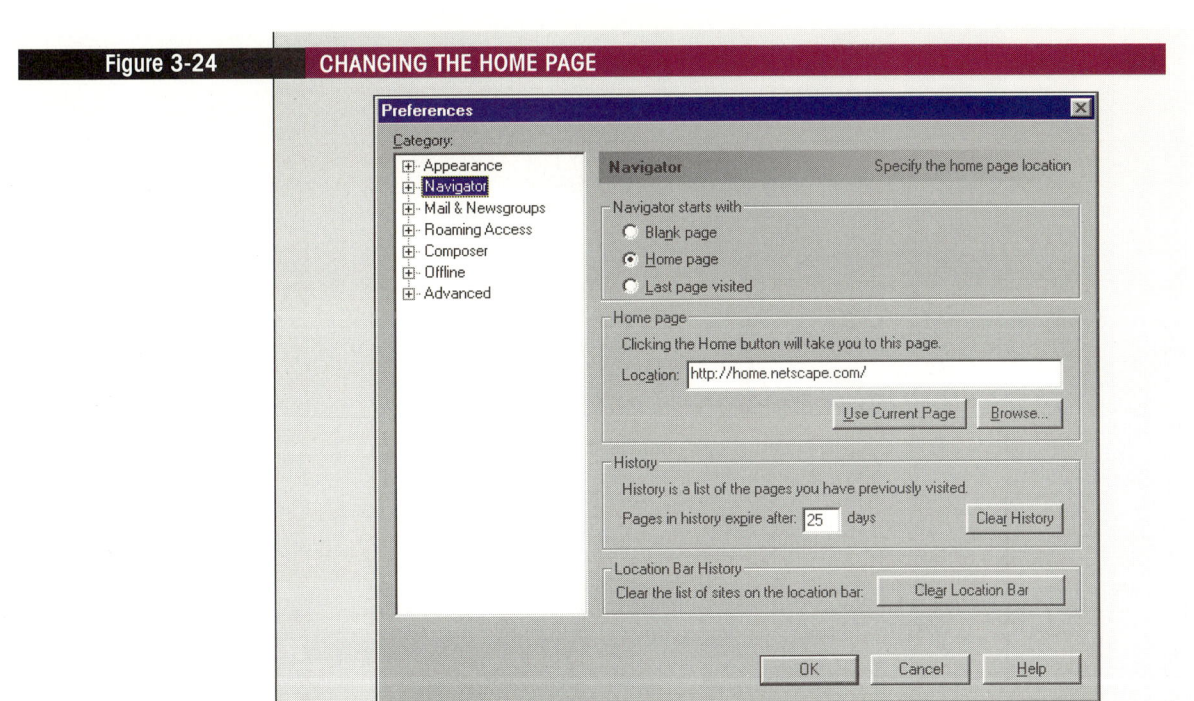

3. To have Navigator open with a **Blank page**, the **Home page** you specify, or the **Last page visited**, click the corresponding option button in the Navigator starts with section of the Preferences dialog box.

   TROUBLE? You might not be able to change these and the following settings if you are using a computer in your school lab or at your office. Some organizations set the home page defaults on all of their computers and lock those settings.

   To specify a home page, select the text in the Location field in the Home page section of the Preferences dialog box shown in Figure 3-24 and enter the URL of the Web page you would like to use. If you loaded the Web page that you would like to be your new home page into Navigator before beginning these steps, you can click the Use Current Page button to place its URL into the Location field. You also can specify an HTML document on your computer or LAN by clicking the Browse button and selecting the disk drive and folder location of that HTML document.

4. Click the **Cancel** button to close the dialog box without making any changes.

Printing a Web Page

The **Print** button on the Navigation toolbar lets you print the current Web frame or page. You can use this button to make a printed copy of most Web pages. (Some Web pages disable the Print command.)

> **REFERENCE WINDOW** RW
>
> **Printing the current Web page**
> - Click the Print button on the Navigation toolbar.
> - Use the Print dialog box to choose the printer you want to use, the pages you want to print, and the number of copies you want to make of each page.
> - Click the OK button to print the page(s).

To print a Web page:

1. Click in the main (right) frame of the Student Online Companion page to select it.

2. Click the **Print** button on the Navigation toolbar to open the Print dialog box shown in Figure 3-25.

Figure 3-25   PRINT DIALOG BOX

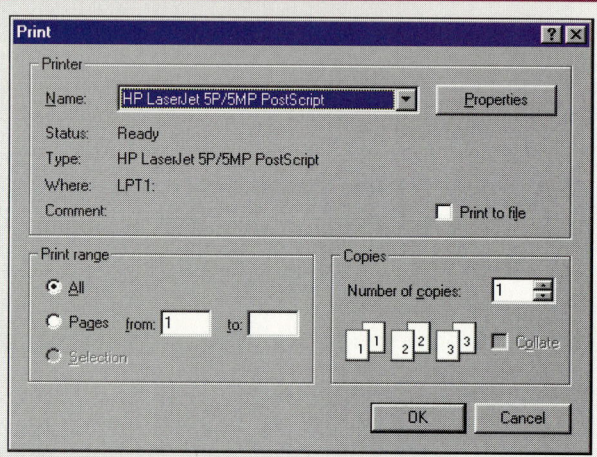

[Print dialog box screenshot showing Printer Name: HP LaserJet 5P/5MP PostScript, Status: Ready, Type: HP LaserJet 5P/5MP PostScript, Where: LPT1:, Print range options (All, Pages from/to, Selection), Number of copies, Collate, OK, Cancel]

3. Make sure that the printer in the Name text box shows the printer you want to use; if necessary, click the Name list arrow to change the selection.

4. Click the **Pages** option button in the Print range section of the Print dialog box, type **1** in the **from** text box, press the **Tab** key, and then type **1** in the **to** text box to specify that you want to print only the first page.

5. Make sure that the Number of copies text box shows that you want to print one copy.

6. Click the **OK** button to print the Web page and close the Print dialog box.

Changing the Settings for Printing a Web Page

You already have seen how to print Web pages using the basic options available in the Print dialog box. You also learned how to store a bookmark so you can return to a Web page later. Usually, the default settings in the Print dialog box are fine for printing a Web page, but you can use the Page Setup dialog box to change the way a Web page prints. Figure 3-26 shows the Page Setup dialog box, and Figure 3-27 describes its settings.

Figure 3-26   PAGE SETUP OPTIONS FOR PRINTING WEB PAGES

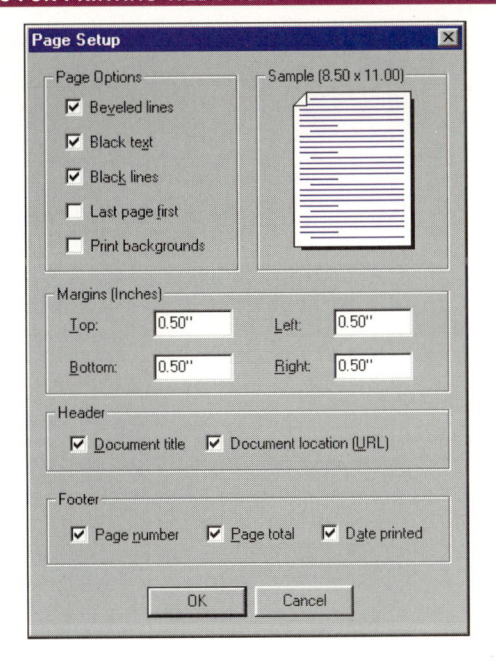

Figure 3-27   PAGE SETUP DIALOG BOX OPTIONS

OPTION	DESCRIPTION	USE
Black Text	Prints all of the text on a Web page as black.	Use when the Web page contains text set in light colors, so it will be legible when printed.
Black Lines	Prints all of the lines on a Web page as black.	Use when the Web page contains light-colored lines, so they will be legible when printed.
Last Page First	Reverses the normal order in which pages are printed.	Some printers eject pages face up. Using this setting will correctly collate the Web page printout.
Print backgrounds	Prints a Web page background, if there is one on the page.	You should leave this option off unless you are using a color printer. Backgrounds can render text and images illegible, and dark colors can waste your printer's toner or ink.
Margins	Use to change the margin of the printed page.	Normally, you should leave the default settings, but you can change the right, left, top, or bottom margins as needed.
Header	Prints the Web page's document title and/or document location (URL).	Selecting these options lets you print the name and location of the page for later reference.
Footer	Prints the Web page's page number, the total number of pages, or the date that the page is printed.	Selecting these options provides a record of the page number, total number of pages, and the date that you printed the page.

When printing long Web pages, another print option that is extremely useful for saving paper is to reduce the font size of the Web pages before you print them. To do this, click Edit on the menu bar, click Preferences, click the Fonts category, and then use the Size list arrow to decrease the size of the font used in the Web page. See Figure 3-28.

Figure 3-28   USING THE PREFERENCES DIALOG BOX TO CHANGE THE WEB PAGE FONT SIZE

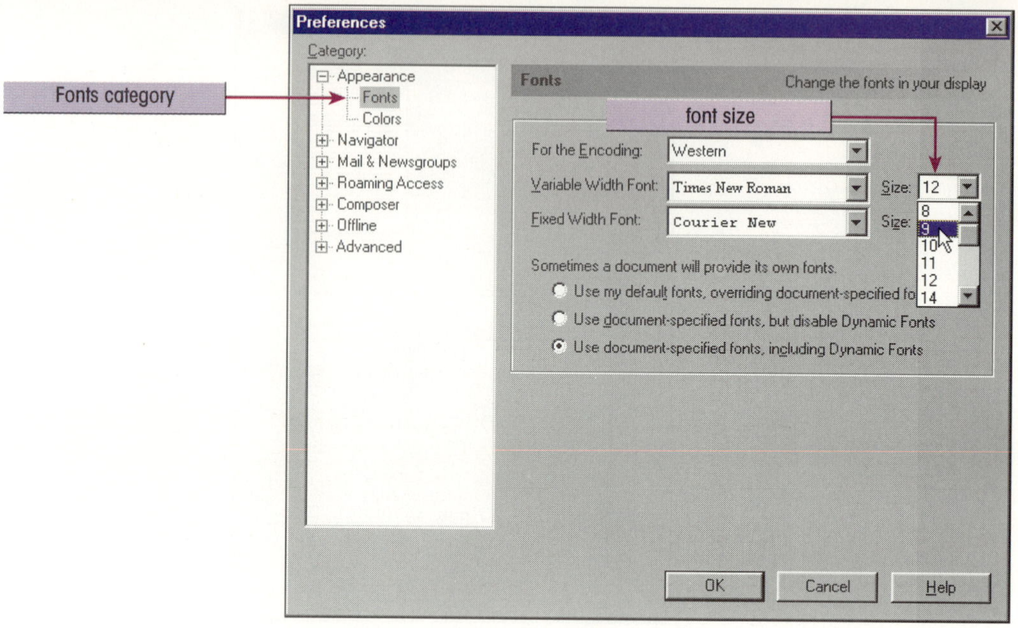

Checking Web Page Security Features

The **Security** button on the Navigation toolbar lets you check some of the security elements of a Web page. This button displays either an open padlock icon or a closed padlock icon. The icon on the Security button will correspond to the icon displayed in the left section of the status bar at the bottom of the Web page to indicate whether the Web page was encrypted during transmission from the Web server. **Encryption** is a way of scrambling and encoding data transmissions that reduces the risk that a person who intercepts the Web page as it travels across the Internet will be able to decode and read the page's contents. Web sites use encrypted transmission to send and receive information, such as credit card numbers, to ensure privacy. You can obtain more information about the details of the encryption used on a Web page by examining the Security Info dialog box that opens when you click the Security button on the Navigation toolbar. Figure 3-29 shows the Security Info dialog box for an encrypted Web page after the user clicked the Security button on the Navigation toolbar.

TUTORIAL 3 BROWSER BASICS WEB 3.35 INTERNET

Figure 3-29 SECURITY INFO WINDOW FOR AN ENCRYPTED WEB PAGE

Getting Help in Netscape Navigator

The Netscape Communicator suite includes a comprehensive online Help facility for all of the programs in the suite, including Navigator. You open the Help Contents window to use Help.

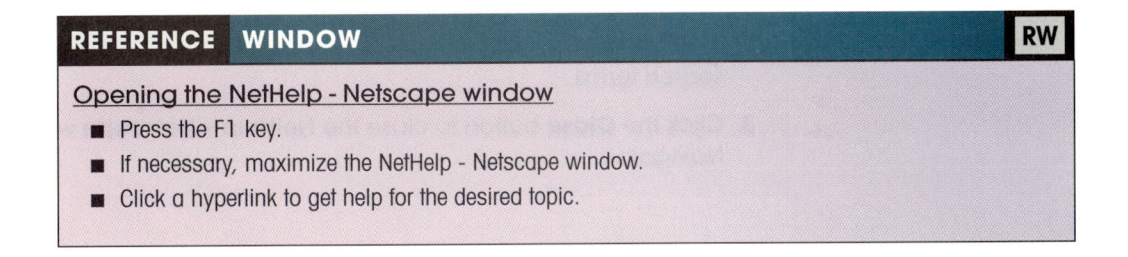

REFERENCE WINDOW RW

Opening the NetHelp - Netscape window
- Press the F1 key.
- If necessary, maximize the NetHelp - Netscape window.
- Click a hyperlink to get help for the desired topic.

To open the Navigator help window:

1. Press the **F1** key, and then click the **Maximize** button on the NetHelp - Netscape window, which provides help for all the programs in the Netscape Communicator Suite.

2. Click the **Browsing the Web** hyperlink to get help for the Navigator program. Examine the page shown in Figure 3-30, and use the scroll box or scroll down button to move down the page.

Figure 3-30 OPENING THE NETHELP - NETSCAPE WINDOW

- Contents icon
- Index icon
- hyperlinks to Help contents
- Back button
- Forward button
- Print Help topic button
- Exit Help button

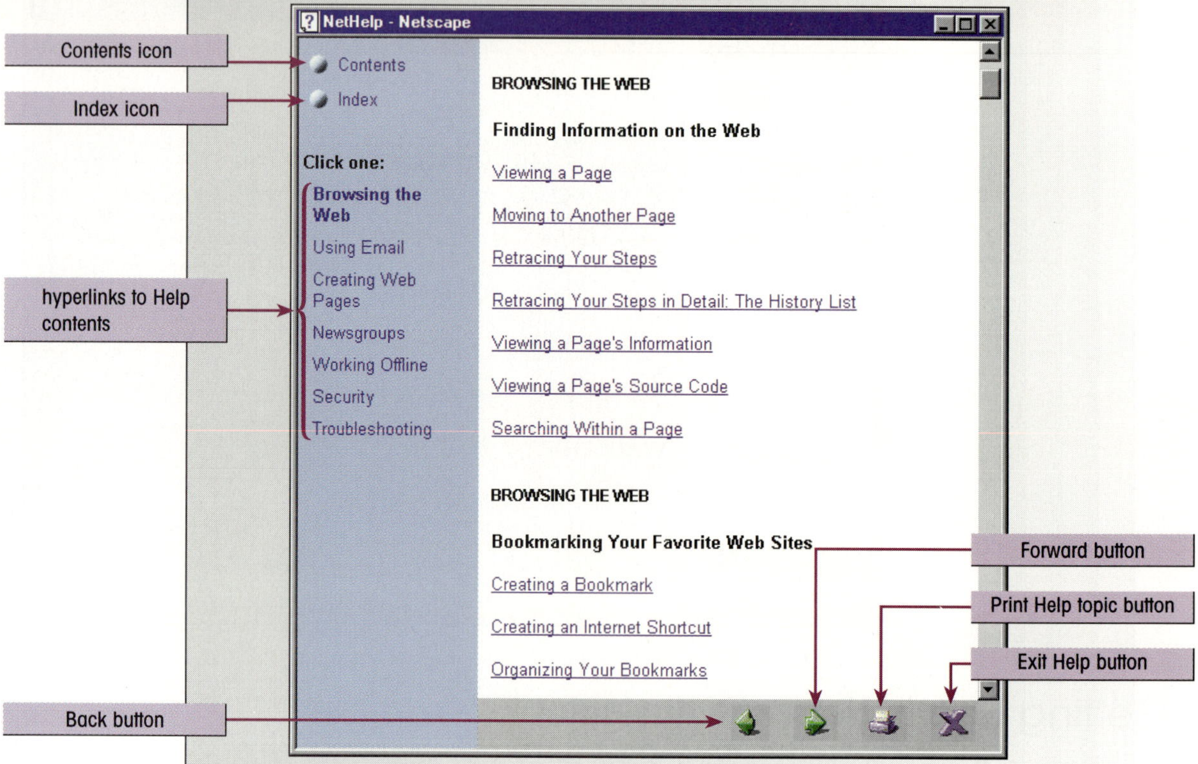

You can click any of the Contents hyperlinks to obtain help on the topics listed. You can also click the Index icon to obtain an alphabetized, searchable list of hyperlinks to specific terms used in the Netscape Help pages, or you can click the Find icon, which opens the standard Windows Find dialog box, and enter search terms.

3. Click the **Close** button to close the NetHelp – Netscape window and return to Navigator.

You are now convinced that you have all of the tools you need to successfully find information on the Web. Marianna probably will be interested in seeing the Pennsylvania Quintet Web page, but you are not sure if she will have Internet access while she's touring. Maggie says that you can save the Web page on disk, so Marianna can open the page locally in her Web browser using the files you saved on that disk.

Using Navigator to Save a Web Page

You have learned how to use most of the Navigator tools for loading Web pages and saving bookmarks. Now, Maggie wants you to learn how to save a Web page. Sometimes, you will want to store entire Web pages on disk; at other times, you will only want to store selected portions of Web page text or particular graphics from a Web page.

Saving a Web Page

You like the Pennsylvania Quintet's Web site and want to save the page on disk so you can send it to Marianna. That way, she can review it without having an Internet connection. To save a Web page, you must have the page open in Navigator.

REFERENCE WINDOW

Saving a Web page to a floppy disk
- Open the Web page in Navigator.
- Click File on the menu bar, and then click Save As to open the Save As dialog box.
- Click the Save in list arrow, and change to the drive on which to save the Web page.
- Accept the default filename, or change the filename, if you want; however, retain the file extension .htm or .html.
- Click the Save button to save the Web page to the floppy disk.

To save the Web page on your Data Disk:

1. Use your bookmark to return to the Pennsylvania Quintet page.

2. Click **File** on the menu bar, and then click **Save As** to open the Save As dialog box.

3. Click the **Save in** list arrow, click the drive that contains your Data Disk (usually, this is 3½ Floppy (A:)), and then double-click the **Tutorial.03** folder. You will accept the default filename of paquintet.htm.

4. Click the **Save** button. Now the HTML document for the Pennsylvania Quintet's home page is saved on your Data Disk. When you send it to Marianna, she can open her Web browser and then use the Open command on the File menu to open the Web page.

If the Web page contains graphics, such as photos, drawings, or icons, you should note that these items will not be saved with the HTML document. To save the graphics, right-click them in the browser window, click Save Image As, and then save the graphic to the same location as the Web's HTML document. The graphics file is specified to appear on the HTML document as a hyperlink, so you might have to change the HTML code in the Web page to identify its location. Copying the graphics files to the same disk as the HTML document will *usually* work.

Saving Web Page Text to a File

Maggie suggests that you might want to know how to save portions of Web page text to a file, so that you can save only the text from the Web page and use it in other programs. You will use WordPad to receive the text you will copy from a Web page, but any word processor or text editor will work.

Marianna just called to let you know that the quintet will play a concert in Cleveland on a Friday night, and she asks you to identify other opportunities for scheduling local concerts during the following weekend. Often, museums are willing to book small ensembles for weekend afternoon programs, and Marianna has given you the URL for the Cleveland Museum of Art. You will visit the site and then get the museum's address and telephone number so you can contact it about scheduling a concert.

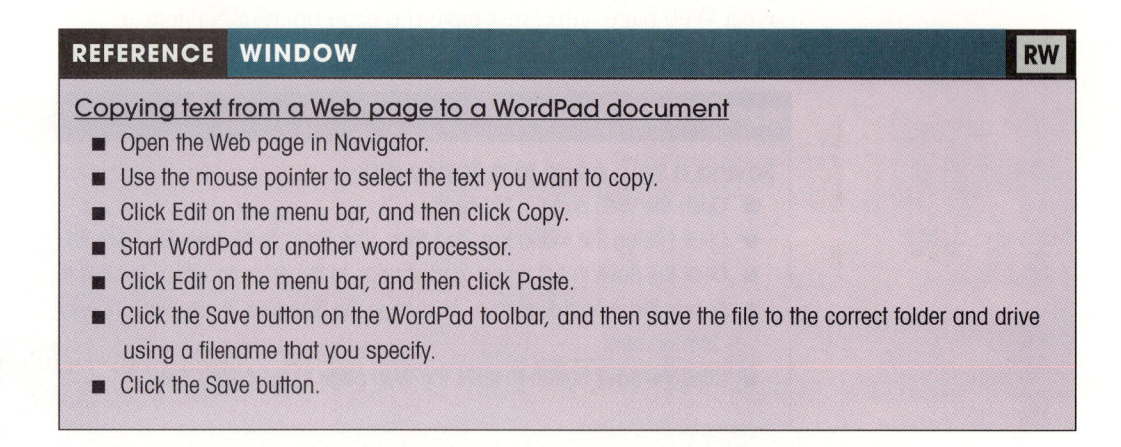

REFERENCE WINDOW RW

Copying text from a Web page to a WordPad document
- Open the Web page in Navigator.
- Use the mouse pointer to select the text you want to copy.
- Click Edit on the menu bar, and then click Copy.
- Start WordPad or another word processor.
- Click Edit on the menu bar, and then click Paste.
- Click the Save button on the WordPad toolbar, and then save the file to the correct folder and drive using a filename that you specify.
- Click the Save button.

To copy text from a Web page and save it to a file:

1. Use the **Back** button to return to the Student Online Companion page, and then click the **Cleveland Museum of Art** link to open that Web page in the browser window.

2. Click the **address** hyperlink in the left frame on the Web page to open the museum information page in the main (right) frame.

3. Click and drag the mouse pointer over the address and telephone number to select it, as shown in Figure 3-31.

Figure 3-31   SELECTING TEXT ON A WEB PAGE

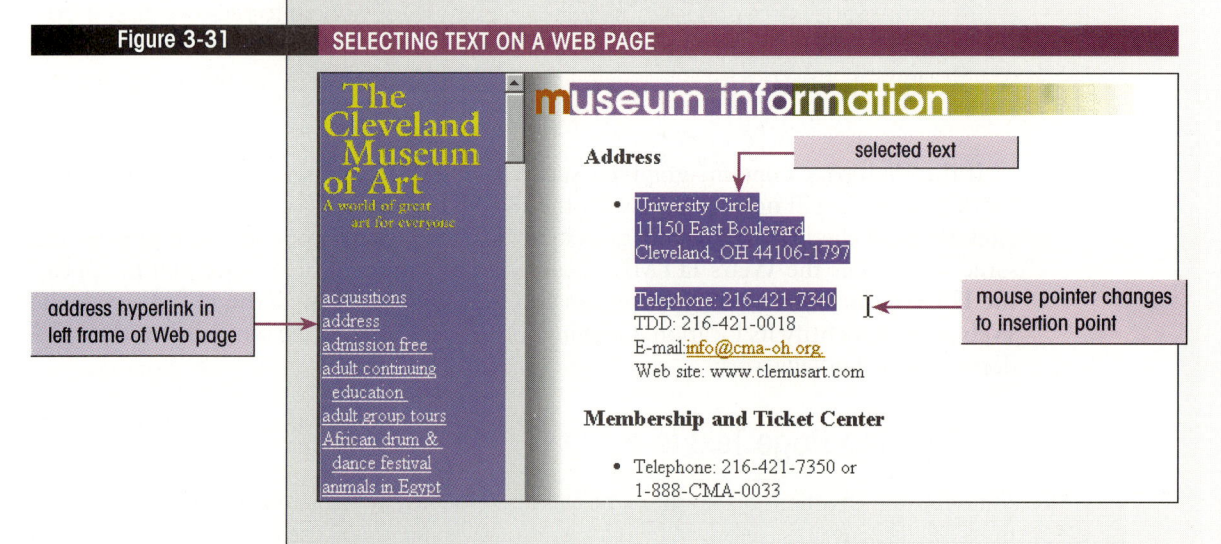

- address hyperlink in left frame of Web page
- selected text
- mouse pointer changes to insertion point

museum information

Address
- University Circle
  11150 East Boulevard
  Cleveland, OH 44106-1797

Telephone: 216-421-7340
TDD: 216-421-0018
E-mail: info@cma-oh.org
Web site: www.clemusart.com

Membership and Ticket Center
- Telephone: 216-421-7350 or 1-888-CMA-0033

Left frame links: acquisitions, address, admission free, adult continuing education, adult group tours, African drum & dance festival, animals in Egypt

The Cleveland Museum of Art — A world of great art for everyone

4. Click **Edit** on the menu bar, and then click **Copy** to copy the selected text to the Windows Clipboard.

Now, you can start WordPad and paste the copied text into a new document.

To start and copy the text into WordPad:

1. Click the **Start** button on the taskbar, point to **Programs**, point to **Accessories**, and then click **WordPad** to start the program and open a new document.

2. Click the **Paste** button on the WordPad toolbar to paste the text into the WordPad document, as shown in Figure 3-32.

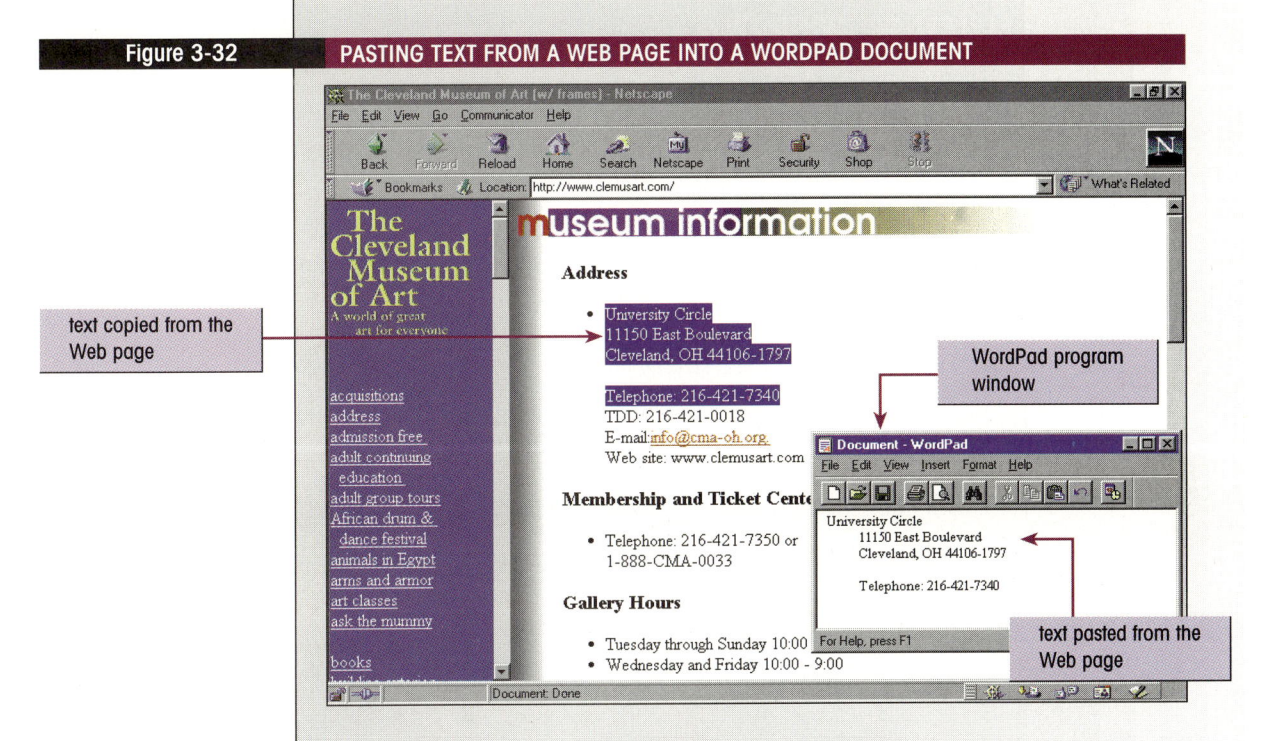

Figure 3-32   PASTING TEXT FROM A WEB PAGE INTO A WORDPAD DOCUMENT

text copied from the Web page

WordPad program window

text pasted from the Web page

TROUBLE? If the WordPad toolbar does not appear, click View on the menu bar, click Toolbar to turn it on, and then repeat Step 2. Your WordPad program window might be a different size from the one shown in Figure 3-32, which does not affect the steps.

3. Click the **Save** button on the WordPad toolbar to open the Save As dialog box.

4. Click the **Save in** list arrow, change to the drive that contains your Data Disk, and then double-click the **Tutorial.03** folder.

5. Select any text that is in the File name text box, type **CMoA-Address.txt**, and then click the **Save** button to save the file. Now, the address and phone number of the museum is saved in a file on your Data Disk for future reference.

6. Click the **Close** button on the WordPad title bar to close it.

Later, you will contact the museum. As you examine the hyperlinks in the left frame of the Cleveland Museum of Art Web page, you notice a hyperlink titled "how to get here." Clicking the "how to get here" hyperlink loads a page that contains directions and information about transportation to the museum. You find that it includes a hyperlink to a street map of the area surrounding the museum.

Saving a Web Page Graphic to Disk

You decide that the Web page with directions and transportation information might be helpful to Marianna, so you decide to save the map graphic on your disk. You can then send the file to Marianna so she has a resource for getting to the museum.

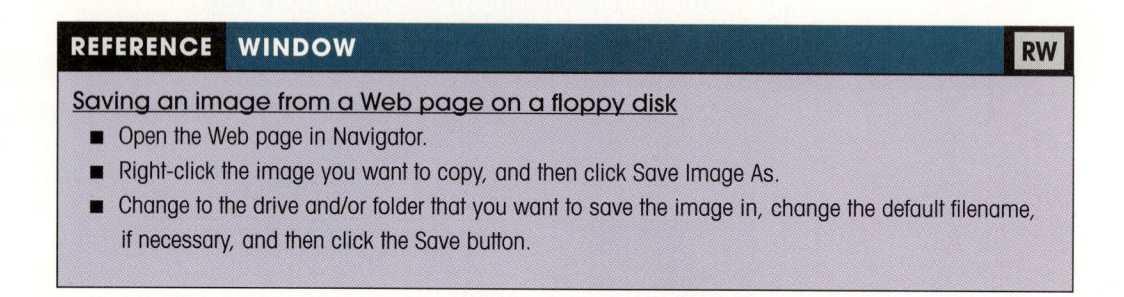

REFERENCE WINDOW

Saving an image from a Web page on a floppy disk
- Open the Web page in Navigator.
- Right-click the image you want to copy, and then click Save Image As.
- Change to the drive and/or folder that you want to save the image in, change the default filename, if necessary, and then click the Save button.

To save the street map image on a floppy disk:

1. Click the **how to get here** hyperlink in the left frame of the Cleveland Museum's home page, and then click the **street map** hyperlink on the Getting around - Directions and Transportation Web page in the main (right) frame. Do not click the hyperlink to the Adobe download version of the map.

2. Right-click the map image to open its shortcut menu, as shown in Figure 3-33.

Figure 3-33   SAVING THE MAP IMAGE TO DISK

map image — shortcut menu for the map image

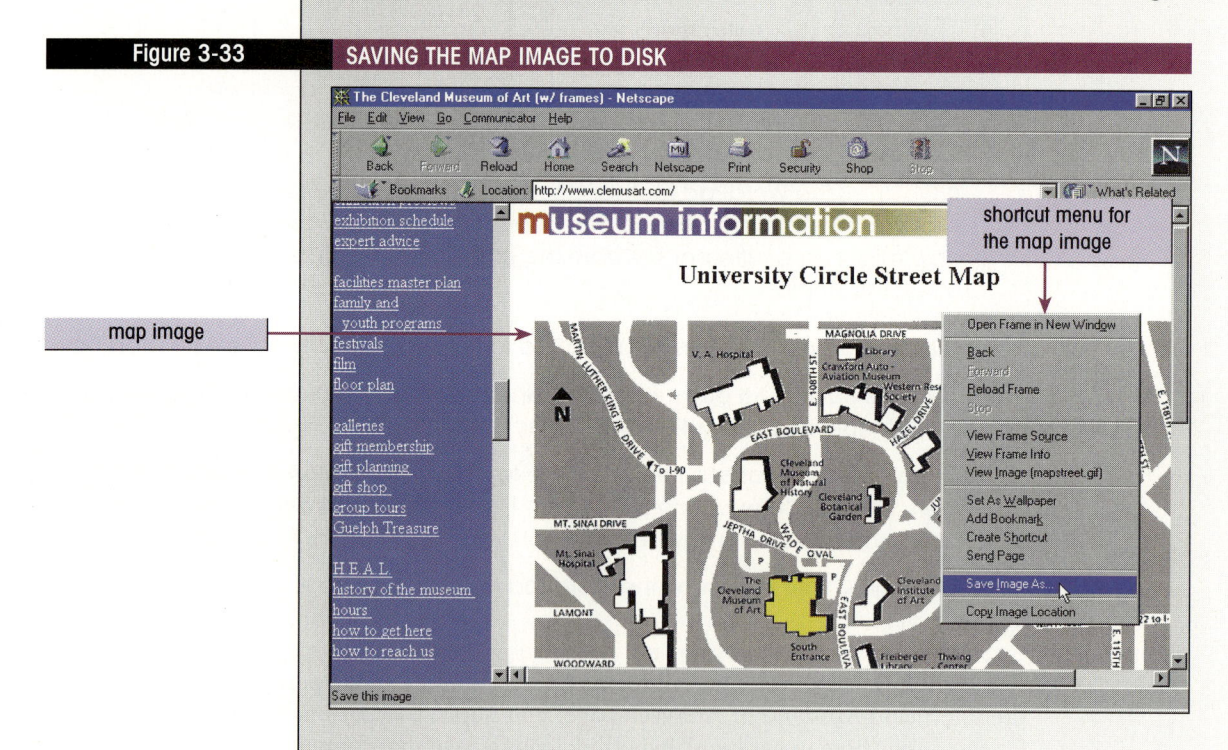

3. Click **Save Image As** on the shortcut menu to open the Save As dialog box.

TUTORIAL 3 BROWSER BASICS WEB 3.41 INTERNET

> 4. Click the Save in list arrow, change to the drive that contains your Data Disk, and double-click the **Tutorial.03** folder, if necessary. You will accept the default filename, mapstreet, so click the **Save** button. Now the image is saved on your Data Disk, and you can send the file to Marianna. Marianna can use her Web browser to open the image file and print it.
>
> 5. Close your Web browser and your dial-up connection, if necessary.

Now you can send a disk to Marianna so she has the Pennsylvania Wind Quintet Web page and a map that shows her how to get to the museum. Marianna is pleased to hear of your progress in using the Web to find information for the quintet.

Session 3.2 QUICK CHECK

1. Describe three ways to load a Web page in the Navigator browser.
2. You can use the _____ in Navigator to visit previously visited sites during your Web session.
3. When would you use the Reload command?
4. What happens when you click the Home button on the Navigation toolbar?
5. Some Web servers _____ Web pages before returning them to the client to prevent unauthorized access.
6. True or False: You can identify an encrypted Web page when viewing it in Navigator.
7. What is a Netscape Navigator bookmark?

If your instructor assigns Session 3.3, continue reading. Otherwise, complete the Review Assignments at the end of this tutorial.

SESSION 3.3

In this session, you will learn how to configure the Microsoft Internet Explorer Web browser and use it to display Web pages. You will learn how to use Internet Explorer to follow hyperlinks from one Web page to another and how to record the URLs of sites to which you would like to return. Also, you will print and save Web pages.

Starting Microsoft Internet Explorer

Microsoft Internet Explorer is Microsoft's Web browser that installs with Windows 95, Windows 98, or Windows 2000. This introduction assumes that you have Internet Explorer installed on your computer. You should have your computer turned on and open to the Windows desktop to begin.

> ### To start Internet Explorer:
>
> 1. Click the **Start** button on the taskbar, point to **Programs**, point to **Internet Explorer**, and then click **Internet Explorer**. After a moment, Internet Explorer opens.

TROUBLE? If you cannot find Internet Explorer on the Programs menu, check to see if an Internet Explorer shortcut icon appears on the desktop, and then double-click it. If you do not see the shortcut icon, ask your instructor or technical support person for help. The program might be installed in a different folder on your computer.

2. If the program does not fill the screen entirely, click the **Maximize** button on the Internet Explorer program's title bar. Your screen should look like Figure 3-34.

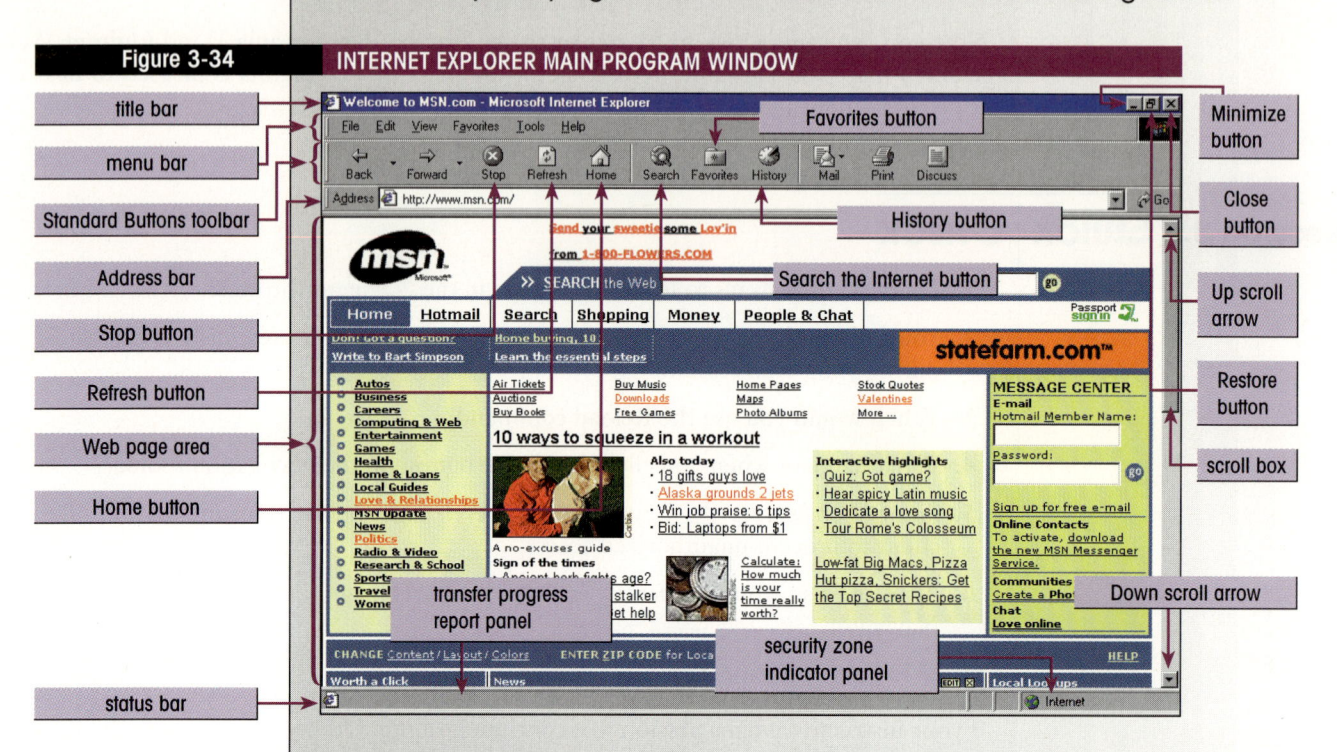

Figure 3-34 INTERNET EXPLORER MAIN PROGRAM WINDOW

Labels: title bar, menu bar, Standard Buttons toolbar, Address bar, Stop button, Refresh button, Web page area, Home button, transfer progress report panel, status bar, Favorites button, History button, Search the Internet button, security zone indicator panel, Minimize button, Close button, Up scroll arrow, Restore button, scroll box, Down scroll arrow

TROUBLE? Figure 3-34 shows the Microsoft Network home page, which is the page that Internet Explorer opens the first time it starts. Your computer might be configured to open to a different Web page or no page at all.

TROUBLE? If you do not see the bars shown in Figure 3-34, click View on the menu bar, point to Toolbars, and then click the name of the bar that you want to turn on.

Internet Explorer includes a Standard Buttons toolbar with 12 buttons. Many of these buttons execute frequently used commands for browsing the Web. Figure 3-35 shows these buttons and describes their functions.

Figure 3-35 STANDARD BUTTONS TOOLBAR BUTTON FUNCTIONS

BUTTON	BUTTON NAME	DESCRIPTION
Back	Back	Moves to the last previously visited Web page
Forward	Forward	Moves to the next previously visited Web page
Stop	Stop	Stops the transfer of a new Web page
Refresh	Refresh	Reloads the current page
Home	Home	Loads the program's defined start page
Search	Search	Opens a Search frame in the Internet Explorer window, which displays a Web search engine chosen by Microsoft
Favorites	Favorites	Opens the Favorites frame in the Internet Explorer window, which allows you to return to Web pages that you have saved as favorites
History	History	Opens the History frame in the Internet Explorer window, which allows you to choose from a list of Web pages that you have visited recently
Mail	Mail	Opens the e-mail program specified in the Internet Options settings
Print	Print	Prints the current Web page
Edit	Edit	Opens the current Web page for editing in the default HTML page editor (button varies depending on the default page editor)
Discuss	Discuss	Opens a link to a discussion server (if your computer is connected to one)

Now that you understand how to start Internet Explorer, you tell Maggie that you are ready to start using it to find information on the Internet. To find information, you need to know about the different Internet Explorer functions.

Status Bar

The **status bar** at the bottom of the window includes several panels that give you information about Internet Explorer's operations. The first panel—the **transfer progress report**—presents status messages that show, for example, the URL of a page while it is loading. When a page is completely loaded, this panel displays the text "Done" until you move the mouse over a hyperlink. This panel displays the URL of any hyperlink on the page when you move the mouse pointer over it. This panel also shows a blue **graphical transfer progress indicator** that moves from left to right in the right side of the panel to indicate how much of a Web page has loaded while Internet Explorer is loading it from a Web server. This indicator is especially useful for monitoring progress when you are loading large Web pages.

The third status bar panel displays a locked padlock icon when the browser loads a Web page that has a security certificate. You can double-click on the padlock icon to open a dialog box that contains information about the security certificate for a Web page.

The fourth (rightmost) status bar panel displays the **security zone** to which the page you are viewing has been assigned. As part of its security features, Internet Explorer lets you classify Web pages by the security risk you believe they present. You can open the Internet Security Properties dialog box shown in Figure 3-36 by double-clicking the third status bar panel. This window lets you set four levels of security-enforcing procedures: High, Medium, Medium-Low, and Low. In general, the higher level of security you set for your browser, the slower it will operate. Higher security settings also disable some of the browser features. You can click the Custom Level button to configure the way each security level operates on your computer.

Figure 3-36   INTERNET SECURITY PROPERTIES DIALOG BOX

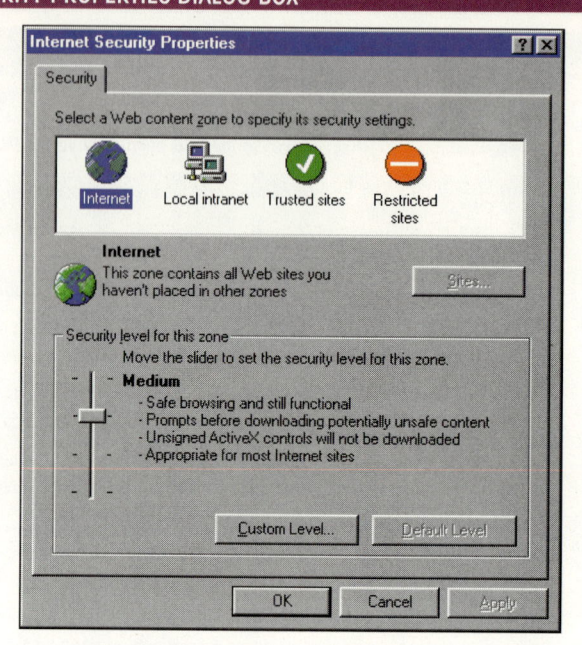

Menu Bar

In addition to the standard Windows commands, the menu bar also provides access to Favorites. The **Favorites** menu command lets you store and organize URLs of sites that you have visited.

Hiding and Showing the Internet Explorer Toolbars

Internet Explorer lets you hide its toolbars to show more of the Web page area. The easiest way to increase the display area for a Web page is to click View (on the menu bar), then click Full Screen.

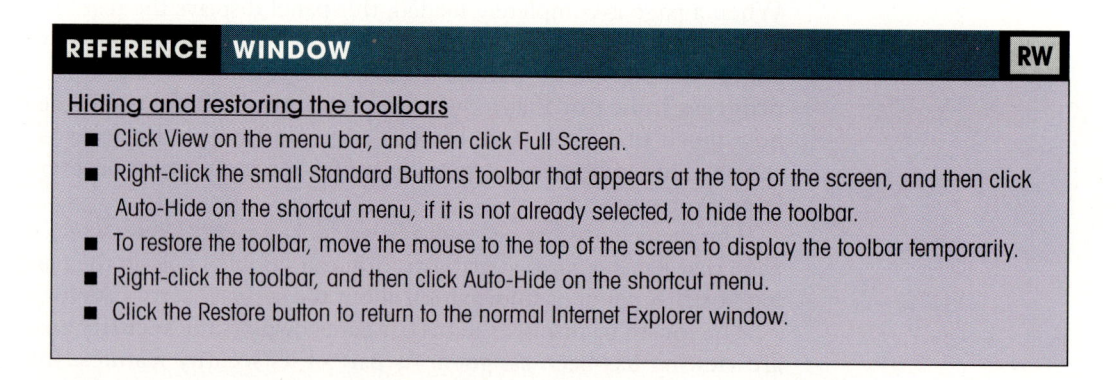

REFERENCE WINDOW

Hiding and restoring the toolbars
- Click View on the menu bar, and then click Full Screen.
- Right-click the small Standard Buttons toolbar that appears at the top of the screen, and then click Auto-Hide on the shortcut menu, if it is not already selected, to hide the toolbar.
- To restore the toolbar, move the mouse to the top of the screen to display the toolbar temporarily.
- Right-click the toolbar, and then click Auto-Hide on the shortcut menu.
- Click the Restore button to return to the normal Internet Explorer window.

To use the Full Screen command and Auto Hide:

1. Click **View** on the menu bar, then click **Full Screen**.

2. Right-click the small Standard Buttons toolbar that appears at the top of the screen to open the shortcut menu, and then click **Auto-Hide** on the shortcut menu if it is not already checked.

3. Move the mouse pointer away from the top of the screen for a moment. Now, you can see more of the Web page area. When the toolbar disappears, return the mouse pointer to the top of the screen to display it again.

4. With the toolbar displayed, right-click the toolbar and then click **Auto-Hide** on the shortcut menu. This removes the check mark from the Auto-Hide entry on the menu and turns the toolbar on again.

5. Click the **Restore** button to return to the normal Internet Explorer window.

You can use the commands on the View menu (and its Toolbars submenu) to **toggle**, or turn on and off, the individual toolbars. Also, you can use the Customize command on the View/Toolbars menu to change the appearance of the toolbars. For example, you can show the Standard Buttons toolbar buttons with or without the text labels that describe each button's function.

Entering a URL in the Address Bar

Maggie tells you that you can use the **Address Bar** to enter URLs directly into Internet Explorer. Marianna gave you the URL for the Pennsylvania Quintet, so you can see its Web page.

REFERENCE WINDOW

Entering a URL in the Address Bar
- Click at the end of the current text in the Address Bar, and then backspace over the text that you want to delete.
- Type the URL of the location that you want.
- Press the Enter key to load the URL's Web page in the browser window.

To load the Pennsylvania Quintet's Web page:

1. Click in the Address Bar; if there is text in the Address Bar, click at the end of the text, and then press the **Backspace** key to delete it.

   TROUBLE? Make sure that you delete all of the text in the Address Bar so the text you type in Step 2 will be correct.

2. Type **http://www.course.com/newperspectives/internet2/** in the Address Bar to go to the Student Online Companion page on the Course Technology Web site. In this book, you will go to the Course Technology site and then click hyperlinks to go to individual Web pages.

3. Press the **Enter** key. After you press the Enter key, the Student Online Companion Web page loads, as shown in Figure 3-37. When the entire page has loaded, the graphical transfer progress indicator in the status bar will stop moving and the transfer progress report panel will display the text "Done."

Figure 3-37   STUDENT ONLINE COMPANION WEB PAGE

TROUBLE? If a Dial-Up Networking dialog box opens after you press the Enter key, click the Connect button. You must have an Internet connection to complete the steps in this tutorial.

4. Click the link for the book you are using to open the main page, click the **Tutorial 3** link to open the page that contains the links for this tutorial, and then click the **Session 3.3** link in the left frame.

5. Click the link to the **Pennsylvania Quintet** in the right frame. The Web page opens, as shown in Figure 3-38.

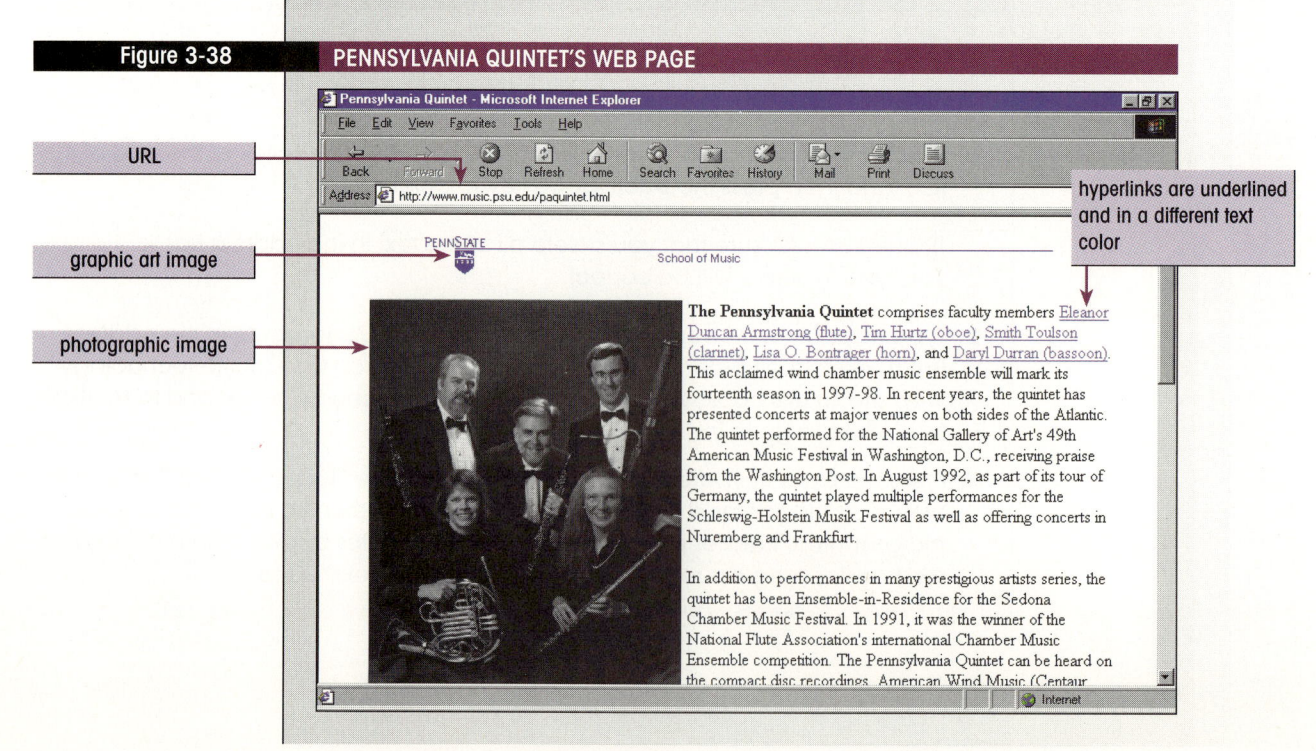

Figure 3-38   PENNSYLVANIA QUINTET'S WEB PAGE

- URL
- graphic art image
- photographic image
- hyperlinks are underlined and in a different text color

> **TROUBLE?** The Pennsylvania Quintet might change its Web page, so your Web page might look different from the one shown in Figure 3-38. If this Web page is deleted from the server, you might see an entirely different Web page. However, the steps should work the same.
>
> 6. Read the Web page, and then click the **Back** button to return to the Student Online Companion page.

You like the format of the Pennsylvania Quintet's home page, so you want to make sure that you can go back to that page later if you need to review its contents. Maggie explains that you can write down the URL so you can refer to it later, but an easier way is to use the Favorites feature to store the URL for future use.

Using the Favorites Feature

Internet Explorer's **Favorites feature** lets you store and organize a list of Web pages that you have visited so you can return to them easily. The **Favorites** button on the Standard Buttons toolbar opens the Favorites frame shown in Figure 3-39. You can use the Favorites frame to open URLs you have stored as Favorites.

Figure 3-39 FAVORITES FRAME

- Favorites button
- closed favorites folder
- open favorites folder

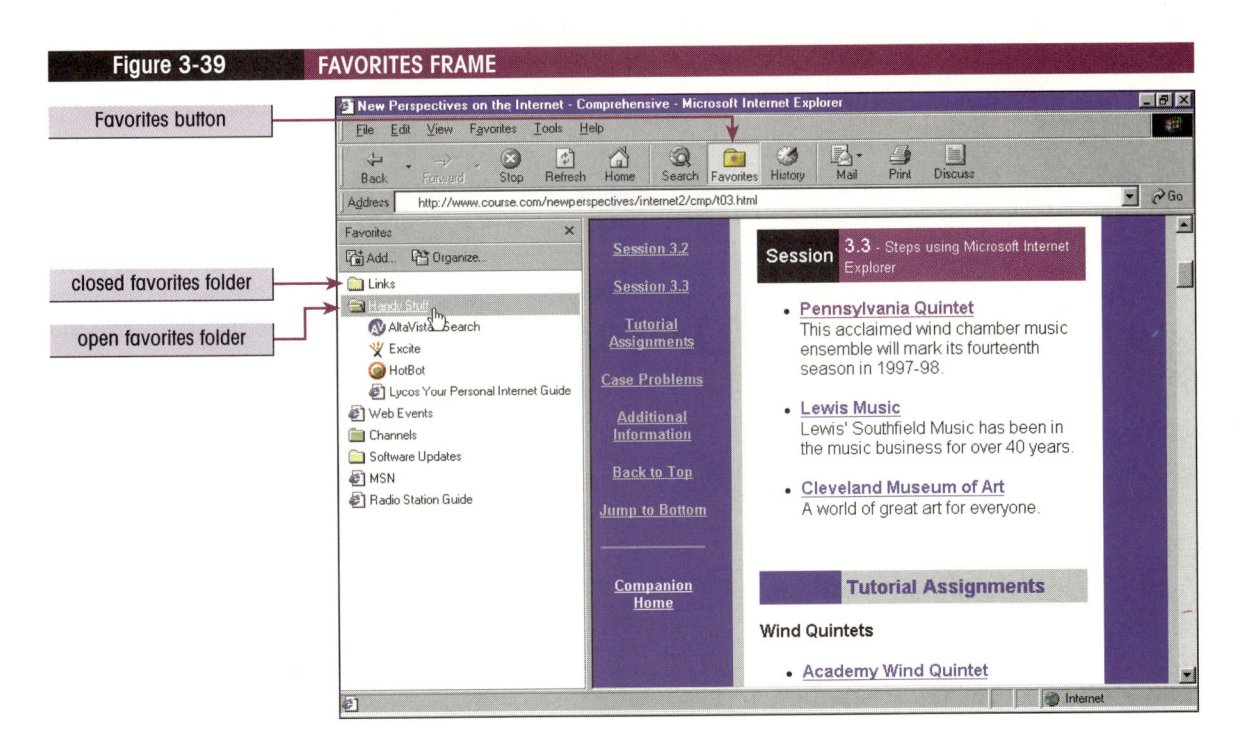

Figure 3-39 shows the hierarchical structure of the Favorites feature. This user stored four search engine Web pages in a folder named "Handy Stuff." You can organize your favorites in the way that best suits your needs and working style.

You decide to save the Pennsylvania Quintet's Web page as a favorite in a Wind Quintet Information folder.

> **REFERENCE WINDOW**
>
> **Creating a new Favorites folder**
> - Open the Web page in Internet Explorer.
> - Click the Favorites button on the Standard Buttons toolbar to open the Favorites frame.
> - Click Favorites on the menu bar, and then click Add to Favorites.
> - If the Create in window of the Add Favorite dialog box is not displayed, click the Create in button in the Add Favorite dialog box.
> - Click the Favorites folder, and then click the New Folder button.
> - Type the name of the new folder in the Folder name text box, and then click the OK button.
> - Click the OK button in the Add Favorite dialog box.

To create a new Favorites folder:

1. Click the **Forward** button on the Standard Buttons toolbar to return to the Pennsylvania Quintet Web page.

2. Click the **Favorites** button on the Standard Buttons toolbar to open the Favorites frame.

3. Click **Favorites** on the menu bar, and then click **Add to Favorites** to open the Add Favorite dialog box.

4. If the Create in window of the Add Favorite dialog box is not displayed, click the **Create in** button.

5. Click the **Favorites** folder in the Create in window, and then click the **New Folder** button to create a new folder in the Favorites folder.

6. Type **Wind Quintet Information** in the Folder name text box of the Create New Folder dialog box, and then click the **OK** button to close the Create New Folder dialog box. See Figure 3-40. Notice that the page name appears automatically in the Name text box in the Add Favorite dialog box. You can change the page name if you wish by editing the suggested page name.

TUTORIAL 3 BROWSER BASICS   WEB 3.49   INTERNET

Figure 3-40   **CREATING A NEW FAVORITES FOLDER**

new folder in Favorites frame →

new folder in Add Favorite dialog box →

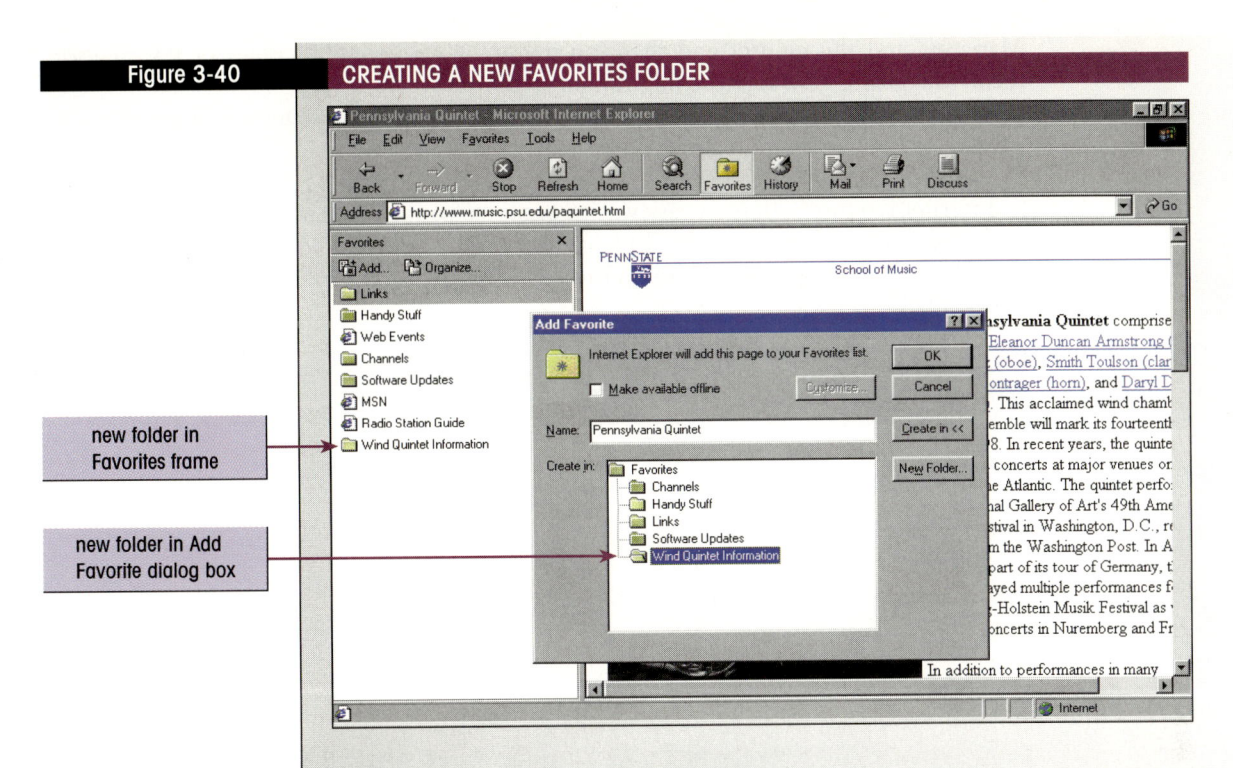

7. Click the **OK** button to close the Add Favorite dialog box. Now, the favorite is saved in Internet Explorer. You can test the favorite by opening it from the Favorites frame.

8. Click the **Back** button on the Standard Buttons toolbar to return to the previous page, click the **Wind Quintet Information** folder in the Favorites frame to open it, and then click **Pennsylvania Quintet**. The Pennsylvania Quintet page opens in the browser, which means that you created the favorite correctly.

   TROUBLE? If the Pennsylvania Quintet page does not open, click Favorites on the menu bar, click the Wind Quintet Information folder, right-click the Pennsylvania Quintet favorite, and then click Properties. Click the Internet Shortcut tab and make sure that a URL appears in the Target URL text box. If there is no URL, then click the OK button to close the dialog box, click Favorites on the menu bar, click the Wind Quintet Information folder, right-click the Pennsylvania Quintet folder, and then click Delete. Repeat the steps to recreate the favorite, and then try again. If you still have trouble, ask your instructor or technical support person for help.

As you use the Web to find information about wind quintets and other sites of interest for the group, you might find yourself creating many favorites so you can return to sites of interest. When you start accumulating favorites, it is important to keep them organized, as you will see next.

Organizing Favorites

You explain to Maggie that you have created a new folder for Wind Quintet Information in the Internet Explorer Favorites frame and stored the Pennsylvania Quintet's URL in that folder. Maggie suggests that you might not want to keep all of the wind quintet-related information you gather in one folder. She notes that you are just beginning your work for

Marianna and the quintet and that you might be collecting all types of information for them. Maggie suggests that you might want to put information about the Pennsylvania Quintet in a separate folder named East Coast Ensembles under the Wind Quintet Information folder. As you collect information about other performers, you might add folders for Midwest and West Coast ensembles, too.

Internet Explorer offers an easy way to organize your folders in a hierarchical structure—even after you have stored them. To rearrange URLs or even folders within folders, you use the Organize Favorites command on the Favorites menu.

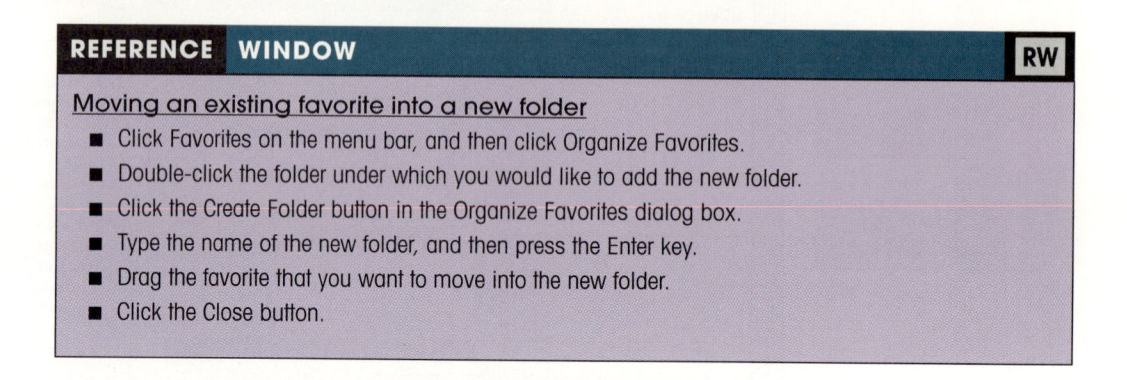

REFERENCE WINDOW	RW

Moving an existing favorite into a new folder
- Click Favorites on the menu bar, and then click Organize Favorites.
- Double-click the folder under which you would like to add the new folder.
- Click the Create Folder button in the Organize Favorites dialog box.
- Type the name of the new folder, and then press the Enter key.
- Drag the favorite that you want to move into the new folder.
- Click the Close button.

To move an existing favorite into a new folder:

1. Click **Favorites** on the menu bar, and then click **Organize Favorites**.

2. Double-click the **Wind Quintet Information** folder in the Organize Favorites dialog box.

3. Click the **Create Folder** button in the Organize Favorites dialog box.

4. Type **East Coast Ensembles** to replace the "New Folder" selected text, and then press the **Enter** key to rename the folder.

5. Click and drag the Pennsylvania Quintet favorite to the new East Coast Ensembles folder, and then release the mouse button. Now, the East Coast Ensembles folder contains the favorite, as shown in Figure 3-41.

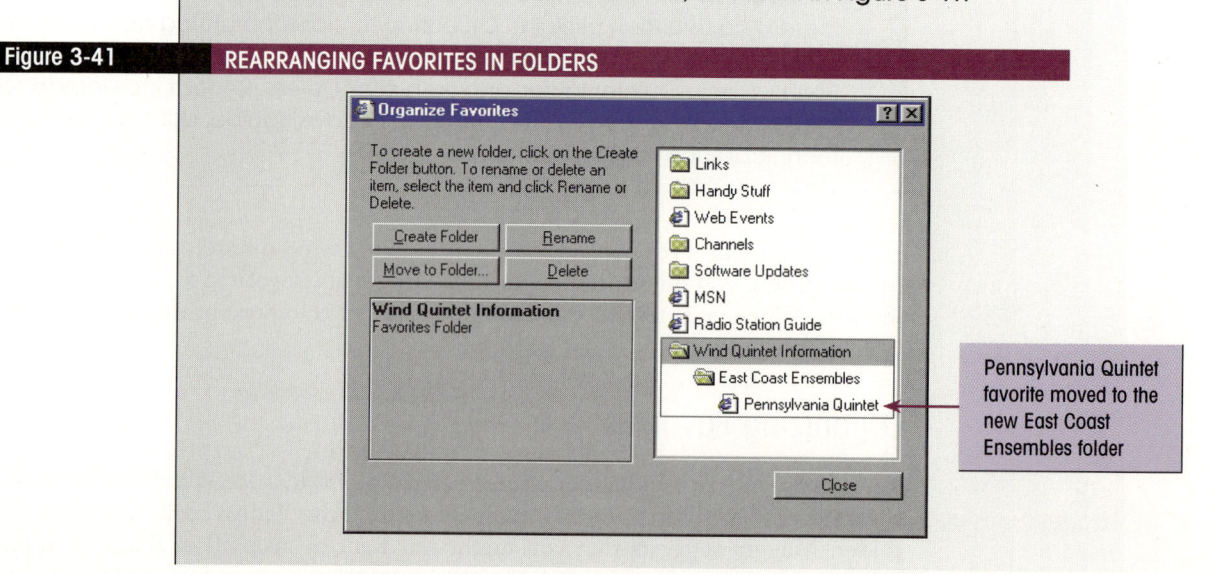

Figure 3-41 REARRANGING FAVORITES IN FOLDERS

Pennsylvania Quintet favorite moved to the new East Coast Ensembles folder

6. Click the **Close** button to close the Organize Favorites dialog box. The Favorites frame is updated automatically to reflect your changes.

7. Click the **Favorites** button on the Standard Buttons toolbar to close the Favorites list.

Hyperlink Navigation with the Mouse

Now you know how to use the Internet to find information that will help you with the Sunset Wind Quintet. Maggie tells you that the easiest way to move from one Web page to another is to use the mouse to click hyperlinks that the authors of Web pages embed in their HTML documents. You can also right-click the mouse on the background of a Web page to open a shortcut menu that includes navigation options.

REFERENCE WINDOW RW

Using hyperlinks and the mouse to navigate between Web pages
- Click the hyperlink.
- After the new Web page has loaded, right-click on the Web page's background.
- Click Back on the shortcut menu.

To follow a hyperlink to a Web page and return using the mouse:

1. Click the **Back** button on the Standard Buttons toolbar to go back to the Student Online Companion page, click the **Lewis Music** link to open that page, and then point to the **Instrument Accessories** hyperlink shown in Figure 3-42 so your pointer changes to 👆.

Figure 3-42   LEWIS MUSIC HOME PAGE

hyperlinks

URL

2. Click the **Instrument Accessories** hyperlink to load the page. Watch the first panel in the status bar—when it displays the text "Done," you know that Internet Explorer has loaded the full page.

3. Right-click anywhere in the Web page area that is not a hyperlink to display the shortcut menu, as shown in Figure 3-43.

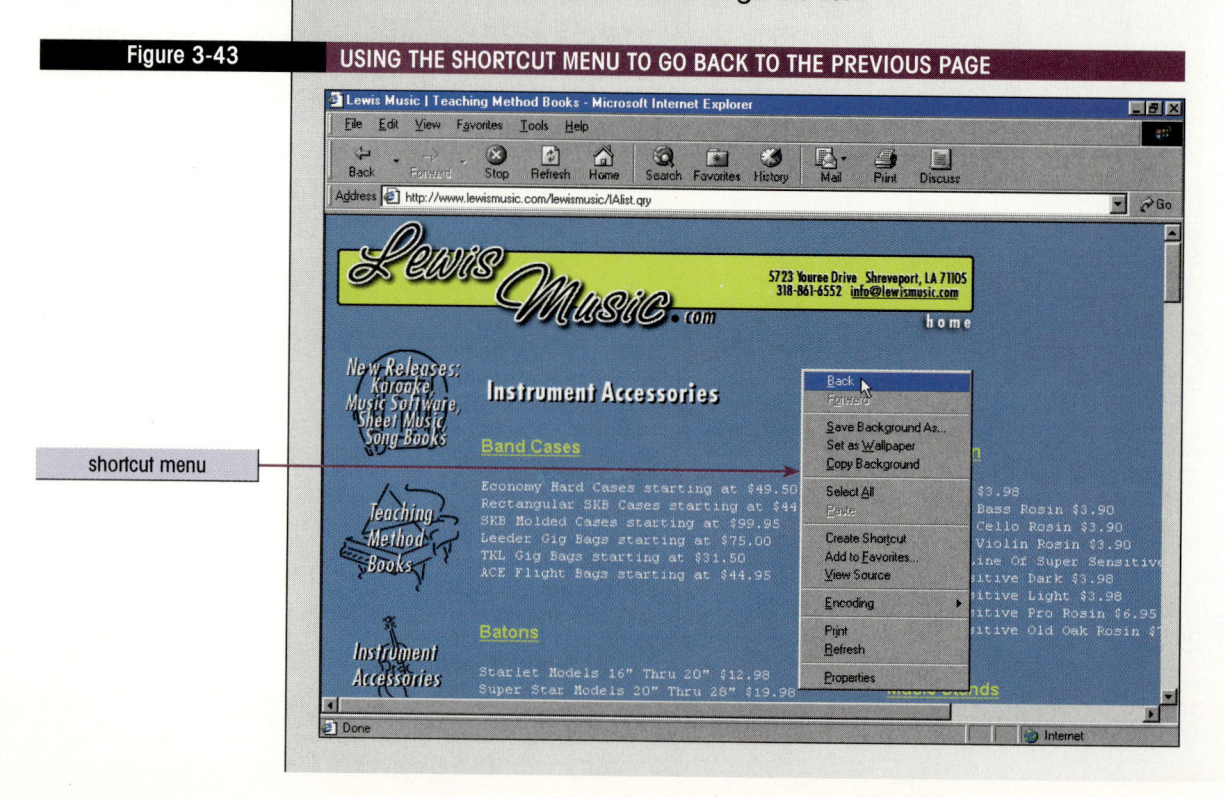

Figure 3-43   USING THE SHORTCUT MENU TO GO BACK TO THE PREVIOUS PAGE

shortcut menu

> **TROUBLE?** If you right-click a hyperlink, your shortcut menu will display a shorter list than the one shown in Figure 3-43, and the Back item will not appear in the menu. If you do not see the shortcut menu shown in Figure 3-43, click anywhere outside of the shortcut menu to close it, and then repeat Step 3.
>
> **TROUBLE?** Web pages change frequently, so the Instrument Accessories page you see might look different from the one shown in Figure 3-43, but right-clicking anywhere on the Web page area that is not a hyperlink will still work.
>
> 4. Click **Back** on the shortcut menu to return to the Lewis Music home page.
> 5. Repeat Step 4 to return to the Student Online Companion page.

You are beginning to get a good sense of how to move from one Web page to another and back again, but Maggie tells you that you have mastered only one technique of many. She explains that the Standard Buttons toolbar and the menu bar offer many tools for accessing and using Web sites.

Using the History List

In Session 3.1 you learned that the Back and Forward buttons let you move to and from previously visited pages. You also can open a full copy of the history list.

> ### To view the history list for this session:
>
> 1. Click the **History** button on the Standard Buttons toolbar. The history list opens in a hierarchical structure in a separate window on the left side of the screen. The history list stores each URL you visited during the past week or during a specified time period. It also maintains the hierarchy of each Web site; that is, pages you visit at a particular Web site are stored in a separate folder for that site. To return to a particular page, click that page's entry in the list. You can see the full URL of any item in the History frame by moving the mouse pointer over the history list item, as shown in Figure 3-44.

Figure 3-44   **EXPLORING THE HISTORY LIST**

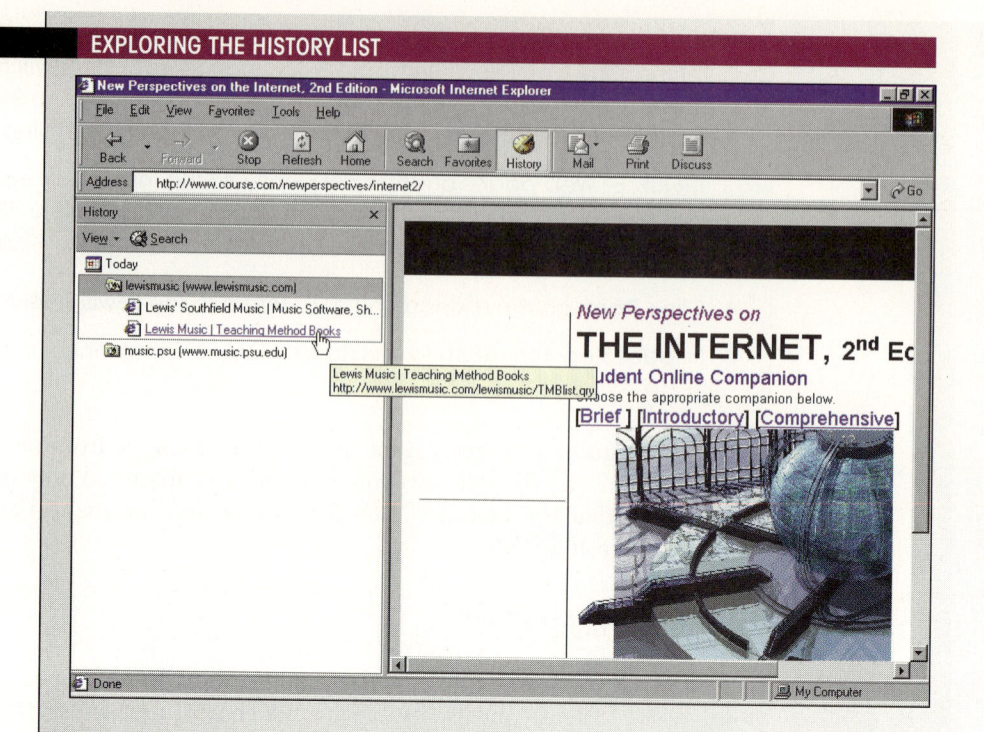

TROUBLE? Your History frame might be a different size from what appears in Figure 3-44. You can resize the window by clicking and dragging its left edge either right or left to make it narrower or wider.

2. Click the **Close** button on the History frame title bar to close it.

You can right-click any entry in the Internet Explorer history list and copy the URL or delete it from the list. Internet Explorer stores each history entry as a shortcut in a History folder, which is in the Windows folder.

Refreshing a Web Page

The **Refresh** button makes Microsoft Internet Explorer load a new copy of the current Web page that appears in the browser window. Internet Explorer stores a copy of every Web page it displays on your computer's hard drive in a **Temporary Internet Files** folder in the Windows folder. This increases the speed at which Internet Explorer can display pages as you move back and forth through the history list because the browser can load the pages from a local disk drive instead of reloading the page from the remote Web server. When you click the Refresh button, Internet Explorer contacts the Web server to see if the Web page has changed since it was stored in the cache folder. If it has changed, Internet Explorer gets the new page from the Web server; otherwise, it loads the cache folder copy.

Returning to Your Start Page

The **Home** button displays the home (or start) page for your copy of Internet Explorer. You can change the setting for the Home toolbar button, as you will see next.

TUTORIAL 3 BROWSER BASICS   WEB 3.55   INTERNET

REFERENCE WINDOW	RW

Changing the Home toolbar button settings
- Click Tools on the menu bar, and then click Internet Options.
- Click the General tab.
- Select whether you want Internet Explorer to open with the current page, its default page, or a blank page by clicking the corresponding button in the Home page section of the Internet Options dialog box.
- If you want to specify a home page, type the URL of that Web page in the Address text box.

To modify your home page:

1. Click **Tools** on the menu bar, and then click **Internet Options** to open the dialog box shown in Figure 3-45.

Figure 3-45   CHANGING THE DEFAULT HOME PAGE

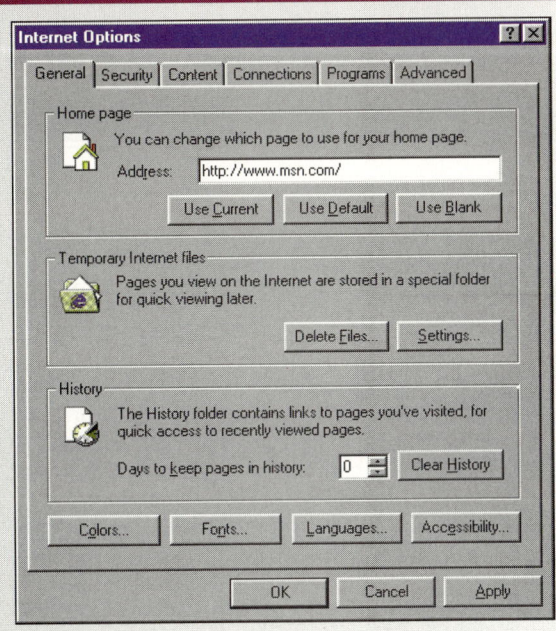

[Screenshot of Internet Options dialog box with General tab selected, showing Home page section with Address field containing http://www.msn.com/, Use Current, Use Default, Use Blank buttons; Temporary Internet files section with Delete Files and Settings buttons; History section with Days to keep pages in history: 0 and Clear History button; Colors, Fonts, Languages, Accessibility buttons; OK, Cancel, Apply buttons.]

To use the currently loaded Web page as your home page, click the Use Current button. To use the default home page that was installed with your copy of Internet Explorer, click the Use Default button. If you don't want a page to open when you start your browser, click the Use Blank button. If you want to specify a home page other than the current, default, or blank page, type the URL for that page in the Address Bar.

TROUBLE? You might not be able to change these settings if you are using a computer in your school lab or at your office. Some organizations set the home page defaults on all of their computers and then lock those settings.

2. Click the **Cancel** button to close the dialog box without making any changes.

In the next section, you will learn how to print the Web page so you have a permanent record of its contents.

Printing a Web Page

The **Print** button on the Standard Buttons toolbar lets you print the current Web frame or page. You will learn more about saving and printing Web pages later in this session, but you can use the Print command to make a printed copy of most Web pages. (Some Web pages disable the Print command.)

REFERENCE WINDOW | RW

Printing the current Web page
- Click the Print button on the Standard Buttons toolbar to print the current Web page with the default print settings.

or

- Click File on the menu bar, and then click Print.
- Use the Print dialog box to choose the printer you want to use, the pages you want to print, and the number of copies you want to make of each page.
- Click the OK button to print the page(s).

To print a Web page:

1. Click in the main (right) frame of the Student Online Companion page to select it.
2. Click **File** on the menu bar, and then click **Print** to open the Print dialog box.
3. Make sure that the printer in the Name text box shows the printer you want to use; if necessary, click the Name list arrow to change the selection.
4. Click the **Pages** option button in the Print range section of the Print dialog box, type **1** in the **from** text box, press the **Tab** key, and then type **1** in the **to** text box to specify that you only want to print the first page.
5. Make sure that the Number of copies text box shows that you want to print one copy.
6. Click the **OK** button to print the Web page and close the Print dialog box.

Changing the Settings for Printing a Web Page

You have seen how to print Web pages using the basic options available in the Print dialog box. Usually, the default settings in the Print dialog box are fine for printing a Web page, but you can use the Page Setup dialog box to change the way a Web page prints. Figure 3-46 shows the Page Setup dialog box, and Figure 3-47 describes its settings.

Figure 3-46 PAGE SETUP DIALOG BOX

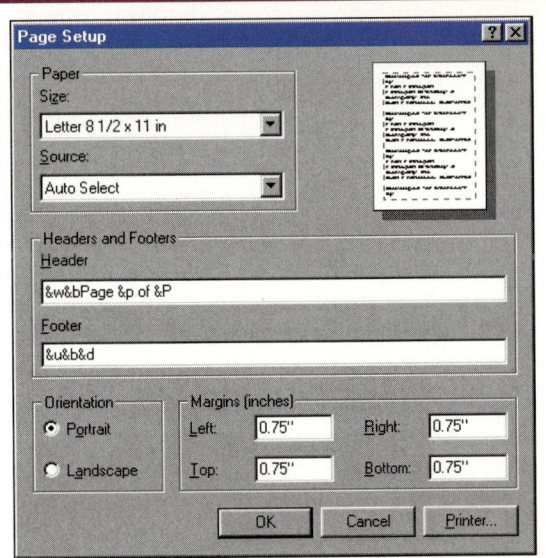

Figure 3-47 PAGE SETUP DIALOG BOX OPTIONS

OPTION	DESCRIPTION	USE
Paper Size	Changes the size of the printed page.	Use the Letter size default unless you are printing to different paper stock, such as Legal or A4.
Paper Source	Changes the printer's paper source.	Use the default AutoSelect Tray unless you want to specify a different tray or manual feed for printing on heavy paper.
Header	Prints the Web page's title, URL, date/time printed, and page numbers at the top of each page.	To obtain details on how to specify exact header printing options, click the Header text box to select it, and then press the F1 key.
Footer	Prints the Web page's title, URL, date/time printed, and page numbers at the bottom of each page.	To obtain details on how to specify exact footer printing options, click the Footer text box to select it, and then press the F1 key.
Orientation	Selects the orientation of the printed output.	Portrait works best for most Web pages, but you can use landscape orientation to print the wide tables of numbers included on some Web pages.
Margins	Changes the margin of the printed page.	Normally, you should leave the default settings, but you can change the right, left, top, or bottom margins as needed.

When printing long Web pages, another print option that is extremely useful for saving paper is to reduce the font size of the Web pages before you print them. To do this, click View on the menu bar, click Text Size, and then click either Smaller or Smallest on the pop-out menu.

Checking Web Page Security Features

You can check some of the security elements of a Web page by clicking File on the menu bar, clicking Properties, and then clicking the Certificates button. Internet Explorer will display security information for the page, if it is available, to advise you of the overall security of the page that appears in the browser window.

Encryption is a way of scrambling and encoding data transmissions that reduces the risk that a person who intercepts the Web page as it travels across the Internet will be able to decode and read the page's contents. Web sites use encrypted transmission to send and receive information, such as credit card numbers, to ensure privacy. When Internet Explorer loads an encrypted Web page, a padlock symbol appears in the third pane of the status bar at the bottom of the Internet Explorer window.

Getting Help in Microsoft Internet Explorer

Microsoft Internet Explorer includes a comprehensive online Help facility. You can obtain help by opening the Internet Explorer Help window.

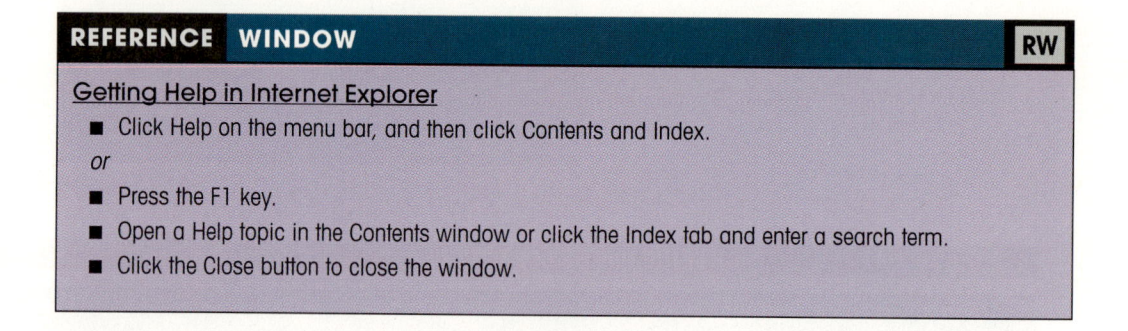

REFERENCE WINDOW

Getting Help in Internet Explorer
- Click Help on the menu bar, and then click Contents and Index.

or

- Press the F1 key.
- Open a Help topic in the Contents window or click the Index tab and enter a search term.
- Click the Close button to close the window.

To open the Internet Explorer Help window:

1. Click **Help** on the menu bar, and then click **Contents and Index** to open the Internet Explorer Help window.

2. If necessary, click the **Maximize** button on the Internet Explorer Help window so it fills the desktop.

3. Click the **Contents** tab in the Contents frame, click **Finding the Web Pages You Want**, and then click **Listing your favorite pages for quick viewing** to open that help topic in the Help window. Notice that the page that opens in the Help frame contains other links to related categories that you can explore. See Figure 3-48.

Figure 3-48 MICROSOFT INTERNET EXPLORER HELP WINDOW

- Hide/Show button closes and reopens the Contents frame
- Help navigation buttons
- click to close Help
- hyperlinks to detailed Help topics
- Contents frame
- Help frame

4. Click the **Close** button to close the Internet Explorer Help window.

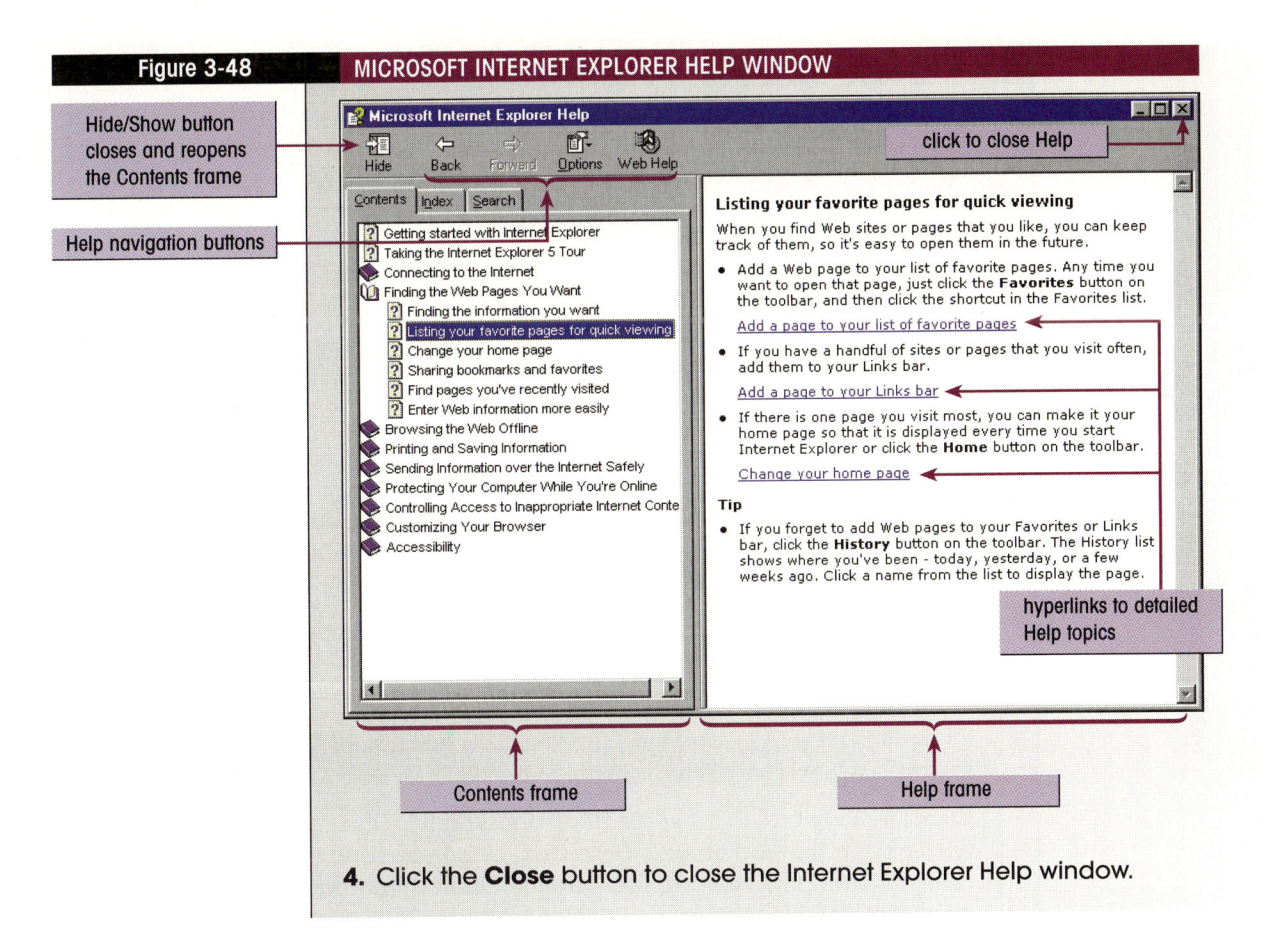

You are now convinced that you have all of the tools you need to successfully find information on the Web. Marianna probably will be interested in seeing the Pennsylvania Quintet Web page, but you are not sure if she will have Internet access while she's touring. Maggie says that you can save the Web page on disk, so Marianna can open the page locally in her Web browser using the files you save on that disk.

Using Internet Explorer to Save a Web Page

You have learned how to use most of the Internet Explorer tools for loading Web pages and saving bookmarks. Now, Maggie wants you to learn how to save a Web page. Sometimes, you will want to store entire Web pages on disk; other times, you will only want to store selected portions of Web page text or particular graphics from a Web page.

Saving a Web Page

You like the Pennsylvania Quintet's Web site and want to save the page on disk so you can send it to Marianna. That way, she can review it without having an Internet connection. To save a Web page, you must have the page open in Internet Explorer.

> **REFERENCE WINDOW**
>
> **Saving a Web page to a floppy disk**
> - Open the Web page in Internet Explorer.
> - Click File on the menu bar, and then click Save As to open the Save Web Page dialog box.
> - Click the Save in list arrow, and then change to the drive on which to save the Web page.
> - Accept the default filename, or change the filename, if you want; however, retain the file extension .htm or .html.
> - Click the Save button to save the Web page on the disk.

To save the Web page on your Data Disk:

1. Use the **Favorites** button to return to the Pennsylvania Quintet page. (You saved the favorite in the East Coast Ensembles folder, which is in the Wind Quintet Information folder.)

2. Click **File** on the menu bar, and then click **Save As** to open the Save Web Page dialog box.

3. Click the **Save in** list arrow, click the drive that contains your Data Disk (usually this is 3½ Floppy (A:)), and then double-click **Tutorial.03** folder. You will accept the default filename of Pennsylvania Quintet.

4. Click the **Save** button. Now the HTML document for the Pennsylvania Quintet's home page is saved on your Data Disk. When you send it to Marianna, she can open her Web browser and then use the Open command on the File menu to open the Web page.

5. Close the Favorites frame.

If the Web page contains graphics, such as photos, drawings, or icons, they will not be saved with the HTML document. To save a graphic, right-click it in the browser window, click Save Picture As, and then save the graphic to the same location as the Web's HTML document. The graphics file is specified to appear on the HTML document as a hyperlink, so you might have to change the HTML code in the Web page to identify its location. Copying the graphics files to the same disk as the HTML document will *usually* work.

Saving Web Page Text to a File

Maggie suggests that you might want to know how to save portions of Web page text to a file, so that you can save only the text from the Web page and use it in other programs. You will use WordPad to receive the text you will copy from a Web page, but any word processor or text editor will work.

Marianna just called to let you know that the quintet will play a concert in Cleveland on a Friday night, and she asks you to identify other opportunities for scheduling local concerts during the following weekend. Often, museums are willing to book small ensembles for weekend afternoon programs, and Marianna has given you the URL for the Cleveland Museum of Art. You will visit the site and then get the museum's address and telephone number so you can contact it about scheduling a concert.

TUTORIAL 3 BROWSER BASICS WEB 3.61 INTERNET

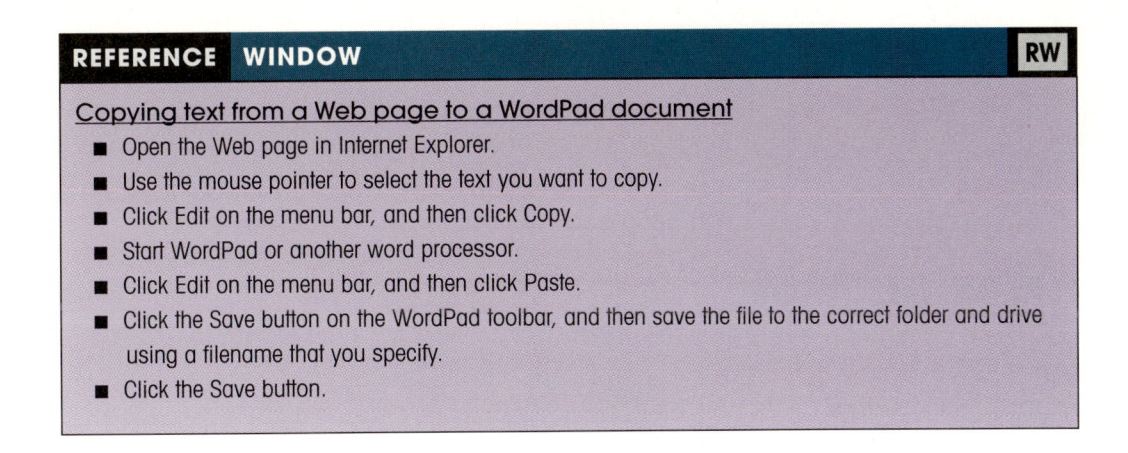

> **REFERENCE WINDOW** | RW
>
> **Copying text from a Web page to a WordPad document**
> - Open the Web page in Internet Explorer.
> - Use the mouse pointer to select the text you want to copy.
> - Click Edit on the menu bar, and then click Copy.
> - Start WordPad or another word processor.
> - Click Edit on the menu bar, and then click Paste.
> - Click the Save button on the WordPad toolbar, and then save the file to the correct folder and drive using a filename that you specify.
> - Click the Save button.

To copy text from a Web page and save it to a file:

1. Use the **Back** button to return to the Student Online Companion page, and then click the **Cleveland Museum of Art** link to open that Web page in the browser window.

2. Click the **address** hyperlink in the left frame on the Web page to open the museum information page in the main (right) frame.

3. Click and drag the mouse pointer over the address and telephone number to select it, as shown in Figure 3-49.

Figure 3-49   SELECTING TEXT ON A WEB PAGE

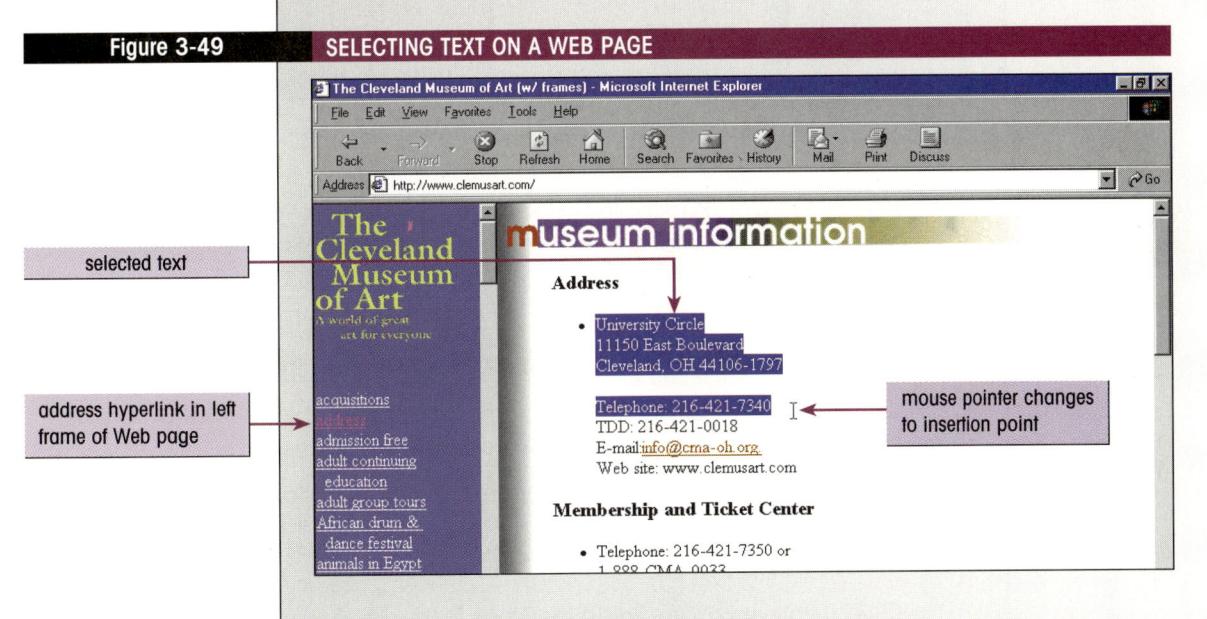

- selected text
- address hyperlink in left frame of Web page
- mouse pointer changes to insertion point

4. Click **Edit** on the menu bar, and then click **Copy** to copy the selected text to the Windows Clipboard.

Now, you can start WordPad and paste the copied text into a new document.

To start and copy the text into WordPad:

1. Click the **Start** button on the taskbar, point to **Programs**, point to **Accessories**, and then click **WordPad** to start the program and open a new document.

2. Click the **Paste** button on the WordPad toolbar to paste the text into the WordPad document, as shown in Figure 3-50.

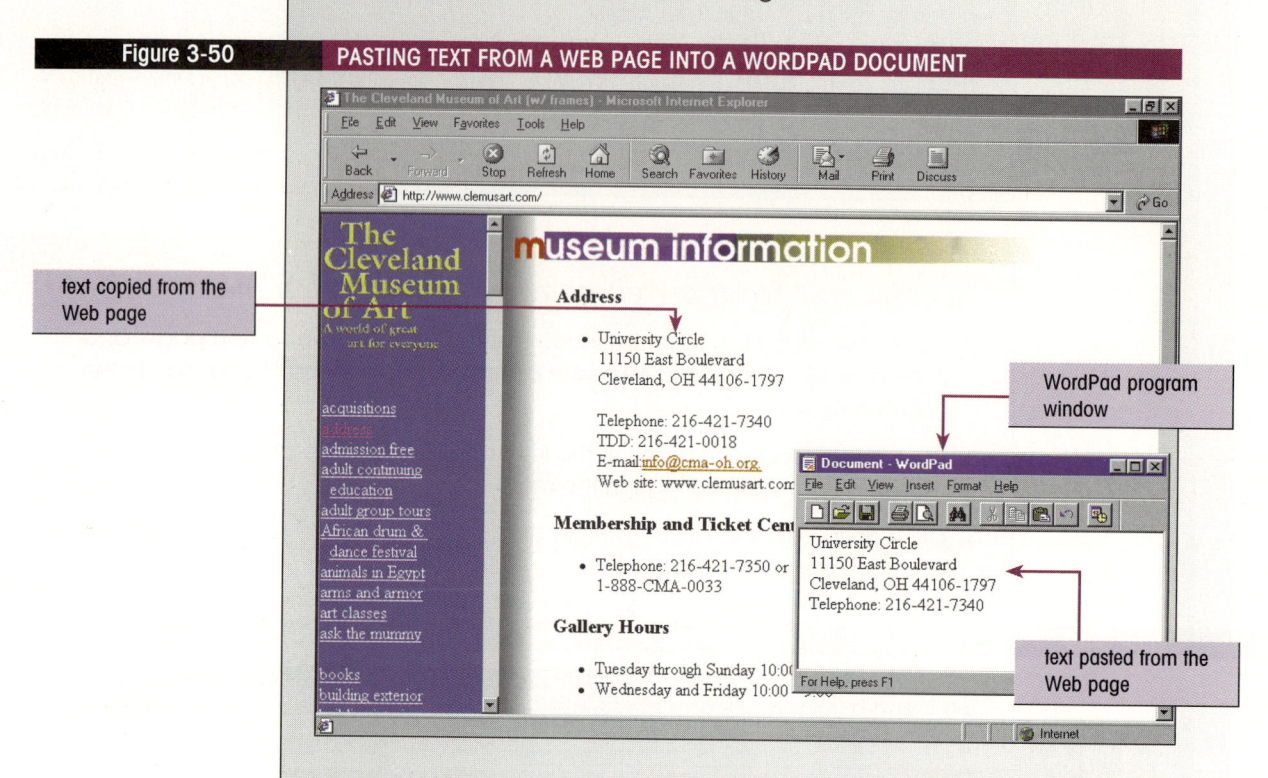

Figure 3-50   PASTING TEXT FROM A WEB PAGE INTO A WORDPAD DOCUMENT

- text copied from the Web page
- WordPad program window
- text pasted from the Web page

TROUBLE? If the WordPad toolbar does not appear, click View on the menu bar, click Toolbar to turn it on, and then repeat Step 2. Your WordPad program window might be a different size from the one shown in Figure 3-50, which does not affect the steps.

3. Click the **Save** button on the WordPad toolbar to open the Save As dialog box.

4. Click the **Save in** list arrow, change to the drive that contains your Data Disk, and then double-click the **Tutorial.03** folder, if necessary.

5. Select any text that is in the File name text box, type **CMoA-Address.txt**, and then click the **Save** button to save the file. Now, the address and phone number of the museum is saved in a file on your Data Disk for future reference.

TROUBLE? If you also completed the steps in Session 3.2, then a dialog box will open and ask if you want to replace the existing CmoA-Address.txt file on your Data Disk. Click the Yes button to replace it.

6. Click the **Close** button on the WordPad title bar to close it.

TUTORIAL 3 BROWSER BASICS WEB 3.63 INTERNET

Later, you will contact the museum. As you examine the hyperlinks in the left frame of the Cleveland Museum of Art Web page, you notice a hyperlink titled "how to get here." Clicking the "how to get here" hyperlink loads a page that contains directions and information about transportation to the museum. You find that it includes a hyperlink to a street map of the area surrounding the museum.

Saving a Web Page Graphic to Disk

You decide that the Web page with directions and transportation information might be helpful to Marianna, so you decide to save the map graphic on your disk. You can then send the file to Marianna so she has a resource for getting to the museum.

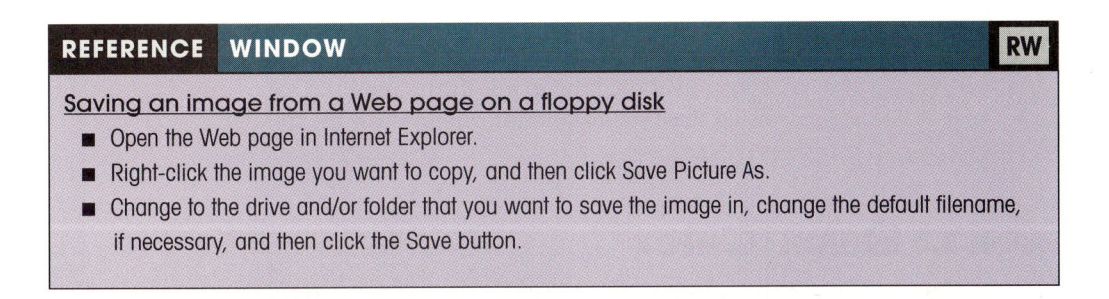

REFERENCE WINDOW

Saving an image from a Web page on a floppy disk
- Open the Web page in Internet Explorer.
- Right-click the image you want to copy, and then click Save Picture As.
- Change to the drive and/or folder that you want to save the image in, change the default filename, if necessary, and then click the Save button.

To save the street map image on a floppy disk:

1. Click the **how to get here** hyperlink in the left frame of the Cleveland Museum's home page, and then click the **street map** hyperlink on the Getting around - Directions and Transportation Web page in the main (right) frame. Do not click the hyperlink to the Adobe download version of the map.

2. Right-click the map image to open its shortcut menu, as shown in Figure 3-51.

Figure 3-51 SAVING THE MAP IMAGE TO DISK

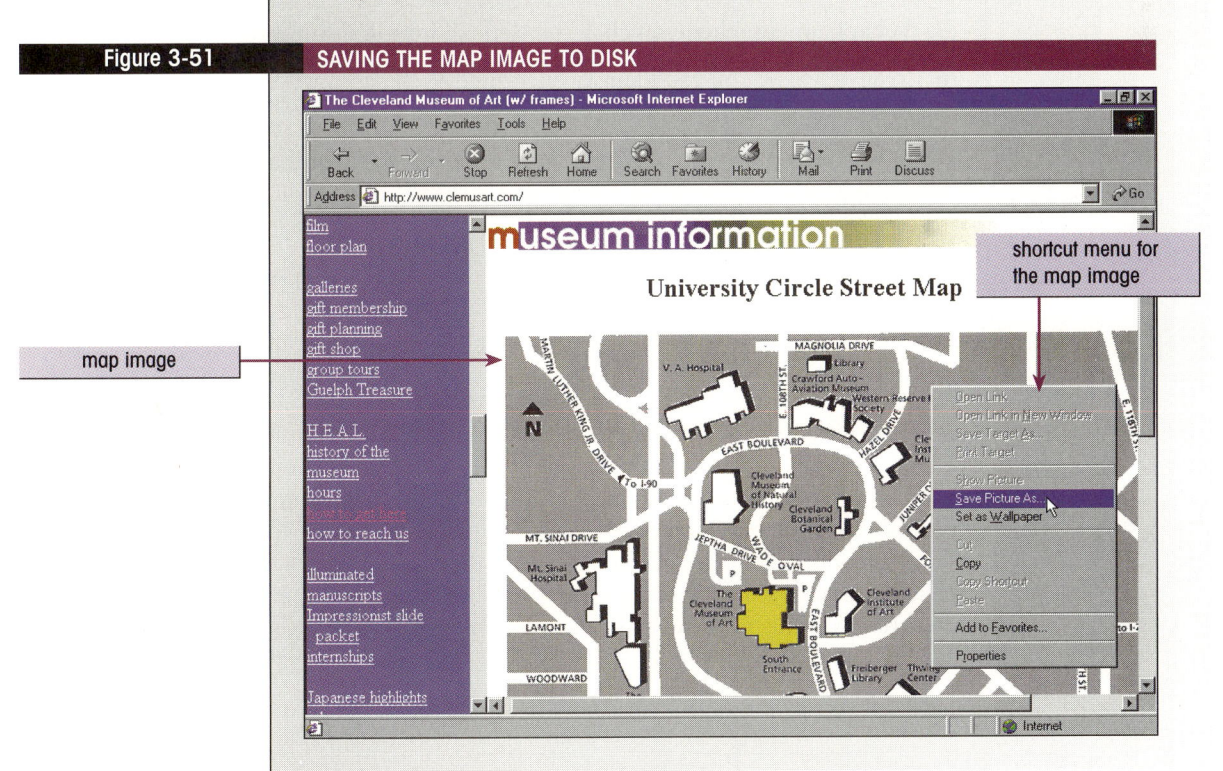

3. Click **Save Picture As** on the shortcut menu to open the Save Picture dialog box.

4. If necessary, click the **Save in** list arrow, change to the drive that contains your Data Disk, and then double-click the **Tutorial.03** folder. You will accept the default filename, mapstreet, so click the **Save** button. Now the image is saved on your Data Disk, and you can send the file to Marianna. Marianna can use her Web browser to open the image file and print it.

   TROUBLE? If you also completed the steps in Session 3.2, then a dialog box will open and ask if you want to replace the existing mapstreet.gif file on your Data Disk. Click the Yes button to replace it.

5. Close your Web browser and your dial-up connection, if necessary.

Now, you can send a disk to Marianna so she has the Pennsylvania Quintet Web page and a map to show how to get to the museum. Marianna is pleased to hear of your progress in using the Web to find information for the quintet.

Session 3.3 QUICK CHECK

1. Describe two ways to increase the Web page area in Internet Explorer.
2. You can use the _____ button in Internet Explorer to visit previously visited sites during your Web session.
3. Click the _____ button on the Standard Buttons toolbar to open a search frame that contains a number of different searching options.
4. List the names of two additional Favorites folders you might want to add to the Wind Quintet Information folder as you continue to gather information for the Sunset Wind Quintet.
5. What happens when you click the Refresh button in Internet Explorer?
6. True or False: You can identify encrypted Web pages when viewing them in Internet Explorer.
7. Describe two ways to obtain help on a specific topic in Internet Explorer.

Now you are ready to complete the Review Assignments using the browser of your choice.

REVIEW ASSIGNMENTS

Marianna is pleased with the information you gathered thus far about other wind quintet Web pages and potential recital sites. In fact, she is thinking about hiring someone to create a Web page for the Sunset Wind Quintet. So that she has some background information for her meetings with potential Web designers, Marianna would like you to compile some information about the Web pages that other small musical ensembles have created. Although you have searched for information about wind quintets, a large number of string quartets (two violinists, a violist, and a cellist) play similar venues.

Do the following:

1. Start your Web browser, go to the Student Online Companion (http://www.course.com/newperspectives/internet2), click the link for your book, click the Tutorial 3 link, and then click the Review Assignments link in the left frame.

2. Click the hyperlinks listed under the category headings Wind Quintets, String Quartets, and Other Small Musical Ensembles to explore the Web pages for each entry.

3. Choose three interesting home pages, and print the first page of each. Create a bookmark or favorite for each of these sites, and then answer the following questions for these three sites.

4. Which sites include a photograph of the ensemble? Which photographs are in color and black and white? Which sites show the ensemble members dressed in formal concert dress?

5. Choose your favorite ensemble photograph and save it in the Tutorial.03 folder on your Data Disk.

6. Do any of the sites provide information about the ensemble's CDs? If so, which ones? Is this information on the home page, or did you click a hyperlink to find it?

7. Do any of the sites offer CDs or other products for sale? If so, which ones? Is this information on the home page, or did you click a hyperlink to find it?

8. Write a one-page report that summarizes your findings for Marianna. Include a recommendation regarding what the Sunset Wind Quintet should consider including in its Web site.

9. Close your Web browser and your dial-up connection, if necessary.

CASE PROBLEMS

Case 1. Businesses on the Web Business Web sites range from very simple informational sites to comprehensive sites that offer information about the firm's products or services, history, current employment openings, and financial information. An increasing number of business sites offer products or services for sale using their Web sites. You just started a position on the public relations staff of Value City Central, a large retail chain of television and appliance stores. Your first assignment is to research and report on the types of information that other large firms offer on their Web sites.

Do the following:

1. Start your Web browser, go to the Student Online Companion (http://www.course.com/newperspectives/internet2), click the link for your book, click the Tutorial 3 link, and then click the Case Problems link in the left frame.

2. Use the Case Problem 1 hyperlinks to open the business sites on that page.

3. Choose three of those business sites that you believe would be most relevant to your assignment.

4. Print the home page for each Web site that you have chosen.

5. Select one site that you feel does the best job in each of the following five categories: overall presentation of the corporate image, description of products or services offered, presentation of the firm's history, description of employment opportunities, and presentation of financial statements or other financial information about the company.

6. Prepare a report that includes one paragraph describing why you believe each of the sites you identified in the preceding step did the best job.

7. Close your Web browser, and log off the Internet, if necessary.

Case 2. Browser Wars Your employer, Bristol Mills, is a medium-sized manufacturer of specialty steel products. The firm has increased its use of computers in all of its office operations and in many of its manufacturing operations. Many of Bristol's computers currently run either Netscape Navigator or Microsoft Internet Explorer; however, the chief financial officer (CFO) has decided the firm can support only one of these products. As the CFO's special assistant, you have been asked to recommend which Web browser the company should choose to support.

Do the following:

1. Start your Web browser, go to the Student Online Companion (http://www.course.com/newperspectives/internet2), click the link for your book, click the Tutorial 3 link, and then click the Case Problems link in the left frame.

2. Use the Case Problem 2 hyperlinks to learn more about these two widely used Web browser software packages.

3. Write a one-page memo to the CFO (your instructor) that outlines the strengths and weaknesses of each product. Recommend one program and support your decision using the information you collected.

4. Prepare a list of features that you would like to see in a new Web browser software package that would overcome important limitations in either Navigator or Internet Explorer. Do you think it would be feasible for a firm to develop and use such a product? Why or why not?

5. Close your Web browser, and log off the Internet, if necessary.

Case 3. Citizens Fidelity Bank You are a new staff auditor at the Citizens Fidelity Bank. You have had more recent computer training than other audit staff members at Citizens, so Sally DeYoung, the audit manager, asks you to review the bank's policy on Web browser cookie settings. Some of the bank's board members expressed concerns to Sally about the security of the bank's computers. They understand that the bank has PCs on its networks that are connected to the Internet. One of the board members learned about browser cookies and was afraid that an innocent bank employee might connect to a site that would write a dangerous cookie file on the bank's computer network. A browser cookie is a small file that a Web server can write to the disk drive of the computer running a Web browser. Not all Web servers write cookies, but those that do can read the cookie file the next time the Web browser on that computer connects to the Web server. The Web server can then retrieve information about the Web browser's last connection to the server. None of the bank's board members knows very much about computers, but all of them became concerned that a virus-laden cookie could significantly damage the bank's computer system. Sally asks you to help inform the board of directors about cookies and to establish a policy on using them.

Do the following:

1. Start your Web browser, go to the Student Online Companion (http://www.course.com/newperspectives/internet2), click the link for your book, click the Tutorial 3 link, and then click the Case Problems link in the left frame.

2. Use the Case Problem 3 hyperlinks to Cookie Information Resources to learn more about cookie files.

3. Prepare a brief outline of the content on each Web page you visit.

4. List the risks that Citizens Fidelity Bank might face by allowing cookie files to be written to their computers.

5. List the benefits that individual users obtain by allowing Web servers to write cookies to the computers that they are using at the bank to access the Web.

6. Close your Web browser, and log off the Internet, if necessary.

Case 4. Columbus Suburban Area Council The Columbus Suburban Area Council is a charitable organization devoted to maintaining and improving the general welfare of people living in Columbus suburbs. As the director of the council, you are interested in encouraging donations and other support from area citizens and would like to stay informed of grant opportunities that might benefit the council. You are especially interested in developing an informative and attractive presence on the Web.

Do the following:

1. Start your Web browser, go to the Student Online Companion (http://www.course.com/newperspectives/internet2), click the link for your book, click the Tutorial 3 link, and then click the Case Problems link in the left frame.

2. Follow the Case Problem 4 hyperlinks to charitable organizations to find out more about what other organizations are doing with their Web sites.

3. Select three of the Web sites you visited and, for each, prepare a list of the site's contents. Note whether each site included financial information and whether the site disclosed how much the organization spent on administrative, or nonprogram activities.

4. Identify which site you believe would be a good model for the Council's new Web site. Explain why you think your chosen site would be the best example to follow.

5. Close your Web browser, and log off the Internet, if necessary.

Case 5. Emma's Start Page Your neighbor, Emma Inkster, was an elementary school teacher for many years. She is now retired and has just purchased her first personal computer. Emma is excited about getting on the Web and exploring its resources. She has asked for your help. After you introduce her to what you have learned in this Tutorial about Web browsers, she is eager to spend more time gathering information on the Web. Although she is retired, Emma has continued to be very active. She is an avid bridge player, enjoys golf, and is one of the neighborhood's best gardeners. Although she is somewhat limited by her schoolteacher's pension, Emma loves travel to foreign countries and especially likes to learn the languages of her destinations. She would like to have a start page for her computer that would include hyperlinks that would help her easily visit and return regularly to Web pages related to her interests. Her nephew knows HTML and can create the page, but Emma would like you to help her design the layout of her start page. You know that Web directory sites are designed to help people find interesting Web sites, so you begin your search with them.

Do the following:

1. Start your Web browser, go to the Student Online Companion (http://www.course.com/newperspectives/internet2), click the link for your book, click the Tutorial 3 link, and then click the Case Problems link in the left frame.

2. Follow the Case Problem 5 hyperlinks to Web directories to learn what kind of organization they use for their hyperlinks.

3. You note that many of the Web directories use a similar organization structure for their hyperlinks and categories; however, you are not sure if that organization structure would be ideal for Emma. You decide to create categories that suit Emma's specific interests. List five general categories around which you would organize Emma's start page. For each of those five general categories, list three subcategories that would help Emma find and return to Web sites she would find interesting.

4. Write a report of 100 words in which you explain why the start page you designed for Emma would be more useful to her than a publicly available Web directory.

5. Close your Web browser, and log off the Internet, if necessary.

LAB ASSIGNMENTS

One of the most popular services on the Internet is the World Wide Web. This Lab is a Web simulator that teaches you how to use Web browser software to find information. You can use this Lab whether or not your school provides you with Internet access.

1. Click the Steps button to learn how to use Web browser software. As you proceed through the Steps, answer all of the Quick Check questions that appear. After you complete the Steps, you will see a Quick Check Summary Report. Follow the instructions on the screen to print this report.

2. Click the Explore button on the Welcome screen. Use the Web browser to locate a weather map of the Caribbean Virgin Islands. What is its URL?

3. A SCUBA diver named Wadson Lachouffe has been searching for the fabled treasure of Greybeard the pirate. A link from the Adventure Travel Web site, www.atour.com, leads to Wadson's Web page called "Hidden Treasure." In Explore, locate the Hidden Treasure page and answer the following questions:

   a. What was the name of Greybeard's ship?
   b. What was Greybeard's favorite food?
   c. What does Wadson think happened to Greybeard's ship?

4. In the Steps, you found a graphic of Jupiter from the photo archives of the Jet Propulsion Laboratory. In the Explore section of the Lab, you can also find a graphic of Saturn. Suppose one of your friends wanted a picture of Saturn for an astronomy report. Make a list of the blue, underlined links your friend must click in the correct order to find the Saturn graphic. Assume that your friend will begin at the Web Trainer home page.

5. Enter the URL http://www.atour.com to jump to the Adventure Travel Web site. Write a one-page description of this site. In your paper include a description of the information at the site, the number of pages the site contains, and a diagram of the links it contains.

6. Chris Thomson is a student at UVI and has his own Web pages. In Explore, look at the information Chris has included on his pages. Suppose you could create your own Web page. What would you include? Use word-processing software to design your own Web pages. Make sure you indicate the graphics and links you would use.

QUICK CHECK ANSWERS

Session 3.1

1. False
2. format text and create hyperlinks
3. The main page of a Web site, the first page that opens when you start your Web browser, or the page that opens the first time you start a particular Web browser
4. Any two: graphics image, sound clip, or video files
5. Candidate's name and party affiliation, list of qualifications, biography, position statements on campaign issues, list of endorsements with hyperlinks to the Web pages of individuals and organizations that support her candidacy, audio or video clips of speeches and interviews, address and telephone number of the campaign office, and other similar information
6. A computer's IP address is a unique identifying number; its domain name is a unique name associated with the IP address on the Internet host computer responsible for that computer's domain.
7. "http://" indicates use of the hypertext transfer protocol, "www.savethetrees.org" is the domain name and suggests a charitable or not-for-profit organization that is probably devoted to forest ecology, and "main.html" is the name of the HTML file on the Web server.
8. A Web directory contains a hierarchical list of Web page categories; each category contains hyperlinks to individual Web pages. A Web search engine is a Web site that accepts words or expressions you enter and finds Web pages that include those words or expressions.

Session 3.2

1. Any three of: type the URL in the Location field, click a hyperlink on a Web page, click the Back button, click the Forward button, click the Bookmarks button and select from the menu, or click Communicator on the menu bar then click Tools and double-click the History listing entry
2. history list
3. when you believe the Web page might have changed since you last visited it
4. Navigator loads the page that is specified in the Home page section of the Preferences dialog box (which you can open from the Edit menu)
5. encrypt
6. True
7. Navigator feature that lets you store and organize a list of Web pages that you have visited

Session 3.3

1. Hide its toolbars or click the Full Screen command on the View menu.
2. History
3. Search
4. Midwest Ensembles, West Coast Ensembles
5. Internet Explorer contacts the Web server to see if the currently loaded Web page has changed since it was stored in its cache folder. If the Web page has changed, it obtains the new page; otherwise, it loads the cache folder copy.
6. True
7. press F1, click Help on the menu bar

APPENDICES

New Perspectives on

THE INTERNET

2nd Edition

APPENDIX E   WEB E.03
Eudora

APPENDIX F   WEB F.01
Pine

EUDORA

Eudora E-Mail Client

Eudora is an e-mail client program that runs on your computer, either a Windows or a Macintosh operating system, and communicates with the mail server that is on the Internet. You can use Eudora only if you are connected directly to the Internet on a university network (usually in a lab) or have a PPP or SLIP connection through an Internet service provider (ISP).

Qualcomm, the company that publishes Eudora, offers a free, downloadable version of Eudora, called Eudora Light, on its Web site. You can download the free version of Eudora Light to complete these steps, or your school might have the complete Eudora Pro package installed in the lab. (The steps will be slightly different depending on which version of Eudora Light you are using, but they should work the same.) A link to the Qualcomm Corporation home page appears in the Student Online Companion Web page for Appendix E.

Note: The steps in this appendix assume that you have read and understand Session 2.1 in Tutorial 2, which covers introductory e-mail concepts.

To start and initialize Eudora for use on a public computer:

1. Click the **Start** button on the taskbar, point to **Programs**, point to **Eudora Pro**, and then click **Eudora Pro**. Eudora starts on your computer.

   TROUBLE? If you do not see Eudora Pro on your Programs menu, then Eudora is not installed on your computer, or it is installed in a different location. Ask your instructor or technical support person for help.

   TROUBLE? If a Note dialog box opens and asks if you want to change Eudora to your default mail program, click the No button.

   TROUBLE? If the Tip of the Day dialog box opens, click the Close button to close it.

   TROUBLE? If the New Account Wizard dialog box opens, click the Cancel button to close it.

2. Click **Tools** on the menu bar, and then click **Options** to open the Options dialog box. If necessary, click the **Getting Started** category button to display the start-up options.

   TROUBLE? If you are using Eudora Light, your steps might differ. Ask your instructor or technical support person for help.

3. Click in the Real name text box, and then type your first and last name, separated by a space.

   TROUBLE? If your account information already appears in the Options dialog box, skip to Step 8.

4. Press the **Tab** key to move to the Return address text box, and then type your full e-mail address (such as barbgoldberg@yahoo.com).

5. Press the **Tab** key to move to the Mail Server (Incoming) text box, and then type the address of your incoming mail server. Usually, the mail server address is the word *mail* or *pop*, followed by a period, and then the remainder of your domain address (such as pop.yahoo.com). Ask your instructor or technical support person for the correct incoming mail server name to use.

6. Press the **Tab** key to move to the Login Name text box, and then type your login name, which is the same as your username or user ID. Type only your login name (such as barbgoldberg), and not the domain name. See Figure E-1.

Figure E-1　ACCOUNT INFORMATION FOR BARBARA GOLDBERG

7. Press the Tab key to move to the **SMTP Server (Outgoing)** text box, and then type the address of your outgoing mail server. Usually, the mail server address is the word *mail* or *smtp* followed by a period, and then the remainder of your domain address (such as mail.yahoo.com). Ask your instructor or technical support person for the correct outgoing mail server name to use.

8. Click the **Checking Mail** category button.

9. Click the **Save password** check box, if necessary, to clear it. Clearing the Save password check box prevents Eudora from remembering your password so other users on this computer cannot access your account information after you exit the program.

10. Click the **Incoming Mail** category button.

11. Click the **Leave mail on server** check box, if necessary, to place a check mark in it. When checked, any mail you download and read also stays on the main server so you can reread the mail from **any** computer. If you leave the Leave mail on server check box cleared, then the mail is deleted the first time you read your mail on any PC. It is available only on the original PC on which you read it.

12. Click the **OK** button to save the new settings and close the Options dialog box.

Now, you have created your user account. If you are using a public computer, you can click the Forget Password(s) command on the Special menu to erase your password so no one can use it to access your e-mail account.

Creating a Message in Eudora

You use the **Composition window**, which includes a title bar, toolbar, the message header, and the message body, to send a message.

The title bar first displays the text "No Recipient, No Subject" until you enter information into the message. The title bar then displays the recipient's e-mail address and the subject of the message. The Composition window toolbar includes buttons that allow quick access to many message features, such as the priority (importance) of your message, text styles, and the ability to send your message.

The message header in the Composition window contains the To, From, Subject, Cc, Bcc, and Attached lines. The message body appears below the message header, and it contains your message.

To send a message using Eudora:

1. Click the **New Message** button on the toolbar. Eudora opens the Composition window.

2. Click the To line, and then type **barbgoldberg@yahoo.com**, which is the recipient's full e-mail address consisting of a user name and domain name separated by the @ sign. Notice that the From line already contains your full e-mail address.

   Note: For these steps, you will send an e-mail message to a real mailbox owned by Barb Goldberg. However, please note that all messages sent to this account are deleted without being read. If you have questions, then you should e-mail your instructor or technical support help at your institution.

3. Press the **Tab** key to move to the Subject line, and then type **Sample Eudora Message**.

4. Press the **Tab** key to move to the Cc line, and then type your full e-mail address so you will receive a copy of the message that you send.

   TROUBLE? If you make a typing mistake, use the arrow keys to move the insertion point to a previous line, or within a line, and then correct the mistake. If the arrow keys do not move the insertion point up or down in the message header, press Shift + Tab or the Tab key to move the insertion point up or down, respectively.

5. Press the **Tab** key twice to move the insertion point to the message body, and then type **Please let me know that you received this message. I am testing the Eudora mail client program.**

6. Press the **Enter** key twice to insert a blank line, and then type your first and last names to sign the message. See Figure E-2.

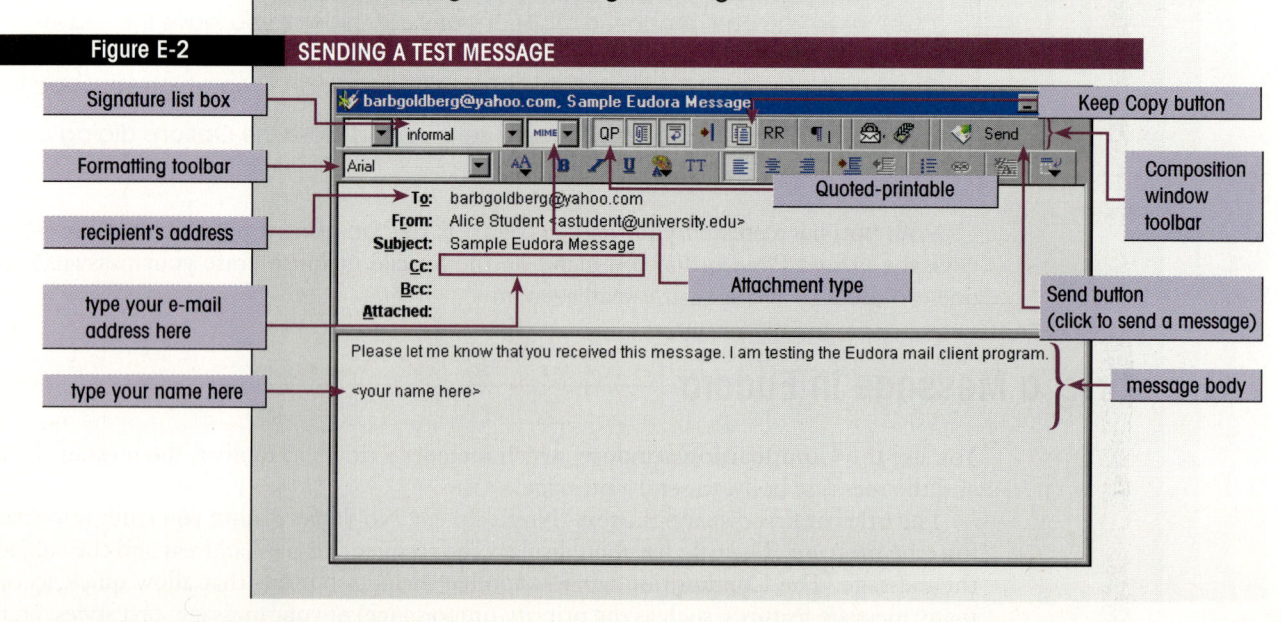

Figure E-2   SENDING A TEST MESSAGE

Now, you can send the message. Be sure to double-check the message body, the recipient's address, and the Cc address to ensure they are correct.

APPENDIX E EUDORA   WEB E.07   INTERNET

To check your mail send options and send your message:

1. Click **Tools** on the menu bar, and then click **Options** to open the Options dialog box. Click the **Sending Mail** category button to display the options shown in Figure E-3.

Figure E-3 CHECKING SENDING MAIL PREFERENCES

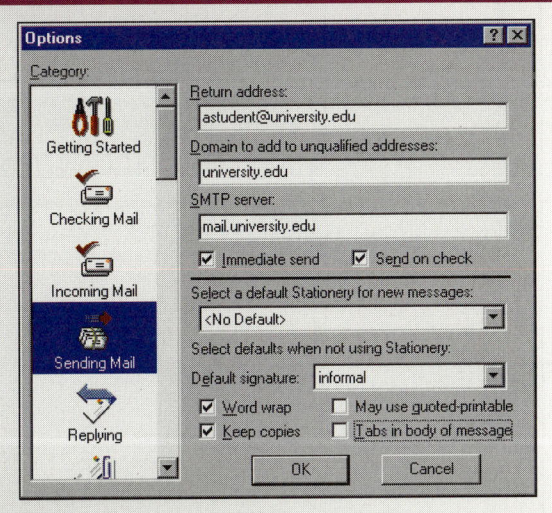

Your message might not be sent to the mail server immediately, depending on how Eudora is configured on your computer. Eudora might queue the message and send it later at your command, or it might send the message when you exit the program. Clicking the Immediate send check box will send mail immediately when you click the Send button. If you clear this check box, then mail will be sent only when you check for incoming mail. You will configure your program to send mail immediately after clicking the Send button.

2. If necessary, click the **Immediate send** check box so it contains a check mark, and then click the **OK** button to close the Options dialog box.

3. Click the **Send** button on the Composition window toolbar to send the message.

Receiving Mail

Eudora can save delivered mail in any of several standard or custom mailboxes on your PC. Depending on your configuration, Eudora periodically communicates with the mail server to see if you have new mail. When you start Eudora, it checks to see if you have any new mail messages. Before Eudora can check for new e-mail, you must enter a password. When you enter your password, asterisks display for each character you type to keep your password hidden. After clicking the OK button, Eudora requests that the mail server deliver your new mail to your PC. Within a few seconds, any new messages appear in the In box and their summary information displays in a window.

To manually check for mail:

1. Click the **Check Mail** button on the Composition window toolbar to retrieve all new mail messages. After a few moments, any new mail messages are transferred to your PC and appear in your In box. See Figure E-4.

Figure E-4 — READING NEW MAIL

local mailboxes

unread messages indicated by blue dots

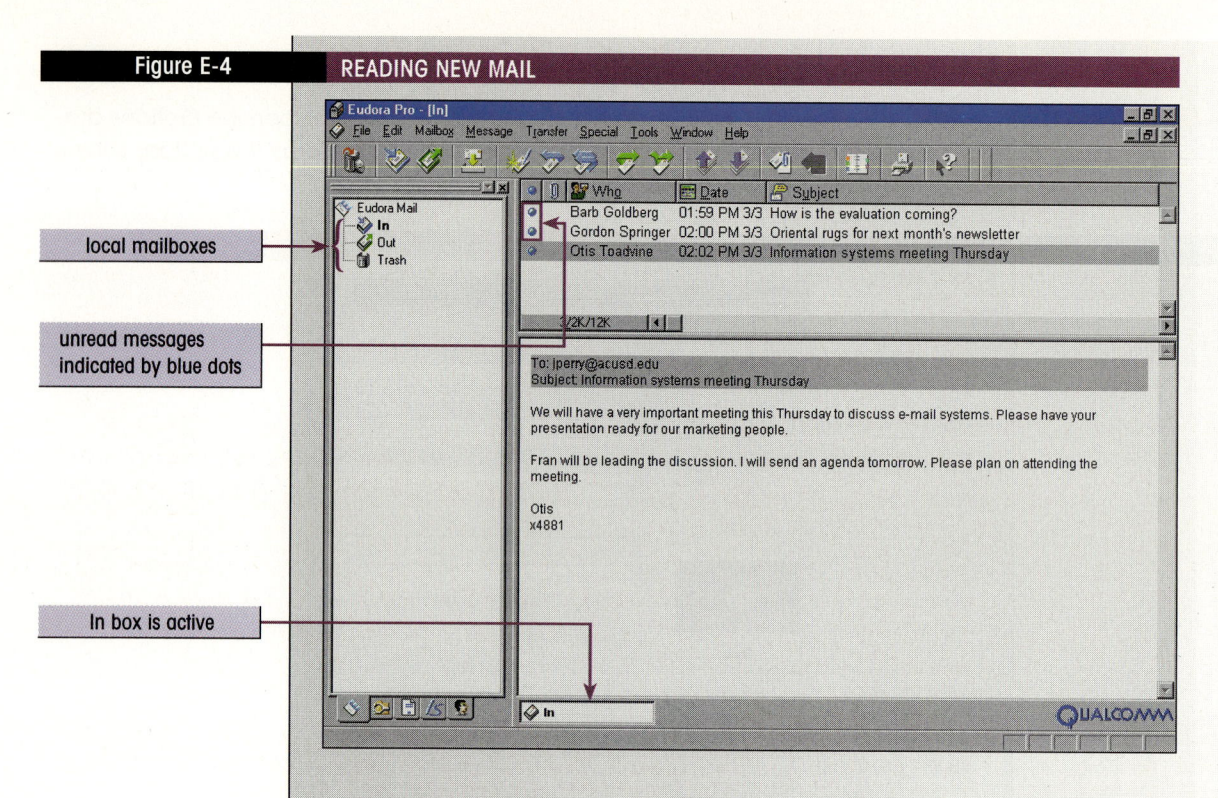

In box is active

TROUBLE? If the Enter Password dialog box opens, type your password in the Password text box, and then click the OK button to continue. If you do not know your password, ask your instructor or technical support person for help.

TROUBLE? If you do not see the In box, double-click the In folder in the left panel of the window to open it.

Notice several features of the In box. Unread messages contain a dot to their left in the message header pane. On the left side of the display is a list of available mailboxes. You can create, delete, or rename mailboxes. Mailboxes let you organize your mail by type; you might create different mail folders to store messages from different individuals or to group messages by project.

You should receive a copy of your **Sample Eudora Message** message when you check for new mail. Wait until you see this message summary line in the upper panel, and then continue with Step 2.

2. Double-click the **Sample Eudora Message** message summary line to open the message into a larger content pane with a title bar, toolbar, and a message body. If the message already appears highlighted, then press the spacebar or the Enter key to open the message.

3. Read the message, and then click the message close button to redisplay the message summary lines. Double-click any other message summary lines you received to read them.

You can save new messages in different mailboxes by right-clicking the message summary line and then clicking Transfer on the shortcut menu. You then click the destination mailbox to move the message to its new location. For now, you will leave the new messages in your In mailbox and close it.

4. Click the **Close** button for the In box window to close it. (Be careful not to click the Eudora application close button, which will close the entire program, not just the In box.)

After you receive new mail, you can leave it in your In box and on the server, or you can treat it like other documents (that is, printing, deleting, or filing it).

Printing a Message

To print an e-mail message, select the message summary line that you want to print, click the Print button, and then use the Print dialog box to select the desired print options.

To print an e-mail message:

1. Double-click the **In box** to open it.

2. Click the **Sample Eudora Message** message summary line in the upper panel again, if necessary, to select it. The top few lines of the message appear in the content pane.

3. Click the **Print** button on the toolbar. The Print dialog box opens. You can use this dialog box to change the default printer, the number of copies to print, or the pages to print, if necessary. The default settings are correct, so click the **OK** button to print the message summary line and body.

Your message prints. Now, file the message into a mailbox that you will create.

Filing a Message

Eudora mailboxes provide a convenient way to file your e-mail messages by category. If the mailboxes do not appear on the screen, click Mailboxes on the Tools menu. Normally, the Mailboxes window will appear on the left side of the screen. You can move mail from the In mailbox to any other mailbox or folder to file it.

To create a new mailbox:

1. Click **Mailbox** on the menu bar, and then click **New**. The New Mailbox dialog box opens.

2. Type **Marketing** in the Name the new mailbox text box, and then click the **OK** button to create the new Marketing mailbox. When you create a new mailbox, a menu command is also added to the Transfer menu.

3. Click **Transfer** on the menu bar. Notice that →**Marketing** appears on the menu.

4. Press the **Esc** key to close the Transfer menu without taking any action.

After you create the Marketing mailbox, you can transfer mail to it. Besides copying or transferring mail from the In box, you can select and transfer any message to another box. The only difference between transferring a message and copying it is that a transferred message is removed from its original mailbox and is moved to its new location. When you copy a message, it remains in its original mailbox, and a copy is placed in another mailbox. Copying a message is useful when you need to file a message in more than one mailbox.

You also can create a new mailbox and transfer mail to it in one step by selecting New from the Transfer menu and then entering a new mailbox name. After you click the OK button, Eudora automatically transfers the selected messages to the new mailbox.

To transfer a message to a mailbox:

1. If necessary, open your In box by double-clicking the **In** mailbox on the left side of the screen, and then click the **Sample Eudora Message** message summary line to select it.

2. Click **Transfer** on the menu bar (see Figure E-5), and then click →**Marketing**. Eudora transfers the selected message to the Marketing mailbox.

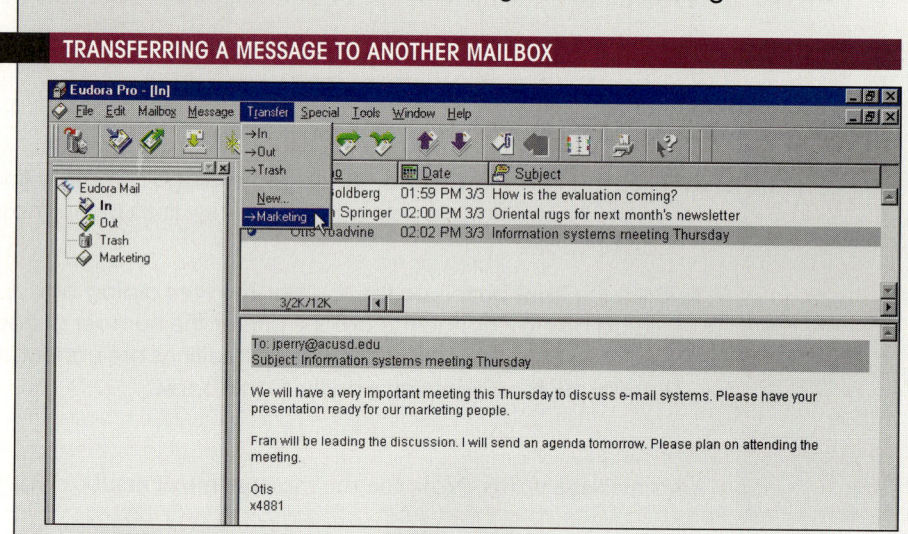

Figure E-5 TRANSFERRING A MESSAGE TO ANOTHER MAILBOX

If you transfer one or more messages to the wrong mailbox, you can cancel the transfer by clicking Undo on the Edit menu immediately after the transfer. The Undo command text will reflect the exact transfer and actually be Undo Transfer from In to Marketing.

If you want to copy a message into a separate mailbox, click Transfer on the menu bar, and then hold down the Shift key and click the mailbox name in which to store the copy of the message.

Forwarding a Message

You can forward any message that you receive to one or more recipients. To forward an existing mail message to another user, open the mailbox containing the message, select the message, and then click the **Forward** button on the toolbar. Your e-mail address and name automatically appear in the From line of the message header, and the Subject line is amended with the text **Fwd** or **Forward** to indicate that the message is being forwarded. Simply fill in the To line and then click the Send button in the Composition window to send the message.

Replying to a Message

When you reply to a message, Eudora automatically formats a new, blank message and addresses it to the sender. To reply to a message, select a message in any mailbox, and then click the **Reply** button on the toolbar. Eudora will open a new message window and place the original sender's address in the To line and your address in the From line. You can leave the Subject line as is or modify it.

Deleting a Message

To prevent you from inadvertently deleting important messages, Eudora requires you to complete two steps to delete a message from your PC. First, you temporarily delete a message by placing it in the Trash, which is a special mailbox on your system. You then permanently delete a message by emptying the trash.

To delete a message and a mailbox:

1. Double-click the **Marketing** mailbox to open it, and then click the **Sample Eudora Message** message summary line in your Marketing mailbox to select it. You can select more than one message by holding down the Ctrl key and then clicking each message's summary line.

2. Click the **Delete Message(s)** button on the toolbar. You also can press the Delete key to delete selected message(s). The deleted message is sent to the Trash mailbox.

   TROUBLE? If you accidentally send a message to the Trash mailbox, double-click the Trash mailbox folder to open it, select the message that you need to restore, click Transfer on the menu bar, and then click →In. The message is transferred to your In mailbox, where you can access it and file it into another folder as necessary.

3. Repeat Steps 1 and 2 to delete any other messages that you received or filed during this session.

4. Right-click the **Marketing** mailbox, and then click **Delete** on the shortcut menu to delete the Marketing mailbox that you created.

5. To delete all messages in the Trash mailbox and permanently remove them from your PC, click **Special** on the menu bar and then click **Empty Trash**. Click **Yes** to empty the trash. After you empty the trash, you cannot recover the deleted messages.

Even after you delete a message, the deleted message still occupies space. Normally, Eudora recovers this space automatically. However, you can force this space recovery to happen by clicking the Compact Mailboxes command on the Special menu.

You can set up Eudora to warn you whenever you are about to transfer unread, queued, or unsent messages to the Trash mailbox. If you hear a warning sound or see a warning message box when you attempt to empty the Trash mailbox, check to make sure you have read all the messages before permanently deleting them. When Eudora finds unread mail in the Trash mailbox, the mailbox name appears in bold type. If this occurs, open the Trash mailbox and read any bolded messages.

Maintaining an Address Book

You can use an address book to create individual and group addresses.

To create an address book entry:

1. Click the **Address Book** button on the toolbar to open the Address Book window.

2. Click the **New** button in the left panel of the Address Book window.

3. Type your first name in the What do you wish to call it? text box in the New Nickname dialog box, and then click the **OK** button.

4. Click the **Address(es)** tab, and then type your e-mail address in the large panel on the right.

5. Click the **Info** tab, and then type your first and last names in the Name text box.

6. Click **File** on the menu bar, and then click **Save** to save the new entry.

7. Click the **Close** button on the Address Book title bar. The Address Book closes.

When you want to send a message to someone listed in your address book, you can type that person's nickname or his or her full name, and Eudora will address the message automatically.

You also can use Eudora to create a distribution list (or a group mailing list). A distribution list is a single nickname that represents more than one individual e-mail address. To create a distribution list, open the address book, click the New button, type the list's nickname in the New Nickname text box, click the OK button, click the Addresses tab, and then type the e-mail addresses for each person in the group and separate them with a comma. To save your list, click File on the menu bar, and then click Save.

You also can create individual nicknames for everyone on the distribution list, and then use each person's nickname, and *not* his or her individual e-mail address, to create the distribution list. That way, if a person's e-mail address changes, you can change it in one place so all the distribution lists that include that person's e-mail address will be updated automatically. This technique is the best way to enter distribution list names in the address book.

Exiting Eudora

Before you leave the computer on which you are working, be sure to exit Eudora. If you are using a public computer, it is *very* important to erase your name and account from selected Eudora text boxes.

To erase your name and account from Eudora text boxes:

1. Click **Tools** on the menu bar, and then click **Options**. The Options dialog box opens.

2. Click the **Getting Started** icon, and then drag your mouse pointer across the Real name text to select it.

3. Press the **Delete** key to erase the contents of the text box.

4. Repeat Steps 2 and 3 for the Return address text box and for the Login Name text box.

5. Click the **OK** button to save your changes and close the Options dialog box.

After deleting your personal information, you can exit Eudora.

To exit Eudora:

1. Click **File** on the menu bar, and then click **Exit**. Eudora closes.

PINE

Pine E-Mail Client

Pine, or **Program for Internet News and E-mail**, is a popular e-mail client program developed for UNIX computers. It is also available on Windows 95/98 PCs. Originally, Pine was conceived and developed by the University of Washington in Seattle in 1989 as a simple mailer that runs on minicomputers. Since then, Pine has been refined and improved for use on the PC. Pine has a simple character-based interface that is easy to learn and use. It also is one of the most widely used e-mail programs in colleges and universities. Because you are likely to use Pine at your school, it is helpful to understand how to use it.

Using Pine to Send a Message

Your instructor or technical support person will give you specific instructions for starting the Pine program on your system. Normally, you log on to a computer system with your user name and password, and then you type "pine" on UNIX-based systems to start it. After starting the program, the Pine Main Menu window appears, as shown in Figure F-1. The first line indicates the Pine version number, screen name, and other useful information, such as the current folder and the number of new messages. The main part of the Pine window is the work area, and the message and prompt line appear at the bottom of the window. Menu commands for using Pine appear as the last two lines on the screen.

Figure F-1   PINE MAIN MENU

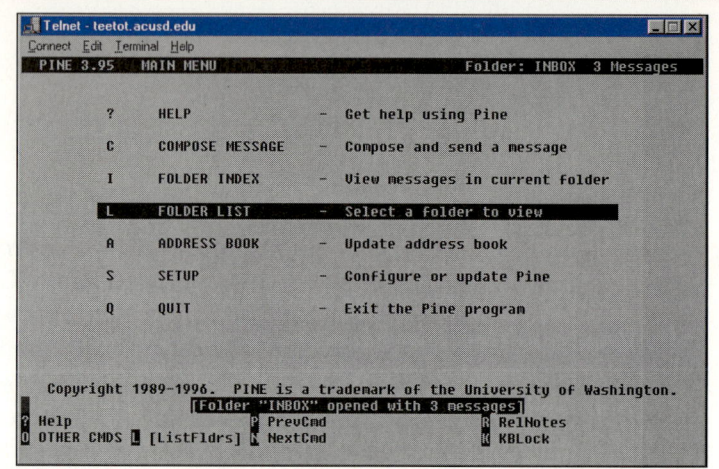

The Main Menu window is the starting point for all Pine e-mail activities. You can use the Main Menu window to seek help, compose and send a message, read incoming mail, manage your mail folders, maintain an address book, perform Pine system setup activities, and exit the Pine program. Every action in Pine springs from one or two keystrokes—the mouse is of little use while you are using Pine.

The first screen Pine displays should look similar to Figure F-1. The key you type to invoke any of the menu commands appears to the left of each option or command name. You can type either uppercase or lowercase letters. However, do *not* press the Enter key after typing a menu command key. You will send a message next.

Note: The steps in this appendix assume that you have read and understand Session 2.1 in Tutorial 2, which covers introductory e-mail concepts.

To create a message:

1. Start Pine, and then if necessary, type **M** to go to the Main Menu window.

   TROUBLE? If you press the Enter key after typing a menu command key (such as M), an error will occur. Do not press the Enter key after typing menu command keys.

2. Type **C** to open the Compose Message window.

3. Type **barbgoldberg@yahoo.com** on the To line. Press the **Enter** key to move to the Cc line.

Note: For these steps, you will send an e-mail message to a real mailbox. However, please note that all messages sent to the barbgoldberg account are deleted without being read.

TROUBLE? If you make a typing mistake, use the arrow keys to move the insertion point to the character following the one that you need to delete, and then press the Backspace key to delete the character. The Delete key sometimes does not work on character-based systems.

4. Type your full e-mail address on the Cc line, and then press the **Enter** key. You won't send an attachment with your message, so press the **Enter** key again to go to the Subject line.

5. Type **Sample Pine Message** in the Subject line, and then press the **Enter** key to move to the Message Text line.

6. Type the simple message **I am using Pine to compose and send this e-mail message.**

7. Press the **Enter** key twice to move down two lines in the message body.

8. Type your first and last names to sign your message. See Figure F-2.

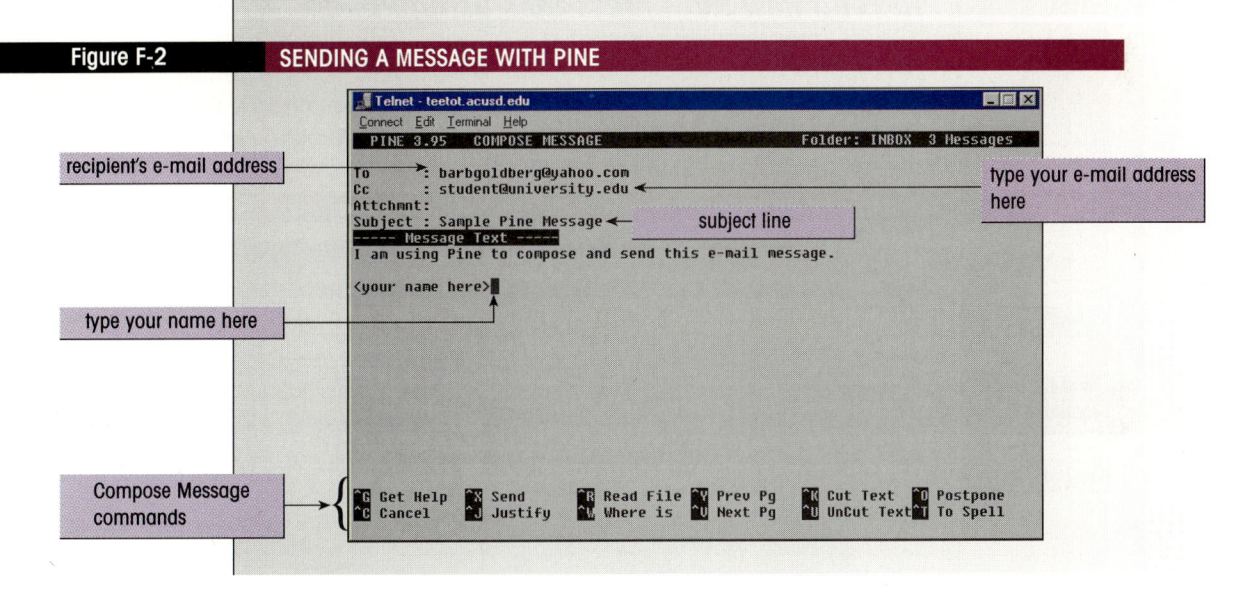

Figure F-2 — SENDING A MESSAGE WITH PINE

- recipient's e-mail address
- type your e-mail address here
- subject line
- type your name here
- Compose Message commands

Notice the commands at the bottom of the Compose Message window. The command ^X stands for Ctrl + X, which sends the message.

Once you are satisfied that the message is complete—check the recipient's e-mail address—and that the message body is correct, then you can send the message.

To send the message:

1. With the Compose Message window still open, press **Ctrl + X**. A prompt line asks if you want to send the message.

2. Type **Y** to send the message. The message is sent to the recipient(s), and the Compose Message window closes.

When you need to send the same message to several people, type all of the e-mail addresses in the To line and separate them with commas.

Pine is different from other e-mail clients because it sends mail immediately without queuing it first. Your only opportunity to cancel sending a message is to type N at the prompt when asked to send the message. If you want to cancel your message, press Ctrl + C. Pine asks you to confirm the cancel operation with a prompt beginning with "Cancel message…". Confirm you want to cancel the message by typing C. Pine closes the Compose Message window.

Using Pine to Receive Mail

Pine helps manage your mail by saving messages in a folder. Pine supplies several folders including those named INBOX, received, and sent. The INBOX folder holds all unread received mail. The sent mailbox holds mail you have sent, and the received folder holds mail you have received and read. You can add folders at any time and name them anything you want.

Mail arrives at the server, and Pine retrieves it. Pine does not always signal you when new mail arrives if you are using Pine, so check your mail regularly so you don't miss important messages while you are online.

To read new mail messages using Pine:

1. If necessary, type **M** to open the Main Menu window.
2. Type **I** to open the INBOX folder. The Folder Index window shows new and read messages and messages that are marked for deletion. See Figure F-3.

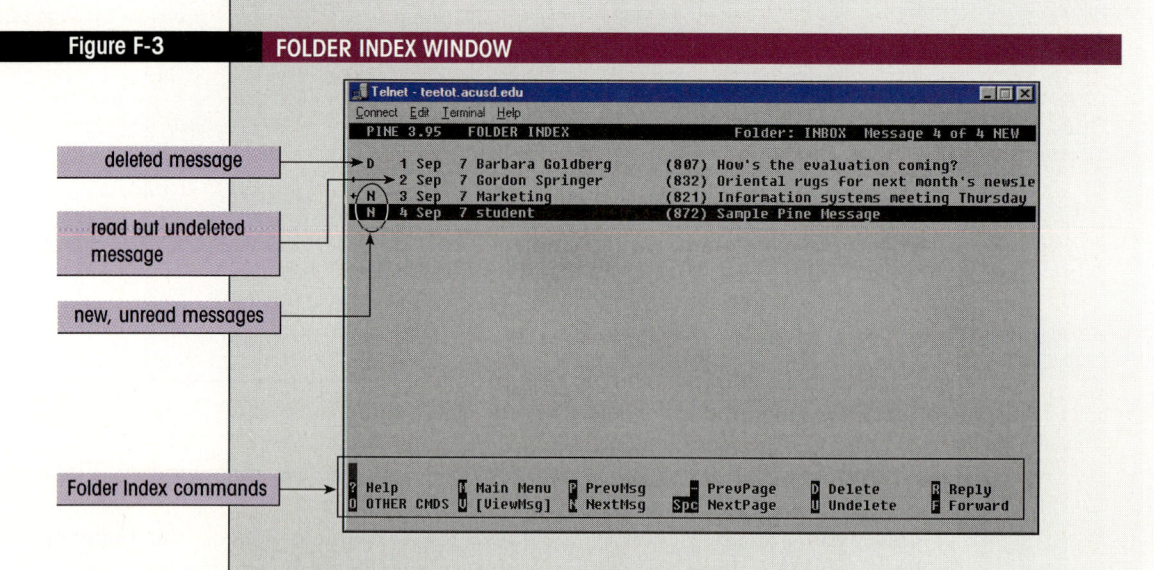

Figure F-3 — FOLDER INDEX WINDOW

Examine Figure F-3 carefully. Each message in the INBOX is numbered. The letters to the left of each message number in the INBOX indicate something about the status of each message. The first message has a "D" indicator, which means that you have read and marked the message for deletion. The second message has no indicator to its left, which indicates that you have read the message but not deleted it. The last two messages shown in Figure F-3 have an "N" status indicator, which indicates the messages are both new and that you have not read them yet.

3. Your Sample Pine Message should be selected—if it is not, use the arrow keys to select it, and then press the **Enter** key to open the selected message summary in its own window. The message opens so you can read its contents. See Figure F-4.

Figure F-4   **READING A MESSAGE**

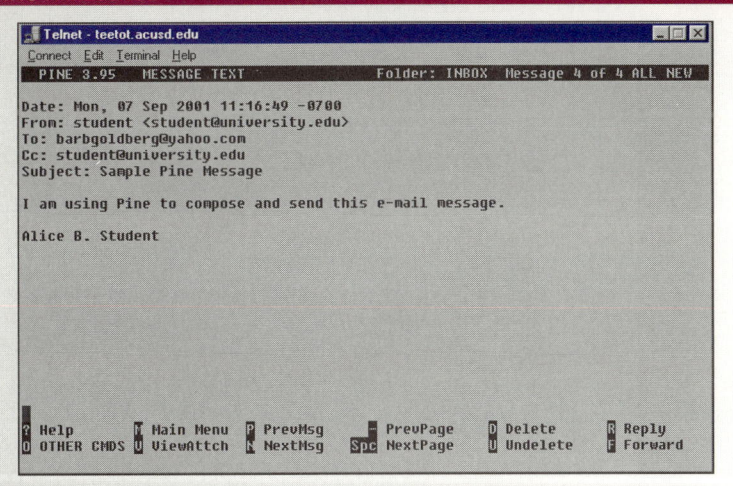

After you read a message, you have many options. For now, you will exit Pine.

4. Type **Q** to quit Pine. The message "Really quit pine?" appears near the bottom of the display.

5. Type **Y** to confirm your intent to leave Pine. The message "Save the 1 read message in "received"?" appears in the message line near the bottom of the display. (Your message might be different.)

6. Type **Y** to save the message you just read in the received folder. The message "Expunge the 1 deleted message from the "INBOX"?" appears. The deleted message is the one you just read.

7. Type **Y** to remove the message from the INBOX permanently. Pine closes, and you return to the system from which you invoked Pine.

Keep in mind a subtle point. Pine stores received messages in the INBOX. Messages remain in the INBOX until you delete them or save them in another folder. That is why Pine deletes the message that you moved to the received folder. Had you chosen *not* to send the message you read in the received folder, then Pine would automatically remove it from the INBOX. Pine removes the "N" status mark from messages you have read but have not yet moved to other folders. These messages remain in the INBOX.

Printing a Message Using Pine

Pine provides three options for printing messages. The first option assumes you have a printer attached to your computer or workstation, whereas another assumes you are using a standard UNIX workstation. Use this option if you are using a dial-up connection to a remote host computer running Pine. The last option provides printing using a predefined print command. Ask your instructor or technical support person for help using this option. If you are using Pine in a university computer lab, the best option is to print to a network printer. Ask your lab administrator to help check your printer setup before you print your e-mail.

To print a message using Pine:

1. Start Pine, and then type **I** to open the Folder Index window and the INBOX.

2. Use the Up and Down arrow keys to select the Sample Pine Message summary line.

3. Press the **Enter** key if you want to open the message to check its contents before printing. (You do not need to open a message in order to print it.)

4. Type **Y** to print the message. The message "Print message <#> using" followed by the printer selection appears on the message line.

   TROUBLE? The print command might not be visible on the first screen of menu commands. Type OK to see other commands in the command lines at the screen's bottom edge.

5. Type **Y** to print the message. If you need to cancel the print operation, either press Ctrl + C or type N for no. Either choice cancels the print command.

6. Type **Q** to quit pine. Respond appropriately to any messages that appear in the message line as you are leaving Pine.

Filing a Pine Message

You can organize your e-mail into different folders by topic, date, or any other category that makes sense to you. Pine even helps keep your INBOX organized chronologically. At the end of every month, Pine prompts you about your folders holding sent mail. Pine first asks if you want to rename your current sent folder. Doing so preserves that month's messages in a uniquely named folder. Second, Pine asks if you want to delete the previous month's sent mail folders and the current month's sent mail folder. You can choose to respond no by typing N to any question or yes by typing Y.

To view your current folders, type L in the Pine Main Menu window. At least three mail folder names appear. They are INBOX, received, and sent. You can move mail from any folder to any other folder. You also can create any new folders you would like and call them any name except an existing folder's name.

To create a new Pine folder:

1. Start Pine and type **L** (ListFldrs) in the Main Menu window to open the Folder List window.

2. Type **A** to add a folder. The prompt "Name of folder to add:" appears at the bottom of the screen.

3. Type **Marketing** to name the new folder, and then press the **Enter** key. Pine creates a new folder and selects it. See Figure F-5.

Figure F-5 CREATING A NEW PINE FOLDER

[Screenshot of Telnet window showing PINE 3.95 FOLDER LIST with INBOX, received, Marketing, sent folders. Status message: "Folder 'Marketing' created". Marketing folder is labeled with a callout.]

4. Type **M** to open the Main Menu.

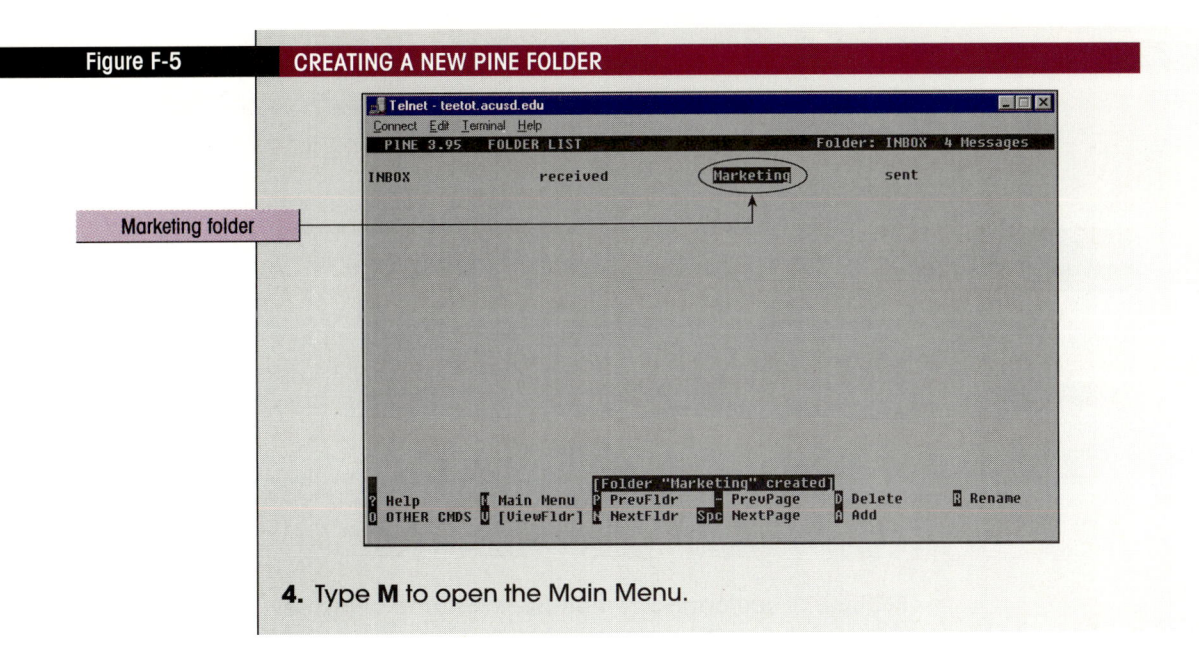

After creating the Marketing folder, you can save messages into it. When you save a message from one folder into another folder, Pine marks the original message for deletion and then moves it to the new folder. If you want to copy a message from one folder into another folder, then you must undelete the message in the original folder by selecting it and typing U for undelete. If you do not undelete the original message, it will be expunged when you exit Pine. Copying a message to different folders is useful if you want to file a message in several folders corresponding to different message categories. Next, you will save a message in the Marketing folder.

To save a message into another folder:

1. Start Pine, and then open the INBOX folder.

   TROUBLE? To open the INBOX, type M to open the Main Menu window and then type I to open the INBOX.

2. Use the Up and Down arrow keys to select the Sample Pine Message summary line in the Folder List.

3. Type **S** to save the highlighted message. The prompt "SAVE to folder (received):" appears at the bottom of the screen.

4. Type **Marketing**, the name of the folder to which you want to transfer the message. See Figure F-6.

Figure F-6 SAVING A MESSAGE TO ANOTHER FOLDER

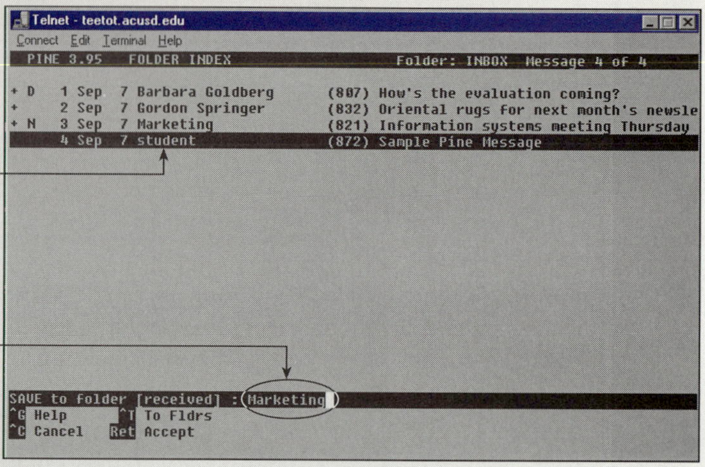

```
Telnet - teetot.acusd.edu
Connect  Edit  Terminal  Help
  PINE 3.95      FOLDER INDEX             Folder: INBOX  Message 4 of 4

  + D  1 Sep  7 Barbara Goldberg    (807) How's the evaluation coming?
  +    2 Sep  7 Gordon Springer     (832) Oriental rugs for next month's newsle
  + N  3 Sep  7 Marketing           (821) Information systems meeting Thursday
       4 Sep  7 student             (872) Sample Pine Message




SAVE to folder [received] : (Marketing)
^G Help         ^T To Fldrs
^C Cancel       Ret Accept
```

- *message being saved in the Marketing folder*
- *folder to which highlighted message is saved*

TROUBLE? If you cannot remember the name of the new folder, press Ctrl + T to display a list of all folder names, select the desired folder, and then press the Enter key.

5. Press the **Enter** key to save the message. Pine displays a message indicating that the message was transferred to the Marketing folder and the original message was marked for deletion.

TROUBLE? If you transfer a message to the wrong folder, just repeat the preceding steps by opening the folder containing the message you transferred. Then, save it to the correct folder.

6. Type **Q** to exit Pine. Pine will ask if you want to expunge messages marked for deletion—including the one you just saved in the Marketing folder—from the INBOX. Because you have a copy of the message in the Marketing folder, you will expunge the original message and any others marked.

7. Type **Y** to expunge messages marked for deletion, including the one you transferred to the Marketing folder.

Forwarding a Message Using Pine

When you forward a message, Pine sends the entire message you received (including the header lines and the body of the message) and adds a line above the entire message indicating that it is a forwarded message. After you add the e-mail address of the person to forward the message to and a subject line and send the message, it is delivered to the addressee just like any other mail message. The original message remains in your INBOX unless you delete it.

To forward an existing mail message to another user, open the INBOX containing the message, highlight the message in the Folder Index window (the INBOX), and then type F to invoke the Forward command. Enter the recipient's e-mail address in the To field, type a short subject, and then enter a brief explanation of why you are forwarding the message in the Message Text area, if necessary. Press Ctrl + X to send the message.

Replying to a Message Using Pine

You use the Pine Reply command to reply to a sender's message. Open the INBOX message to which you want to respond and type R to execute the Reply command. Pine asks you if you want to include the original message in the reply. Type Y to include it, or type N to omit it. If the sender's message has Cc or Bcc recipients, Pine will ask if you want to reply to all recipients. Again, type either Y or N to answer yes or no, respectively. The Compose Message Reply window opens with the header completed, and the insertion point appears in the first position of the Message Text area. Pine automatically inserts the original message sender's e-mail address in the To line of the response. The greater than symbol (>) appears to the left of each line of the original message to distinguish it from the text you supply in response. In addition to writing response lines, you can modify any portion of the sender's message in your response. Often, a responder will delete much of the sender's text, leaving only a snippet of the original message—just enough to provide a context for the response.

Deleting a Message Using Pine

To prevent you from inadvertently deleting important messages, Pine requires you to take two steps to delete an e-mail message. First, you delete a message, which simply marks the message for permanent removal. Second, you permanently remove a message by expunging all messages marked for deletion.

To delete a message using Pine:

1. Start Pine, and then type **L** to display your e-mail folders.
2. Press the right arrow key enough times to select the Marketing folder.
3. Press the **Enter** key to open the Marketing folder to reveal the message you saved.
4. Use the Up and Down arrow keys to select your Sample Pine Message summary line, and then type **D** to mark the highlighted record for deletion. The letter "D" appears in the left column of the message line and the next message summary line, if there is one, is selected. See Figure F-7.

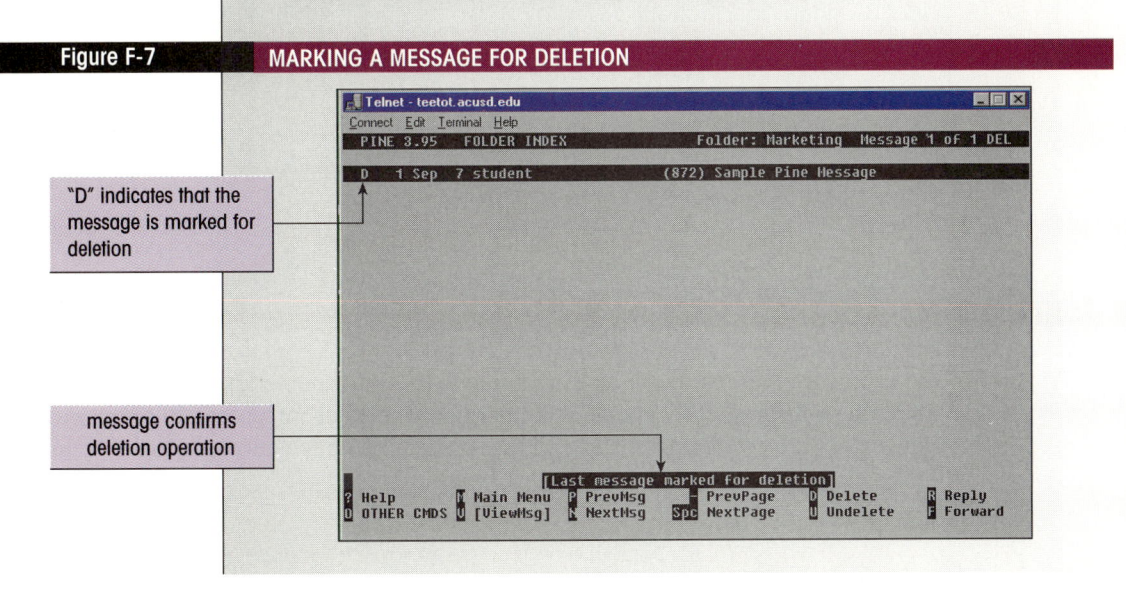

Figure F-7   MARKING A MESSAGE FOR DELETION

"D" indicates that the message is marked for deletion

message confirms deletion operation

> **TROUBLE?** If you mark the wrong message for deletion, type **U** to send the Undelete command and remove the deletion mark. You can undelete a message any time before you expunge all messages.
>
> 5. Repeat Step 4 to delete any other messages that you received during this session.
> 6. Type **M** to return to Pine's Main Menu window. If you want to quit Pine at this point and do not want to delete marked messages permanently, type **N** when Pine asks if you want to expunge the deleted messages.

You can mark a message in any folder for deletion. Next, you will expunge all messages marked for deletion.

> ### To expunge a Pine message:
> 1. Type **Q** to quit Pine.
> 2. Type **Y** at the "Really quit pine?" prompt.
> 3. If Pine asks you if you want to save a message or messages in the received folder, type Y if you want to move messages from the INBOX folder to the received folder. Otherwise, type N and the group of messages—unmarked ones—will remain in the INBOX.
> 4. Type **Y** to expunge all marked messages at the "Expunge the 1 deleted message from "INBOX"?" prompt. All messages marked for deletion disappear, and control returns to the program from which you started Pine.

Besides deleting individual e-mail messages, you can delete entire e-mail folders. Next, you will delete the Marketing folder.

> ### To delete a Pine e-mail folder:
> 1. Start Pine, if necessary, and type **L** to open the FOLDER LIST.
> 2. Use the right and left arrow keys to select the Marketing folder.
> 3. Type **D** to delete the Marketing folder. A message displays near the bottom of the display: Really delete "Marketing" (the currently open folder)?
> 4. Type **Y** to confirm the deletion. The Marketing folder is removed.
> 5. Type **M** to return to Pine's Main Menu window.

Maintaining an Address Book in Pine

You can use an address book to create individual and group addresses. After you have a few entries in your Pine address book, you can refer to them at any point while you are composing, replying to, or forwarding a message. Pine sorts address book entries in order by full name.

To create an address book entry:

1. Start Pine, and make sure that you are in the Main Menu window.

2. Type **A** to open the Address Book window.

   TROUBLE? If you see the message "(Empty)" in the Address Book window, don't worry. That simply means that you do not yet have any e-mail addresses stored in your address book.

3. Type **A** to add a new entry.

4. Type your first name on the Nickname line, and then press the **Enter** key.

5. Type your last name, a comma, a space, and your first name (such as Goldberg, Barbara) on the Fullname line, and then press the **Enter** key three times to move to the Addresses line.

6. Type your full e-mail address in the Addresses line. Notice the instructions below the entry to help you save it. See Figure F-8.

Figure F-8   CREATING A NEW ADDRESS BOOK ENTRY

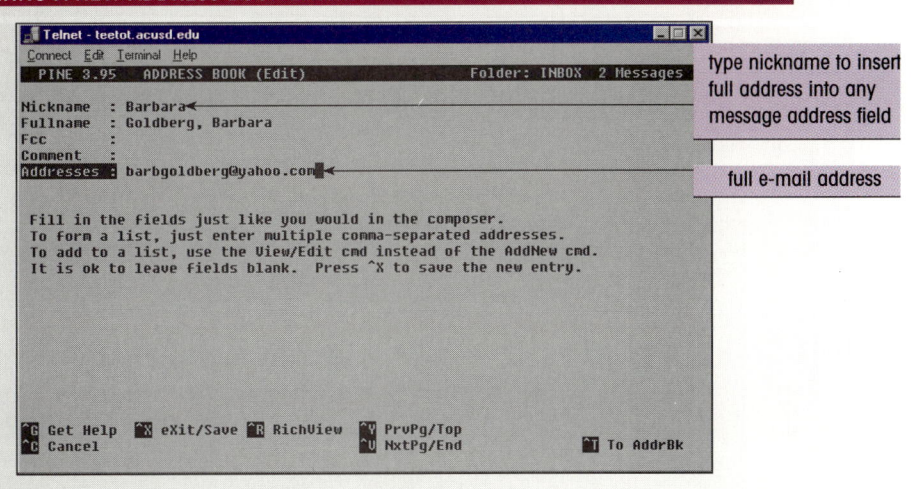

type nickname to insert full address into any message address field

full e-mail address

   TROUBLE? If you make a mistake in any entry, use the arrow keys to move to the line and correct the mistake.

7. Press **Ctrl + X** to save the new entry, and then type **Y** to confirm exiting and saving the new entry. The address book shows the new entry in alphabetical order by the Fullname field.

   TROUBLE? If you change your mind and do not want to save the entry, press Ctrl + C to cancel saving the entry, and then type Y to confirm cancellation.

8. Type **M** to go to the Main Menu window.

When you want to send a message to someone who is listed in your address book, you can type that person's nickname or his or her full name, and Pine will address the message automatically.

You also can use Pine to create a distribution list of e-mail addresses. To do this, type A to open the Address Book window, type A to add a new address, type the list's name on the Nickname line and press the Enter key to move to the Addresses line, and then type the individual e-mail addresses and separate them with commas. Press Ctrl + X to save the new entry, and then type Y to exit and save changes. The address book reappears with the distribution list address visible. You can see the individual addresses in the group address by selecting the entry.

Exiting Pine

When you are finished using Pine, you should exit the program. Furthermore, if you have used Telnet to log into a UNIX system running Pine, be sure to log out of your account. The next steps illustrate how to exit the Pine e-mail system. Consult with your instructor about logging off the system at your school.

To exit Pine:

1. Type **Q**, and then respond to any prompts to exit Pine and return to the system from which you started.

2. Type **Y** when the "Really quit pine?" message appears.

3. If additional messages appear near the bottom of the display (they are easy to overlook), respond by typing Y (for yes) or N (for no) as appropriate. Example messages include "Save read message in "received"?" or "Expunge the deleted message from "INBOX"?" The "Pine finished" message confirms you exited the program.

GLOSSARY/INDEX

A

acceptable use policies (AUPs),
   WEB 1.20–21
   The policy of a school or employer that specifies the conditions under which its students and/or employees can use their Internet connections.

Address Bar
   entering URLs in, WEB 3.45–47
   Element of the Internet Explorer browser window into which you can enter the URL or a Web page that you would like to open.

address books, WEB 2.12
   adding e-mail addresses to
      in Netscape Messenger,
         WEB 2.29–30
      in Outlook Express,
         WEB 2.47–49
   multi-address entries in
      in Netscape Navigator,
         WEB 2.49–50
      in Outlook Express,
         WEB 2.31–33
   The collection of e-mail addresses maintained by an e-mail program and stored conveniently. Often, nicknames can be assigned to address book entries so they are easy to recall and insert into e-mail message headers.

addressing. *See also* **e-mail addresses**
   domain name, WEB 3.06–3.08
   IP (Internet Protocol), WEB 2.07,
      WEB 3.06, WEB 3.07

ADSL, WEB 1.18–19

Advanced Research Projects Agency (ARPA or DARPA), WEB 1.08
   The U.S. Department of Defense agency that sponsored the early research and development of technologies and systems that later became the Internet.

anchor tags, WEB 3.03
   An HTML tag that links multiple HTML documents to each other. The connection between two HTML documents is called a hypertext link, a hyperlink, or, simply, a link.

Andreessen, Marc, WEB 1.15

ARPA, WEB 1.08

ARPANET
   defined, WEB 1.08
   e-mail messages over, WEB 1.09
   history, WEB 1.10, WEB 1.12
   The experimental WAN that DARPA established in 1969 to connect universities and research institutions so they could share computer resources.

Asymmetric Digital Subscriber Line (ADSL), WEB 1.18–19
   A new type of digital subscriber line (DSL) that offers transmission speeds ranging from 16 to 640 Kbps from the user to the telephone company and from 1.5 to 9 Mbps from the telephone company to the user.

Asynchronous Transfer Mode (ATM), WEB 1.19
   A high-bandwidth (622 Mbps) data transmission connection used as part of the Internet backbone.

attachments, to e-mail messages
   defined, WEB 2.05
   saving
      in Netscape Messenger,
         WEB 2.22–23
      in Outlook Express,
         WEB 2.40–41
   sending
      in Netscape Messenger,
         WEB 2.19–20
      in Outlook Express, WEB 2.38
   viewing
      in Netscape Messenger,
         WEB 2.22–23
      in Outlook Express, WEB 2.40
   A file encoded so that it can be carried over the Internet safely when attached to an e-mail message.

AUPs (acceptable use policies),
   WEB 1.20–21

Auto Hide feature
   in Internet Explorer, WEB 3.44–45

B

Back button, WEB 3.14, WEB 3.29

bandwidth, WEB 1.18–19
   defined, WEB 1.18
   for Internet connection types,
      WEB 1.18–19
   measurement of, WEB 1.18
   The amount of data that can travel through a communications circuit in one second.

Bcc (blind carbon copy), WEB 2.03,
   WEB 2.04–2.05

Because It's Time (originally, "There") Network (BITNET),
   WEB 1.09, WEB 1.10
   A network of IBM mainframe computers at universities founded by the City University of New York.

Berners-Lee, Timothy, WEB 1.14,
   WEB 1.15

BITNET, WEB 1.09, WEB 1.10

bits per second (bps), WEB 1.18
   The basic increment in which bandwidth is measured.

blind carbon copy (bcc),
   WEB 2.04–2.05, WEB 3.03
   A copy of an e-mail message sent to a primary recipient without the Bcc recipient's address appearing in the message. The message's original recipient is unaware that others received the message.

bookmark folders
   creating, WEB 3.24–25
   saving bookmarks in, WEB 3.25–27

bookmarks. *See also* **favorites**
   creating, WEB 3.23–24
   defined, WEB 3.14
   using, WEB 3.14, WEB 3.15
   A feature of Navigator that allows you to save the URL of a specific page so you can return to it.

Bookmarks button, WEB 3.23

Bookmarks window
   examining bookmark hierarchy in,
      WEB 3.23–24

bps (bits per second), WEB 3.18

Bush, Vannevar, WEB 1.14

C

cable modems
   connecting to Internet with,
      WEB 1.21–22
   defined, WEB 1.21
   Converts a computer's digital signals into radio-frequency analog signals that are similar to television transmission signals. The converted signals travel to and from the user's cable company, which maintains a connection to the Internet.

cable television
   connecting to the Internet with,
      WEB 1.19, WEB 1.21–22

cables
   connecting computers to Internet
      with, WEB 1.06

cache folder, WEB 3.14

Calliau, Robert, WEB 1.14,
   WEB 1.15

carbon copies (Cc)
   sending, in Netscape Messenger,
      WEB 2.19
   sending, in Outlook Express,
      WEB 2.38
   A copy of an e-mail message sent to other people in addition to the primary recipient.

carbon copy (Cc) line, WEB 2.03,
   WEB 2.04

Category 1 cable, WEB 1.06
A type of twisted-pair cable that telephone companies have used for years to carry voice signals. Category 1 cable is inexpensive and easy to install but transmits information much more slowly than other types of cable.

Category 5 cable, WEB 1.06
A type of twisted-pair cable developed specifically for carrying data signals rather than voice signals. Category 5 cable is easy to install and carries signals between 10 and 100 times faster than coaxial cable.

Cerf, Vincent, WEB 1.09

CERN, WEB 1.14

circuit switching, WEB 1.08
A centrally controlled, single-connection method for sending information over a network.

circuits
defined, WEB 1.08

Clark, James, WEB 1.15

client computers, WEB 1.05
A computer that is connected to another, usually more powerful, computer called a server. The client computer can use the server computer's resources, such as printers, files, or programs. This way of connecting computers is called a client/server network.

client/server local area networks, WEB 1.05–1.06
A way of connecting multiple computers, called client computers, to a main computer, called a server computer. This connection method allows the client computers to share the server computer's resources, such as printers, files, and programs.

coaxial cable, WEB 1.06, WEB 1.07
An insulated copper wire that is encased in a metal shield and then enclosed in plastic insulation. The signal-carrying wire is completely shielded so it resists electrical interference much better than twisted-pair cable does. Coaxial cable also carries signals about 20 times faster than twisted-pair cable, but it is considerably more expensive.

commercial e-mail services
history of, WEB 1.11

Composition window
in Netscape Navigator, WEB 2.15
The Netscape Messenger window in which you create e-mail messages.

CompuServe, WEB 1.11

Computer Science Network (CSNET), WEB 1.09
An internet funded by the NSF for educational and research institutions that did not have access to the ARPANET.

connections to the Internet, WEB 1.17–22
bandwidth, WEB 1.18–19
service providers, WEB 1.17
through cable television companies, WEB 1.21–22
through employers, WEB 1.20
through Internet service providers (ISPs), WEB 1.21
through schools, WEB 1.20
via satellite, WEB 1.22

copies of e-mail messages, WEB 2.04–2.05
blind carbon copies, WEB 2.04
carbon copies, WEB 2.04, WEB 2.19, WEB 2.38
sending to another folder, WEB 2.26–27

copyright, WEB 3.16
The legal right of the author or other owner of an original work to control the reproduction, distribution, and sale of that work.

country domain names, WEB 3.07–3.08

CSNET, WEB 1.09, WEB 1.10

D

DARPA, WEB 1.08

Deleted Items folder
in Outlook Express, WEB 2.34, WEB 2.45–47

deleting
e-mail messages, WEB 2.11
in Netscape Messenger, WEB 2.27–28
in Outlook Express, WEB 2.45–47
mail folders
in Netscape Messenger, WEB 2.28
in Outlook Express, WEB 2.47

demodulation, WEB 1.20
The process of converting an analog signal to a digital signal.

Digital Subscriber Line or Digital Subscriber Loop (DSL), WEB 1.18
A protocol used by some telephone companies that allows higher bandwidth data transmissions than standard telephone service does.

directories, Web. See Web directories

distribution lists, WEB 2.12
creating in Outlook Express, WEB 2.49–50
A single address book nickname that refers to a collection of two or more e-mail addresses. Also known as a group mailing list.

DNS (domain name server) software, WEB 3.7
A program on an Internet host computer that coordinates the IP addresses and domain names for all of the computers attached to it.

domain names, WEB 3.06–08
country, WEB 3.07–3.08
defined, WEB 3.07
top-level, WEB 3.07–3.08
A unique name that is associated with a specific IP address by a program that runs on an Internet host computer.

domain name servers, WEB 3.07
The Internet host computer that runs DNS software to coordinate the IP addresses and domain names for every computer attached to it.

Down scroll arrow, WEB 3.11

DSL, WEB 3.18

dumb terminals, WEB 2.8
An otherwise "smart" computer that passes all your keystrokes to another computer to which you are connected and does not attempt to do anything else.

E

educational institutions
Internet connections through, WEB 1.20

electronic mail. See e-mail

e-mail, WEB 2.01–2.50. See also e-mail messages; mailing lists
commercial services, WEB 1.10–11
configuring Netscape Messenger for, WEB 2.15–18
configuring Outlook Express for, WEB 2.34–36
defined, WEB 1.04, WEB 2.02
history of, WEB 1.09
mail client software, WEB 2.02
protocols, WEB 2.02
Web-based, WEB 2.08–2.09
The transmission of messages over communications networks, such as the Internet.

e-mail addresses, WEB 2.06–2.08
adding to address books
in Netscape Messenger, WEB 2.29–30
in Outlook Express, WEB 2.47–49

in Cc and Bcc lines of e-mail
  messages, WEB 2.04
defined, WEB 2.06
distribution lists, WEB 2.12
host names, WEB 2.07
in From line of e-mail messages,
  WEB 2.04
in To line of e-mail messages,
  WEB 2.04
user names, WEB 2.07
e-mail attachments. *See* attachments,
  to e-mail messages
e-mail clients, WEB 2.08–2.09. *See
  also* **Microsoft Outlook Express;
  Netscape Messenger**
  free, WEB 2.08–2.09
  setting up, WEB 2.09
  shareware, WEB 2.08
  using, WEB 2.09–2.11
e-mail messages. *See also*
  attachments, to e-mail messages;
  e-mail
  archives of, WEB 2.10
  with attachments, WEB 2.05,
    WEB 2.19–20, WEB 2.22–23,
    WEB 2.38, WEB 2.40–41
  Bcc line, WEB 2.04–2.05
  Cc line, WEB 2.04–2.05
  components of, WEB 2.03–2.06
  copies of, WEB 2.03,
    WEB 2.04–2.05
    in Netscape Messenger,
      WEB 2.18–19
    in Outlook Express,
      WEB 2.36–37
  copying and moving
    in Netscape Messenger,
      WEB 2.26–27
    in Outlook Express,
      WEB 2.44–45
  deleting, WEB 2.11
    in Netscape Messenger,
      WEB 2.27–28
    in Outlook Express,
      WEB 2.45–47
  filing, WEB 2.10
  forwarding, WEB 2.10–2.11
    in Netscape Messenger,
      WEB 2.24–25
    in Outlook Express, WEB 2.43
  guidelines for writing, WEB 2.09
  leaving on server, WEB 2.17
    From line, WEB 2.04
    To line, WEB 2.03, WEB 3.04
  marking as delivered, WEB 2.10
  marking as read, WEB 2.10
  message body, WEB 2.03,
    WEB 2.05
  message header, WEB 2.03

opening
  in Outlook Express, WEB 2.40
printing, WEB 2.10
  in Netscape Messenger,
    WEB 2.27
  in Outlook Express, WEB 2.45
queued, WEB 2.09
  in Netscape Messenger,
    WEB 2.20
  in Outlook Express, WEB 2.39
quoted, WEB 2.11
receiving, WEB 2.10
  in Netscape Messenger,
    WEB 2.21–22
  in Outlook Express,
    WEB 2.39–40
replying to, WEB 2.11
  in Netscape Messenger,
    WEB 2.23–24
  in Outlook Express,
    WEB 2.41–42
signature files, WEB 2.05–2.06
spell checking
  in Netscape Messenger,
    WEB 2.20
  in Outlook Express, WEB 2.39
Subject line, WEB 2.04
e-mail programs, WEB 2.08–2.09
encryption, WEB 3.34, WEB 3.58
  A way of scrambling and encoding
  data transmissions that reduces the
  risk that a person who intercepted
  the Web page as it traveled across
  the Internet would be able to decode
  and read the transmission's contents.
Englebart, Douglas, WEB 1.14
error messages
  for nonworking hyperlinks,
    WEB 3.05
Ethernet networks, WEB 1.18
ExciteMail, WEB 2.08

F

Fast Ethernet, WEB 1.18
Favorites, WEB 3.47–51. *See also*
  bookmarks
  creating new folders, WEB 3.48–49
  defined, WEB 3.14
  organizing, WEB 3.49–51
  using, WEB 3.14, WEB 3.15
  A feature of Internet Explorer that
  allows you to save the URL of a
  specific page so you can return to it.
Favorites button, WEB 3.47
**Federal Networking Council (FNC),
  WEB 1.11**
**fiber-optic cable, WEB 1.06,
  WEB 1.07**

  A type of cable that transmits
  information by pulsing beams of
  light through very thin strands of
  glass. Fiber-optic cable transmits
  signals much faster than coaxial cable
  does and, because it does not use
  electricity, is immune to electrical
  interference. Fiber-optic cable is
  lighter and more durable than
  coaxial cable, but it is harder to work
  with and much more expensive.
file attachments. *See* attachments, to
  e-mail messages
**File Transfer Protocol (FTP),
  WEB 1.09**
filing e-mail messages, WEB 2.10
  with filters, WEB 2.10
  in Netscape Messenger,
    WEB 2.26–27
  in Outlook Express, WEB 2.44–45
filters
  filing e-mail messages with,
    WEB 2.10
  An automatic method of filing
  incoming mail into one or several
  mailboxes or folders based on
  characters found in the message
  header or message body.
floating component bar
  in Netscape Messenger, WEB 3.18
floppy disks
  saving bookmark files to,
    WEB 3.26–27
  saving Web pages to, WEB 3.37,
    WEB 3.40–41, WEB 3.63–64
**FNC (Federal Networking Council),
  WEB 1.11**
Folder list
  in Outlook Express, WEB 2.34
  A list of e-mail folders for receiving,
  saving, and deleting mail messages.
formal signatures
  for e-mail addresses, WEB 2.06
  An e-mail signature that typically
  contains the sender's name, title,
  company name, company address,
  telephone and fax numbers, and
  e-mail address.
**Forward button, WEB 3.14,
  WEB 3.29**
forward slash (/), WEB 3.09
**forwarding e-mail messages,
  WEB 2.10–11**
  in Netscape Messenger,
    WEB 2.24–25
  in Outlook Express, WEB 2.43
  The process of sending a copy of an
  e-mail message to another recipient
  whom you specify without the
  original sender's knowledge.

From line, WEB 2.04
Contains the e-mail address of a message's sender.
Full Screen command
in Internet Explorer, WEB 3.44–45

G

Get Msg button
in Netscape Messenger, WEB 2.21
gigabits per second (Gbps), WEB 1.18
A measure of bandwidth; 1,073,741,824 bits per second (bps).
Go command
in Netscape Messenger, WEB 3.29
graphical transfer process indicator
in Internet Explorer, WEB 3.43
Element of the Internet Explorer status bar that indicates how much of a Web page has loaded from the Web server.
graphical user interface (GUI), WEB 1.15
of Web browsers, WEB 3.10
A way of presenting program output to users that uses pictures, icons, and other graphical elements instead of just displaying text.
group address entries
creating in Outlook Express, WEB 2.49–50
group mailing lists, WEB 2.12. *See also* **distribution lists**
GUI. *See* **graphical user interface (GUI)**

H

Help
in Internet Explorer, WEB 3.58–59
in Netscape Messenger, WEB 3.35–36
hierarchical structures
of bookmarks window, WEB 3.23–24
The organized, inverted tree containing folders and files on a computer.
History button
in Internet Explorer, WEB 3.53
history list, WEB 3.14
viewing in Internet Explorer, WEB 3.53–54
viewing in Netscape Navigator, WEB 3.29
A file in which the Web browser stores the location of each page you visit as you navigate hyperlinks from one Web page to another.

Home button
in Web browsers, WEB 3.12, WEB 3.30
home pages
default
in Internet Explorer, WEB 3.54–55
in Netscape Navigator, WEB 3.30–31
defined, WEB 3.05
displaying
in Internet Explorer, WEB 3.54
in Netscape Navigator, WEB 3.30
modifying default
in Internet Explorer, WEB 3.55
in Netscape Navigator, WEB 3.30–31
returning to, in Internet Explorer, WEB 3.54–55
use of term, WEB 3.06
The main page that all of the pages on a particular Web site are organized around and to which they link back; or the first page that opens when a particular Web browser program is started; or the page that a particular Web browser program loads the first time it is run. This page usually is stored at the Web site of the firm or other organization that created the Web browser software. Home pages under the second and third definitions also are called start pages.
host name suffix, WEB 2.07
host names, WEB 2.07
A user-friendly name that uniquely identifies a computer connected to the Internet. You can use it in place of an IP address.
HotMail, WEB 2.08
HTML. *See* **Hypertext Markup Language (HTML)**
http://, WEB 3.09
hyperlinks. *See also* **links**
defined, WEB 1.14
A connection between two HTML pages. Also known as a link or a hypertext link.
hypermedia links, WEB 3.05
A connection between an HTML document and a multimedia file, such as a graphics, sound clip, or video file.
hypertext
defined, WEB 1.14
origins of, WEB 1.14
A page-linking system described by Ted Nelson in the 1960s in which text on one page links to text on other pages.

hypertext links. *See* **links**
Hypertext Markup Language (HTML), WEB 1.14, WEB 3.03
defined, WEB 3.03
reading documents, WEB 1.15
A language that includes a set of codes (or tags) attached to text that describe the relationships among text elements
hypertext servers, WEB 1.14
A computer that stores HTML documents and lets other computers connect to it and read those documents.
Hypertext Transfer Protocol (HTTP), WEB 3.09

I

IETF (Internet Engineering Task Force), WEB 1.11
images
as links, WEB 3.05
saving from Web pages, WEB 3.16
saving to disk, WEB 3.37, WEB 3.40–41, WEB 3.63–64
IMAP (Internet Message Access Protocol), WEB 2.02
A protocol for retrieving e-mail messages from a mail server.
Inbox
in Netscape Messenger, WEB 2.13
in Outlook Express, WEB 2.34
index.html, WEB 3.09
The default name for the HTML document that serves as a Web site's home or main page.
informal signatures
for e-mail messages, WEB 2.06
An e-mail signature that sometimes contains graphics or quotations that express a more casual style found in correspondence between friends and acquaintances.
Integrated Services Digital Network (ISDN), WEB 1.18
A type of DSL that allows data transmission at bandwidths of up to 128 Kbps.
interconnected network (internet), WEB 1.07
A general term for *any* network of networks. Also known as an internet (lowercase i).
Internet. *See also* **World Wide Web**
commercial use of, WEB 1.10–11, WEB 1.15
communication tools available on, WEB 1.04
connection options, WEB 1.17–22
defined, WEB 1.04, WEB 1.07

Federal Networking Council's definition of, WEB 1.10
first use of term, WEB 1.09
growth of, WEB 1.11–13
history of, WEB 1.07–1.11
information resources available on, WEB 1.04
original networks composing, WEB 1.10
privatization of, WEB 1.12
structure of, WEB 1.13–14
traffic on, WEB 1.13
A specific worldwide collection of interconnected networks whose owners have voluntarily agreed to share resources and network connections.

Internet 2, WEB 1.19
A network being developed by a group of universities and the NSF that will have backbone bandwidths that exceed 1 Gbps.

Internet access providers (IAPs), WEB 1.17. *See also* **Internet service providers (ISPs)**
Firms that purchase Internet access from network access points and sell it to businesses, individuals, and smaller IAPs. Also known as an Internet service provider (ISP).

Internet Accounts dialog box
in Outlook Express, WEB 2.35–36

Internet addresses, WEB 2.06. *See also* **e-mail addresses**

Internet Connection window
in Outlook Express, WEB 2.35–36

Internet Engineering Task Force (IETF), WEB 1.11
A self-organized group that makes technical contributions to the Internet and related technologies. It is the main body that develops new Internet standards.

Internet Explorer. *See* **Microsoft Internet Explorer**

internet (interconnected network), WEB 1.07. *See also* **interconnected network**

Internet Message Access Protocol. *See* **IMAP**

Internet Protocol (IP), WEB 1.09
A part of the TCP/IP set of rules for sending data over a network.

Internet Protocol (IP) addressing, WEB 2.07, WEB 3.06, WEB 3.07
A series of four numbers separated by periods that uniquely identifies each computer connected to the Internet.

Internet Security Properties dialog box, WEB 3.43–44

Internet service providers (ISPs), WEB 1.17. *See also* **Internet access providers (IAPs)**
advantages and disadvantages of, WEB 1.21
connecting to the Internet through, WEB 1.21

Internet Worm, WEB 1.11
A program launched by Robert Morris in 1988 that used weaknesses in e-mail programs and operating systems to distribute itself to some of the computers that were then connected to the Internet. The program created multiple copies of itself on the computers it infected, which then consumed the processing power of the infected computers and prevented them from running other programs.

intranets, WEB 1.11
A LAN or WAN that uses the TCP/IP protocol but does not connect to sites outside the host firm or organization.

IP addresses. *See* **Internet Protocol (IP) addressing**

ISDN service, WEB 1.18

ISPs. *See* **Internet service providers (ISPs)**

J

Joint Academic Network (Janet), WEB 1.10
An internet established by U.K. universities.

Juno, WEB 2.08, WEB 2.09

K

Kahn, Robert, WEB 1.09
kilobits per second (Kbps), WEB 1.18
A measure of bandwidth; 1,024 bps.

kilobytes, WEB 2.05
A unit of measure that is approximately 1,000 characters.

L

LANS. *See* **local area networks (LANs)**

line-splitters, WEB 1.22
A device that divides combined signals from a cable television company into their television and data components.

links. *See also* **hyperlinks**
color of, WEB 3.04
defined, WEB 1.14, WEB 3.03
display of, WEB 3.04
following, WEB 3.27–31, WEB 3.51–53
in Internet Explorer, WEB 3.51–53
in Netscape Navigator, WEB 3.27–31
graphic images as, WEB 3.05
locating on a page, WEB 3.05
uses of, WEB 3.05

LISTSERV, WEB 1.09
Software for running mailing lists on IBM mainframe computers.

local area networks (LANs), WEB 1.05–106
connecting computers to, WEB 1.06–1.07
defined, WEB 1.07
wireless, WEB 1.07
Any of several ways of connecting computers to each other when the computers are located close to each other (no more than a few thousand feet apart).

location field
entering URLs in, WEB 3.20, WEB 3.21
The Navigator control into which you can enter the URL of a Web page that you would like to open.

Location toolbar
in Netscape Navigator, WEB 3.19–27
bookmarks, WEB 3.23–27
entering URLs in, WEB 3.21–23
hiding and showing, WEB 3.21
The Navigator toolbar that contains the Location field, the page proxy icon, and the Bookmarks button.

M

mail client software, WEB 2.02
An e-mail program that requests mail delivery from a mail server to your PC.

mail folders
in Netscape Messenger
creating, WEB 2.26
deleting, WEB 2.28
transferring mail to, WEB 2.27
in Outlook Express
creating, WEB 2.44
deleting, WEB 2.47
transferring mail to, WEB 2.45

mail servers, WEB 2.02
configuring, in Netscape Messenger, WEB 2.16–17

mailing lists
creating in Netscape Messenger, WEB 2.31–33
defined, WEB 1.09, WEB 2.03, WEB 2.31

group, WEB 2.12
modifying in Netscape Messenger, WEB 2.33
A list of names and e-mail addresses for a group of people who share a common interest in a subject or topic.

mainframe computers, WEB 1.06
A computer that is larger and more expensive than either a minicomputer or a PC. Businesses and other organizations use mainframe computers to process large volumes of work at high speeds.

Maximize button, WEB 3.17
in Internet Explorer, WEB 3.42

MCI Mail, WEB 1.11

megabits per second (Mbps), WEB 1.18
A measure of bandwidth; 1,048,576 bps.

Memex, WEB 1.14
A memory-extension device envisioned by Vannevar Bush in 1945 that stored all of a person's books, records, letters, and research results on microfilm. The idea included mechanical aids to help users consult their collected knowledge quickly and flexibly.

menu bar
in Internet Explorer, WEB 3.44
in Web browsers, WEB 3.12

message body (e-mail), WEB 2.03, WEB 2.05
The content of an e-mail message.

Message Center window
in Netscape Messenger, WEB 2.13–14

message content panel
in Netscape Messenger, WEB 2.13

message headers (e-mail), WEB 2.03
The part of an e-mail message containing information about the message's sender, receiver, and subject.

message header summaries
in Netscape Messenger, WEB 2.13
Subject lines from the e-mail messages in a mail folder that are displayed in a list.

Message List window
in Netscape Messenger, WEB 2.13

Message window
in Netscape Messenger, WEB 2.14–15

Messenger. *See* **Netscape Messenger**
Microsoft Corporation, WEB 1.15
Microsoft Internet Explorer, WEB 1.15. *See also* **Web browsers**
elements of, WEB 3.10–12

entering URLs in Address Bar, WEB 3.45–47
Favorites feature, WEB 3.47–51
Help facility, WEB 3.58–59
hiding and showing toolbars in, WEB 3.44–45
history list, WEB 3.53–54
hyperlink navigation with mouse, WEB 3.51–53
menu bar, WEB 3.44
printing Web pages in, WEB 3.56–57
refreshing Web pages in, WEB 3.54
returning to start page in, WEB 3.54–55
saving Web pages in, WEB 3.59–64
security features, WEB 3.57–58
Standard Buttons toolbar, WEB 3.42–43
starting, WEB 3.41–42
status bar, WEB 3.43–44
toolbar buttons, WEB 3.42–43
A popular Web browser program. Also known as Internet Explorer.

Microsoft Outlook Express, WEB 2.33–50
address books, WEB 2.47–50
configuring for e-mail, WEB 2.34–36
deleted Items folder in, WEB 2.34
deleting messages, WEB 2.45–47
features, WEB 2.33–34
filing messages, WEB 2.44.45
Folder list in, WEB 2.34
forwarding messages, WEB 2.41, WEB 2.43
Inbox folder in, WEB 2.34
Internet Connection Wizard, WEB 2.35–36
printing messages in, WEB 2.45
receiving and reading messages in, WEB 2.39–40
replying to messages, WEB 3.41–42
saving and opening attached files in, WEB 2.40–41
sending messages in, WEB 2.36–39
Sent Items folder in, WEB 2.34
An e-mail client program that works with Internet Explorer Web browser software. Also known as Outlook Express.

MILNET (Military Network), WEB 1.10
The part of ARPANET, created in 1984, reserved for military uses that required high levels of security.

MIME (Multipurpose Internet Mail Extensions), WEB 2.02
A protocol specifying how to encode nontext data, such as graphics and sound, so you can send them over the Internet.

minicomputers, WEB 1.06
A computer that is larger and more expensive than a PC. Businesses and other organizations use minicomputers to process large volumes of work at high speeds.

modems
cable, WEB 1.21–22
defined, WEB 1.20
A device that converts a computer's digital signal to an analog signal (modulation) so it can travel through a telephone line and also converts analog signals arriving through a telephone line to digital signals that the computer can use (demodulation).

modulation, WEB 1.20
The process of converting a digital signal to an analog signal.

modulator-demodulator. *See* **modems**

Morris, Robert, WEB 1.11

Mosaic, WEB 1.15
The first program with a GUI that could read HTML and use HTML documents' hyperlinks to navigate from page to page on computers anywhere on the Internet. Mosaic was the first Web browser that became widely available for PCs.

mouse, WEB 1.14
hyperlink navigation with, WEB 3.27–29, WEB 3.51–53

MUDs, WEB 1.09

multi-address entries
in address books, WEB 2.12
in Netscape Messenger, WEB 2.31–33
in Outlook Express, WEB 2.49–50

Multipurpose Internet Mail Extensions. *See* **MIME**
multiuser dimensions. *See* **MUDs**
multiuser domains. *See* **MUDs**
multiuser dungeons. *See* **MUDs**

N

NAPs, WEB 1.19
Internet connections, WEB 1.19

National Science Foundation Network
NSFnet, WEB 1.10, WEB 1.12, WEB 1.13

National Science Foundation (NSF), WEB 1.19

Navigation toolbar, WEB 3.19–20
The Navigator toolbar that contains buttons for commonly used Web browsing commands.

NCP (Network Control Protocol), WEB 1.08
Nelson, Ted, WEB 1.14
Netscape Communications, WEB 1.15
Netscape Communicator Suite, WEB 2.13
 Help in, WEB 3.32–36
 The suite of programs developed by Netscape Communications Corporation that includes the Navigator Web browser and the Messenger e-mail program.
Netscape Message Center window, WEB 2.13–14
 Contains a list of the current user's mailboxes, mail folders, and discussion groups.
Netscape Messenger, WEB 2.13–33
 address books, WEB 2.29–33
 Composition window, WEB 2.15
 configuring for e-mail, WEB 2.15–18
 defined, WEB 2.13
 deleting e-mail messages, WEB 2.27–28
 filing e-mail messages, WEB 2.26–27
 forwarding e-mail messages, WEB 2.24–25
 Message Center window, WEB 2.13–14
 Message List window, WEB 2.13
 Message window, WEB 2.14–15
 Preferences window, WEB 2.15–`6
 receiving and reading messages, WEB 2.21–22
 replying to e-mail messages, WEB 2.23–24
 sending e-mail messages, WEB 2.18–20
 starting, WEB 2.13
 windows, WEB 2.13–15
 The e-mail client program that is an integral part of the Netscape Communicator suite. Also known as Messenger.
Netscape Navigator, WEB 1.15
 changing default home page, WEB 3.30–31
 creating bookmarks in, WEB 3.23–24
 elements of, WEB 3.10–12
 floating component bar, WEB 3.18
 Help in, WEB 3.35–36
 hiding and showing toolbar, WEB 3.21
 history list, WEB 3.29
 hyperlink navigation in, WEB 3.27–31
 Location toolbar, WEB 3.19–27
 print options in, WEB 3.31–34
 saving Web pages in, WEB 3.36–41

 security features, WEB 3.34–35
 starting, WEB 3.17–18
 toolbar buttons, WEB 3.19–20
 A popular Web browser program. Also known as Navigator.
network access points. *See* **NAPs**
network backbone, WEB 1.10
 The long-distance lines and supporting technology that transport large amounts of data between major network nodes.
Network Control Protocol (NCP), WEB 1.08
 A set of rules for formatting, ordering, and error-checking data used by the ARPANET and other early forerunners of the Internet.
network interface cards (NICs), WEB 1.05
network operating system, WEB 1.05
 Software that runs on a server computer that allows other computers, called client computers, to be connected to it and share its resources, such as printers, files, or programs.
networks, WEB 1.05–1.11
 circuit switching, WEB 1.08
 connecting to, WEB 1.06–1.07, WEB 1.17
 interconnecting, WEB 1.10
 local area, WEB 1.05–1.06
 packet switching, WEB 1.08
 wide area, WEB 1.07
 wireless, WEB 1.07
New Card button
 in Netscape Messenger address book, WEB 2.29–30
New Contact button
 in Outlook Express, WEB 2.47
New Mail button
 in Outlook Express, WEB 2.37
New Msg button
 in Netscape Messenger, WEB 2.15
newsgroups, WEB 1.09
 defined, WEB 1.09
 mail from, in Netscape Messenger, WEB 2.14
 Topic categories on the Usenet News Service. Also known as forums or Internet discussion groups.
nicknames
 in address books, WEB 2.11
 in Netscape Messenger, WEB 2.29
 in Outlook Express, WEB 2.47
 as e-mail addresses, WEB 2.07
NSFnet
 defined, WEB 1.10
 privatization of the Internet and, WEB 1.12, WEB 1.13

O

open architecture, WEB 1.08–1.09
 An approach that allows each network in an internet to continue using its own protocols and data transmission methods for moving data internally.
Outbox folder
 in Outlook Express, WEB 2.34
 The e-mail folder that holds messages waiting to be sent.
Outlook Express. *See* **Microsoft Outlook Express**

P

packet switching, WEB 1.08
 A method for sending information over a network in which files and messages are broken down into packets that are labeled electronically with codes for their origins and destinations. The packets are sent through the network, each possibly by a different path. The packets are reassembled at their destination.
Page proxy icon
 in Netscape Navigator, WEB 3.23
Page Setup dialog box
 in Internet Explorer, WEB 3.56–57
 in Netscape Navigator, WEB 3.32–33
personal computers (PCs)
 as servers, WEB 1.06
Pine, WEB 2.08
plain old telephone service (POTS), WEB 1.18
 The standard telephone service provided by telephone companies to business and individual customers for voice communications. This service allows users to transmit data by using a modem at a bandwidth of between 28.8 and 56 Kbps.
plus sign
 clicking, to show hierarchical listings, WEB 2.16
point-to-point protocol (PPP), WEB 1.20
 A set of rules for transmitting data that makes a PC's modem connection appear to be a TCP/IP connection.
POP (Post Office Protocol), WEB 2.02, WEB 2.09
 One of the Internet-defined procedures that handles incoming e-mail messages. POP is a standard, extensively used protocol that is part of the Internet suite of recognized protocols.

POTS. *See* **plain old telephone service (POTS)**
PPP connections, WEB 1.20
Preferences window
    in Netscape Messenger, WEB 2.15–16
Preview Pane
    in Outlook Express, WEB 2.34
Print button
    in Web browsers, WEB 3.15
printing
    e-mail messages, WEB 2.10
        in Netscape Messenger, WEB 2.27
        in Outlook Express, WEB 2.45
    Web pages, WEB 3.15
        in Internet Explorer, WEB 3.56–57
        in Netscape Navigator, WEB 3.31–34
protocols
    defined, WEB 1.08
    for e-mail, WEB 2.02
    A collection of rules for formatting, ordering, and error-checking data sent across a network.

Q

queued e-mail messages, WEB 2.09
    in Netscape Messenger, WEB 2.20
    in Outlook Express, WEB 2.39
    E-mail messages that are held temporarily by the client before processing.
quoted e-mail messages, WEB 2.11
    That portion of the body of a sender's original message that you include in your reply to the sender. Usually, you add your comments to the message.

R

receiving e-mail messages
    in Netscape Messenger, WEB 2.21–22
    in Outlook Express, WEB 2.39–40
Refresh button, WEB 3.14
    in Internet Explorer, WEB 3.54
Reload button, WEB 3.14
    in Netscape Navigator, WEB 3.30
reloading Web pages, WEB 3.30–31
Reply All button
    in Netscape Messenger, WEB 2.23
replying to e-mail messages, WEB 2.11
    in Netscape Messenger, WEB 2.23–24

in Outlook Express, WEB 2.41–42
A response to an e-mail message you receive.
routers, WEB 1.08
    A computer on a packet-switching internet that accepts packets from other networks and determines the best way to move each packet forward to its destination.
routing algorithms, WEB 1.08
    The program on a router computer in a packet-switching internet that determines the best path on which to send packets., WEB 1.08

S

satellite Internet connections, WEB 1.19, WEB 1.22
Save Image As command, WEB 3.37
Save Picture As command, WEB 3.64
saving e-mail attachments
    in Netscape Messenger, WEB 2.22–23
    in Outlook Express, WEB 2.40–41
saving images
    from Web pages, WEB 3.37, WEB 3.40–41
saving Web pages
    in Netscape Navigator, WEB 2.36–41
    in Web browsers, WEB 3.15–16
scroll bars
    in Web browsers, WEB 3.11
Search the Internet button, WEB 3.14
security
    in Internet Explorer, WEB 3.43, WEB 3.57–58
    in Netscape Navigator, WEB 3.34–35
    The protection of assets from unauthorized access, use, alteration, or destruction.
Security zone, WEB 3.44
    Classification levels of Web page security risk in Internet Explorer.
sending e-mail messages
    with attachments
        in Netscape Messenger, WEB 2.19–20
        in Outlook Express, WEB 2.38
    copies, WEB 2.04
    in Netscape Messenger, WEB 2.18–20
    in Outlook Express, WEB 2.36–39
Send/Recv button
    in Outlook Express, WEB 2.39

Sent Items folder
    in Outlook Express, WEB 2.34
    A folder that contains copies of your sent e-mail messages.
serial line Internet protocol (SLIP), WEB 1.20
    A set of rules for transmitting data that makes a PC's modem connection appear to be a TCP/IP connection.
server computers, WEB 1.05
    A computer that accepts requests from other computers, called clients, that are connected to it and shares some or all of its resources, such as printers, files, or programs, with those client computers. This way of connecting computers is called a client/server network.
SGML, WEB 1.15
shareware, WEB 2.08
    Free or inexpensive software that you can try for an evaluation period before you purchase it.
signature (e-mail), WEB 2.05–2.06
    One or more lines in an e-mail message that identify more detailed information about the sender (such as his or her name, address, and phone number).
signature files, WEB 2.05
Simple Mail Transfer Protocol. *See* **SMTP**
SLIP connections, WEB 1.20
SMTP (Simple Mail Transfer Protocol), WEB 2.02, WEB 2.09
    One of the Internet-defined procedures that determines which path your message takes on the Internet.
SMTP servers
    configuring, in Netscape Messenger, WEB 2.17, WEB 2.20
    configuring, in Outlook Express, WEB 2.35
spell checking e-mail messages
    in Netscape Messenger, WEB 2.20
    in Outlook Express, WEB 2.39
Standard Buttons toolbar
    in Internet Explorer, WEB 3.42–43
Standard Generalized Markup Language (SGML), WEB 1.15
    The document description language on which HTML is based. Organizations have used SGML for many years to manage large document-filing systems.
start pages. *See also* **Home pages**
    defined, WEB 3.06

displaying in Netscape Navigator, WEB 3.30–31
returning to, in Internet Explorer, WEB 3.54–55
The page that opens when a particular Web browser program is started or the page that a particular Web browser program loads the first time it is run. Usually, this page is stored at the Web site of the firm or other organization that created the Web browser software. *See also* home page.

status bar
in Internet Explorer, WEB 3.43–44
in Web browsers, WEB 3.12

Stop button
on Web browsers, WEB 3.15

Subject line, in e-mail, WEB 2.04
A brief summary of a message's content.

T

tags, HTML, WEB 1.15, WEB 3.03

T1 connections, WEB 1.19
A high-bandwidth (1.544 Mbps) data transmission connection used as part of the Internet backbone and by large firms and ISPs as a connection to the Internet.

T3 connections, WEB 1.19
A high-bandwidth (44.736 Mbps) data transmission connection used as part of the Internet backbone and by large firms and ISPs as a connection to the Internet.

TCP/IP. *See* **Transmission Control Protocol/Internet Protocol (TCP/IP)**

telephone service
Internet connections and, WEB 1.18–19, WEB 1.20

Telnet, WEB 1.09
protocol, WEB 3.09
The part of the TCP/IP protocol set that lets users log on to their computer accounts from remote sites.

Temporary Internet Files
in Internet Explorer, WEB 3.54
The name of the folder (in the Windows folder) in which Internet Explorer stores copies of Web pages you have viewed recently.

text, Web page
copying and saving, WEB 3.37–39, WEB 3.62

title bar
in Web browsers, WEB 3.11

toggle commands, WEB 3.20, WEB 3.45
A type of control in a program that works like a push button on a television set; you press the button once to turn on the television and press it a second time to turn it off.

To line, in e-mail, WEB 2.03–2.04
Part of a message header that contains an e-mail message recipient's full e-mail address.

Tomlinson, Ray, WEB 1.09

toolbar buttons
in Internet Explorer, WEB 3.42–43
in Netscape Navigator, WEB 3.19–20

top-level domains, WEB 3.08
proposed, WEB 3.08
The last part of a domain name, which is the unique name that is associated with a specific IP address by a program that runs on an Internet host computer.

transfer progress indicator, WEB 3.44
A section of the status bar in Internet Explorer that presents status messages, such as the URL of a page while it is loading, the text "Done" after a page has loaded, or the URL of any hyperlink on the page when you move the pointer over it.

transfer protocols, WEB 3.09
The set of rules that computers use to move files from one computer to another on an internet. The most common transfer protocol used on the Internet is HTTP.

Transmission Control Protocol, WEB 1.09
A part of the TCP/IP set of rules for sending data over a network.

Transmission Control Protocol/Internet Protocol (TCP/IP)
addresses available under, WEB 1.13
defined, WEB 1.09
growth of the Internet and, WEB 1.09
A combined set of rules for data transmission. TCP includes rules that computers on a network use to establish and break connections; IP includes rules for routing of individual data packets.

Trash mailbox
emptying, in Netscape Messenger, WEB 2.27–28

twisted-pair cable, WEB 1.06, WEB 1.07
The type of cable that telephone companies have used for years to wire residences and businesses, twisted-pair cable has two or more insulated copper wires that are twisted around each other and enclosed in another layer of plastic insulation.

U

Uniform Resource Locators (URLs)
components of, WEB 3.09
defined, WEB 3.08
entering in Internet Explorer Address Bar, WEB 3.45–47
entering in location field in Netscape Navigator, WEB 3.21
The four-part addressing scheme for an HTML document that tells Web browser software which transfer protocol to use when transporting the document, the domain name of the computer on which the document resides, the pathname of the folder or directory on the computer in which the document resides, and the document's filename.

Up Scroll arrow
in Web browsers, WEB 3.11

URLs. *See* **Uniform Resource Locators (URLs)**

U.S Department of Defense (DOD), WEB 1.07–1.08, WEB 1.10, WEB 1.12

Usenet (User's News Network), WEB 1.09
A network that allows anyone who connects to the network to read and post articles on a variety of subjects.

user names
defined, WEB 2.07
selection of, WEB 2.07
The character string that identifies a person to a particular computer system or family of systems.

User's News Network. *See* **Usenet**

W

WANs. *See* **wide area networks (WANs)**

Web. *See* **World Wide Web**

Web-based e-mail, WEB 2.08–2.09

Web browsers, WEB 3.02–3.05. *See also* **Microsoft Internet Explorer; Netscape Navigator**
defined, WEB 1.15, WEB 3.02

development of, WEB 1.14–15
display of HTML documents by, WEB 1.14–15
elements of, WEB 3.10–12
history list, WEB 3.14
Home button, WEB 3.12
menu bar, WEB 3.12
scroll bars, WEB 3.11
status bar, WEB 3.12
title bar, WEB 3.11
Software that lets users read (or browse) HTML documents and move from one HTML document to another through the text formatted with hypertext link tags in each file. HTML documents can be on the user's computer or on another computer that is part of the WWW.

Web clients
defined, WEB 3.02
A computer that is connected to the Web and runs software called a Web browser that enables its user to read HTML documents on other computers, called Web servers, that also are connected to the Web.

Web directories, WEB 3.14
A Web site that contains a list of Web page categories, such as education or recreation. The hyperlinks on a Web directory page lead to other pages that contain lists of subcategories that lead to other category lists and Web pages that relate to the category topics.

webmasters, WEB 3.16
The title often used for the person who is responsible for maintaining a Web page or Web site.

Web page area
in Web browsers, WEB 3.1
The portion of a Web browser window that displays the contents of the HTML document or other file as a Web page.

Web pages. *See also* **Web sites**
copying and saving text from, WEB 3.37–39
copyright law and, WEB 3.16
hypertext in, WEB 3.03–2.04
printing, WEB 3.15,
in Internet Explorer, WEB 3.56–57
in Netscape Navigator, WEB 3.31–34
refreshing, WEB 3.54
reloading, WEB 3.30–31
returning to, WEB 3.15
saving, WEB 3.16
to file, WEB 3.37–39
in Internet Explorer, WEB 3.59–64
in Netscape Navigator, WEB 3.36–41
security issues, WEB 3.57–58
stopping transfer of, WEB 3.15

Web search engines
defined, WEB 3.14
stopping transfer of, WEB 3.15
A Web site that allows you to conduct searches of the Web to find specific words or expressions. The result of a search engine's search is a Web page that contains hyperlinks to Web pages that contain text or expressions that match those you entered.

Web servers
defined, WEB 3.02
A computer that is connected to the Web and contains HTML documents that it makes available to other computers connected to the Web.

Web sites. *See also* **Web pages**
defined, WEB 1.15, WEB 3.05, WEB 3.06
growth of, WEB 1.15–16

Computers that are connected to the Internet and that store HTML documents. All Web sites taken together make up the Web.

wide area networks (WANs), WEB 1.07
Any of several ways of connecting individual computers or networks to each other over distances greater than those included in LANs.

wireless networks, WEB 1.07
A way of connecting computers to each other that does not use cable. Instead, a wireless network uses wireless transmitters and receivers that plug into network interface cards (NICs).

workplace
Internet connections through, WEB 1.20

World Wide Web
commercial use of, WEB 1.15
defined, WEB 1.04
growth of, WEB 1.15–16
history of, WEB 1.14–16
A worldwide system of hyperlinked HTML documents on the Internet.

WWW. *See* **World Wide Web**

X

Xanadu, WEB 1.14
A global system for online hypertext publishing and commerce outlined by Ted Nelson in his book, *Literary Machines*.

Y

Yahoo!Mail, WEB 2.08, WEB 2.09

TASK REFERENCE

NETSCAPE NAVIGATOR TASKS

TASK	PAGE #	RECOMMENDED METHOD	WHERE USED
Address book entry, create	WEB 2.29	See Reference Window "Adding an address to the address book"	Messenger
Address book group, create	WEB 2.31	See Reference Window "Creating a mailing list"	Messenger
Attached file, save in Netscape Message window	WEB 2.22	See Reference Window "Saving an attached file"	Messenger
Bookmark folder, create	WEB 3.24	See Reference Window "Creating a Bookmarks folder"	Navigator
Bookmark, create	WEB 3.25	Click the Bookmarks button, click Add Bookmark	Navigator
Bookmark, create in a specific folder	WEB 3.25	See Reference Window, "Creating a bookmark in a bookmarks folder"	Navigator
Bookmarks file, save to floppy disk	WEB 3.26	See Reference Window, "Saving a bookmark to a floppy disk"	Navigator
Bookmarks window, open	WEB 3.24	Click the Bookmarks button, click Edit Bookmarks	Navigator
E-mail name, set up your	WEB 2.17	Click Edit, click Preferences, click Identity in the Mail & Newsgroups category, type your first and last names, type your full e-mail address, click OK	Messenger
File, attach in Composition window	WEB 2.19	Click the Attach button, click File, locate the file, click Open	Messenger
Font size of a Web page, change	WEB 3.33	Click Edit, click Preferences, click the Fonts category, use the Size list arrow to change font size, click OK	Navigator
Help, get	WEB 3.35	See Reference Window "Opening the NetHelp - Netscape window"	Navigator
History list, open	WEB 3.29	Click Communicator, point to Tools, click History	Navigator
Home page, change default	WEB 3.30	See Reference Window "Changing the default home page"	Navigator
Home page, return to	WEB 3.30	Click the Home button	Navigator
Mail folder, create	WEB 2.26	Click File, click New Folder	Messenger
Mail folder, delete	WEB 2.28	Click the folder to select, right-click the folder, click Delete Folder, click OK	Messenger
Mail preferences, set servers	WEB 2.16	Click Edit, click Preferences, click Mail & Newsgroups category, click Mail Servers, type SMTP and POP server names, click OK	Messenger

TASK REFERENCE

TASK	PAGE #	RECOMMENDED METHOD	WHERE USED
Mail, compose	WEB 2.19	Click the New Msg button	Messenger
Mail, copy to another folder in Message List window	WEB 2.26	Click Message, point to Copy Message, click destination folder	Messenger
Mail, delete	WEB 2.27	Right-click the message summary, click Delete Message	Messenger
Mail, delete permanently	WEB 2.28	Click File, click Empty Trash on Local Mail	Messenger
Mail, forward from Message List window	WEB 2.24	Click the Forward button	Messenger
Mail, move to another folder in Message List window	WEB 2.27	Click File button, click destination folder	Messenger
Mail, print message	WEB 2.27	Right-click the message summary, click Print Message	Messenger
Mail, read in Message List window	WEB 2.21	Click the message summary line	Messenger
Mail, receive messages in Message List window	WEB 2.21	Click the Get Msg button, type your user name and password, click OK	Messenger
Mail, reply to all recipients in Message List window	WEB 2.23	Click the message summary line, click the Reply All button	Messenger
Mail, reply to sender in Message List window	WEB 2.23	Click the message summary line, click the Reply button	Messenger
Mail, send from Composition window	WEB 2.20	Click the Send button	Messenger
Mail, spell check in Composition window	WEB 2.20	Click the Spelling button	Messenger
Messenger, start	WEB 2.15	Click the Start button, point to Programs, point to Netscape Communicator, click Netscape Messenger	
Navigator window, maximize	WEB 3.17	Click the Maximize button	Navigator, Messenger
Navigator window, minimize	WEB 3.11	Click the Minimize button	Navigator, Messenger
Navigator window, restore maximized	WEB 3.11	Click the Restore button	Navigator, Messenger
Navigator, close	WEB 3.11	Click the Close button	Navigator, Messenger
Navigator, start	WEB 3.17	Click the Start button, point to Programs, point to Netscape Communicator, click Netscape Navigator	

TASK REFERENCE

TASK	PAGE #	RECOMMENDED METHOD	WHERE USED
Page print settings, change	WEB 3.32	Click File, click Page Setup	Navigator
Start page, return to	WEB 3.30	Click the Home button	Navigator
Toolbar, hide	WEB 3.20	Click View, point to Show, deselect toolbar to hide	Navigator
Toolbar, show	WEB 3.20	Click View, point to Show, select toolbar to show	Navigator
URL, enter and go to	WEB 3.21	See Reference Window "Entering a URL in the Location field"	Navigator
Web page graphic, save	WEB 3.40	See Reference Window "Saving an image from a Web page on a floppy disk"	Navigator
Web page in history list, move forward to previous	WEB 3.19	Click the Forward button	Navigator
Web page in history list, return to previous	WEB 3.27	Click the Back button	Navigator
Web page text, save	WEB 3.38	See Reference Window "Copying text from a Web page to a WordPad document"	Navigator
Web page, print all pages	WEB 3.31	Click the Print button	Navigator
Web page, print one or a few pages	WEB 3.32	See Reference Window "Printing the current Web page"	Navigator
Web page, reload	WEB 3.30	Click the Reload button	Navigator
Web page, save to floppy disk	WEB 3.37	See Reference Window "Saving a Web page to a floppy disk"	Navigator
Web page, stop loading	WEB 3.15	Click the Stop button	Navigator

MICROSOFT INTERNET EXPLORER TASKS

TASK	PAGE #	RECOMMENDED METHOD	WHERE USED
Address book entry, create	WEB 2.47	See Reference Window "Entering a new e-mail address in the address book"	Outlook Express
Address book group, create	WEB 2.49	See Reference Window "Creating a group address entry"	Outlook Express
Attached file, save	WEB 2.41	See Reference Windows "Saving an attached file"	Outlook Express
Favorite, move to a new folder	WEB 3.50	See Reference Window "Moving an existing favorite into a new folder"	Internet Explorer
Favorites folder, create	WEB 3.48	See Reference Window "Creating a new Favorites folder"	Internet Explorer
Favorites frame, open	WEB 3.47	Click the Favorites button	Internet Explorer
File, attach in New Message window	WEB 2.38	Click the Attach button, locate the file, click Attach	Outlook Express
Font size of Web page, change	WEB 3.57	Click View, point to Text Size, click the desired size option	Internet Explorer

TASK REFERENCE

TASK	PAGE #	RECOMMENDED METHOD	WHERE USED
Help, get	WEB 3.58	See Reference Window "Getting Help in Internet Explorer"	Internet Explorer
History list, open	WEB 3.53	Click the History button	Internet Explorer
Home page, change default	WEB 3.55	See Reference Window "Changing the Home toolbar button settings"	Internet Explorer
Home page, return to	WEB 3.54	Click the Home button	Internet Explorer
Internet Explorer window, maximize	WEB 3.42	Click the Maximize button	Internet Explorer, Outlook Express
Internet Explorer window, minimize	WEB 3.11	Click the Minimize button	Internet Explorer, Outlook Express
Internet Explorer window, restore maximized	WEB 3.11	Click the Restore button	Internet Explorer, Outlook Express
Internet Explorer, close	WEB 3.11	Click the Close button	Internet Explorer, Outlook Express
Internet Explorer, start	WEB 3.41	Click the Start button, point to Programs, click Internet Explorer	
Mail account, set up	WEB 2.35	Click Tools, click Accounts, click the Mail tab, click the Add button, click Mail, follow steps in the Internet Connection Wizard	Outlook Express
Mail folder, create	WEB 2.44	Click File, point to Folder, click New	Outlook Express
Mail folder, delete	WEB 2.47	Right-click the folder, click Delete	Outlook Express
Mail, compose	WEB 2.37	Click the New Mail button	Outlook Express
Mail, copy to another folder	WEB 2.45	Click the message summary, click Edit, click Copy to Folder	Outlook Express
Mail, delete	WEB 2.46	Click the message summary, click the Delete button	Outlook Express
Mail, delete permanently	WEB 2.46	Open Deleted Items folder, click the message summary of message to delete, click the Delete button	Outlook Express
Mail, forward from Inbox window	WEB 2.43	Click the Forward button	Outlook Express
Mail, move to another folder	WEB 2.45	Click the message summary, drag the message to destination folder	Outlook Express
Mail, print	WEB 2.45	Click the message summary, click the Print button	Outlook Express
Mail, read	WEB 2.39	Click the message summary	Outlook Express
Mail, reply to author from Inbox window	WEB 2.42	Click the message summary, click the Reply button	Outlook Express

TASK REFERENCE

TASK	PAGE #	RECOMMENDED METHOD	WHERE USED
Mail, send and receive	WEB 2.39	Click the Send/Recv button	Outlook Express
Mail, send from New Message window	WEB 2.39	Click the Send button	Outlook Express
Mail, spell check in New Message window	WEB 2.39	Click Tools, Spelling	Outlook Express
Outlook Express, start	WEB 2.34	Click the Start button, point to Programs, click Outlook Express	
Page print settings, change	WEB 3.56	Click File, click Page Setup	Internet Explorer
Start page, return to	WEB 3.54	Click the Home button	Internet Explorer
Toolbar, hide or show	WEB 3.44	See Reference Window "Hiding and restoring the toolbars"	Internet Explorer
URL, enter and go to	WEB 3.45	See Reference Window "Entering a URL in the Address Bar"	Internet Explorer
Web page graphic, save	WEB 3.63	See Reference Window "Saving an image from a Web page on a floppy disk"	Internet Explorer
Web page in history list, move forward to previous	WEB 3.48	Click the Forward button	Internet Explorer
Web page in history list, return to previous	WEB 3.47	Click the Back button	Internet Explorer
Web page text, save	WEB 3.61	See Reference Window "Copying text from a Web page to a WordPad document"	Internet Explorer
Web page, print all pages	WEB 3.56	Click the Print button	Internet Explorer
Web page, print one or a few pages	WEB 3.56	See Reference Window "Printing the current Web page"	Internet Explorer
Web page, refresh	WEB 3.54	Click the Refresh button	Internet Explorer
Web page, save to floppy disk	WEB 3.60	See Reference Window "Saving a Web page to a floppy disk"	Internet Explorer
Web page, stop loading	WEB 3.15	Click the Stop button	Internet Explorer

EUDORA TASKS

TASK	PAGE #	RECOMMENDED METHOD	WHERE USED
Eudora, exit	WEB E.12	Click File on the menu bar, click Exit	
Eudora, start	WEB E.04	Click the Start button, point to Programs, point to Eudora Pro, click Eudora Pro	
Mail, create address book entry	WEB E.11	Click the Address Book button, click the New button, type nickname, click OK, click Address(es) tab, type e-mail address, click Info tab, type first and last names, click File, click Save	

TASK REFERENCE

TASK	PAGE #	RECOMMENDED METHOD	WHERE USED
Mail, delete message	WEB E.11	Select the message, click the Delete Message(s) button	
Mail, forward	WEB E.10	Select the message, click the Forward button	
Mail, print	WEB E.09	Select the message, click the Print button	
Mail, reply to message	WEB E.10	Select the message, click the Reply button	
Mail, retrieve and read	WEB E.07	Click the Check Mail button, enter password, double-click the message summary	
Mail, send message	WEB E.07	Click the Send button	
Mail, transfer message to another mailbox	WEB E.10	Select the message, click Transfer on the menu bar, click the target mailbox	
Mailbox, create	WEB E.09	Click Mailbox on the menu bar, click New, type the new mailbox name, click OK	

PINE TASKS

TASK	PAGE #	RECOMMENDED METHOD	
Mail, compose	WEB F.02	Type C at the Main menu	
Mail, create a folder	WEB F.06	From the Main menu, type A, type the name of the folder, press Enter	
Mail, create address book entry	WEB F.11	From the Main menu, type A, type A again, enter address information in the appropriate lines, press Ctrl + X, type Y	
Mail, delete message	WEB F.09	Open a mail folder, select a message summary line, type D	
Mail, expunge message	WEB F.10	From the Main menu, type Q, type Y, type Y again	
Mail, forward	WEB F.08	Open a message, type F, fill in recipient's address, press Ctrl + X, then press Y	
Mail, print	WEB F.06	Open a message, press Y twice	
Mail, quit	WEB F.12	From the main menu type Q, type Y	
Mail, retrieve and read	WEB F.04	From the Main menu, type I, use arrow keys to select the message summary, press Enter	
Mail, send	WEB F.03	With the Compose Message window open, press Ctrl + X	